# International Financial Management

## Second Edition

JOHN HOLLAND

**BLACKWELL**

*Business*

First edition published 1986
Second edition published 1993

Blackwell Publishers
108 Cowley Road
Oxford OX4 1JF
UK

Three Cambridge Center
Cambridge, Massachusetts 02142
USA

*British Library Cataloguing in Publication Data*
A CIP catalogue record for this book is available from the British Library.

*Library of Congress Cataloging-in-Publication Data*
Holland, John, 1947–
    International financial management / John Holland. – 2nd ed.
        p.   cm.
    Includes bibliographical references (p.        ) and indexes.
    ISBN 0-631-17421-4
        1. International finance.   2. International business enterprises-
-Finance.   I. Title.
HG3881.H615   1993
658. 15–dc20                    *1734784*              93-14795
                                                                      CIP

Typeset in Ehrhardt on 11 on 13 pt by TecSet Ltd, Wallington, Surrey

Printed in Great Britain by BPCC Wheatons, Exeter

# Contents

List of Figures                                                                     vii

List of Tables                                                                       ix

Preface to the Second Edition                                                        xi

1   The International Dimensions of Corporate Financial
    Management  14 - 25                                                              1
2   The International Financial System                                              29
3   The Parity Relationships, Imperfections and IFM Decisions                      77
4   The Foreign Exchange Risk Management Problem                                   118
5   FERM, Economic Exposure and Adapting Strategic and
    Operational Decisions    exclude 150 - 155                                     147
6   FERM and Internal Financial Techniques                                         174
7   FERM and the Use of External Risk Management
    Instruments                    = 0                                             202
8   Corporate Foreign Investment Decisions                                         231
9   The Analysis of the Capital Budgeting Decision                                 265
10  The StrathKelvin Company: A Case in International Capital
    Budgeting                                                                      288
11  International Sources of Finance for the Firm                                   318
12  The Debt Financing Decision                                                    339
13  Global Financing Decisions                                                     365
14  Financial Planning and Corporate Strategy  910 - 423                           406

Appendix 1:   Linear Programming Run for Netting Problem                           427

Appendix 2:   BASIC Listing of Capital Budgeting Model                             433

Appendix 3:   BASIC Listing of Financing Model                                     441

Appendix 4:   Simulation Run Using the Financing Model          450

References                                                     454

Index                                                         464

# List of Figures

| | | |
|---|---|---|
| 1.1 | Wheel model of multinationality | 4 |
| 1.2 | Matrix organizational structure for ICI | 6 |
| 1.3 | International financial management decisions in the MNC | 15 |
| 1.4 | Organization of finance function | 17 |
| 2.1 | Institutional elements of the international financial and monetary system | 30 |
| 2.2 | Valuing option contracts | 55 |
| 2.3 | The role of the bank in international markets | 68 |
| 3.1 | Equilibrium relationship between interest rate, inflation rate and exchange rates | 79 |
| 3.2 | Example investment alternatives | 80 |
| 3.3 | Equilibrium relationships in algebraic form | 82 |
| 3.4 | Extended equilibrium framework | 98 |
| 5.1 | Effects of exchange rate changes on Rolls-Royce's competitive strategy | 152 |
| 5.2 | Operations of first example UK firm | 158 |
| 5.3 | Operations of second example UK firm | 160 |
| 5.4 | Operations of combined firm | 162 |
| 6.1 | Internal financial system of an MNC | 175 |
| 6.2 | Cross-border financial transactions for an MNC: internal and external | 178 |
| 6.3 | Possible model for netting problem | 198 |
| 7.1 | Hero Books: no cover of transaction exposure | 204 |
| 7.2 | Here Books: forward cover of transaction exposure | 205 |
| 7.3 | Hero Books: money market cover of transaction exposure | 206 |
| 7.4 | Hero Books: option cover of transaction exposure | 207 |
| 8.1 | Conventional view of political risk | 241 |

| | | |
|---|---|---|
| 8.2 | World institutions and the MNC | 247 |
| 8.3 | European institutions and the MNC | 249 |
| 8.4 | Theoretical basis for the MNC's strategic investment choices | 253 |
| 8.5 | Procedure for the global strategic analysis of overseas expansion opportunities | 254 |
| 9.1 | Convergence of cash flow classification schemes on the APV model | 276 |
| 9.2 | Cash flows for example project | 277 |
| 9.3 | Combinations of cash flow types and environmental assumptions | 283 |
| 10.1 | Structure of spreadsheet model | 301 |
| 11.1 | Wheel model of financial centre advantages | 320 |
| 11.2 | The Eurolending process in the retail market | 322 |
| 11.3 | The bank role in the issue of a Eurobond | 329 |
| 11.4 | The role of banks in the Euronote market | 332 |
| 11.5 | Principles of an interest rate swap | 334 |
| 11.6 | Principles of a currency swap | 336 |
| 11.7 | Principles of a debt for equity swap | 337 |
| 12.1 | Choices in overseas debt financing | 347 |
| 12.2 | Summary of example financing choices | 358 |
| 12.3 | Simple simulation financing model | 363 |
| 13.1 | The trade-off of objectives in a global financing decision | 389 |
| 14.1 | Shareholder wealth relationships | 419 |
| 14.2 | IFM framework used in this book | 424 |

# List of Tables

| 1.1 | Classification of firms by involvement in domestic and international markets | 3 |
|---|---|---|
| 1.2 | Orthodox theoretical concepts and their application to IFM theory | 14 |
| 2.1 | Historical changes in exchange rate systems | 32 |
| 2.2 | Foreign exchange quotation examples | 47 |
| 2.3 | London spot rates and forward rates against the pound | 50 |
| 2.4 | London spot rates and forward rates against the dollar | 53 |
| 2.5 | Aggregate market values | 60 |
| 2.6 | Capitalization of the major domestic equity markets, 1980 and 1990 | 61 |
| 2.7 | Borrowings on the international capital market, 1988–1992 | 73 |
| 3.1 | Examples of market circumstances | 96 |
| 4.1 | Strategies for foreign exchange risk management | 124 |
| 4.2 | FERM decisions in two periods | 137 |
| 4.3 | Reactive and proactive options in FERM decision taking | 138 |
| 5.1 | Shareholder wealth or value questions in relation to FERM decisions | 167 |
| 5.2 | Constraints in relation to FERM decisions | 170 |
| 6.1 | Obstacles to trade and transaction costs in financial services markets | 180 |
| 6.2 | Active opportunistic strategy for subsidiary in appreciating currency country | 184 |
| 6.3 | Active opportunistic strategy for subsidiary in depreciating currency country | 185 |
| 6.4 | Payments and receipts within a multinational enterprise | 192 |
| 6.5 | Net receipts and payments within MNC | 194 |

6.6   Netting transfer requirements and transfer costs                194
6.7   Possible netting solution                                        195
6.8   Results of linear programming run for netting problem            196
6.9   Interpretation of linear programming run: netting solution       196
6.10  Sensitivity of payments and receipts constraints in netting
      problem                                                          197
6.11  Sensitivity of costs of transfer in netting problem             197
8.1   Advantages of alternatives in overseas involvement              239
13.1  Strategies for global financing management                      372

# Preface to the Second Edition

The rapid growth of the multinational corporation (MNC) and of international trade since the Second World War has brought about a major change in the way in which financial problems arise for the internationally involved enterprise. In particular, major challenges and opportunities have presented themselves to MNCs and other international enterprises owing to new developments in international capital markets, the increased concern shown by managers with respect to exchange rate and interest rate fluctuations and the growth of overseas corporate investment. The increased internationalization of the firm and its finance function has accentuated the need for a decision framework to help managers cope with the attendant increased complexity of their international foreign exchange risk and cash management, investment, financing and dividend decisions. This internationalization of business has also highlighted the significance of the finance function in the internationally involved industrial and commercial corporations.

The second edition of this major text presents a comprehensive and up-to-date coverage of the modern theory and practice of international financial management. The book places special emphasis on broad policy issues as well as detailed analysis of specific international financial management decision areas. It also makes extensive use of the experiences of real firms to analyse many of the difficult questions of international financial management (IFM). These case firms are used throughout the book to explore the main issues of IFM and to examine the role of the finance executive and treasurer in the internationally involved enterprise.

Chapter 1 discusses the novel complexities faced by financial managers as they move from a domestic to an international arena. In chapter 2 the institutional nature of the international monetary and financial system is described, including the role of international banks, the functions of supranational bodies, and the main features of markets for foreign exchange, international bonds and equities, and various futures and options products. This is followed by an analysis of recent changes in world financial markets. Chapter 3 provides a neo-classical perspective on how this system prices foreign exchange and financial assets. The theories outlined are then used to draw implications for IFM decision making. This chapter demonstrates the value of orthodox financial theory in providing a conceptual framework for IFM decision making. The chapter then considers deviations from this view of well functioning markets and assesses the evidence for imperfections in international markets for capital, currency and financial services. Chapters 4 to 13 explore the central corporate IFM decisions under a series of assumptions ranging from imperfections to well functioning foreign exchange, international capital and product markets. This includes the foreign exchange risk management (FERM) decisions in chapters 4, 5, 6 and 7, capital budgeting in chapters 8, 9 and 10, and financing decisions in chapters 11, 12 and 13. In each of these decision areas, the role of computer based models as decision aids is demonstrated and examples of sensitivity analysis of the decisions are presented. The design of the models is based on the decision rules outlined in the chapters, and the models place greater analytical and computational power in the hands of the financial manager facing increasingly complex international financial management problems. In chapter 14, the major international financial management decisions are viewed together in a financial planning framework.

# 1

# The International Dimensions of Corporate Financial Management

*Intro*

The rapid growth of the multinational corporation (MNC) since the Second World War has brought about a major change in the way in which international trade is conducted. The development of the MNC was not anticipated within the classical theory of international trade in which only goods and services were thought to be internationally mobile. Today, factors of production such as labour and capital are seen to move freely across national borders. The multinational corporation is the agent of this change and fully exploits its unique ability to move managerial teams, research and development knowledge and capital across borders.

This increased importance of the MNC has highlighted the significance of the finance function in the large industrial and commercial corporations. In particular, major challenges and opportunities have presented themselves to MNCs owing to the emergence of international capital markets, the increased concern shown by managers with respect to exchange rate and interest rate fluctuations and the growth of overseas corporate investment. The increased internationalization of the firm and its finance function has accentuated the need for a decision framework to help managers cope with the attendant increased complexity of their cash management, investment, financing and dividend decisions.

This chapter attempts to outline such a framework and to identify the organizational and market context in which financial decisions are made in the MNC. Thus in section 1.1 the nature of the MNC is outlined. This leads to a discussion in section 1.2 on the nature of the MNC's environment and on various assumptions employed in the field of international financial management (IFM) to simplify our view of this environment. This set of assumptions, concerning well functioning

markets, imperfections in markets, and the firm as an active economic
agent, provides a framework to analyse financial decisions in the MNC. In
section 1.3, the major financial decisions in the international firm are
identified, and in section 1.4 the role of finance theory in supporting such
decision making is explored. Section 1.5 investigates the nature of the
MNC finance and treasury function and its role in implementing financial
decisions for the enterprise. Section 1.6 reviews the major topics covered in
each chapter of the book.

## 1.1 The Nature of the MNC Firm

Multinational companies such as ICI, Volkswagen, Ford, BP, Unilever,
BSN, IBM and Nestlé, are complex and ever changing phenomena.
However, these enterprises can be distinguished from domestic firms by
their international dimension. More specifically, we can define an MNC as
an enterprise with a global vision that seeks

1   a high degree of international involvement in world product, factor
    and financial markets
2   a high degree of co-ordination of international business operations and
    functions such as treasury.

We can illustrate the first element of multinationality by classifying firms
according to their degree of involvement in international product, factor
and capital markets. The classification is further broken down by
separating equity and debt sources and by having ownership of foreign
subsidiaries as an extra category. The former extension is designed to
highlight shareholder issues and the latter indicates a key extra dimension
to the firm's involvement in international product and factor markets.
Given such a framework, firms can be classified as in table 1.1 according to
their degree of involvement in international product, factor and capital
markets.

   The first point to make about the classification scheme in the table is that
it does not imply a model of MNC evolution. Certainly a plausible case can
be made that, as a firm increases its involvement in international product
and factor markets, the tendency to establish foreign subsidiaries becomes
strong. This in turn is likely to encourage the firm to consider international
sources of capital. However, many alternative paths to full multinational
status, i.e. MNC III, are possible. In chapter 8 we will see that a wide range

**Table 1.1** Classification of firms by involvement in domestic and international markets

| Type of firm | Product markets | Factor markets | Foreign subsidiaries | Debt capital | Equity capital |
|---|---|---|---|---|---|
| Do I | D | D | — | D | D |
| Do II | I | I | — | D | D |
| MNC I | I | I | I | D | D |
| MNC II | I | I | I | I | D |
| MNC III | I | I | I | I | I |

D, high involvement domestically; I, high involvement internationally.

of theories seek to explain the development of MNCs. Thus it is clear that this classification scheme does not cover all aspects of multinationality. It does however provide a useful basis for managers to identify the degree of international involvement of their firm.

The second element of multinationality considers the degree of co-ordination the firm exercises over its international business operations and functions such as treasury. This can be expanded to include many co-ordination factors such as

- the degree of integration of global operational decisions
- the degree of integration of global financial decisions
- the global flexibility of real and financial decisions

The enterprise that can integrate its many overseas production and marketing operations has a distinct global capability compared with a relatively uncoordinated multidomestic enterprise. The enterprise that can co-ordinate the treasury operations of its overseas subsidiaries has a capability to exploit world financial markets in a way that is not available to a firm that allows its overseas treasurers a high degree of autonomy. In all of these cases, firms may qualify as multinationals by virtue of their high degree of international involvement. However, those firms with the higher degree of international co-ordination are better placed to achieve the aims of a global strategy. Firms with such co-ordinative attitude and capability reveal their global intent and distinguish themselves from internationally involved firms with a more limited domestic or (world) regional vision.

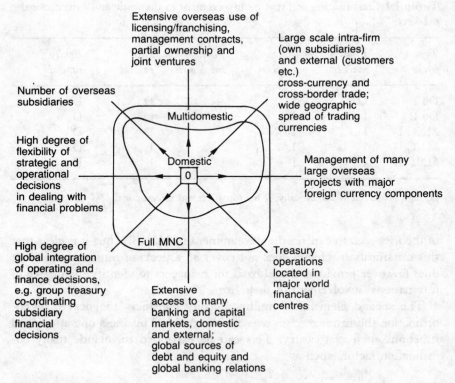

**Figure 1.1** Wheel model of multinationality

They treat all parts of the world as a potential marketplace and see this as their 'home'.

An additional multinationality factor exists if an enterprise can alter real decisions such as global sourcing or the geographic location of its subsidiaries in response to, say, currency risk. These principles of control and flexibility extend to the relationship between all financial and real decisions faced by the MNC. Extensive global control and flexibility can broaden the global scope of MNCs and distinguish them from their less well co-ordinated and less flexible MNC counterparts.

Figure 1.1 combines many of these factors in a descriptive wheel model of multinationality. Clearly enterprises will differ in terms of the multinationality factors shown in the figure. In general, the more an enterprise moves out to the end of each spoke of the wheel, the more multinational it becomes.

In practice the scale of direct foreign investment (DFI) or the number of overseas subsidiaries has often led or determined many of the above factors, and this has been employed as a common measure of multinationality. Thus the scale of in-house cross-border, cross-currency trading is likely to increase with an increasing number of integrated overseas subsidiaries and with increasing control over overseas treasury operations. However, these are not exclusive multinationality criteria. For example, a firm may have a few small scale overseas operations but, because of its extensive exporting and licensing activities, may score high on the other criteria for multinationality.

The wholly domestic firm is likely to have low measures on all of the factors and is shown in figure 1.1 as a small 'square' consisting of a clustering of low factor scores around the centre of the diagram. A multidomestic firm scores low on the integration and flexibility criteria, but high on the number of overseas units. This may lead to a mixture of high and low scores on the other criteria. A mature MNC is likely to score high on all left hand side criteria, that is integration, flexibility and the number of overseas units. This is likely to lead to high scores on the other criteria, and such a firm is illustrated by the larger 'square' in figure 1.1. As a result these three different types of firm are likely to exhibit major differences in the scale and variety of foreign currency cash flows, in their need for overseas funds and in the general complexity of their international financial management problems. They will also differ in their capability to recognize and deal with such problems.

## Case study: ICI

ICI is a very large and complex UK based MNC. It has seven major businesses, each of which operates internationally through a wide range of subsidiaries. The global spread of the firm began with its old empire links and now extends through the US, Europe and the Pacific Rim regions. The firm lies at the heart of the global chemical industry. It has a broad science base and very large R&D expenditure designed to maintain the competitive edge of the firm in this market. ICI sells its wide array of chemical and pharmaceutical products in 150 countries. In 1992 it had extensive production facilities around the world, and manufactured in over 35 countries in over 600 locations. Sales were £13.7 billion in 1990 of which £6 billion were in the UK and the rest overseas. In 1992 it had 125,000 employees of which 75,000 were outside the UK.

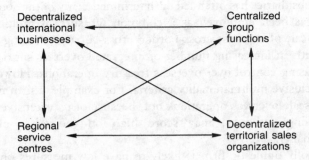

**Figure 1.2** Matrix organizational structure for ICI

Given this complexity, a matrix organizational structure has been set up to ensure that ICI can exploit whatever integrative advantages are available to it without compromising flexibility and managerial autonomy advantages (figure 1.2). The matrix structure recognizes the complex interactions that can occur between product, territory and function. It has been designed to encourage clarity and flexibility of decision making at the centre and in the subsidiaries, and to control the costs of decision making and service provision through the group.

Maximum authority is devolved to business and territorial managers. Thus decentralized decision making is matched to profit centre goals for these units. Decentralized functions carried out in the seven major businesses include production, marketing, R&D, distribution, purchasing, selling and promotion. However, functional centralized control is exercised over finance, treasury, strategy, senior management appointments, patents, trademarks, litigation, insurance and pensions. The centralized functions and the business and territorial units, where appropriate, share some (regionally centralized) services such as accounting and sales administration (Henderson and Rogerson 1987). Thus where there is synergy between business units, and cost efficiency across units can be improved, some centralization is necessary. This policy is supported by keeping management lines open and by reporting as directly and as simply as possible. The matrix is the means by which ICI avoids the costs of a large centralized group (and territorial unit bureaucracies) coupled with extensive overheads in each business.

## 1.2. The International Economic Environment: Market Forces and the MNC as a Purposeful and Active Economic Agent

The financial, political and business environment of the MNC contains many components and these will be discussed in detail in the following chapters. For the present we can recognize that this complexity is brought about because such firms

1  operate across and within different political, legal, taxation and cultural systems
2  operate across and within a wider range of product and factor markets, each with differing levels of competition and efficiency
3  trade in a wide range of currencies, and have frequent resort to foreign exchange markets
4  have access to a wide range of domestic capital markets, and to unregulated international capital markets. These markets may also exhibit differing degrees of efficiency and integration with each other.

The complex nature of the MNC's financial, political and business environment leads to the use of various simplifying assumptions in the field of international financial management (IFM). These include 'market forces' assumptions concerning well functioning markets and imperfections in markets, as well as assumptions about the firm as an active economic agent.

Two major classes of market forces assumptions are employed in the IFM literature. The first comprises neo-classical assumptions about the nature of international trade, and about the behaviour of inflation, interest rates and exchange rates. These provide the basis from which to develop idealized equilibrium theories about international trade, and about common pricing (parity) links between international capital, foreign exchange, product and factor markets. The second class consists of assumptions about deviations from the ideal parity conditions. These normally take the form of assumptions about imperfections in the capital, foreign exchange, product and factor markets. Such imperfections are deemed to create profit opportunities for firms, especially those with a high involvement in these markets. Deviations from parity conditions will be discussed in detail in chapter 3, where possible profit opportunities open to the firm will be identified.

Under both sets of assumptions the conventional aim of financial decision making is to maximize shareholder wealth. Conventionally, these decisions have been classified into the strategic investment, financing and dividend decisions, and the tactical decisions such as cash management and working capital management (e.g. Brealey and Myers 1981). The analysis of the environment has concentrated mainly on the capital market, both as a source of funds and as a means to measure the discount rate for capital investments.

In the idealized world of the first set of market forces assumptions, the only decisions that matter are the investment and the funding decisions. The former is the source of value for the enterprise. The financing decision does not add value but it does make the investment decision possible. A wide range of ancillary financial decision areas are considered irrelevant in that they should have no impact on shareholder wealth. Thus there is no need to expend scarce managerial resources on decision areas such as

- capital structure decisions
- dividend decisions – on group dividend to external shareholders or internal dividends from subsidiaries
- cash management or working capital management decisions
- currency or interest rate risk management decisions.

There is a considerable theoretical literature outlining the arguments for the irrelevance of decision areas such as capital structure and dividend policy and currency risk under these ideal circumstances (e.g. Dufey and Srinivasulu 1983).

The second set of market forces assumptions points to a world in which there are many imperfections such as taxes, bankruptcy costs, market failure or disequilibrium, and government intervention in financial markets. These conditions can reduce or add to the fundamental value created by the investment decision. The presumption remains that the investment decision continues to be the primary source of value. The central role of funding and other financial decisions is to support investment decisions and to fully exploit the shareholder value available from real assets. Under these circumstances, financial decision making should concentrate on identifying and correctly valuing investment projects, on avoiding financial distress, and on estimating and securing the cash flows expected from the real business. When these imperfections are thought to exist there is the possibility of additional value being created by careful manipulation of funding and the other supporting financial decisions. Thus in the capital structure decision, tax imperfections can be a source of value by exploiting additional borrowing capacity. Cheap finance may also be available from government sources or from segmented capital markets. However, additional value achieved from the exploitation of imperfections in financial markets is likely to be transient and quickly arbitraged away once known. These opportunities therefore provide a bonus for the finance function rather than a primary rationale or activity.

These two major sets of market forces assumptions – neo-classical and imperfections – underpin the conventional framework for identifying the central problems in and decision techniques of IFM. They both share the common view that the major explanations for IFM problems lie in a market framework, perfect or otherwise. In these two sets of assumptions the firm is seen as either passively accepting market forces, or alternatively reacting to market imperfections. However, a significant part of the IFM literature now emphasizes the active role of the firm in fashioning the economic environment to its own requirements through its unique control over information, technology or markets. This development is particularly strong in the general area of theorizing about the nature of MNCs and in the areas dealing with political risk, direct foreign investment, and the formulation of strategy by MNCs. This perspective emphasizes the purposeful nature of the MNC and its impact on the economic environment. The joint firm–market view of economic phenomena developed by Williamson (1975; 1977) and the literature on strategic and financial planning provide alternative frameworks from which to assess the significance (or otherwise) of IFM issues.

In conclusion, the three sets of assumptions about the economic environment to be employed in this text are

1 neo-classical assumptions – efficient and linked pricing between markets
2 deviations from neo-classical ideal conditions – imperfect markets
3 Joint market–firm behaviour – MNCs as strategically active economic agents.

The market forces perspective (including deviations) dominates the analyses of IFM decision making in chapters 2 to 13 and is a major theme of the book. However, the alternative view of the MNC as a purposeful and active economic agent is employed throughout the text and is used to draw further implications for IFM decision making, especially in the context of integrated financial planning and strategic analysis.

## 1.3 Financial Decisions in the International Firm

It is clear from sections 1.1 and 1.2 that increasing multinationality involves a firm in a complex financial, political and economic environment. This in turn can lead to a host of novel international financial management problems and an increased level of complexity in conventional areas of financial management. At this stage, the degree of international involvement classification scheme in table 1.1 and the sets of environmental assumptions from section 1.2 can be used to tentatively identify some of the novel issues created by the additional complexity of IFM phenomena.

The wholly domestic firm (i.e. domestic I in table 1.1) appears to have no international involvement at all, and it apparently faces the conventional range of domestic financial management problems. However, if capital markets are assumed to be fully integrated with one world pricing mechanism for risky financial securities, then even this firm must take a global perspective. If its owners hold diversified portfolios in a world capital market in which a world risk/return trade-off exists, then its managers should employ the world-wide opportunity cost of funds when measuring discount rates for investment projects. The wholly domestic firm may face further internationally based problems if MNCs are competing in its home market. The competitive presence of MNCs may affect the cash flows it expects from existing investments and from new proposals. This may occur directly via world-wide competition or indirectly through exchange rate changes affecting the competitive position.

If we turn to the active importer or exporter (domestic II in table 1.1), this trading activity may involve receipts and payments in foreign currencies and therefore the possibility of exposure to transaction risk, i.e. the risk that these receipts and payments will be adversely affected by unexpected changes in currency values. Various strategies for minimizing risk from transactions exposure are employed by practitioners. These include the purchase and sale of currencies in foreign exchange markets at some future transaction date (forward hedges), or the use of the money markets to hedge or avoid the perceived foreign exchange rate risk.

However, when one turns to MNC I, a major change has occurred in the decision problems facing the company. The decision to invest overseas marks a dramatic change for many companies. The complexity of this decision is witnessed by the vast and burgeoning literature on the theory of direct foreign investment (DFI). The firm now faces different legal, political and cultural systems impinging on its day-to-day operational decision making. This added complexity introduces a new dimension to the risk of managing subsidiaries, i.e. political risk. This is the risk that host governments may periodically interfere in the subsidiaries' operations, and that this interference will have an adverse effect on the returns on DFI as received by the parent. The theory of DFI and the analysis of political risk are wholly new issues raised in IFM, and domestic financial management theory offers little in this respect. Further potential problems associated with the DFI decision include the effect of unanticipated exchange rate changes on future overseas cash flows (economic exposure) and on accounting measurements of events prior to the exchange rate changes (accounting or translation exposure). The large MNC with many overseas subsidiaries can avoid some foreign exchange risk by the internal transfer of funds within the firm. The ability to combat foreign exchange risks in this way is a unique feature of MNCs and of the field of IFM, and this will be explored in chapters 5, 6 and 7.

MNC II and MNC III in table 1.1 complete the full internationalization of the firm as it first enters a range of domestic debt markets and unregulated 'offshore' debt markets and then seeks equity funds in several domestic stock exchanges. The firm may now face exchange rate risk on its sources of capital as well as its uses of capital. This also raises further questions about capital structure and the cost of financing of such sophisticated MNCs. The expanded choice of external financing sources also enhances the ability of the MNC to use its internal financial transfer system to exploit these choices.

These MNCs will also differ in terms of the degree of co-ordination the firm exercises over its international business operations and functions such as treasury. This, in turn, is likely to have an effect on the way in which financial problems can be dealt with in an MNC. Centralized treasury operations with a capability to exploit internal financial flows or world financial markets can simplify some financial problems for the treasurer and create new kinds of financial management opportunities. In addition, an enterprise that can co-ordinate its global sourcing of, say, semi-finished components or can centrally adjust its currencies of invoicing is also better placed to deal with the complexities of IFM. MNCs without these capabilities may find that they are particularly vulnerable to problems such as currency risk. Their ability to recognize these problems, and to respond to them in a way that protects shareholder wealth, may be much impaired. They may therefore have to make extensive use of externally supplied banking services to remedy their internal weaknesses.

Questions such as currency risk, subsidiary versus group capital structure, and global treasury co-ordination are accentuated by the nature of MNCs and their world of complex and varied international financial and banking markets. However, many international financial management decisions are similar to equivalent domestic financial management questions. This suggests that domestic financial management theory can provide a useful starting point for IFM. In particular, it will be shown in chapters 4 to 13 that international capital budgeting and financing decisions have many similarities with the equivalent domestic decisions. However, exchange rate risk, political interference and the wide variety of international capital markets do create unique problems in international capital budgeting, financing, liquidity management and working capital decision areas. The differences between the domestic decision and its international counterpart will therefore be drawn out in these chapters. Dividend decisions in MNCs can be separated into subsidiary dividends paid to the parent and MNC dividends paid to shareholders of the parent. The former decision will involve the cross-border transfer of funds and has many novel IFM implications. The latter decision involving the home country dividend decision of the MNC is assumed to be little influenced by the multinationality of the firm and is considered to be comparable to the dividend decision of the domestic company. The subsidiary dividend question is therefore considered in this text as part of the analysis of the intra-firm transfer of funds. The overall MNC dividend decision is assumed to be adequately covered in the domestic financial management literature and a detailed discussion is therefore omitted from this text.

As a result the novel issues in IFM appear to include

- foreign exchange rate behaviour
- determinants of direct foreign investment decisions
- political risk analysis
- integration and efficiency of international capital markets
- differences between various domestic capital markets.

The extensions to the class of decisions to be found in domestic financial management include

- foreign exchange risk management
- interest rate risk management in many funding currencies

- capital budgeting, including identifying cash flows and discount rates
- capital structure and financing decisions in international capital markets
- cash and working capital management in many currencies, including intra-firm transfers of funds and the subsidiary dividend decision.

The extent to which these issues and the associated decision needs arise in the firm are clearly dependent on the degree of international involvement of the firm, the degree of control over the operations and financial decisions of subsidiaries, and the nature of the international economy. These problems impinge upon domestic companies to some degree, but are central to firms with increasing degrees of multinationality. In the following chapters an attempt will be made to identify the conditions under which these IFM decision problems become significant to the firm. The emphasis will be on the internationally involved firm and the key strategic decision areas identified above, i.e. capital budgeting, foreign exchange risk management (FERM) and financing decisions. The tactical decisions dealing with working capital management will also be partially covered in the foreign exchange risk management area. Dividend decisions for MNCs will be covered to the extent that they relate to intra-company transfers, but the overall MNC dividend decision in the major home base is otherwise assumed to be comparable to that of the domestic firm.

## 1.4 Fundamental Concepts of Finance and IFM

The strong similarities between domestic and international financial management questions suggest that financial management theory developed primarily in a domestic context can provide a valuable framework and set of concepts for IFM. As a result, international financial management theory attempts to satisfy the complex financial decision needs of corporate treasurers by making extensive use of the central concepts of orthodox theory. These include an emphasis on cash flow concepts and the need to reward investors for the time value of money and risk, and the use of the net present value (NPV) rule. IFM also exploits the distinction between systematic and unsystematic risk, and makes use of models such as the capital asset pricing model (CAPM) to assess the price for risk, as well as extending the implications of market efficiency to a host of international financial markets. Table 1.2 provides some examples of how these fundamental concepts are employed throughout this book.

**Table 1.2** Orthodox theoretical concepts and their application to IFM theory

| Concepts | Examples of international application areas |
|---|---|
| *At market level* | |
| CAPM | Integration and segmentation issues in world financial markets |
| Systematic/unsystematic risk | Diversification effects across a world portfolio; reference market for risk; significance of total risk for managers |
| Market efficiency | In external markets for bank deposits, currency, Eurobonds and equities |
| Law of one price | Parity relationships in international financial markets |
| Arbitrage | Between future and forward markets; between tax systems; between banking systems |
| *At firm or transaction level* | |
| NPV | International capital budgeting; valuing Eurobonds or syndicated loans |
| Value additivity | Use of adjusted present value rule in capital budgeting; value penalty loss due to lack of management of currency risk |
| Options | Currency options, real options in international capital budgeting |

These basic concepts of finance are an important means to comprehend many of the complexities in the world of international finance. As such they can provide a valuable guide to financial decision making in this complex world. These concepts will be extensively employed throughout chapters 2 to 13 and form the foundations of the market forces perspective on international financial management.

## 1.5 The Role and Nature of the Finance and Treasury Function

Concepts of finance and an identification of the major financial decisions in the international firm are key elements of a book on international financial management. However, these ideas must be understood and implemented by an organizational unit. This section investigates the nature of the MNC

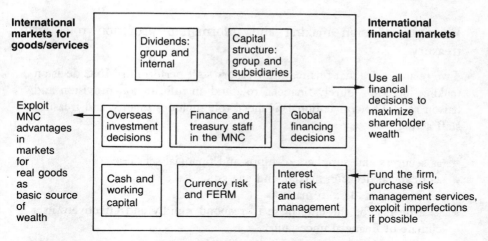

**Figure 1.3** International financial management decisions in the MNC

finance and treasury function and its central role in conducting financial policy for the enterprise.

Figure 1.3 places the international financial management problems of the MNC in the context of real and financial markets. The investment decision is the fundamental source of value for the firm and is the centre of attention for the board, managing directors and operational staff. The aim of overseas investment is to create value by matching the unique advantages of the enterprise in, say, product design, production technology or marketing with the special advantages of overseas locations. The latter may include access to very large markets, cheap raw materials or the lower cost of labour. The exploitation of these location specific advantages in markets for real goods and services is the province of operational managers and is the core basis for creating additional shareholder wealth.

This decision is supported by a host of international financial management decisions. These make the investment decision feasible and are the means to protect and enhance the wealth created. The links between all of the decision areas form much of the substance of chapters 5 to 13, with chapter 14 investigating these links in some detail.

Finance staff, more specifically the finance director (or chief financial executive), and treasury staff are involved in all of these international financial management decision areas. The treasurer and finance director can be seen as the 'staff in the middle' between real markets for goods, services, labour etc. and financial markets.

## Financial decision making and information provision roles of treasury

Two related roles that finance and treasury staff perform in MNC decision making include a purely financial role and an information provision and liaison role. The conventional financial role includes finance and treasury staff acting

- as securers and suppliers of funds and financial services
- as financial decision makers and analysts
- as financial traders in markets
- as a means for the enterprise to respond rapidly and effectively in a climate of financial uncertainty.

This financial role involves the finance and treasury staff satisfying the expected and unexpected financial service needs of the firm and dealing with the financial risks facing the firm, subject to strategic aims. Their specialism lies in financial matters, and many of their day-to-day activities are located at the boundary between the firm and financial markets. In some cases, such as in currency trading, treasury staff may be wholly oriented to the marketplace and know little about the nature of the enterprise in which they work.

The second role involves finance and treasury staff providing information to and liaising with board members, and mediating between divisional and subsidiary managers and other operational managers. Finance and treasury staff can therefore collect information from senior and operational staff on the financial needs, and financial risks, arising from strategic and operational decisions. They can also co-ordinate discussions between operational and finance staff on the implications of perceived financial risks for the firm. Thus exchange rate forecasts and their implications for sourcing, pricing and currency risk may require joint decisions on changes to operational decisions and to financial hedging. The extent of this liaison role for finance/treasury staff depends on the scale and significance of financial risks facing the firm. Firms with high operational flexibility and facing extensive financial risks are more likely to exploit such liaison possibilities. Finance and treasury staff must be able to speak both the language of the financial marketplace and that of the real business of the firm if they wish to succeed in this information provision and liaison role.

## Treasury and finance function organization

In practice, the finance function consists of a diverse group of finance related staff undertaking a wide range of financial, accounting and tax decisions. The treasurer generally forms part of the team reporting to the finance director along with the chief accountant. Figure 1.4 (adapted from Hodson 1984: E1/13) illustrates the organization of finance in a typical large corporation. One or more of these departments may be combined depending on many practical factors faced by each company. As a result the financial and information/liaison roles identified above are likely to be distributed across a range of finance, treasury and operational managers.

Figure 1.4 also illustrates that close liaison will often be required between treasury and financial accounting and management accounting staff as well as with tax specialists. This liaison may involve decisions on hedging currency and interest rate risks on the balance sheet, on identifying project cash flows and on assessing the tax implications of new projects and of financing decisions.

The division of these tasks will vary between firms. However, the finance director will generally focus on links between strategic issues and international financial management decisions. This could involve the evaluation of significant new overseas projects, new acquisitions, global financing policy, and the identification of broad guidelines for risk management.

The treasurer will generally be concerned with working capital and cash management, global financing of the company and its subsidiaries, interest rate and currency risk management, and managing the relationships with the principal suppliers of financial goods and services. The most important of these suppliers are the firm's bankers, whose products/services include

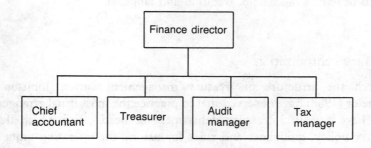

**Figure 1.4** Organization of finance function (adapted from Hodson 1984: E1/13)

bank lending, underwriting of securities, cheque clearing and money transmission services, corporate finance advice, and the provision of risk management advice and services. As a result the treasurer will dominate the purely financial role identified above. He or she will spend much of his or her time as an active transactor in financial markets and will act as a key intermediary between the firm and financial markets. The treasurer is therefore likely to have a strong cost reduction or profit maximization orientation, giving rise to decisions that have an immediate impact on the profit and loss of the business.

The finance director role is closer to the heart of the business. It involves liaison with the board and divisional and subsidiary managers in terms of the role of finance and financial services in enhancing or protecting shareholder wealth.

In practice the division of duties here will vary across organizations depending on factors such as the size and individual philosophy of the organization and the degree of complexity of its financial problems. Whatever organizational form the treasury takes in a company, the main treasury activities will evolve around the above core areas and related issues.

Channon and Jalland (1979) point out that treasury management in the MNC is substantially different from that in purely domestic firms. They observe that the treasurer in an MNC must cope with an additional range of problems not faced in one country trading, such as international taxation rates, variations in local capital markets, exchange control restraints, and specific legal and accounting convention constraints prevailing in individual countries. Moreover, international executives face a number of special difficulties, notably of time, distance and culture, which complicate their task. Distance results in delays and reduced reliability in communication; time-zone differences result in significant problems for short run foreign exchange and cash management; while cultural variations lead to problems of custom, tradition and language.

## Treasury centralization

Though the structure of treasury management varies, Johnson and Batchelor (1988) have observed that in practice the most usual arrangement is to have a central treasury department at head office which defines treasury policy, guidelines and rules for use by the operating units. The decision on whether to centralize or decentralize depends on a host of practical requirements. Some of the factors that are likely to influence the centralization of the finance and treasury function are as follows:

*Environmental*
- good access possible to major world financial centres
- large number of national controls such as exchange controls or transfer pricing rules

*Strategic*
- strong desire to avoid financial distress
- operational decisions already centralized

*Corporate*
- high degree of control over currencies of sale or purchase
- large scale or volume of international financial transactions, both external to firm with customers and suppliers and internal to firm between subsidiaries
- high sophistication of internal financial transfer system
- strong ethnocentric views of group management
- wide geographic spread of the operating units
- sophisticated funding and financial service needs of subsidiaries/ affiliates.

Clearly the finance/treasury function should be structured to accommodate the requirements of the commercial operations of the firm. However, the treasury structure does not have to be dictated by the structure of those operations. Thus operating units may be decentralized, but the scale of treasury operations and transactions, and the concentration of supply in a few major financial centres, may give the central group treasury major advantages in reducing internal and external transaction costs. The ICI case described earlier indicates that centralization advantages may not exist at the level of operational decisions in an MNC but do exist for treasury. As a result, group treasury has a stronger incentive to centralize than other functions. These centralizing forces may only apply to areas such as foreign exchange risk management and this may mean that other treasury activities such as bank lending can be decentralized. The centralizing forces may also lead to treasury acting as a profit rather than a cost centre. If treasury develops the capability to exploit market imperfections and thus make profits in its own right, then this can become the benchmark for treasury performance. One problem that can arise here is that a purely profit seeking treasury can lose sight of the business aims of the firm, and this can lead to poor treasury support for strategic and operational decisions.

There are advantages to both treasury centralization and decentralization. According to Sweeney and Rachlin (1984), a centralized treasury allows close control of financial issues at headquarters. It also ensures consistency and compliance with the corporation's global policies. On the other hand, decentralization ensures local management involvement and accountability. It also means that any central treasury functions will be small in number and less bureaucratic than a large centralized corporate treasury. Although companies may try to build a compromise solution that incorporates the best aspects of centralization and decentralization, modern treasuries, at least in international enterprises, are generally constructed on the basis that the advantages of a centralized structure outweigh those of a decentralized structure.

The ICI group treasury is a good example of a centralized system. The treasury team consisted of about 40 people in 1987 (Henderson and Rogerson 1987). About half were involved mainly in short term cash and currency management or the provision of trade finance. The focus of the other members of the team included medium term and long term funding for the group and individual subsidiaries as well as general liability management duties. Advice was also provided on acquisitions, divestments and other major investment projects. Bank relationships were carefully managed at this point to avoid the costs of over-banking and to provide the spread and flexibility of services required by the subsidiaries and the group. The aim was to develop a treasury team that was capable of responding quickly to the financial needs of the business world-wide as well as able to exploit attractive funding opportunities.

The existence of such a sophisticated treasury function can be seen as a central component of a flexible financing, financial services supply and risk management policy. It provides the means to implement financial policy. In addition, its responsiveness to unanticipated demands can be seen as a key means to deal with uncertainty in financial markets.

## Recent changes in the treasury function

Treasury centralization is one manifestation of the growing sophistication of the treasury function of MNCs over the past decade. This has been stimulated by many recent changes in international financial and banking markets. These changes are discussed in section 2.2. For the present, a brief insight into these changes and their impact on the treasury function will be outlined.

The increased volatility of foreign exchange rates and interest rates and the changing transaction costs experienced by treasurers in the 1970s and 1980s have played a role in changing the corporate treasury function. The emergence of freely floating currencies (after 1973) and the increased variety of foreign exchange risk management products are related to the growth of foreign exchange functions in MNC treasuries. These changes have heightened the currency dimension of strategic, operational and financial decisions. This in turn has increased the significance of currency information, advice and liaison roles for treasury in relation to all of these decision areas. It has also increased the significance of foreign exchange trading functions and foreign exchange risk management functions within the modern treasury. The changes have focused treasurers' minds on the special qualities of certain external modes of supply. Banks with special skills in currency supply, risk management products and advice may be preferred as 'lead' or 'close relationship' banks. Similar problems and treasury responses have occurred throughout the 1980s with respect to interest rate volatility. This problem has highlighted the role of treasury in dealing with interest rate risks, especially in terms of their impact on the liability management of the firm. Deregulation of world financial markets and innovations in new financial instruments have also played a key role in encouraging the development of the treasury function (Lessard 1989). These changes are discussed in greater detail in chapter 2.

The changes in international financial markets have combined with the growing internationalization of business to provide fertile ground in which new treasury skills have flourished. The increasing internationalization of business and the growing complexity of financial problems have accentuated the importance of a sophisticated treasury capable of dealing with financial uncertainty. The emergence of sophisticated treasury functions in many MNCs has underlined the role of treasury as a co-ordinator and in some cases producer of internal supplies of financial services. This has also focused attention on the need to proactively manage external suppliers of funds and financial services.

In addition, many changes in the costs of financial transacting have occurred in the past two decades. In firms the sophistication of treasury trading and information technology has dramatically improved over the past decade (Knight and Barnett 1990) and this has increased the scope for internal transacting. In markets, the growth of security funding (securitization) compared with bank funding indicates that transaction costs have been lowered for direct financing via markets compared with indirect financing via financial intermediaries (Lewis and Davis 1987: 380). The reduction in transaction costs has meant that internal treasury sourcing of funds and financial services and direct market transacting bypassing banks have become more important over the decade.

## Treasury as an In-House Bank

These environmental change factors have probably also played a part in encouraging centralized treasury operations in MNCs. Such centralized, professionally managed treasuries have the potential to perform many of the functions traditionally handled by the organization's banker(s). It is this kind of treasury which is now referred to as an 'in-house bank' (IHB). This involves centralizing the group's treasury function so as to manage the financial resources and liabilities from a central focal point, and thus to act as a banker to the rest of the group (i.e. all its subsidiaries) and to provide a united group front to the conventional banks in the placing or raising of funds (Beerel 1987). It is clear from this definition that the word 'bank' refers to the internalization by the modern corporate treasury of functions which previously were performed by its banker(s).

The sophisticated treasury or in-house bank is now able to produce or source some financial services internally. In a large MNC group, the group treasury can now act as a financial intermediary between the wide range of surplus/deficit MNC subsidiaries on the one hand and banks and capital markets on the other. The group treasury has a sophisticated information system which enables it to know the position (known exposures in various currencies, potential exposures, financing needs, cash flow surpluses etc.) for each subsidiary and across the whole group.

More specifically, the IHB can handle nearly all aspects of external supply with banks and other financial institutions for the subsidiaries. This includes corporate finance advice, foreign exchange business, and short term and long term funding. For example, currency risk management and foreign exchange trading can be wholly managed by the specialist in-house bank. The company can identify the subsidiaries' exchange rate exposures and then write (internal) forward exchange contracts for the subsidiaries (i.e. between the group and the subsidiary). The company can then decide if it needs to cover its net group position by entering forward exchange rate contracts with a bank.

The emergence of centralized and sophisticated treasury operations in MNCs has significant implications for international financial management. These organizational units are likely to

- be efficient at generating relevant information for IFM decisions
- be experienced at recognizing and managing complex IFM problems
- be able to provide specialist financial advice to the board and subsidiary managers and to assess the implications of financial risks for strategic and operational decisions
- have a high degree of co-ordination over internal financial decisions
- have a high degree of control over external suppliers of funds and financial services
- be able to transact in financial services at 'fair' market rates
- be able to respond quickly to financial price and supply uncertainty.

Treasury is the organizational means to implement many of the rules, guidelines and concepts of international financial management theory. This book recognizes the significance of the treasury function. It therefore attempts to outline the central concepts and decision rules for the international financial manager and to place them in the context of such an organizational function.

## 1.6 The Structure of the Book and Major Topics Covered

This chapter has briefly identified the additional complexities that financial managers face as they move from a domestic to an international arena. In the following chapters the novel issues and problems of IFM are analysed in some detail. In so doing, much of the literature on IFM will be summarized.

In chapter 2 the institutional nature of the international monetary and financial system is described, including the role of international banks, the functions of supranational bodies, and the main features of markets for foreign exchange, international bonds and equities, and various futures and options products. This is followed by an analysis of recent changes in world financial markets, in bank regulation and in the world debt crisis. The changes have brought about new levels of complexity and new degrees of freedom for the international finance executive and treasury staff. This in turn has meant that more highly skilled managers are required in this function. The aim in subsequent chapters is to provide the insights necessary for the development of these skills.

This is followed in chapter 3 by a presentation of the neo-classical perspective on how this system prices foreign exchange and financial assets. The theories outlined are then used to draw implications for IFM decision making. This chapter demonstrates the value of orthodox financial theory in providing a conceptual framework for IFM decision making. Concepts such as the 'law of one price' and market efficiency are applied to foreign exchange and international capital markets and are shown to be of considerable value in interpreting complex market and institutional phenomena.

The neo-classical framework is then applied to the three key decision areas of international financial management. These are foreign exchange risk management, financing decisions, and capital budgeting decisions. If the equilibrium relationships hold then many of the issues of international financial management are shown to be illusions. Coping with the problems of IFM therefore becomes a question of using existing domestic financial management (DOFM) theory and the parity relationships to see through these illusions to the fundamental financial problems common to all firms.

Chapter 3 then considers deviations from this view of well functioning markets and assesses the evidence for imperfections in international markets for capital, currency and financial services. If these imperfections occur, they create sources of profit or additional value for the firm and there is much for financial managers to do with respect to IFM issues. This chapter identifies the limitations of the orthodox view and highlights the need for financial managers to actively respond to profitable opportunities in international factor, product, foreign exchange and capital markets. These possibilities will be investigated by looking again at the three decision areas identified above. This forms the substance of chapters 4 to 13.

Chapters 4 to 13 explore the central corporate IFM decisions under a series of assumptions ranging from imperfections to well functioning foreign exchange, international capital and product markets. This includes the foreign exchange risk management (FERM) decisions in chapters 4, 5, 6 and 7, capital budgeting in chapters 8, 9 and 10, and financing decisions in chapters 11, 12 and 13. In these chapters, the role of computer based models as decision aids is demonstrated and examples of sensitivity analysis of the decisions are presented. The design of the models is based on the decision rules outlined in the chapters, and the models place greater analytical and computational power in the hands of the financial manager facing increasingly complex international financial management problems.

In the first part of chapter 4, major deviations from the parity relationships are shown to make corporate foreign exchange risk management relevant to both managers and investors. This section will also outline an active opportunistic strategy for foreign exchange risk management consistent with the pursuit of shareholder wealth maximization. The second part of the chapter is concerned with outlining the general nature of the foreign exchange risk management problem. This problem will then be explored in some detail.

The next three chapters look at examples of some of the major techniques of foreign exchange risk management. This will include strategic and operational responses (chapter 5), various internal financial techniques (chapter 6) as well as forward market hedges, money market hedges and currency options (chapter 7).

Chapter 5 considers how a firm can fashion its strategic and operational decisions as part of a set of responses to currency risk. In section 5.1 we consider how adaptations to strategy can reduce economic exposure to currency risk. Section 5.2 looks at operational responses. In section 5.3 we consider a model of the overall FERM problem and how a firm can choose between a wide variety of real and financial FERM methods.

A high degree of flexibility in strategic and operational decisions is essential for FERM. This flexibility often depends on corporate or industry specific factors and manifests itself as unique corporate advantages. The widely diversified MNC is likely to have major advantages here, especially when its marketing and production managers can exploit their specialized knowledge of the firm's imperfect product and factor markets to support currency risk management.

In chapter 6 we consider internal financial techniques including netting, leading and lagging, and matching as an asset and liability management technique (Prindl 1976; McRae and Walker 1980). Internal techniques are primarily used to alter the company's exposure but may also be used to create profit opportunities for the firm by allowing it to make informed bets against exchange rate movements. The firm's capability to employ many of these internal techniques depends on the existence of a sophisticated internal financial system in the MNC. The nature of this system is the topic for section 6.1. Sections 6.2 and 6.3 are concerned with the use of the internal financial techniques in currency risk management.

In chapter 7 we consider the use of market based risk management instruments in FERM. These include forward contracts, short term borrowing and currency options. External techniques are generally used to insure against a loss due to an exposed position, but may also be used to 'bet against' perceived deviations in exchange rates or interest rates.

In chapter 8 we consider the overseas investment decision. In section 8.1 we consider the various theories of direct foreign investment (DFI) and seek to explain the corporate rationale behind decisions, in particular the manner in which overseas projects are likely to generate additional wealth for the owners of the firm. In section 8.2 we consider the nature of political risk and its impact on the overseas investment decision. In section 8.3 we consider how these theory sources can be used to guide the search for valuable overseas investment opportunities. In section 8.4 we consider how MNCs have developed their global strategy and the impact of strategy on the search for overseas investment opportunities.

Chapter 8 reveals some of the limitations of the market forces perspective. This leads to an analysis in which the financial manager is viewed as a member of an enterprise which is able to create and maintain market imperfections. However, corporate market power is shown to be constrained by political risk considerations. This view, in which the firm exercises considerable power, albeit constrained by political forces, is in sharp contrast to the market forces perspective adopted in chapters 2 to 7 and 9 to 13.

In chapter 9 we are concerned with analysis of the overseas capital budgeting decision. The global capital strategic analysis discussed in the previous chapter provides a key context for this chapter in that it aids the search for valuable overseas investment opportunities. In contrast, this chapter assumes that information on the overseas investment opportunity is available. It therefore focuses on theoretical models for the valuation of capital budgeting projects. This chapter provides the basis for the development in chapter 10 of a computer based model as a decision aid for managers involved in this complex decision area.

In chapter 10 we discuss the StrathKelvin company – a case in international capital budgeting. The StrathKelvin company is a British based MNC specializing in the manufacture and sale of a variety of electronic consumer goods. The problem the firm faces involves a decision to invest in a large production facility overseas. The case is used to explore how an MNC can generate information on cash flows and includes a detailed calculation of the net present value of the project. The example calculation is also used to explore the design of a spreadsheet model and the role of sensitivity analysis in decision making.

In chapter 11 we consider the wide variety of sources of funds for the international enterprise. We begin in section 11.1 by describing the main characteristics of international financial centres. These centres are important sources of many different kinds of finance. In the case of the very large centres such as London and New York they are the dominant locations for raising syndicated Euroloans, Eurobonds and commercial paper. In section 11.2 we investigate the typical funding vehicles employed in these markets. The focus here is on the way in which firms raise syndicated Euroloans, Eurobonds and commercial paper as well as the central role of the international bank in these markets. In section 11.3 we describe the use of interest rate and currency swaps in risk management in the MNC treasury.

In chapter 12 we analyse the overseas financing decision. This is a complex decision problem in its own right. For example, in the case of the MNC financing overseas subsidiaries it involves choices (for the parent company) between home currency (HC) financing, local currency (LC) financing for subsidiaries, foreign currency (FC) financing (foreign to home and subsidiary), and internal transfers of funds. The basic decision model for evaluating these choices is the conventional NPV model. The goal is therefore to maximize the net present value of a bond sale or debt issue.

In chapter 13 we consider how an MNC can finance its world-wide operations. This requires an initial consideration of the complexities of the global funding decision and an analysis of the funding implications of efficient and inefficient financial markets. This is followed by an investigation of the capital structure decision for the MNC. The identification of the overall corporate capital structure and local subsidiary capital structure norms provides the boundaries within which the firm can pursue a value maximization goal for the financing decision. These sections provide the basis to analyse the global financing policy of the MNC. This policy considers how funding decisions can interact with risk management decisions and capital structure constraints and how together they can alter the riskiness of the firm's cash flows and the value of the firm. ICI is employed as a detailed case to illustrate these issues.

The three decision frameworks outlined in section 1.2 include pure market forces, well functioning and efficient markets in an imperfect world, and the view of the MNC as an active and purposeful economic agent. These views are complementary in many respects and can be of considerable value to the financial manager of the internationally involved enterprise. They will be used throughout these chapters to discuss in detail the state of the art of international financial decision making. A market forces perspective dominates the analysis of financial decision making. However, where possible and relevant the active and purposeful behaviour of the MNC is emphasized. Thus in chapter 8 the implications for IFM decision making of various theories of MNC economic behaviour are considered. This chapter also highlights the role of political risk analysis in the development of corporate strategy.

Chapter 14 reviews the previous chapters and outlines a corporate financial strategy under each major set of assumptions concerning the economic and political environment. This provides an essential context for integrating the major IFM decisions in the internationally involved enterprise.

# 2

# The International Financial System

In this chapter we begin in section 2.1 by investigating the nature of the international financial and monetary system. This section will be primarily concerned with describing the system by identifying its major institutional elements and the manner in which they relate to each other. In section 2.2 we describe recent changes in this system. The aim of the chapter is to ensure that the student of international financial management can understand this key context for financial decision making and its impact on the development of the corporate finance and treasury function.

The description of the major institutional elements, including governments, supranational institutions, financial markets, financial institutions and multinational firms, provides one means to understand the unity of this system. In addition we will see that the growing role of inter-governmental co-operation in these financial and banking markets provides further insight into how these components interact. Market forces will also be introduced as a key unifying feature of this system but will be explored in more detail in chapter 3. Finally, the concept of the international bank as a new kind of financial firm, organized around all of these financial markets, will be employed as another unifying principle.

## 2.1 The International Monetary and Financial System

The international monetary and financial system is a key source of funds, foreign exchange and liquidity for the internationally involved enterprise. It contains many interacting and rapidly evolving institutional elements and these are briefly outlined in figure 2.1.

The major institutional categories identified in the diagram are supranational bodies, governments and their agents, markets, financial

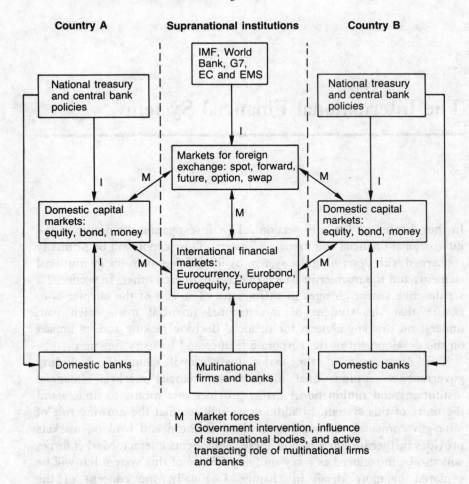

**Figure 2.1** Institutional elements of the international financial and monetary system

institutions and MNCs. All of these institutions are linked in some way either through the pressures of market forces or through the influence of governments or supranational institutions.

In the simple two country model outlined in figure 2.1, countries A and B are assumed to have well developed domestic financial systems. Borrowers and lenders in these countries can transact domestically, or in each other's markets by going through the foreign exchange market or by dealing in the 'offshore' international markets. Thus these markets are linked in some way and economic events in one country or region may well affect market prices in all markets.

Governments and supranational institutions also play a part in influencing and directly controlling parts of this system. Individual governments may, through their central bank and treasury officials, control their domestic capital markets and intervene in dealings in their currencies. Governments may also act together in this way through some *ad hoc* agreement or within the confines of an international arrangement such as the European monetary system (EMS). Other supranational institutions such as the International Monetary Fund (IMF) and the World Bank play a part in influencing monetary arrangements in countries and therefore influence the way in which the foreign exchange markets can transact.

An important issue with respect to this system is whether it represents a single fully integrated market for funds and foreign exchange or whether it operates as a series of linked but segmented markets. If it is the former then the analysis of the system for the financial manager of the MNC enterprise is much simplified. This financial management issue will be discussed in chapter 3 and the evidence for and against integration is also presented in chapter 3. Related to this issue is the significance or otherwise of governmental and supranational interference in and control over parts of the system. This will be assessed in chapter 3.

For the present, this chapter will take a closer look at the elements of this system and some of the key interactions between these elements. In particular, in this section we consider international monetary arrangements, government intervention, the functioning of the major international financial markets and the role of banks. Throughout this chapter, government intervention, and the influence of supranational bodies, are seen as possible sources of distortion and regulation in markets. The transacting, arbitrage and speculative practices of MNCs, international banks and individuals are seen as activities which can improve the functioning of market forces.

In section 2.2 we consider recent changes in world financial markets, bank regulation and the world debt crisis. These have increased the complexity of this system by creating new links between the international markets for capital and currency, widening the opportunities for transacting and arbitrage by multinational banks and firms, and increasing the degree of international co-operation in managing the system. These changes have created new degrees of freedom for the international finance executive and treasury staff. They have also increased the significance of the finance function for the international enterprise (Castellanos 1990).

## International monetary arrangements

A brief historical progression of changes in exchange rate systems is shown in table 2.1. In the late nineteenth century the major trading nations fixed their currencies in terms of gold. Exchange rates were therefore fixed and these countries had essentially one common currency. When national gold reserves came under pressure, governments pursued contractionary policies to reduce the impact of trade on reserves; when the reserves grew, expansionary policies were adopted. Despite some limitations of this system, the gold standard worked reasonably well until the First World War disrupted international trade with the result that the main Western countries suspended convertibility of their currencies into gold. After the First World War some countries, notably Britain, attempted to return to the gold standard, with a high cost in terms of unemployment. This and other parallel developments, such as the emergence and then collapse of large scale international capital flows, were contributory factors to the Great Depression (Krueger 1983: 2). International monetary events were seen to have played a significant role in the Depression and so, during and after the Second World War, plans were laid to bring some order to the world monetary system.

In July 1944, international negotiations were held at Bretton Woods, New Hampshire, to identify the basis of the new monetary system. The participants envisaged an international monetary system that would determine exchange rate parities on the basis of consultations. This was meant to be a sharp contrast to the nationalistic 'beggar thy neighbour' policies that had contributed to the chaos of the 1930s. To this end a new

**Table 2.1** Historical changes in exchange rate systems

| | |
|---|---|
| 1821–1914 | Gold standard |
| 1914–1918 | First World War |
| 1919–1925 | Suspension of gold |
| 1925–1931 | Return to gold |
| 1931–1939 | Beggar thy neighbour |
| 1939–1945 | Second World War |
| 1944–1973 | Bretton Woods system |
| 1973–1985 | Floating of major currencies |
| 1985–1992 | Co-ordination via EMS, G7, IMF |
| 1992–1993 | EMS crisis |

exchange rate system was set up with the US dollar at its centre, and the International Monetary Fund (IMF) was established to monitor adherence to the Bretton Woods agreement.

The post-war system was designed to be one of fixed but adjustable exchange rates. Member nations of the IMF were expected to 'peg' their currencies within a narrow band of internationally agreed parities. The US pegged the dollar in terms of gold and all other nations pegged their currencies in terms of the US dollar.

The IMF was endowed with a pool of funds which could be lent to countries experiencing temporary balance of payments difficulties. The intention was to avoid devaluations unless fundamental changes such as long term trade imbalances had occurred in the economic position of the country. The IMF and the country concerned were encouraged to negotiate a new set of domestic policies designed to bring the balance of payments back into balance. Changes in exchange rate parities were expected only when it seemed unlikely that a change in domestic policies would relieve fundamental payment imbalances.

In practice, countries with balance of payment problems were generally reluctant to devalue and those with surpluses were not under pressure to revalue (Krueger 1983: 4). Pressure on countries in either situation grew in the 1960s with the increased mobility of capital across much expanded national and international capital markets. Speculative runs on currencies were increasingly common as foreign exchange market participants became adept at guessing when currency realignments were inevitable. In many cases this constituted a risk free bet for foreign exchange market agents as governments defended their currencies with most of their reserves.

The breakdown of the Bretton Woods system began when convertibility of the US dollar into gold ended in August 1971. In December 1971 the Smithsonian Agreement resulted in a major devaluation of the US dollar and multilateral adjustments in the major exchange rate parities. The US dollar crises of 1973 finally finished off Bretton Woods, when the major currencies abandoned the adjustable peg and floated their currencies against the US dollar.

Since then countries have adopted a wide range of exchange rate practices, including independent floats, group floating, pegging against a major currency, and pegging against a 'basket' of currencies such as the IMF's special drawing right (SDR) basket. The January 1976 Jamaica IMF meeting recognized these new exchange rate practices and accepted that the choice of exchange rate arrangements was up to the individual country.

It did however provide general guidelines for the management of exchange rate systems. Each member has to notify the IMF of any changes it makes and these should be made in such a way as to promote exchange rate stability. The IMF monitors the new system to ensure that it is effective and to ensure that members fulfil their obligations under the new arrangements. If the IMF feels that abuse is occurring it can initiate consultations with the country concerned and suggest changes in both exchange rates and internal domestic economic policies.

IMF members have exercised a considerable degree of latitude in their choice of currency exchange arrangements. These include pegging, crawling pegging, group floating, independent floating and various other variations on these themes.

Many countries, particularly less developed countries (LDCs), have chosen to peg their currencies either to a single currency, or to specially weighted baskets of currencies, or to the basket of currencies used by the IMF to calculate the value of its SDRs. One benefit of the last approach is that the IMF provides national exchange authorities with daily information on the value of the SDR basket. Pegged rates are generally managed on a daily basis through direct intervention in the foreign exchange market or indirectly by foreign exchange controls over transactions. Countries that peg to a particular currency such as the US dollar or the French franc are free to choose the intervention currency and the width of the intervention band within which they will intervene to defend their currency. Countries that peg relative to a basket of currencies intervene to manage a weighted average value of their currency. The currency weights are commonly based on the significance of their major trading partners. Central bankers and treasurers often intervene to stabilize currency fluctuations when they are outside certain limits such as $\pm 2$ per cent of the weighted average, and they generally employ a single currency such as the US dollar in their dealings.

Some variations on these themes are also employed. A few countries pursue a crawling peg policy in which frequent devaluations are made relative to the reference currency. Changes in indicators such as relative inflation rates or balance of payments position prompt an incremental change in the peg. Another example is where the currency basket employed by the IMF for the calculation of the value of SDRs is used as the reference point for pegging. The daily SDR rates published by the IMF are used to set the buying and selling rates, and a major currency such as the US dollar may be used to intervene when the currency moves outside the limits set by the country concerned.

The major industrial countries of the world such as the UK, Germany, the US, Japan and Canada allowed their currencies to float independently in the foreign exchange markets in the period after 1973. Market supply and demand forces therefore determined exchange rates and the historical link between exchange rate policy and domestic economic policies was broken in these cases. This was quite deliberate on the part of these countries. Their experience in managing exchange rates in the post-war system convinced them that such actions distracted attention from and distorted domestic economic policies.

During this 'pure floating' period the central banks and treasurers of floating currency countries intervened to differing degrees in foreign exchange markets, to limit daily variations in the exchange rates of their currencies. Interventionist practices differed between these countries, ranging from close control over daily variations to little or no intervention. For example, from 1981 onwards the US monetary authorities only intervened to smooth markets whenever they appeared to be 'disorderly'. The US monetary authorities, during the Reagan years, took the view that the value of the US dollar against other currencies was a matter for market forces and any action by the US government was likely to be costly and generally futile. This attitude changed with the Bush and Clinton leadership, especially in periods when the US dollar rapidly depreciated against the currencies of other major Western countries. In the post-Reagan era, disorderly conditions in the foreign exchange markets have promoted increasing exchange rate co-operation between the US authorities and other major Western countries. The New York Plaza Agreement in 1985 and the Louvre Accord in Paris in 1987 marked the return to co-operative monetary agreements on the part of the US authorities. This policy continued under the Clinton presidency.

During the period after the breakdown of Bretton Woods, other countries with floating currencies adopted a policy of 'leaning against the wind'. The central bank and treasury transacted directly or indirectly in the foreign exchange markets to minimize short term variations and to influence longer term trends in the exchange rate. Japan presented the major example of this practice in the early 1980s, but in 1985 began to act more in concert with other Western monetary and foreign exchange authorities as part of an international search for more orderly foreign exchange markets.

## Co-ordination and control in the foreign exchange and capital markets

The IMF has indicated that the main purpose of official intervention in exchange markets by member states is to counteract disorderly conditions which may consist of disruptive short term movements in a country's exchange rate. One situation in which this is thought to occur is when the bid–offer quote for a currency widens, reflecting increased uncertainty about the currency in question. Large fluctuations in exchange rates in association with a low volume of trading and an unwillingness by traders to buy a particular currency are also assumed to indicate disorderly conditions.

This broadly defined IMF guideline leaves considerable room for interpretation. In practice, countries pursue the orderly market goal in tandem with other goals when intervening in foreign exchange markets. 'Leaning against the wind' is one strategy designed to keep exchange rates in line with perceived long term trends. Other intervention policies include establishing target exchange rates and using the exchange rate to influence domestic currency reserves and monetary aggregates.

Co-ordination amongst nations has been the main feature of currency arrangements since the mid 1980s. This reflects a dissatisfaction with the high volatility of floating rate regimes and a harking back to the benefits of historically more stable arrangements. Since the mid 1980s a central feature of this co-ordinated action has been close liaison by the group of seven (G7) largest industrialized countries. G7 acts as an umbrella group for the seven key EC and North American countries and Japan when liaising on currency arrangements. The European monetary system (EMS) or exchange rate mechanism (ERM) is a wholly European example of such co-ordination and has a history going back to the end of the 1970s. This arrangement involves much more than co-operation and is an important example of a treaty based currency arrangement. The shared EC, North American and Japanese membership of G7 ensures that co-ordination is possible between these EC currency arrangements and other major world currencies. The IMF plays a central co-ordinating role for the major industrialized nations in this currency co-operation as well as holding a brief for the rest of the world and its desired currency arrangements.

The G7 leading industrial nations, namely Japan, the US, Canada, Italy, the UK, Germany and France, are at the heart of this co-operative system. They form an important bridge between the major trading blocs of the developed world and together can muster vast resources in support of their agreed currency arrangements. For example, their ability to co-ordinate purchases (sales) of say dollars to boost (deflate) the dollar far exceeds that of the US authorities. This can act as a deterrent to arbitrageurs or speculators in large banks and multinational treasuries if these market participants believe that the central bank authorities, acting together, have more funds at their disposal than they do. For example, the US dollar, after soaring against all major currencies in September 1984, suddenly went into reverse on Friday 21 September as the German Bundesbank sold approximately $500 million. This trend towards central bank co-operation in the 1990s will be boosted by the successful negotiation of the Uruguay round of the General Agreement on Tariffs and Trade (GATT) and the avoidance by the major trading blocs – Japan and the Pacific Rim, the USA plus Canada and Mexico, and the EC plus the European Free Trade Association (EFTA) – of exchange rates as part of a protectionist policy. The aim is that the lessons of the 1930s and the consequences of 'beggar thy neighbour' policies on this vast scale can be avoided.

The European monetary system (EMS) is a significant attempt on the part of Europeans to return to a Bretton Woods type of currency arrangement. This is much more than a voluntary co-operative exchange agreement in that it is underpinned by legal agreements between the member states. From March 1979 all members of the EC, except the UK, were active participants in this scheme. The UK was a member of the system for purposes of calculation of the value of the European currency unit (ECU) but it did not fix the pound relative to the ECU. The UK joined the system as a full member in October 1990 but suspended the pound from full membership in September 1992. The Irish pound (the punt) was eventually affected by this, and was devalued in the ERM by 10 per cent at the end of January 1993. The member countries float jointly against other currencies and internally peg their currencies to the ECU as a common reference unit. The EMS has partly a political and partly an economic purpose, in that it is seen as a first step to monetary union and ultimately political union, as well as a contribution to the stabilization of exchange rates within the EC (Boisseau 1990).

A central feature of the operation of the EMS is that par values of each currency are measured in terms of the ECU. This currency basket contains agreed proportions of each EC member's currency, with each weight based on the significance of the economy and currency concerned. Each currency has a central rate set against the ECU and so no one currency serves as the reference currency for the EMS system. From 8 October 1990 to 16

September 1992, sterling joined the exchange rate mechanism of the
European monetary system at a central rate of 0.696904 against the ECU
and a bilateral central rate of £1 = DM2.95. The Deutschmark exchange
rate is commonly used as the reference rate rather the ECU rate. This use
of the mark as the *de facto* anchor of the EMS has arisen because of the
significance of the mark within the EC and world trading zones. The
central ECU rates are used with upper and lower levels for intervention
purposes. For most currencies these consist of a narrow band of ±2.25 per
cent variation either side of the bilateral central rates. Between October
1990 and September 1992, the UK pound had a wider band of ±6 per
cent. Thus the pound could move within the range DM2.7780 to
DM3.1320 without requiring intervention from the UK and German
central banks. However, each member of the EMS is obliged to sell its
currency if it moves towards the upper limit and to buy if it drifts towards
the lower limit. In practice several countries might act together to bring a
currency back to within its agreed limits. This may take the form of the
German Bundesbank and the monetary authorities in say France, Holland,
Spain, Italy and the UK liaising in the purchases and sales of their
currencies in foreign exchange markets. Alternatively, these partners may
borrow or lend each other's currencies to boost or deplete their reserves.
Such action is more likely when bilateral exchange rates within the EMS
are tending to move to their agreed limits. If problems are occurring
between an EMS currency and say the US dollar then similar co-ordinated
action may be taken, possibly with the agreement of the American
authorities and within existing G7 agreements.

If fundamental changes are occurring in the economy of an EC member
country and it seems that its currency will not stay within the agreed limits,
then there are further arrangements to allow for devaluation or revaluation
of currencies within the EMS system. These are negotiated between the
members and generally involve adjustments of all the bilateral central rates.
However, this may be avoided by a country as it realizes that the exchange
rate issue can become embroiled in EC 'horse trading' and that devaluation
benefits are exceeded by other political costs such as increased EC control
over other aspects of national life. Central bank intervention and the use of
domestic interest rate changes were all employed during the EMS currency
crisis of mid September 1992, in which the currency traders of the large
international banks (acting on behalf of their customers in commercial and
financial enterprises concerned about the pound and lira values of their
financial assets) questioned the existing EMS parities and tested the
reserves and the staying power of the central bankers of the EC, the US

and Japan. The high degree of turbulence in the currency markets at this time particularly affected the lira, the peseta and the pound and led to suspension of the pound and the lira from the EMS, effectively allowing them to freely float on the world currency markets. This latter option can be seen as an important safety valve for the EMS when facing massive speculative capital flows targeted on specific currencies such as the pound. It can also provide some insight into the EMS exchange rates acceptable to currency markets and is likely to lead to a stable realignment of rates within the system. Devaluing in this way because of market forces may also reduce the political costs identified above for EC countries when devaluing through an administrative mechanism in the EMS.

The Maastricht summit meeting of EC leaders in December 1991 endorsed the introduction of a single EC currency to be managed by an independent European central bank. The immediate target for this was 1997, with 1999 being the latest date for implementation if member states cannot meet the strict economic criteria for convergence of economic policies. Britain negotiated a special opt-out clause which gave it alone the right to decide whether and when it joined the single currency. Danish rejection of Maastricht in June 1992 and UK suspension of the pound from the EMS on 16 September 1992 may delay implementation of these arrangements. Alternatively, those countries with a stronger committment to the Single European Act and the Maastricht arrangements may decide to create a two tier EC in which they accelerate these changes, leaving the others to catch up at some point in the future.

Another form of government intervention has been when countries erect various controls and barriers to capital flows and foreign exchange transactions between themselves and other countries. Controls such as these have not normally worked to any great extent. For example, the West German authorities attempted to insulate their capital market in the early 1970s, but abandoned this on floating the mark. The UK abolished its similar exchange control system in 1979, making it one of the most open economies for international capital flows. EC policy was to eradicate all such controls within the Community by 1990 as part of its plan for a unified EC currency. However, Spain, Ireland, Greece and Portugal had an extended January 1993 deadline in this respect. These exchange controls probably played a significant role in protecting these currencies from speculative flows during the September 1992 EMS crisis. Ireland renewed its controls in 1993, but this did not protect the Irish pound from a subsequent 10 per cent devaluation within the EMS at the end of January 1993. Finally, it should be noted that governments may also indirectly

vene in foreign exchange markets by their domestic economic policies.
Thus changes in monetary policy or fiscal policy are likely to have an
immediate impact on expectations about inflation and interest rates and
therefore exchange rates.

It is clear from the above description of exchange rate arrangements that
market forces and actions by central banks and treasuries will interact and
jointly affect exchange rates. Floating currencies are subject to official
intervention by their own authorities and in the case of major currencies by
the co-ordinated actions of G7 and EC monetary authorities. In addition,
pegged and group floating currencies are also strongly influenced by their
reference floating currencies. Thus there are close links between all of these
currencies regardless of whether they float independently, float in a group
or are pegged in some way, and these links are manifest through market
forces, single government intervention and co-ordinated intervention.
Theories identifying the general nature of these market forces will be
discussed in chapter 4, and the evidence for these market forces will be
outlined and the implications of various market imperfections, such as
government intervention, will be analysed.

## The foreign exchange market

The foreign exchange market is a world-wide market and does not have
one centralized location. The foreign exchange departments of large
international commercial banks are linked across the world on a 24 hour
basis, through a sophisticated network of communication systems. Major
commercial centres such as London, Amsterdam, Frankfurt, Milan, Paris,
New York, Toronto, Bahrain, Tokyo, Hong Kong and Singapore are
particularly active in this market and have provided the communication
links and continuous trading necessary for a global 24 hour market. Bank of
England surveys in 1989 and 1992 of turnover in all major foreign
exchange centres confirm London's premier position in this market and its
clear dominance in a European context (*Bank of England Quarterly Bulletin*,
November 1990 and November 1992). In April 1992, $300 billion was
traded in London on a net daily basis, an increase of 60 per cent on the
1989 $187 billion figure. The equivalent 1992 figures were for New York
$192 billion, Tokyo $128 billion, Singapore $74 billion and, way down the
list, Germany (Frankfurt) $57 billion. The last figure concealed the
emerging role of the mark in this trading, with DM/$ trading accounting
for 23 per cent of transactions in the foreign exchange markets, followed by
£/$ trading at 19 per cent. The 1992 survey also revealed that there had

been a significant growth in cross-currency deals involving the mark and in ECU deals, both within Europe. The latter may have declined since the September 1992 ERM crisis. The growth in these markets between 1989 and 1992 in a period of slow growth in the real world economy stemmed from the financial risk management needs of large MNCs and international banks. In particular, the forward market had grown and accounted for 50 per cent of the market, with a 14 per cent fall in spot deals in 1989–92. The shift from spot to forward and to other currency products such as futures and options was partially explained by the increasing transacting capabilities of corporate treasury departments which increased their share of turnover from 10 to 26 per cent from 1989 to 1992.

The participants in the market include central banks, commercial banks, brokers, corporations and individuals. The central banks both monitor market movements and sentiment and intervene according to government policy and the prevailing situation. The currency dealing rooms of large international banks such as CitiCorp of New York, Westpac of Sydney, Deutsche Bank of Frankfurt, or Barclays Bank of London form the heart of the foreign exchange market. Trading between the commercial banks, either directly or indirectly via brokers, constitutes the vast majority of transactions in the market. The banks' involvement stems from their need to provide a wide range of currency services to their corporate, governmental, bank and personal customers. These services range from simple payment and cheque clearing services in many currencies to more sophisticated currency risk management products. A bank's presence in the currency markets and other financial markets also creates the opportunity for the bank to construct many composite services based on each market's specific set of services. The regional dealing rooms and branch offices of the international banks satisfy local demands for these services and collect local surpluses. The central dealing room of the bank will co-ordinate and balance out these global deficits and surpluses produced by its customers. The scale of this currency dealing makes these banks very big players in sales and purchases of their home country and other major currencies. As a result, they can act as market makers in these currencies and can continuously provide buy/sell rates on a global basis. In general, banks prefer to be matched in terms of the currency composition of their financial assets and liabilities or, if not, to use the currency markets to neutralize or hedge a risky currency exposure. However, their currency resources are such that they can bear some risk by holding a small surplus of one currency over a short period in the expectation that the exchange rate change will be favourable to them. Too large a net exposure over too long a period can be very risky for these banks and so traders will work within certain exposure limits for each currency. The EMS crises of September 1992 and early 1993 are good examples of events which can provide a relatively risk free bet for bank traders. In September 1992 the major international banks probably traded right up to their exposure limits as they sold pounds and bought marks prior to the expected sterling devaluation. After the devaluation, they probably sold marks for pounds to bring their balance sheets back into a matched position. The banks also probably traded in a similar way on their corporate customers' behalf. The net losers here were the central bankers and their depleted reserves.

Brokers play a unique supporting role to the banks in the inter-bank market in that they seek out and match potential buyers and sellers of foreign exchange. They also provide information on market prices and relevant 'news' to parties to the bargain so that a trade can take place with confidence. One piece of information they do not release before the deal is the names of the buyers and sellers. This is done to prevent the market at large knowing whether they are involved in buying or selling. If this were publicly known then the advantage the broker has about prospective purchasers and sellers and possibly about favourable prices would be dissipated. The brokers make their commission from the banks on the basis of this information, and under competitive conditions the commission reflects the costs of seeking potential traders plus a profit margin. Banks generally deal with several brokers to ensure that competition exists, and the brokers know that the bank they are dealing with has access to several sources of information on exchange rates. This regular flow of information to the market and intense trading competition make this market one of the most effective in establishing a world-wide exchange price for its commodity, currencies or purchasing power. Thus the price of say the £/$ exchange rate is likely to be the same in the various world financial centres at any time. The 1990 Bank of England survey showed that brokers' share of transactions fell in London in the period 1986–9 as the banks increased direct transactions between themselves and with their customers, and as some of their large corporate customers bypassed both banks and brokers and dealt direct with each other. However, the survey indicates that the brokers continue to intermediate a significant proportion of business in London.

Large MNCs are active traders in the foreign exchange markets in their own right. In some cases they have currency dealing rooms to match the operations of large banks and, as indicated above, they can trade directly with each other, avoiding the banks as intermediaries. In general, they deal through the commercial banks and normally develop long term currency trading relationships with particular banks. These banks provide MNCs and other corporate customers with access to the banks' foreign exchange information system for current currency prices. Competition between the banks in this way ensures that a company knows it is getting a fair market rate for a particular transaction. Wealthy individuals also trade in the foreign exchange market (again through the banks) but on a small scale compared with corporations.

Given the range of the above participants it is clear that the foreign exchange market performs many different functions. These include the following:

1 Purchasing power is transferred across different countries and therefore the feasibility of international trade and investment is enhanced.
2 The market acts as a central focus whereby prices are set for various currencies.
3 The foreign exchange market provides the means by which investors can hedge or minimize the risk of loss due to adverse exchange rate changes.
4 The market allows traders to identify risk free opportunities and arbitrage these away. Thus $/DM price differences between, say, forward and future currency prices, in a single financial centre or across financial centres, can be exploited in this way.
5 A controversial feature of the market is the speculative activity of investors who seek profits by taking exposed positions when exchange rates are expected to change in their favour. Thus in this sense it provides an investment function for bank and corporate traders who are prepared to expose their enterprise to currency risk.

To satisfy these needs, the market consists of three major sectors: the spot market, the forward and futures markets, and the currency options market. In the spot market, currencies are bought and sold at once for delivery within a few days. The spot market therefore deals in currencies or purchasing powers of different countries. When UK pounds are exchanged for US dollars in Frankfurt, the currencies do not leave their country of origin and the transaction only reflects a change of ownership. Banks do physically transfer currencies across borders for the use of travellers, but this is unnecessary in the sophisticated inter-bank foreign exchange market in which currency in the form of bank deposits can be shifted to the new owner's account.

In the forward market, a contract concerning a currency transaction in the future is established between buyer and seller. The rates at which currencies are to be exchanged in the future are contractually agreed some time prior to the exchange. Thus the rate three months ahead may be agreed today, but the exchange involving the delivery of the currency (of say dollars) and payment (say in pounds) takes place after three months.

The currency futures market is similar to the forward market in that it deals in future currency prices and future exchanges of currency. The Chicago International Money Market (IMM) has been in operation since 1971. Similar markets were set up in New York in 1978 and 1979. The London International Financial Futures Exchange (LIFFE) was opened in 1984. This has at times traded in currency futures and options, but now concentrates on interest rate futures (and options on these) in various currencies such as Euromarks or Eurodollars. LIFFE has faced competition in Europe from a similar futures exchange in Paris (MATIF), the emergence of a new futures exchange in Frankfurt, and increasing co-operation between these two exchanges. Despite trading a large daily volume of futures contracts, LIFFE recognized that it had to become much larger to deal with the rest of the European competition. With this in mind it moved to a large new trading floor in London (above Cannon Street station) in December 1991 and subsequently merged with its other London competitor, the London Traded Options Market (LTOM), to become LIFFE-LTOM. This merger may lead to the re-emergence of trading in currency futures and options on LIFFE-LTOM.

Currency futures markets trade in fixed size contracts for major currencies such as the US dollar, the pound sterling and the yen. The contracts are for standard amounts (e.g. on the IMM, £62,500 and DM125,000) of currency and are available for delivery at fairly limited periods in the future. Their use for corporate hedging purposes is restricted by these factors and by the relatively small size of the contracts and the narrow range of currencies offered. In contrast the forward market, sustained by large banks, deals in any convertible currency as long as a reasonable level of trading or liquidity is present. The forward market also has a maturity structure corresponding to most normal business days and trading takes place on a 24 hour global basis. The currency futures market is likely to be of greater value to the firm with predictable foreign currency cash flows and having limited access to the forward markets. Large MNCs generally prefer to use the forward market and to purchase tailored forward contracts to match 'lumpy', varying duration, foreign currency cash flows.

In the currency option markets, the corporate treasury can buy the right, but not the obligation, to sell or buy currency forward, if required. This option, to decide whether to buy or sell currency, is particularly important when the firm is unsure about the timing or size of a foreign currency receipt or payment. For example, many large UK firms generate considerable US dollar income from their export business to the US and from dollar sales by their US subsidiaries. These dollar cash inflows are likely to contain well known transaction exposures as well as uncertain short term dollar cash inflows. The latter may stem from new sales, fixed foreign currency price lists and many other short term contingencies facing the firm in its overseas markets.

The known transaction exposure can be hedged in the forward markets. The uncertain dollar cash flow component may be hedged by buying the right, but not the obligation, to buy pounds at an agreed dollar price (i.e. by buying a pound call option) if the dollar receipts arise. Alternatively, if the firm believes that it might require dollars in the near future it can buy the right, but not the obligation, to sell pounds at an agreed dollar price (i.e. buy a pound put option) if the need for dollars arises. The contractually agreed exchange price is fixed at the start of the contract and the exchange is possible at this rate over the life of the contract. These options are available over an agreed exercise period, say up to three months ahead. In the case of the US style option, the holder or buyer of the (US style) option can exercise his or her right, but not obligation, to buy (call) or sell (put) foreign currency at any time up to the expiration date of the contract. In the case of the European option, exercise occurs at the end of the option's duration. Further details are given later in this section.

The bulk of these contracts are traded on North American exchanges such as the Philadelphia Stock Exchange. These organized exchange markets are similar to futures markets, in that standardized contracts with fixed currency amounts, maturities and expiry dates are employed with trading taking place by open outcry on the exchange floor. Banks are active traders here as well as specialized brokers and some multinational transactors. Examples of the standard amounts of foreign currency traded include currency option contract sizes of DM62,500 or £31,250, with the option price or premium quoted in US cents per unit of the underlying foreign currency (marks or pounds). We can see from the latter case that the UK treasurer has to treat the pound as the underlying foreign currency for the purposes of dealing with this exchange. Thus in the example above of the UK firm with a large US dollar cash inflow it may appear more logical to buy a dollar put option. However, the trading conventions on the Philadelphia Exchange mean that the treasurer will buy the exactly equivalent pound call option contract. Both provide the right, but not the obligation, to sell dollars (buy pounds).

Options are also sold 'over the counter' (OTC) in a manner similar to currency forward contracts. OTC contracts have very flexible terms arranged by negotiation between the (normal bank) supplier and the corporate buyer. Thus the currencies to be bought and sold can vary according to the corporate customer's needs and do not have to correspond to exchange market conventions. Amounts, duration of the option, and price can all be negotiated and matched to the corporate customer's exposure. There is no public secondary market in OTC currency options but trading is conducted by telephone using 'indicative' prices available on screen systems provided by large international (commercial and invest-ment) banks. MNCs are major users of OTC options and are key participants in the screen markets. These OTC markets are closely linked to spot and forward markets in currency in which the banks and MNCs also play central roles. The organized currency option exchanges provide an important public pricing mechanism for the MNC treasurer and may also provide a suitable currency option contract for foreign cash flows of known size but uncertain likelihood of occurrence.

### Quotation conventions for foreign exchange

The two conventions for quoting exchange rates are the direct and indirect methods. The direct quote is the home country cost, in home country currency units, of buying or selling one unit of foreign currency. This is normally employed within Western Europe with the exception of the UK and Ireland. In the US, banks normally use the direct quote internally as the dollar price for a single unit of foreign currencies. The indirect quote is the number of foreign currency units purchased or sold with one unit of home currency. This is the method favoured in London. US banks also use the indirect quote when dealing outside the US. The exceptions to this US practice are the pound, the punt (Irish pound) and the ECU which are quoted direct both internally and externally in the US. The lack of a single convention reflects the history of exchange rate regimes, especially the period of dominance of sterling in the nineteenth century and the early twentieth century and the difficulties of quoting in portions of the old British pound, shillings and pence system (£sd). This was followed by US dollar dominance from the Second World War to the early 1970s.

**Table 2.2** Foreign exchange quotation examples

|  | *London (£)* | *New York ($)* | *Frankfurt (DM)* |
|---|---|---|---|
| Direct quote: HC cost (no. units of buying (or selling) one FC unit | £/FC<br>0.5830£/$[b]<br>0.5163£/C$[b]<br>0.3440£/DM[b] | $/FC<br>1.7155$/£[a]<br>0.8860$/C$[c]<br>0.5896$/DM[c] | DM/FC<br>2.910DM/£[a]<br>1.503DM/C$[a]<br>1.696DM/$[a] |
| Indirect quote: FC units bought or sold with one HC unit | FC/£<br>1.7155$/£[a]<br>1.9360C$/£[a]<br>2.9100DM/£[a] | FC/$<br>0.5830£/$[b]<br>1.1285C$/$[d]<br>1.6960DM/$[d] | FC/DM<br>0.344£/DM[b]<br>0.665C$/DM[b]<br>0.5896$/DM[b] |

FC, foreign currency; HC, home currency.
[a]Local convention normally employed for quoting exchange rates.
[b]This type of quote not normally employed in this market.
[c]Inside the US.
[d]Outside the US.
*Source*: based on data in *Financial Times*, 21 October 1991

In the examples given in table 2.2, the indirect quote in each market column (London, New York, and Frankfurt) is the reciprocal of the direct quote. Thus the same prices are employed in the top half and bottom half of each column, but they are expressed according to different conventions.

In the table, the three indirect London quotes have been taken from the *Financial Times* (Monday 21 October 1991, p. 29): these are the three opening spot rates on Friday 18 October 1991. The other rates in the table have been calculated from these three by using the idea of cross-rates as follows. The underlined rates are the three given rates. Thus the DM/$ rate is calculated as (2.91DM/£)/(1.7155$/£) = 1.696DM/$ or, as a reciprocal, 0.5896$/DM.

$$\underline{1.7155\$/£}$$

C$/$ = 1.1285                    DM/$ = 1.696

$$\underline{1.9360C\$/£} \qquad\qquad \underline{2.9100DM/£}$$

DM/C$ = 1.5031

These calculations presume that there are no transaction costs when trading currencies between these three major financial centres and there are no barriers to trading in currencies. As a result the prices are likely to be the same, with the reciprocal of the exchange rate in one quoting convention equalling the value in the other convention. In practice, transaction costs may mean that prices differ slightly between these three centres at any time.

*Bid and offer rates*

In foreign exchange markets the price of one currency quoted in terms of another is expressed as two rates: the bid rate and the offer rate. The two different rates reflect the fact that the basic maxim in the currency trading business is to 'buy cheap and sell dear'. The difference between these buy and sell prices is the major source of profit for the dealer.

Thus a London trader could be involved in buying and selling dollars using pounds as the means of payment. For example, she could buy cheap dollars at 1.785$/£ (i.e. £0.56 each) and sell dearer dollars at 1.754$/£ (i.e. £0.57 each), and make a 0.031$/£ spread or gross profit on the two exchanges. The bid rate is the lower of the two rates quoted, and the offer or ask rate is the higher. In diagrammatic form:

Bid (lower) rate                Offer or ask (higher) rate
   = 1.754$/£                     = 1.785$/£

Sell dearer dollars   ←——  0.031$/£ profit  ——→  Buy cheap dollars
    for pounds                                  for pounds

The gross trading profit provided by this margin is very small and is limited by fierce competition between the banks. It must cover the trader's basic costs of operating as well as their transaction costs. The net profit is likely to be minuscule compared with the size of the currency deal.

The spread is likely to be very narrow in the actively traded currencies. However, as uncertainty increases the margin becomes wider because currency traders begin to 'buy much cheaper and sell much dearer' than if they were trading in actively traded currencies or in spot or very short term forward deals. This increasing margin creates a larger profit incentive to cope with the larger risk of longer maturity forward deals or of deals involving less well traded currencies.

Finally, we should note that (ignoring transaction costs) the buying rate in one currency centre (or bank trading room) should equal the selling rate in another centre (or bank trading room). If this is not the case, an opportunity for profit exists. For example, if there were a New York quote of 0.5$/DM and a Frankfurt quote of 2.2DM/$ then dealers would arbitrage by recognizing that they would get DM2.2 for their dollar in Frankfurt and DM2 for their dollar in New York. They would buy cheap DM2.2 in Frankfurt with $1 and sell them in New York for $1.1, making a 10 cents profit. Such arbitrage activity will quickly bring prices together in both centres.

*Forward quotes and their premiums and discounts*
Forward foreign exchange quotes follow the same conventions as for spot rates in the same financial centre. The London forward quotes from the *Financial Times* (Monday 21 October 1991, p. 29) for Friday 18 October 1991 are as in table 2.3. In the *FT* the difference between the forward and the spot rate is expressed as a percentage change relative to a spot rate base, i.e.

$$\frac{\text{forward premium}}{\text{or discount}} = \frac{\text{forward} - \text{spot}}{\text{spot}} \times \frac{12}{n} \times 100$$

where $n$ is the number of months remaining in the forward contract. If the three months forward dollar is quoted 'at a premium' to say the pound as a reference currency, then this means that the dollar is expected to become more expensive in pounds compared with the pound price of dollars today (spot). For example:

Today (spot):    $1.724 bought for £1    or    £0.58 to buy $1
Three months:    $1.695 bought for £1    or    £0.59 to buy $1

In this case the purchasing power of the pound is expected to decline or depreciate relative to the dollar over the next three months. In contrast, if the dollar is at 'a discount' then a pound is expected to buy more dollars in the future and the pound's purchasing power is expected to increase relative to the dollar, i.e. appreciating pound or depreciating dollar.

The premium for the dollar against the the pound in table 2.3 can be calculated as follows:

*One month premium*

$$\text{Low}: \quad \frac{0.0075}{1.7245} \times 12 \times 100 = 5.2189\%$$

$$\text{High}: \quad \frac{0.0073}{1.7255} \times 12 \times 100 = 5.07672\%$$

**Table 2.3** London spot rates and forward rates against the pound, 18 October 1991

| | Day's spread | Day's close | One month | % p.a. | Three months | % p.a. |
|---|---|---|---|---|---|---|
| US | $1.7155–1.7255 | $1.7245–1.7255 | 0.75–0.73c pm | 5.15 | 2.08–2.05c pm | 4.79 |
| Germany | DM2.9100–2.9150 | DM2.9100–2.9150 | 3/8–1/4 pf pm | 1.29 | 7/8–5/8 pf pm | 1.03 |
| Japan | Y222.7–224.25 | Y223.25–224.25 | 7/8–5/8 Y pm | 4.02 | 2.25–2.00Y pm | 3.80 |

*Source: Financial Times*, 21 October 1991, p. 29

Average: approximately 5.15% dollar premium on pound

*Three month premium*

$$\text{Low} \quad \frac{0.0208}{1.7245} \times \frac{12}{3} \times 100 = 4.8246\%$$

$$\text{High} \quad \frac{0.0205}{1.7255} \times \frac{12}{3} \times 100 = 4.7522\%$$

Average: approximately 4.788% dollar premium on pound

Thus the dollar is becoming more expensive relative to the pound by about 4.79% per annum, i.e. the dollar is appreciating relative to the pound.

The data in table 2.3 can be used to calculate absolute forward rates. If we assume that the expected change in the exchange rate is quoted relative to the foreign currency (*FT* method), then for indirect quotes:

- If the foreign currency is at a premium, subtract the percentage change from the spot rate to get the absolute forward rate.
- If the foreign currency is at a discount, add the percentage change to the spot rate to get the absolute forward rate.

Thus for the indirect $/£ quote in the table we can calculate the three month forward rate as follows:

|  | Bid | Offer | Difference |
|---|---|---|---|
| Spot | $1.7245 | $1.7255 | 0.10c |
| Premium | −$0.0208 | −$0.0205 | 0.03c |
| Forward | $1.7037 | $1.7050 | 0.13c |

In both bid and offer rates we can see that the pound is expected to secure fewer dollars in the future and thus its purchasing power is expected to decline. In addition, the forward bid–offer spread has widened relative to the spot spread and this is consistent with the greater uncertainty faced in this deal.

In the case of direct quotes we can reverse the rule to calculate the forward rate:

- If the foreign currency is at a premium, add the percentage change to the spot rate to get the absolute forward rate.
- If the foreign currency is at a discount, subtract the percentage change from the spot rate to get the absolute forward rate.

The *Financial Times* also provides exchange rates against the dollar. Table 2.4 shows the dollar figures for Friday 18 October 1991 (*FT*, Monday 21 October 1991, p. 29).

The discount for the mark against the dollar may be calculated as follows:

*One month discount*

$$\text{Low}: \quad \frac{-0.57}{1.6880} \times \frac{12}{1} = -4.0521324\%$$

$$\text{High}: \quad \frac{-0.58}{1.6890} \times \frac{12}{1} = -4.1207808\%$$

Average:  −4.0864% mark discount on dollar

*Three month discount*

$$\text{Low}: \quad \frac{-1.65}{1.6880} \times \frac{12}{3} = -3.9099524\%$$

$$\text{High}: \quad \frac{-1.68}{1.6890} \times \frac{12}{1} = -3.9786856\%$$

Average:  −3.944319% mark discount on dollar

that is, the mark is expected to become cheaper relative to the dollar by about 4% per annum, or the mark is depreciating relative to the dollar.

The absolute one month forward rate for the indirect US quote for DM/$ is calculated as follows:

|          | Bid        | Offer      | Difference |
|----------|------------|------------|------------|
| Spot     | DM1.6880   | DM1.6890   | 0.1pf      |
| Discount | +DM0.0057  | +DM0.0058  | 0.01pf     |
| Forward  | DM1.6937   | DM1.6948   | 0.11pf     |

Thus the dollar is expected to buy more marks in the future and the forward bid–offer margin has widened relative to the spot spread.

**Table 2.4** London spot rates and forward rates against the dollar, 18 October 1991

| | Day's spread | Day's close | One month | % p.a. | Three months | % p.a. |
|---|---|---|---|---|---|---|
| UK £[a] | $1.7155–1.7255 | $1.7245–1.7255 | 0.75–0.73c pm | 5.15 | 2.08–2.05c pm | 4.79 |
| Germany | DM1.6880–1.6965 | DM1.6880–1.6890 | 0.57–0.58pf dis. | −4.09 | 1.65–1.68pf dis. | −3.94 |
| Japan | Y129.45–130.05 | Y129.70–129.80 | 0.13–0.14Y dis. | −1.25 | 0.27–0.28Y dis. | −0.85 |

[a]UK pound, Irish punt and ECU are quoted in US currency. All other currencies quoted per dollar, i.e. indirect quotes.

*Source: Financial Times*, 21 October 1991

*Valuing currency options*

As indicated earlier, the exchange based markets sell call and put options for a range of currencies. The call or put is on the underlying foreign currency such as the mark or the pound, and the premium or option price is quoted in US dollars (normally cents) per unit of foreign currency.

Purchasers of currency options include a UK firm exporting to the US and wishing to sell its dollar reciepts (buy a pound call option), and a UK firm importing from the US and wishing to secure dollars (buy a pound put option) for its purchases. The bank option writer acts as an insurer for the firm and receives a premium for this risk bearing service. The following table illustrates the symmetrical nature of put and call contracts exchanged between a buyer (normally a firm) and writer (normally a bank):

|  | £ call | £ put |
|---|---|---|
| Corporate buyer or holder of option | Right to buy pounds for dollars | Right to sell pounds for dollars |
| Bank writer or seller of option | Obligation to sell pounds for dollars if requested (exercised) by option buyer | Obligation to buy pounds for dollars if requested or exercised by option buyer |

Supply and demand will ultimately determine option prices or premiums. However, within a given supply–demand scenario, four key factors determine currency option prices for a given exercise or contract price:

- spot prices
- volatility
- interest rates in the reference and in the option currency
- duration of the contract.

These factors are at work in influencing option premiums in both the exchange based markets and the OTC markets. The factors influence two principal components of value in the option price: intrinsic value and time value (figure 2.2). Intrinsic value is the difference between the current spot rate and the exercise price. In the case of 'in the money' call options, where the spot rate exceeds the exercise price, the larger the intrinsic value $(S-X)$ the more valuable the option. In the case of a pound call option, as the pound appreciates (e.g. from 1.8 to 1.9\$/£) and becomes more expensive to buy with dollars in the spot market, the option ( at $X = 1.8\$/£$) becomes more valuable. This intrinsic value falls to zero as the pound depreciates and the spot rate approaches the

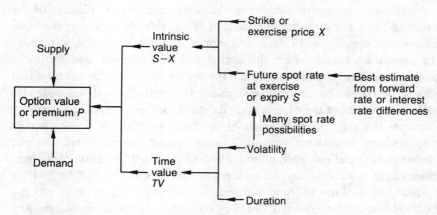

**Figure 2.2** Valuing option contracts

exercise price plus the premium. The reverse logic applies to a pound put option.

In the case of a pound call contract we can see that under different $\$/£$ spot rates the firm and the bank will take different decisions according to whether the contract is in, at or out of the money for the firm (the holder): Time value is a function of volatility and the duration of the contract, for a given exercise price. This reflects the possibility that, over its life and in a volatile currency context, the option will become more valuable than at

|  | *In the money* | *At the money* | *Out of the money* |
|---|---|---|---|
| Firm action | Exercise the option and buy the pounds from the bank Pay the premium | | Use the spot market to buy pounds for dollars Also pay the premium |
| Bank action | Sell the pounds Receive the premium | | Receive the premium |

present. The longer the time to maturity, the more valuable the put or call option. In other words, the longer maturity means that there is more time for a favourable spot rate to occur. This time value element to the contract diminishes to zero as the contract approaches its expiry date.

One of the most important factors here is the volatility of the spot rate. Stable exchange rates are not valuable because this restricts the opportunity for favourable spot rates occurring. Thus the higher the volatility of the exchange rate, the greater the chance of favourable and unfavourable spot rates occurring relative to the exercise price on the option. The former are the conditions under which the option will be exercised, and the more possibilities here, the more valuable the put or the call option contract. It should be noted that the spot rate values that make the call valuable also make the put out of the money and vice versa, but that increasing volatility increases the value of both kinds of contract. Volatility is conventionally estimated by measuring periodic changes (daily, monthly etc.) in the exchange rate and calculating an annualized standard deviation of historic changes. In pracice, an option trader will alter estimates based on historic volatility according to new information affecting fluctuations of the exchange rate. The expected volatility estimate is the only factor affecting option value that cannot be observed from market prices. It is also likely to be the most important ingredient in time value. This explains why banks and firms expend so much effort in estimating volatility.

Interest rate differences in the two currencies are also important because these contain forecasts about the path of the exchange rate to expiry. This forecast provides an insight into intrinsic value over the life of the contract. In addition, a bank that writes calls or puts places itself in an exposed position. Thus the bank's cost of continuously hedging this exposure over the duration of the contract must be incorporated into the time value component of the option premium.

As a derivative product the currency option price can be estimated from other market prices and volatility estimates. These variables are formally incorporated into currency option valuation models such as variants of the Black-Scholes (1972) option model or the Garman-Kohlhagen (1983) model. It is important that the treasurer understands how and why these factors affect currency option prices. It is also important that when they use these variables in an option pricing model they can assess if the premiums charged seem reasonable relative to other market prices.

## The Euro or external markets

The two well established sectors of the Euromarkets are the Eurocurrency market and the Eurobond market. The former refers to funds channelled via financial intermediaries from international lenders to international borrowers. The large multinational banks dominate this business and have played a major role in the development and growth of these offshore markets. The Eurobond market is characterized by direct transactions between borrowers and lenders, although the large banks play a major role in underwriting and placing the bonds.

The Eurocurrency markets provide the short to medium term debt required by banks, corporate customers and government borrowers. The source of these funds is domestic bank deposits whose ownership is transferred to banks outside the controlled domestic monetary systems. These deposits never actually leave their country of origin and all final settlements of Eurodollar transactions take place in New York and Eurosterling in London. The largest owners of these funds during the early 1980s were the governments of the oil producing and exporting countries and the multinational oil companies. The 'Euro' prefix refers to the high volume of these funds circulating in Europe, mainly through London. However this market is world-wide, and sectors of the market exist in the Middle East and the Far East (Asiadollar market).

The Eurocurrency market is therefore created and sustained by the large international banks and operates at two levels. Firstly, there is the very competitive wholesale market centred in London, in which these banks sell their funds to each other at the London inter-bank offering rate (LIBOR). This business is mainly conducted via telephone, and thus only the highest quality banks can operate in the wholesale market. Secondly, smaller banks, corporate borrowers and national governments (in the late 1970s from Eastern Europe and developing countries, and now primarily from the Western industrialized countries) can acquire loans from this market. In this large scale 'retail' loan market the large international banks only lend the offshore deposits after detailed credit investigation of the borrowers.

Loans in a particular currency are priced according to a 'LIBOR plus' basis, with the margin over LIBOR depending on market conditions and the credit quality standing or riskiness of the borrower. The banks generally arrange syndicated loans in this market. Thus the risks of a particular borrower are distributed across several banks. The hope here is that, in the case of delayed repayment or (even worse) default, no single placed in a risky position. Of course, simultaneous default by large sovereign states would negate these diversification benefits seriously affect the position of certain banks. This possibility was at the t of the world banking crises of the 1980s and was still present in the early 1990s with the breakup of the former Soviet Union and a world recession.

The Eurocurrency markets serve three basic functions (Feiger and Jacquillat 1982: 248). Firstly, they are extensively used for foreign exchange hedging purposes as the banks seek to balance out their foreign assets and liabilities. The banks therefore take positions in the Eurocurrency markets to cover the forward commitments they have made with their customers. Secondly, Eurocurrency markets can at times bypass domestic channels of financial intermediation, especially when governments impose tight credit policies. For example, US corporations can acquire Eurodollars in London: these deposits may be US domestic dollar deposits that have been transferred abroad during a US domestic credit squeeze. The third function of the markets is the full international intermediation role of channelling surplus liquid resources from say OPEC countries to those countries or corporations who need to borrow.

A central feature of these markets is the relative absence of governmental controls. Historically, from the early 1950s to the mid 1980s they lay outside the sovereign laws of a country despite physically residing within that country. They were external or 'duty free' markets in that deposits were not 'taxed' by the requirement for specific capital ratios and thus all capital was actively employed. This feature, allied with fierce competition within these markets, has meant that the wholesale Eurocurrency markets in bank deposits and their market price, LIBOR, approach a world pricing mechanism for financial assets of very low risk. In addition, the associated retail markets for loans and LIBOR plus also represent a world pricing mechanism for (syndicated) loans.

Regulation has begun to penetrate these markets via co-operative efforts amongst the major banking nations to establish world standards on capital adequacy and safe levels of liquidity in international banks. National regulatory systems or those of the EC bloc are the means by which these standards are being used to establish controls over the offshore markets (Lewis and Davis 1987: 228).

Finally, we can note the possibility of a link between these capital markets and currency markets. The *Financial Times* publishes Euro-currency interest rates on a daily basis. We can use these figures to

calculate average differences (bid–offer) in interest rates between say the
dollar and the pound and between the dollar and the mark for
Eurocurrency bank deposits on 18 October 1991 as follows:

| Eurodollar | 3 month deposit rate | = | 5.500–5.375 |
| Europound | 3 month deposit rate | = | 10.4375–10.375 |
| Difference | | = | 4.9375–5.000 |
| Average | | = | 4.96875% p.a. |

| Eurodollar | 3 month deposit rate | = | 5.500–5.375 |
| Euromark | 3 month deposit rate | = | 9.375–9.250 |
| Difference | | = | 3.875–3.875 |
| Average | | = | 3.875% p.a. |

These interest rate differences are very close to the annual dollar premium
on the pound (4.79 per cent) or the annual dollar premium on the mark
(3.94 per cent) calculated in the previous section for three month forward
contracts. This suggests that the higher interest rates on mark and pound
deposits are compensating for the loss of purchasing power in these
currencies relative to the dollar. If we used interest rate and forward
premium/discount data for the same instant, these annual percentage
changes would be very close indeed. This pricing link between
Eurocurrency markets (for bank deposits) and currency markets will be
returned to in chapter 4.

The second major sector of the unregulated international capital market
is the Eurobond market. This market permits lenders to lend directly to
borrowers across national borders, without the intermediation of a bank.
Banks can, however, play a major role in arranging the transaction.
Eurobonds differ from foreign bonds in that the latter are issued in one
country in its currency by a foreign borrower. By contrast, the Eurobond is
issued in one currency such as the the dollar, the yen, the pound, the mark
or the Swiss franc (or a currency basket such as the ECU or the SDR) for
sale in many capital markets, with the sale managed by an international
syndicate of bank underwriters. The borrowers or issuers of the bonds
include MNCs, public sector organizations and commercial banks. The
lenders or purchasers of the bond securities are individual and institutional
investors, with the latter group dominating. A secondary market for
Eurobonds has grown rapidly as these financial institutions continuously
seek to adjust their portfolios, and as a result the original lenders are not
committed to a borrower until the final maturity of the bond issue.

Generally, purchasers buy Eurobonds in currencies other than their own, and a major attraction of these bonds for individuals is that in most currencies they are exempt from withholding taxes. Furthermore, the unregulated nature of the market means that its costs are lower and its issuing process much faster than domestic or foreign bond counterparts.

The offshore bond markets are important for the international firm in that they provide a wide variety of medium to long term funds of 3 to 15 years maturity. Fixed coupons or interest rates are common but floating rate notes are also important. As with the Eurocurrency market, until recently the major denominations have been the dollar, the mark, the yen and the ECU. Similar asset pricing tendencies can be assumed to occur, albeit with securities of longer maturity and greater risk.

## Domestic capital markets and links with international markets

The third major sector of the international capital market consists of the set of domestic equity, bond and credit markets within which the international investor can operate. These markets differ from the Eurocurrency and Eurobond markets in that they are subject to the laws of the sovereign state within which they reside. Such regulation may affect the degree of integration of these markets with international and other domestic markets and therefore lead us to question the concept of a world capital market.

At the end of 1980 the major world domestic bond and equity markets were divided fairly equally between the US domestic markets and the rest of the world domestic markets (Ibbotson et al. 1982) as in table 2.5.

Despite the 1987 crash the absolute value of equities multiplied many times over the 1980s. In addition, there was a shift away from US dominance. Using a combination of the Ibbotson et al. (1982) data and the International Stock Exchange (ISE) *Quality of Markets Quarterly* (October–December 1990) we can identify the approximate changes in the market capitalization values of the major domestic equity markets over

**Table 2.5** Aggregate market values (US$ billions)

|          | US     | Rest of world |
|----------|--------|---------------|
| Bonds    | 1111.7 | 1748.3        |
| Equities | 1187.5 | 1049.3        |

*Source*: Ibbotson et al. 1982

**Table 2.6** Capitalization of major domestic equity
markets, 1980 and 1990 (per cent)

|  | *1980* | *1990* |
|---|---|---|
| London | 10.22 | 11.40 |
| Frankfurt | 3.82 | 4.45 |
| Paris | 2.85 | 4.26 |
| US (New York) | 63.89 | 43.62 |
| Tokyo | 19.21 | 36.62 |
|  | 100.00 | 100.00 |

*Sources*: Ibbotson et al. 1982; *Quality of Markets Quarterly*,
October–December 1990

the 1980s as in table 2.6. In 1980 the US equity market was by far the
largest domestic equity market in the world and was three times larger than
its nearest rival, the Japanese market. During 1990 there were periods
when the capitalization of the Tokyo Stock Exchange was higher than the
New York Stock Exchange. These relative values can fluctuate quite
dramatically. For example, the Tokyo Stock Exchange market capitalization fell by 29 per cent in the middle two quarters of 1990. The London
Stock Exchange only fell by 17 per cent over this period. As a result, the
value rankings are not stable over short periods. However, table 2.6 does
chart the rapid rise of the Tokyo Stock Exchange over the 1980s, the
relative decline of US stock markets, and the slow but sure growth of
London and the other European stock exchanges.

The UK has a large domestic and international equity market relative to
the size of its economy. This market is the most international in terms of
foreign companies listed and the extent of foreign equities traded. In
contrast, German equity markets are small relative to the size of the
economy. The UK, Canadian and US domestic capital markets are very
similar to each other in that many domestic firms are quoted and equity is a
significant form of finance. However most of the smaller domestic capital
markets can be characterized as consisting of very few firms which are
widely publicly held (Feiger and Jacquillat 1982: 308). Small group and
family holdings predominate and new equity issues are avoided for fear of
losing control. Bond and bank loan financing dominate especially in
Germany, Belgium and Japan. Banks play a particularly important role in
the provision of long term funds and often are directly involved in

managerial decision making. Finally, several of these domestic capital markets are subject to significant government regulation and control over capital flows. The huge Japanese domestic market has begun to open up in the past decade and is moving away from its restricted access for foreigners and its highly regulated nature. However, the Tokyo Stock Exchange's turnover in international equities was only 10 per cent of that of London in 1988 (*Bank of England Quarterly Bulletin*, November 1990, p. 520).

The domestic markets of the US, the UK, France, Germany, Switzerland and the Netherlands have considerable international importance because they are relatively open to international investors and borrowers. The regulatory climate in these markets is liberal and this makes them attractive to international capital: as a result, the same investors and borrowers are likely to be active in both domestic and offshore markets. For example, a domestic bank can lend to a foreign resident firm, and the foreign resident firm may issue securities in domestic markets, both in the domestic currency. All of this would be subject to local regulation. Alternatively, the bank can lend in foreign currencies to the foreign resident via the unregulated Euromarkets, or the foreign resident can issue securities such as Eurobonds in various currencies in these markets. In contrast, domestic investors can acquire foreign bonds and equities and deposit funds in overseas banks. Thus the potential for arbitrage is very high between certain domestic bond, equity and credit markets and their offshore equivalents. We would therefore expect that the pricing mechanisms between the Euromarkets and the relatively open domestic markets would be closely linked and that this would approximate to one market for the pricing of international capital.

## The role of the banks

Commercial (or in the UK clearing) banks are providers of payment services and they act as financial intermediaries. In the latter role they offer both deposit and lending services. They offer a variety of liabilities such as deposit and current accounts tailored to fit particular savers' preferences, and they lend the funds they receive on a variety of terms which satisfy the needs of a range of borrowers. By pooling risks, by averaging the experience of many individuals and by acquiring the expertise to assess the prospect of profit and loss inherent in lending, banks are able to provide their savers with a combination of interest, ease of repayment and protection against loss that is better than these savers could obtain by lending directly to the ultimate borrowers (Bain 1970). Banks mediate between these borrowers and savers to achieve a profit. However, costs are incurred in this intermediation process and these costs must be met out of the banks' margins between the borrowing and lending interest rates. Banks are able to achieve these margins through economies of scale. However, the margins are always under pressure from the basic costs of the business and from competition.

These basic principles of commercial banking are amply demonstrated in the case of international banks. These institutions are the dominant traders in the Euromarkets and the foreign exchange market and are very active in some domestic credit and bond markets. As indicated earlier, the Eurocurrency market consists of banks, commonly referred to as Eurobanks, which accept deposits and lend in foreign currencies. Most of the banks active in the Eurocurrency market also trade extensively in the foreign exchange markets. The Eurobanks concerned include some of the largest banks in the world, such as BNP, Crédit Agricole and Crédit Lyonnais of France, Bank America Corporation of San Francisco, Citicorp of New York, Deutsche Bank and Dresdener Bank of Germany, Lloyds and Barclays of London, and Sumitomo Bank and Fuji Bank of Tokyo.

Eurobanks are typically London branches of these large international banks and are primarily engaged in intermediation in short term deposits denominated in currencies other than sterling. Eurosterling dealing takes place outside British jurisdiction in locations such as Paris. The large American and Japanese banks have dominated the Eurocurrency business, but major British banks have also been very active throughout the 1980s. Some of the large world commercial banks have also formed 'consortium' banks as special purpose joint ventures set up to deal in the Eurocurrency market (Dufey and Giddy 1978a: 12). From the parent bank's point of view, the Eurobank branch or consortium has been able to operate outside the range of domestic banking regulations and has therefore achieved considerable cost economies owing to the absence of reserve requirements and other regulatory costs. International co-operation on capital adequacy standards has begun to erode this privileged position. As a result, the global financial intermediation activities of international banks are now increasingly subject to some form of international control. A further advantage of Eurobanking stems from the scale of borrowing and lending in this market. This means that major economies of scale can be realized by banks. These factors explain why Eurocurrency deposit and lending rates fall within the equivalent domestic values. Thus the Eurosterling loan rate will be lower than the British domestic bank loan rate and the Eurosterling deposit rate will be higher than the British deposit rate. The resulting very narrow profit margin in the Eurocurrency market is only possible owing to the transaction and regulatory cost savings achievable in this market compared with equivalent domestic markets.

## 2.2 Recent Changes in the World Financial System

Three areas of change in the world financial system are discussed in this section. They include changes in world financial markets, in bank regulation and in the world debt crisis.

### Market based changes

Many changes have occurred in the past decade in international financial markets. Securitization, changes in investor preferences, innovation in capital markets, and changes in the corporate banking market are employed as convenient categories to discuss many interrelated sources of change. These categories are not exhaustive and are not meant to conceal the considerable interaction taking place between these aspects of environmental change and their impact on markets, banks and MNCs. In practice, we will see that the degree of interaction between these categories is very high and the direction of causality of change is often unclear.

*Securitization and disintermediation in international capital and credit markets*
As Eurosecurity markets became more operationally efficient (i.e. achieved lower transaction costs) over the 1980s there was a movement away from syndicated bank Euroloans to a greater use of new forms of security funding, ranging from uncommitted (not underwritten or bank backed) sources such as Eurocommercial paper and Euronotes to committed (bank insured) sources such as note issuance facilities (NIFs) or revolving underwritten facilities (RUFs). This 'securitization' phenomenon can be attributed, in part, to the higher costs of internal transacting (intermediating between borrowers and lenders) incurred by banks in the aftermath of the world debt crisis. In addition, changing investor preferences and changes in financial technology were key factors in

reducing market transaction costs and encouraging this shift in the financing mechanism for firms.

It seems likely that the costs of searching for good credit risks and subsequent bargaining costs escalated considerably from the beginning of the debt crisis. The rescheduling of sovereign debt has also increased the policing and enforcement costs of existing debt contracts and may have affected expectations about such costs for future contracts. The emergence of the Eurocommercial paper markets reflected further reductions in market transaction costs compared with short term paper such as RUFs and NIFs with their costly standby facilities.

Banks are vulnerable to such changes in the market costs of transacting. The changes appear to have eroded the boundary between internal and external transacting and enhanced the benefits to borrowers and to suppliers of capital of dealing directly through markets. In the mid to late 1980s syndicated lending suffered a relative decline and securitized borrowing expanded dramatically. Large international commercial banks responded to these changes by entering the securities business in a substantial way, using London as the jurisdiction in which this business was most effectively conducted.

*Changing investor preferences*
International capital flows changed dramatically in the 1980s. The golden age of petrodollar recycling from 1973 to the early 1980s vanished. During this period commercial banks were responsible for shifting large amounts of money from dollar rich oil exporting nations via syndicated loans to credit hungry nations in the developed and developing world. These latter countries faced increasing payments problems from the higher price of imported energy and this in turn increased their need for credit.

The large oil exporters preferred to place surplus funds with banks rather than take any direct investment risks themselves and this in turn fuelled the syndicated loan boom of this period. From the mid 1980s onwards the main source and impulse in world capital flows involved the shift of funds from Japan to the United States. Japan rapidly emerged as the world's largest creditor nation to the United States, which from 1985 to the early 1990s continued to be a net debtor nation. Thus surplus funds were now in the hands of investors, such as Japanese pension funds and insurance companies, who preferred to buy securities. This meant that the securities markets became more important than the bank loan market as a vehicle for international capital flows. This growth in the securities market was very heavy in the Eurobond market and in the Eurocommercial paper market. One consequence of this change was that the relative importance of traditional commercial banking declined and that of investment banking grew.

### Innovations in markets

The period 1985–90 saw the emergence of a very competitive banking world. Initially international banks competed for market share by lowering their prices, by devising more and more financial innovations and by expanding their range of banking functions. Major innovations in the 1980s include the Eurocommercial paper and Euronote markets, RUFs, NIFs, convertible bonds, swaps, options, financial futures and many other variants of these. The more established Euro and domestic security markets also grew over this period. In particular the Eurobond market developed major new dimensions in its symbiotic relationships with other new markets such as the swaps market and the Euroequity market.

However, since the crash of October 1987 and the implementation of the Basle capital adequacy proposals for banks, innovation has slowed and banks have emphasized a more rational risk/reward balance in corporate banking markets. Gaining market share through unprofitable pricing was no longer a key policy as the need for internally generated capital became paramount. Innovations are still occurring in the marketplace but these are now examined carefully by corporate and other parties to the exchange to see if the bank, when acting as information broker or as financial intermediary, is providing a valuable service or is merely creating a complex product to maximize its fee income. Innovation has begun to slow down in these markets as bankers face up to these new constraints and as corporate users of such products become more aware of their costs and more sceptical of their role in financial management.

The Eurobond market is still a major source of corporate funding despite some setbacks after the 1987 crash. The latter did mean closure of bond departments in some banks. Pricing in this market is now more firmly based on a rational risk/return basis and banks remaining in this market are expected to make profits. The emergence of the swaps market has added a significant new dimension to the Eurobond market. Bonds can be issued in one currency with say a fixed interest profile and be immediately swapped into another currency and varying interest rate profile. This innovation has given the Eurobond market a further stimulus and further reduced corporate reliance on bank loans. (See chapter 11 for more details of swaps.)

Additional security market innovations include the emergence of equity linked (convertible) bonds and Euroequities. The latter are distributed using Eurobond syndication methods and thus allow banks to make multiple uses of their skills.

### Changing roles of investment and commercial banks

Two historic roles of banks in domestic and international capital and credit markets have been those of investment banking and commercial (clearing) banking. Commercial banks are financial intermediaries that borrow money from savers in the form of deposits and relend them to ultimate borrowers by making loans or buying securities. Investment banks are information intermediaries that help corporate borrowers to raise funds directly from savers via the design, issue, underwriting and sale of securities. They are primarily sellers of security design skills, security sale insurance or underwriting services, and placing/selling skills.

Deregulation, the world debt problem, changing investor preferences and innovations in capital markets all contributed in the 1980s to an erosion of these historic roles in international banking. The comprehensive or universal bank, combining both investment and commercial banking functions, can in the 1990s offer companies a full range of services including corporate advisory work, underwriting and syndication services for new security issues, and security trading services as well as traditional commercial banking services. In the 1990s the same institution can operate in many different banking modes across the world financial and banking markets and thus act as a universal international bank. London is a key centre for such activity because it allows US and Japanese banks to operate in this way outside strict domestic restrictions on universal banking.

The central role of the bank in these international corporate loan, bond, commercial paper and swaps markets can best be shown as in figure 2.3. The bottom 'row' of the diagram illustrates conventional deposit taking and lending in corporate markets by commercial or clearing banks. The top 'row' illustrates conventional investment banking as the bank offers information, insurance or security selling services. The two vertical columns illustrate bank swap services in corporate liabilities (LHS) or assets (RHS).

An international bank can arbitrage between many of these markets for its own benefit, and by being at the centre of all of these markets it can offer its customers a full service. Many products in the corporate banking market lie in one of these markets or involve combinations of transactions with these markets or with other related markets such as the foreign

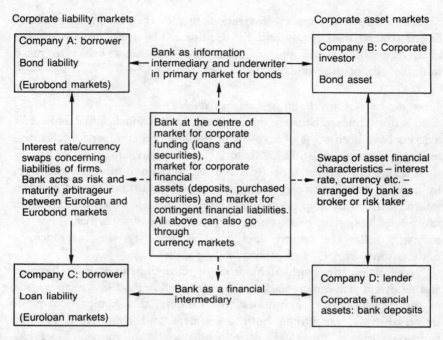

**Figure 2.3** The role of the bank in international markets

exchange market. To this can be added the role of international payment services in supplying a rich source of information on corporate clients in helping the bank to screen high default risks and to identify new areas of financial services business. Reorienting the bank towards these markets and towards the centralization and co-ordination of these cross-market functions is a major competitive advantage sought by large international banks such as Lloyds.

As a result it is clear that the lines of differentiation between the investment bank and the commercial (in the UK clearing) bank are becoming blurred. This has mainly occurred in the UK market but the phenomenon has begun to spread to other European banking markets as the barriers came down within the EC with the advent of '1992' and the December 1991 Maastricht Agreement. In addition, there was much debate in the US in 1992 about the adaptation or removal of the Glass Steagall Act and the domestic barriers to universal banking. This has been rejected, but if US practice does change in a significant way, then similar changes are likely in Japanese domestic regulation.

## Deregulation, reregulation and harmonization of the world banking system

### *The Basle or Cooke Committee*

By the mid 1980s there was a consensus that changes in the world of international banking had strengthened the arguments for convergence or harmonization of capital adequacy standards. The concern stemmed both from prudential grounds and also from a concern that in some countries domestic capital requirements gave local banks a competitive advantage.

The Basle or Cooke Committee, comprising the bank supervisors of the group of ten (G10) industrialized countries, had by December 1987 outlined its proposals in this respect. Internationally active banks had until 1992 to achieve a common minimum standard ratio of capital to weighted risk assets of 8 per cent, with core capital (equity and disclosed reserves) of at least 4 per cent. Most national bank supervisors expected their banks to exceed these new minimum standards. In this scheme there are different weightings for 'on balance sheet' assets depending on their perceived (by regulators) credit risk class. 'Off balance sheet' assets have to be translated into their equivalent credit risk class. These include such items as swaps, options, futures, and various forms of underwriting commitments entered into by the banks.

Basle/G10 has equity as top tier capital, and thus increased the emphasis on stock markets as the primary source of risk capital and heightened the significance of profits as a source of capital. This risk asset model (RAM) and the recession of the early 1990s enforced more conservative behaviour on the asset side of the bank balance sheet. Aggressive search for market share in international loan markets or in off balance sheet products was curtailed as all banks faced the same capital adequacy constraints. This renewed focus on quality lending and avoidance of very risky business will probably reduce the variance of bank asset returns. All of these outcomes were seen as desirable by the G10 regulators.

### *The EC and financial and banking markets*

Changes within the EC are but one part of the global change process in the financial system. However, within the EC countries there are quite specific moves to bring about the creation of one of the largest unified markets in financial services and products. In particular the Single European Act (1986) has provided a major impetus to European financial integration. It includes mutual recognition of banking regulation rules and common prudential rules. These regulatory changes are being proposed in tandem with the G10 recommendations. Each member state has to accept the bank regulatory framework of its partners in the EC. The Second Banking Directive requires a bank to report to its home country authorities concerning its EC and overseas activities. In addition the Commission of the EC is committed to a policy of encouraging internal competition and removing significant internal barriers to trade in financial services. Thus any bank or financial services enterprise, legally established in a member state, will be allowed to enter another EC country market without requesting new bank authorization in the country concerned. In parallel with this there is increasing integration of European domestic capital markets and links with the new equity and equity related activity in the Euro or offshore markets. Finally, the gradual removal of exchange controls and the evolution of the EMS, despite the 1992 and 1993 setbacks, are designed to move the EC closer to a single monetary union. These factors together add a considerable European dimension to the changes occurring in world capital and banking markets.

## Sovereign lending and the world debt crisis

One major problem faced by international banks and capital markets throughout the 1980s and 1990s was in the area of lending to sovereign states. High levels of interest rates, massive foreign debts in the non-oil-producing states, poor economic management and performance and the threat of default by some states, all increased the sovereign risk facing banks. At the same time the equity base of the banks declined relative to debt and the ability of banks to absorb losses was much reduced. The scale of the problem was such that it generally encouraged a co-operative attitude amongst the banks, creditor nations, debtor nations and the international agencies, with the occasional eruption of veiled threats between the parties.

However, in the 1990s many of the poorer debtor nations, especially from sub-Saharan Africa, still faced severe problems as their outstanding debt continued to rise even when interest rates fell. This was, in part, due to their increased need for debt as well as the capitalization of interest arrears. It was also exacerbated by the global recession of the early 1990s. The threat of a debtors' cartel, in which these nations agree to simultaneously default or go into arrears, seems to have receded with rescheduling agreements and the losing of the South American part of the debt problem. However, this is still a significant threat hanging over many members of the international banking community, especially with the possibility of the rescheduling of the sovereign debts of Eastern European nations and the new states emerging from the former Soviet Union.

The further significant downturn in the world economy in 1992 and 1993, especially its German and Japanese elements, continued to make it difficult for debtor countries to sustain exports and reduce balance of payments pressures. This, combined with sub-Saharan drought and the political instability in Africa, the former Soviet Union and the former Yugoslavia, has maintained calls for a more radical approach to the debt problem. This in turn could mean increased losses for international banks and promote further activity by the Basle Committee to regulate banks and by implication their activities in the Euromarkets. The latter possibility would strike at the *raison d'être* of the Euromarkets, whilst the former would affect the confidence of lenders and accentuate the problems facing international banks.

In 1985 James Baker, the US Secretary of the Treasury, argued that growth was the major route out of the problem with each debtor nation being dealt with on a case by case basis. It was argued that the IMF and the World Bank should only give support to those countries adopting acceptable growth policies. By 1988 it was clear that this growth had not occurred and that the conditions laid down by the World Bank and the IMF for policy change and debt repayment were not being complied with. In particular, non-compliance with the programmes of these institutions has led them to become major creditors, with their own financial interests at stake. Baker's successor, Nicholas Brady, argued in March 1989 that direct debt reduction was essential to resolve the problem. This reflects a reality in the marketplace where in some cases banks have exchanged their debt (at a discount) for cash, for equity stakes in South American companies, or for (exit) bonds that eliminate the banks' liability to lend more money. Brady argued that these market based solutions can be encouraged by contributions from the World Bank and the IMF. These can also be encouraged by creditor nations and banks reducing legislative disincentives (such as bank tax arrangements) to debt reduction and simplifying and waiving certain (sharing and negative pledge) clauses in the loans. In 1991 a new twist to the problem emerged for these world institutions and the banks with the collapse of communism in the Soviet Union and political turmoil in its old Eastern European and newly independent states. The possibility of loan defaults by a non-existent Soviet Union or its successor states is likely to lead to further unknown demands on these bodies and the commercial banks. In 1993 the recession had spread throughout the developed world, with inevitable effects on the ability of less developed countries (LDCs) to repay debt. The only glimmer of hope here was a reduction of interest rates during this global recession. Central and South American debtor countries appeared to be mostly likely to emerge from this problem. For example, the World Bank affiliate IFC approved a record $622 million in syndicated loans with international commercial banks in the year to 30 June 1990. The change in the banks' attitudes was particularly evident in South America where the IFC syndicated loans of $157 million for projects in six countries.

By 1993 the banks had widely adopted a policy of increasing their bad debt reserves, and this was beginning to reflect 100 per cent of the LDC debt held by some of the very large UK, European and US banks. Banks were also responding to this problem by adopting policies to ensure that they did not face similar problems in the future. They were therefore attempting to strengthen their existing loan portfolio and balance sheet. Thus EC based banks and US banks were focusing on higher quality lending to Western governments and companies and turning away from the heavily indebted countries. International firms began to make more sophisticated use of the Eurolending market by employing more flexible financing arrangements such as multi-option facilities. Euroloan syndication facilities had become very important in funding the surge of takeovers and management buyouts in the latter half of the 1980s, but this role was much reduced by 1993. The loan markets also provided competitive funding facilities to those firms with limited access (limited credit rating) to the Eurobond and other Eurosecurity markets. These firms then used the swaps markets to gain indirect access to the Eurosecurity markets. As a result of these changes, there was a minor revival of the international syndicated loan market in 1987 to 1989. However, as we will see in the next section, the world recession in the early 1990s had a dampening effect.

## International capital markets in 1992

The OECD, in its periodic report *Financial Trends*, summarizes changes in international capital markets. Table 2.7 is taken from the October 1992 report and shows data from 1988 to September 1992.

The major points from this report were as follows. Firstly, the international capital markets in total suffered their first decline in a decade in 1990 but showed good growth again by 1992.

Secondly, international securities including Euro (external) bonds, Euroequities, and medium term uncommitted Euronotes all showed signs

**Table 2.7** Borrowings on the international capital market, 1988–1992 ($ billion)

| Funding instruments | 1988 | 1989 | 1990 | 1991 | Jan.–Sept. 1991 | 1992 |
|---|---|---|---|---|---|---|
| External bonds | 227.1 | 255.7 | 229.9 | 297.4 | 228.6 | 248.6 |
| External equities | 7.7 | 8.1 | 7.3 | 23.6 | 14.8 | 20.6 |
| Syndicated loans | 125.5 | 121.1 | 124.5 | 116.0 | 74.6 | 86.1 |
| Note issuance facilities | 14.4 | 5.5 | 4.3 | 2.1 | 1.1 | 1.3 |
| Other backup facilities (e.g. RUFs) | 2.2 | 2.9 | 2.7 | 5.6 | 5.0 | 3.9 |
| Total securities, loans and underwritten/committed facilities | 376.9 | 393.3 | 368.7 | 444.7 | 324.1 | 360.6 |
| Eurocommercial paper | 57.1 | 54.1 | 48.3 | 35.7 | 25.1 | 15.8 |
| Euronote and other non-underwritten facilities | 19.5 | 19.1 | 17.9 | 44.5 | 30.8 | 62.8 |
| Total uncommitted facilities | 76.6 | 73.2 | 66.2 | 80.2 | 55.9 | 78.6 |
| Overall total | 453.5 | 466.5 | 434.9 | 524.9 | 380.0 | 439.1 |

of growth in 1992, with the medium term Euronotes growing at 35 per cent in the first nine months of 1992. Other securities, such as Eurocommercial paper, continued their decline to mid 1980s levels. Underwritten, backup or committed facilities such as NIFs and RUFs were well below the levels reached in the mid 1980s. In 1991 the Eurobond markets showed particularly good growth in fixed coupon or straight bonds, with currencies such as the ECU becoming more popular as the US dollar declined as the dominant issue currency. The September 1992 ERM crisis reversed this trend as investors sought safer currency havens such as the US dollar.

Thirdly, the syndicated loans markets were depressed in 1991. There were signs of improvement in late 1992 but growth was only coming from specific segments of these markets such as US based leveraged buyouts, with other sectors remaining in the doldrums. The banks were generally only making funds available to top class borrowers including the major countries and their 'blue chip' MNCs. This market can only expect growth as the world economy begins to recover, and when mergers and acquisition activity picks up again in the MNC sector. Lending to LDCs grew over 1990–2 owing to the return of Latin American countries to the market. In 1992 new LDC borrowing was $33.7 billion, with most of the growth being in security funding rather than syndicated lending. The banks are expected to maintain their cautious approach to international syndicated lending, offering stiff spread and fee terms to even the best of borrowers. Despite this, syndicated lending remained a key means of funding, second only to the Eurobond market, with Euronotes emerging as a major funding source.

These statistics reveal the extent to which there has been a shift in funding patterns in the Euro or external markets in recent years and reflect the continuing impact of the global recession in the early 1990s.

## 2.3 Summary

The international monetary and financial system is a fast moving and complex world for the financial manager. Four means of unifying our understanding of this complex system were employed in this chapter:

1   The primary constituent elements of the system were outlined including governments, supranational institutions, financial markets, financial institutions and multinational firms.
2   The growing role of inter-governmental co-operation in co-ordinating action in currency markets and in banking regulation was explored.
3   Market forces were seen as a key unifying feature of this system. These will be explored in more detail in the following chapter.
4   The international bank was seen as a new kind of financial firm organized around all of these financial markets.

Thus the discussion in section 2.1 identified the institutional nature of this system and highlighted the significance and complexity of the system for the multinational enterprise. This section specifically described the main features of the Eurocurrency, foreign exchange, international bonds and equities, and various futures and options markets.

In section 2.2, we considered recent changes in world financial markets, in bank regulation and in the world debt crisis. These have further increased the complexity of this system by creating new links between the international markets for capital and currency, widening the opportunities for transacting and arbitrage by multinational banks and firms and increasing the degree of international co-operation in managing the system.

The international banks have changed quite significantly over the past decade in terms of the range of banking functions and financial products and services offered, and in terms of their attitudes to the pricing and profitability of these services. The period of rapid innovation in financial markets in the 1980s was part of this change in international banks. All of these changes seem to have slowed down dramatically after the 1987 stock market crash and the world recession of the early 1990s. Despite this slowdown the international bank has emerged as a central component in the new global financial system.

The changes in financial and banking markets have both simplified and complicated the task of the international financial manager. The merging of many national financial markets has increased the likelihood that global prices apply to many financial services and sources of funds. Regardless of this there may still be opportunities for financial managers to create value by arbitraging between markets. The development of co-operative management schemes for the world monetary system may reduce the volatility of exchange rates and thus the significance of the foreign exchange risk management problem faced by the firm. At present, this possibility is only likely to apply to those firms that trade in the currencies operating within the 2 per cent band of the EMS. However, the EMS crisis of September 1992, and the Irish pound devaluation within the EMS in January 1993, reminded financial managers of the possibility of unanticipated realignments within the EMS and of the sudden floating or suspension of member currencies. This experience may increase the caution shown by EC based corporate treasurers in the field of foreign exchange risk management. Finally, the expansion of bank functions has combined with a freeing up of national banking systems to broaden the funding and financial service supply system for MNCs and domestic firms alike. Thus whilst the search for bargains in the world of finance has become more difficult, the capabilities of the system to deliver the required financial products has much improved.

In chapter 1 the growing sophistication of the treasury function of MNCs over the past decade was noted. This has been stimulated by the many recent changes in international financial and banking markets outlined above. These have combined with the high volatility of foreign exchanges rates and interest rates, the growing internationalization of business, and changes in treasury technology to provide fertile ground in which new treasury skills have flourished. These changes have increased the significance of the finance function for the international enterprise. The new levels of complexity and new degrees of freedom for the international finance executive and treasury staff mean that more highly skilled managers are required in this function. The aim in the following chapters is to provide the insights necessary for the development of these skills. We begin in the following chapter by attempting to describe the market forces of figure 2.1 through a simple set of linked theories. These parity theories and their institutional and market background form an essential context in which the financial manager performs his organizational task.

# 3

# The Parity Relationships, Imperfections and IFM Decisions

This chapter explores how market forces might function in markets for foreign exchange, funds and other financial services. This aim is achieved in section 3.1 by the use of parity theories to link together variables such as interest rate and inflation rate differences between countries and changes in their exchange rates. The financial parity relationships include

- interest rate (and equity return) parity
- the international Fisher effect
- the unbiased forward rate effect
- the international capital asset pricing model.

The parity relationships are discussed in the context of the institutional and market background in which they are thought to prevail. Thus the parity relationships provide an important framework for summarizing the roles of international banks and multinationals in the foreign exchange, Euro-currency, Eurobond and national equity markets outlined in chapter 2. To complete the framework, the purchasing parity theory is outlined and international trading in goods and services is linked to exchange rate and inflation rate changes.

This neo–classical framework is then applied in section 3.2 to three key decision areas of international financial management. These are foreign exchange exposure risk management, financing decisions and capital budgeting decisions. If the parity or equilibrium relationships hold then many of the issues of international financial management are shown to be illusions. Coping with the problems of IFM therefore becomes a question of using existing domestic finance theory and the parity relationships to see through these illusions to the fundamental financial problems common to all firms. The benefits and limitations of this framework are investigated in the rest of chapter 3 and in subsequent chapters.

In section 3.3 we outline the nature of the imperfections possible in international markets for capital, currency and financial services. These circumstances create sources of profit or additional value for the firm. The evidence for and against the full functioning of the parity relationships is then outlined. This provides some insight into the general circumstances in which these imperfections may occur and their impact on IFM decisions. Section 3.4 summarizes the findings.

## 3.1 An Equilibrium Framework

The description of the international financial system in chapter 2 has isolated supranational influences, direct government action, the economic behaviour of banks and MNCs and market forces as major influences on the functioning of international capital markets and foreign exchange markets. In this section we consider theories of the market forces operating in this financial system. Governments, banks, MNCs and supranational institutions are generally seen as sources of imperfections in the normal functioning of these markets and therefore the causes of deviations from ideal market conditions. Such ideal conditions are described by various parity theories and these form the topics of discussion in this section. Deviations are discussed in later sections of this chapter.

Giddy (1977: 602) has outlined a framework which relates the foreign exchange and international money markets, within the context of market efficiency. This theory of market forces involves the equilibrium relationships expected between interest rates, exchange rates and inflation rates:

> Through the purchasing power parity relationship, the inflation rate differential causes a corresponding rate of change of the exchange rate. If the foreign exchange market is efficient, the forward exchange rate equals the market's expected future exchange rate. Hence the expected rate of change of the exchange rate equals the forward premium or discount, which in turn equals the interest rate differential through the interest rate parity theorem. To close the loop, if the traditional 'Fisher effect' holds, then the interest rate differential equals the expected inflation rate differential.

These relationships can be expressed as follows (Giddy 1977: 604):

*Purchasing power parity (PPP) theorem*
 expected rate of change of spot exchange rate = inflation rate differential
*One country Fisher effect*
 interest rate = real interest rate plus expected inflation rate
*International Fisher effect (IFE)*
 expected rate of change of spot exchange rate = interest rate differential
*Interest rate parity (IRP) theorem*
 forward exchange premium or discount = interest rate differential
*Unbiased forward rate (UBFR) theorem*
 forward exchange premium or discount = expected rate of change of spot exchange rate

The framework for these relationships is shown in figure 3.1.

## Worked example of the parity relationships

The relationships between interest rate, inflation rate, forward premium or discount, and spot rate change expectations expressed in figure 3.1 can best be demonstrated by an example.

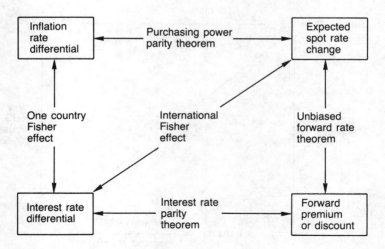

**Figure 3.1** Equilibrium relationship between interest rate, inflation rate and exchange rates

A firm has £1 million to invest for the year ahead. The spot exchange rate today is 1.7037$/£ and the one year forward rate (agreed today) is 1.628$/£. The London sterling interest rate is $10\frac{7}{16}$ per cent for one year bank deposits, and the New York dollar interest rate is 5.5 per cent for one year bank deposits of the same risk. The firm can:

*either*
1   invest £1 million in London at $10\frac{7}{16}$ per cent for one year, giving interest of £104,375 and a total sum of £1,104,375
*or*
2   (a) convert £1 million to dollars at 1.7037$/£ that is $1,703,700; invest this dollar principal in New York for one year at 5.5 per cent, giving interest of $93,704 and a total sum of $1,797,404; *and*
    (b) sell the dollar total forward at the one year forward rate (agreed today) of 1.628$/£ and receive £1,104,057 at the end of the year.

These alternatives are illustrated by figure 3.2.
We can see that the investment in dollar bank deposits or in sterling bank deposits produces approximately the same sterling sum: the dollar bank deposit and the forward rate agreement produce slightly less owing to extra transaction costs. If interest rate parity did not hold in this way then a

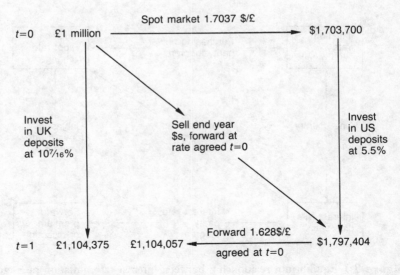

**Figure 3.2** Example investement alternatives

'money machine' would exist: traders would arbitrage between the (Euro) markets for bank deposits and the currency markets, spot and forward, and quickly erode the price advantage in one market. This is one major transacting route (probably with arbitrage and speculative motives) that ensures that exchange rate expectations are fully reflected in both interest rates and forward exchange rates.

We can also see that the future spot rate at the end of one year ($t = 1$) implied by these interest rates is $\$1,797,404/\pounds1,104,375 = 1.6275 \text{ \$/\pounds}$. This is very close to the forward rate set at $t = 0$ and shows how the international Fisher effect incorporates the expected future spot forecast and future spot changes into the interest differential at $t = 0$. These are the same future spot rate expectations as those built into the forward rate premium and so the international Fisher effect and the unbiased forward rate effect share a common forecast of the future spot rate. The interest rate difference can be calculated as follows:

$$\frac{0.055 - 0.104375}{1 + 0.104375} \times 100 = -4.47\%$$

This interest rate difference can be interpreted as:

- the forecast of the spot exchange rate change over the year, i.e. the international Fisher effect
- the forecast of the inflation rate difference expected between the US and the UK over the year, i.e. the domestic Fisher effect across two countries.

Thus both of these forecasts are implied in this interest rate difference.

We have already seen how the forward premium or discount is calculated from the spot rate and the $n$ months forward rate, where $n = 1$, 3, 6, 12 etc.:

$$\frac{\text{forward premium}}{\text{or discount}} = \frac{\text{forward} - \text{spot}}{\text{spot}} \times \frac{12}{n} \times 100$$

Thus in our case we can also calculate the forward premium as

$$\frac{1.628 - 1.7037}{1.7037} \times \frac{12}{12} \times 100 = \frac{-0.0757}{1.7037} \times 100 = -4.45\%$$

The dollar is becoming more expensive relative to the pound by about 4.45% per annum, or the dollar is appreciating relative to the pound. The interest rate difference provided a similar percentage change, and this demonstrates that IRP holds for this example.

Given this example, we can express the parity relationships framework for figure 3.1 in algebraic form as in figure 3.3. In the figure, the annualized version of the forward premium is presented in the bottom right-hand box, i.e. at $n = 12$. The top right-hand box is very similar, except that the forward market price is replaced by an expectation or forecast of the future spot rate for that period. In the bottom left-hand box the interest rate difference is shown as calculated on an annualized rate of change from the UK base.

The UK indirect quoting method is employed, and the pound is used as the reference or base currency from which changes are calculated. Given that the pound is the reference currency, the UK inflation rate and interest

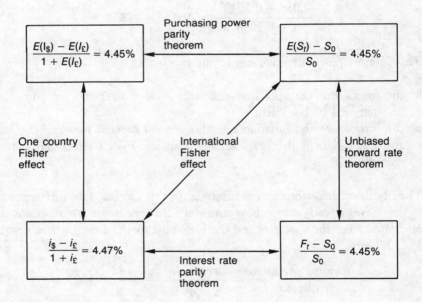

**Figure 3.3** Equilibrium relationships in algebraic form

$E(I_C)$ expected inflation in currency $C$

$i_C$   interest rate in currency $C$

$E(S_t)$ expected spot rate in period $t$

$F_t$   forward rate in period $t$, agreed in period 0

$S_0$   spot rate in period 0

rate are employed as the denominators (bottom) in the left-hand boxes, with foreign currency differences from these UK figures forming the numerators (top). If direct quoting (e.g. £/$) had been used, then the foreign currency (dollars) would be the reference base, with denominators of $1 + E(I_\$)$ and $1 + i_\$$ for the left-hand boxes. All of the above equations would therefore adjust for this. In the example above the US dollar is used as the foreign currency.

## Parity relationships and the world of trade and finance

The parity relationships abstract away from a complex world of financial and real markets. The top two boxes of figure 3.3 relate to PPP and a world of arbitrage in real goods and services. Changes in prices of real goods and services are linked to exchange rate changes through the concept of the 'law of one price' and its handmaiden PPP. This world of real goods and services is tied to the world of finance by the rest of the parity relationships.

The bottom two boxes conceal a considerable amount of trading and arbitrage in a wide range of financial markets. Thus the international Fisher effect involves arbitrage between external financial markets such as the Eurodollar and the Eurosterling markets for bank deposits, and this is the means by which expectations about the future $/£ spot rate are reflected in interest rates. Interest rate parity concerns arbitrage between the Eurocurrency bank deposit markets and the currency markets, both spot and forward. The unbiased forward rate parity relationship refers to arbitrage within and between the spot and forward markets as new information feeds into these sectors of the currency markets and influences expectations about the future path of the spot rate. The one country Fisher relationship deals with the incorporation of inflation expectations into domestic interest rates and the way in which any national differences in this inflation adjustment mechanism can be exploited by arbitrage between domestic markets.

The parity relationships provide the conceptual means to see how these many complex markets can be linked in a relatively simple way. They also demonstrate the power of many of the basic concepts of finance in the international context. Thus concepts of arbitrage, market efficiency and value are central to the parity relationships. These concepts, when tied together in the overall parity framework, provide a valuable addition to the tools of international financial management.

## Purchasing power parity

The PPP relationship is established by international arbitrage in real goods and services. Essentially consumers in different countries are assumed to wish to pay the same price for the same (internationally traded) basket of commodities. Thus, if inflation rates in two countries are expected to change the relative purchasing power in each country, then PPP (relative version) states that the rate of change of the spot exchange rate between these countries will tend over time to equal the expected difference in the inflation rates. As a result, after adjusting prices for the spot exchange rate, consumers in both countries will expect to pay the same price for internationally traded goods and services.

Purchasing parity provides some explanation for the influence of arbitrage in real goods on exchange rates. To provide explanations for the relationship between financial arbitrage and PPP we need to turn from markets for real commodities to financial markets and foreign exchange markets. A brief discussion of the equilibrium relationships expected in these markets, i.e. the Fisher effect, the international Fisher effect, the interest rate parity theorem and the unbiased forward rate theorem, can provide insights into shorter term exchange rate movements.

## Unbiased forward rate

As we have seen, in the forward market a contract is established between buyer and sellers. The rate at which currencies are to be exchanged in the future is contractually agreed some time prior to the exchange. Thus the rate three months ahead may be agreed today, but the exchange takes place after three months. Clearly few foreign exchange transactors will wish to buy or sell currencies forward at a rate which creates a loss for them. Therefore an essential ingredient in trading in the market will be an accurate forecast of spot rates at the various forward dates.

The aggregate effect of speculative competition between these traders is to ensure that the forward premium or discount tends to equal the expected rate of change of the exchange rate. This occurs because commercial and financial transactors who expect to receive foreign currency payments will tend to accept forward exchange deals only at a future spot exchange rate close to that which they expect to prevail at the agreed forward date. As a result the forward rate or premium will continually adjust to reflect new information, and will adjust to equal the expected rate of change of the spot exchange rate over the contract period. In this sense then the foreign exchange market is considered 'efficient' (Dufey and Giddy 1978a: 67) and the forward rate is considered an unbiased predictor of future spot rates.

Levich (1979: 50) defines this phenomenon in more formal statistical terms. The average forecast error (calculated as the difference between today's forward exchange rate for delivery in *n* days and the spot exchange rate *n* days in the future) is small and not statistically different from zero. There is no positive or negative bias in the error term. In addition, any forecast errors are serially uncorrelated and so the time series of the forecast error should not exhibit predictive patterns of positive and negative values. The latter condition reflects the (weak form) informational efficiency of the market in that there is no additional information to be garnered from historic prices.

## Interest rate parity and the international Fisher effect

In the Eurocurrency markets, financial assets of the same risk and maturity, but denominated in different currencies, are bought and sold. Hence it is in these markets, and the closely linked foreign exchange markets, that the equilibrium relationships between interest rates, forward exchange rates and expected exchange rates are thought to be firmly established.

For example, it is through the processes of arbitrage and foreign exchange hedging between the Eurocurrency markets and the currency markets that interest rate differentials tend to equal the forward premium or discount. Differences between, say, the Eurosterling and Eurodollar interest rates will tend to equal the sterling–dollar forward premium or discount, and interest rate parity is continuously maintained.

The international banks are the major traders in these markets. They find it necessary to 'hedge their bets' by either buying/selling forward foreign exchange or buying/selling financial assets denominated in different currencies. There are two major reasons for this financial strategy. Firstly, the banks are unwilling to have significant net (currency) exposed positions in loans or deposits. They see their primary roles as being financial and informational intermediaries, rather than currency risk taking speculators. They will therefore hedge the bulk of their balance sheets by transacting in the foreign exchange or Eurocurrency markets. A second reason for trading continuously in both Eurocurrency and currency markets is to exploit relatively risk free arbitrage opportunities by taking advantage of different effective interest rates (i.e. effective interest rate =

nominal interest rate + forward premium or – forward discount) across Eurocurrency deposits of similar risk and maturity.

This continuous arbitrage in both the Eurocurrency and the foreign exchange markets ensures that interest rate parity is effectively maintained between Eurocurrency interest rate differences and the corresponding exchange rate premiums or discounts.

The international Fisher relationship follows from IRP and UBFR and suggests that through arbitrage the expected rate of change of the exchange rate tends to equal the Eurocurrency interest rate differential. Well informed corporate treasurers will exploit differences between Eurocurrency interest differentials and expected exchange rate changes until they are equal and no opportunity for profit remains.

## The one country Fisher effect

The one country Fisher effect is essentially concerned with the formation of expectations in one country concerning the effect of inflation on its interest rates. It states that in domestic capital markets, investors' expectations about future inflation rates will be directly reflected in the nominal (actual) interest rates quoted. Investors are assumed to require a relatively low real riskless rate of return plus a compensation equal to expected inflation, plus any risk premium appropriate to the financial security or asset.

If we transfer Fisher to the international situation (for say riskless assets), then in equilibrium, and assuming integrated world markets, the expected real return on capital will be the same in different countries. Two countries will therefore offer the same expected real (riskless) interest rate and the differences in their nominal rates will reflect the expected differences in their inflation rates (Brealey and Myers 1981: 692). If this is the case then a single world capital market exists, with the same real rate of interest in different countries.

## International investors and the equilibrium relationships

If we assume that international capital markets are integrated, and that the equilibrium relationships outlined above also operate for equity and other risky financial assets, then this has some major implications for the international investor. For example IRP would suggest that differences in the nominal expected rates of return on equity securities of the same systematic risk, but denominated in different currencies, would equal the forward premium or discount (i.e. equity return parity, ERP). If UBFR also holds they would be indifferent between hedge and no hedge strategies and they would only be exposed to unanticipated changes in the exchange rate (i.e. the changes other than those changes already forecast or anticipated in the forward rate). Given that these changes are unanticipated they are unlikely to be correlated with their market (world) portfolio, and therefore this residual risk may be largely diversified away.

Hedging against exchange risk by investors is of no value in efficient foreign exchange and capital markets because investors will, in the long run, achieve the same expected return under hedge and no hedge strategies. This is because the expected value of the distribution of any gains and losses (forward rate for period $t$ less actual spot rate in period $t$) will be zero in an efficient and unbiased forward foreign exchange market. Investors may, of course, reduce the variability of their returns by hedging, if they are prepared to pay the costs of hedging.

The Fisher relationship suggests that equity returns within countries should adjust completely for domestic inflation. Hence assuming integrated markets, two countries will offer the same expected real risk adjusted (world portfolio basis) returns for identically risky assets. The expected difference in nominal equity returns will reflect expected differences in the two countries' inflation rates. As a result, holders of internationally diversified portfolios can assume that any expected inflation differentials between countries have been taken into account by world equity markets.

## 3.2 Neo-classicism and the Significance of IFM Issues

If the parity relationships hold then there is little for financial managers to do with respect to IFM issues. Many of the issues of IFM are seen to be illusions, as markets rapidly adjust to any changes in interest rates, exchange rates and inflation across the international economy. This will be demonstrated by looking at some of the central areas of IFM, i.e.

- foreign exchange risk management
- financing decisions
- capital budgeting decisions.

## Exchange rate changes and risk management

Exposure to foreign exchange risk can be simply defined along the following lines:

*Economic exposure* is concerned with the impact of unanticipated exchange rate changes on the uncertain foreign currency stream of corporate revenues and costs and ultimately with the impact on the value of the firm.
*Transaction exposure* is the uncertain domestic value of short term corporate receipts and payments denominated in a foreign currency at a certain future date.
*Translation or accounting exposure* is the uncertain domestic value of a net accounting position denominated in a foreign currency at a certain future date.

These brief definitions will be reconsidered in detail in chapter 4.

In the case of economic exposure, if the parity relationships hold the firm is not subject to any additional risk, since through purchasing parity the prices of real goods adjust to offset exchange rate changes, and the interest rates anticipate exchange rate changes via interest rate parity and the international Fisher effect. There is therefore no need to manage real assets and financial liabilities in response to any expected changes because the market anticipates the decision maker and pre-empts any gains. Furthermore, because the forward rate equals the market expected future spot rate, the expected cost or gain of hedging is zero (over many hedging transactions) and hedging is itself of little value.

If managers feel for some reason that they must always hedge their corporate foreign exchange exposure, then they can do this for no extra cost (except minor hedging costs). Thus as Brealey and Myers (1981: 693) note, the unbiased forward rate effect provides the firm with a low cost insurance scheme against the perceived risk of foreign exchange losses. Managers may wish to do this to reduce the variability of cash flows and earning flows. However, if these equilibrium relationships are working, this hedging activity is not of any value to shareholders.

Adler and Dumas (1983) dissent from this point of view and argue that hedging may be of value to both shareholders and managers, even when foreign exchange markets are efficient. In their view, the above advice ignores the risks associated with distributions with zero expected values. Thus the distribution of unanticipated exchange rate gains and losses (relative to the forward rate) may have a mean of zero but very wide variances. This may be repeated at the level of the firm's cash flows and could lead the firm into liquidity problems if large negative changes in exchange rates coincide with the timing of payment of a large foreign currency receivable. It would be little consolation for the managers and owners to know that this large cash flow loss would correct itself with an equivalent cash flow gain 'in the long run'.

A further argument used to demonstrate that foreign exchange risk management is superfluous to investors as owners of the firm is based on the view that if world capital markets are integrated and efficient then:

1 Investors can diversify away any unsystematic risk from currency changes by portfolio construction.
2 Any systematic risk due to currency changes can be priced in efficient markets (foreign exchange and world capital).

As a result, investors are deemed sophisticated enough to 'see through' conventional financial reports to correctly assess the true economic value of the firm (Jacque 1981: 94). In this situation, hedging to minimize earnings variability or translation currency risk is of no value to shareholders.

## Financing decisions

The parity relationships also provide corporate financial managers with a basic reference point and framework for evaluating financing decisions in international capital markets. The competition in these markets and the resulting equilibrium conditions means that managers can use the 'efficient market' argument in an international financing context. Thus, unless corporate management is privy to relevant information not freely available to these markets, it is unlikely that managers can achieve excess returns or secure cheap funds (positive NPV funding) by 'playing' the Eurocurrency market. Under conditions of market efficiency, market based prices and forecasts should be accepted as valid.

For example, if the international Fisher effect (IFE) holds then expected changes in exchange rates will be reflected in say Eurocurrency interest rates, and if purchasing power parity (PPP) holds then exchange rates will offset differential inflation rates. This ensures that the expected cost of debt will be the same when expressed in different currencies, and the currency of denomination will be a matter of indifference to the firm. Factors such as the nature of the local tax system now become predominant, especially if it discriminates in its treatment of interest costs on the basis of the currency of denomination (Stanley 1981: 108).

The above financing strategies are not designed to cope with unexpected changes in exchange rates. Dufey and Giddy (1978a: 77) suggest that managers should respond to this situation by devoting their energies towards matching borrowings and investments with the timing and currency of the funds needed or produced by the firm's operations. This should ensure that any unanticipated change in the return on assets is offset, as far as is possible, by a change in the effective cost of liabilities.

Burmeister (1981) is critical of the operational value of some of these prescriptions. In particular he argues that it is difficult for firms to achieve the compensating effects of IFE, PPP etc. with respect to the financing decision. He investigated the experience of corporations borrowing medium term Euroloans with interest based upon 'LIBOR six month plus' margins. He tried to find if compensating effects did occur between interest rate and exchange rate variations for these corporate loans. His results suggest that IFE did not provide operational decision rules for financial managers. The results did not reject IFE but they did show that financing costs among currencies varied widely, and did not have a sufficient tendency to convergence. Firms did not receive the long term benefits of IFE because of the continuous change brought about by the economic expansion of these firms (Burmeister 1981: 216). This was seen as inevitable in the conventional trading firm, and so Burmeister called for the development of operational decision rules to cope with these IFM financing problems.

## Capital budgeting

If world equity markets are integrated, then securities would be priced according to their systematic or undiversifiable risk within the context of the world market portfolio. A world capital asset pricing model (CAPM) would apply and beta adjusted returns for equity securities of the same risk would be the same world-wide.

World equity returns can be viewed as consisting of the following three major components (Lessard 1981: 124):

- the world real risk free rate
- a local addition for inflation (Fisher effect)
- a risk premium based upon the world portfolio.

'Real' rates are those that occur in an inflation free world, and security risk premiums are determined relative to the diversified risk of the security and the excess of market returns over the risk free rate.

In equation form:

$$1 + \text{expected equity return}$$
$$= (1 + \text{real risk free rate})(1 + \text{real risk premium})(1 + \text{inflation rate})$$

or

$$(1 + E(R_j)) = (1 + \text{nominal risk free rate})(1 + \text{nominal risk premium})$$

where $E(R_j)$ is the expected return on security $j$.

The return on equity is conventionally measured within the international CAPM (ICAPM) and ignores exchange rate risk because of hedging and diversification by international investors (Feiger and Jacquillat 1982: 304). It is constituted as follows:

$$E(R_j) = R_f + \beta_j[E(R_m) - R_f]$$

where $R_f$ is the risk free rate, $E(R_m)$ is the expected rate on the market portfolio, and $\beta_j$ is the beta on security or project $j$, given by

$$\beta_j = \frac{\text{covariance between returns on } j \text{ and those on market portfolio}}{\text{variance of returns on market portfolio}}$$

In this model, the well diversified investor only seeks a premium for systematic risk of his or her returns. Total risk and its unsystematic (diversifiable) risk component do not play a role in determining risk premiums. Beta in the above equation measures the way in which project or security returns move with market returns. This is considered to be a measure of how more or less (systematically) risky the security is than the overall security market. In practical terms it measures how much the price of a particular share moves up and down compared with how the security market moves up and down. A beta of 1 indicates that the security price moves exactly in line with the market. Thus it has the same systematic risk as the security market and should only earn the same excess over the risk free rate. A beta of 2 is very risky and indicates that the holders of the security will require twice the risk premium over the risk free rate demanded of the security market. This is because the security price has had a historic tendency to rise (or fall) by, say, 20 per cent when the market has only risen (or fallen) by 10 per cent. The difficulties in implementing this model are discussed in section 3.3.

If an international capital asset pricing model and the parity relationships hold, the financial manager can use conventional business finance theory directly in international capital budgeting. Clearly the data inputs will be different, but the form of the model is identical (Feiger and Jacquillat 1982: 304). The conventional NPV model is applicable, and the discount rate should be measured using the world CAPM.

## The implications of parity for international financial decisions

The international monetary and financial system is a fast moving and complex world for the financial manager. The discussion in chapter 2 identified the institutional nature of this system and highlighted the need for a theory base to explain this phenomenon. Such a theory perspective was developed in section 3.1, in which equilibrium pricing mechanisms linking international capital markets, domestic capital markets, foreign exchange markets and markets for real goods were discussed.

If these equilibrium parity relationships hold, then many of the issues of international financial management are shown to be illusions. Coping with the problems of IFM therefore becomes a question of using existing (domestic) corporate finance theory and the parity relationships to see through these apparent complexities to the fundamental financial problems common to all firms. Under the equilibrium framework the domestic and international environments coalesce into one. Some exceptions to this view were noted, but in general the theories outlined in section 3.1 suggest that IFM problems are interesting but not significantly different from those of DOFM.

## 3.3 The Imperfections Paradigm

Few thinkers in the field of IFM urge the wholesale adoption of the neo-classical approach. It is generally seen in the literature as a valuable reference point, but in need of adaptation according to circumstances. These circumstances, and the appropriate management response, form the focus of attention of this section and following chapters.

In this section we identify four major classes of deviation, and we discuss the circumstances that would indicate to a financial manager whether short or medium imperfections exist within his or her decision time span. We then consider evidence on the equilibrium framework collected over longer periods and whether this indicates support for or against the parity relationships and ICAPM. This analysis provides the basis in chapters 4 to 13 for identifying possible imperfections and for analysing the implications of parity deviations for foreign exchange risk management, global financing, and international capital budgeting decisions.

## Identifying market imperfections

The implications drawn in section 3.2 for corporate financial decision making flow directly from assuming that the efficiency of foreign exchange markets and international capital markets is such that they approach that of the US and UK equity markets and that few if any imperfections exist in these international markets. In the case of freely floating exchange rates, and unregulated international capital markets such as the Eurodollar and Eurobond markets, this is likely to be a reasonable representation of the situation. However, where government intervention is high, forward exchange markets are not available and capital markets are underdeveloped, the picture is likely to be quite different. The parity relationships and their equilibrium framework can therefore be seen as a useful point of departure in that, when deviations from these interest rate, exchange rate and inflation rate relationships appear, there are opportunities for profit or value creation (Eaker 1977: 607).

For example, the incomplete nature of government controls, and the specialized knowledge of such markets acquired by large multinationals, may place them in a privileged position. In particular it may allow them to exploit opportunities provided by government constraints on equilibrium tendencies for exchange rates and interest rates. Speculative actions by corporations may, in turn, help these markets to return to equilibrium conditions.

The task of international financial management under these conditions is to identify such opportunities and exploit them subject to political constraints. The degree of exploitation will depend upon how far the corporation is prepared to move from its basic trading role in product and factor markets and the extent to which national governments and supranational institutions are expected to take punitive action against individual companies. If a firm decides to fully exploit all foreign exchange and capital market opportunities open to it then it will have become, in part, a financial institution. Alternatively, it may decide to use the opportunities in one part of the international economy to offset threats and losses elsewhere. These strategic decisions and the issue of political interference are outside the scope of this chapter, and it will be assumed here that firms will attempt to maximize the value addition benefits of such profitable opportunities. Chapter 8 will explore the wider issues raised here.

The exploitation of these value addition opportunities requires

1   a thorough understanding of the workings of offshore (or Euro) capital markets and of foreign exchange markets
2   an analysis of likely government actions both in domestic capital markets and in support of exchange rates
3   the identification of equilibrium tendencies in the key financial variables.

A detailed analysis of perceived deviations from parity normally takes the form of assumptions about imperfections in the capital, foreign exchange, product and factor markets. Such imperfections are deemed to create valuable profit opportunities for firms, especially those with a high involvement in these markets. The evidence for and against the existence and persistence of such deviations will be discussed in the next section.

Calvet (1981), in the course of an analysis of one major IFM issue, the direct foreign investment (DFI) decision, has proposed a taxonomy of market imperfections. He distinguished between four major classes of imperfections:

1   market disequilibrium hypotheses
2   government imposed distortions
3   market structure imperfections
4   market failure imperfections.

Calvet's taxonomy can be extended to cover IFM issues other than DFI. Thus these classes of imperfections can be seen to influence the whole range of novel IFM decisions identified in chapter 1 and in section 3.2.

For example, the common feature of group 1 hypotheses can be seen as the short term nature of the disequilibrium conditions and the associated profit opportunities. The reactive response of profit seeking firms and other arbitrageurs to these opportunities will eventually bring about a return to equilibrium conditions. In group 2, governments and supranational institutions are seen to be distorting markets and therefore creating profit opportunities. For example, distortion can take place in markets for foreign exchange, between domestic capital markets, and in markets for real goods.

Group 3 refers to firms departing from perfectly competitive behaviour owing to their power to interfere with market pricing mechanisms. This could be due to oligopolistic behaviour by banks in foreign exchange markets for rarely traded currencies or by large MNCs in real goods markets. Group 4 deals with situations where markets fail, in particular owing to departures from perfect market assumptions regarding production techniques and commodity properties (Calvet 1981: 44). This refers to situations where it is not possible to create a market in a particular currency or form of credit or where no market exists for intermediate real goods or intangibles such as technical know-how.

Calvet has used this classification scheme to specifically consider imperfections in the product and factor markets. In this chapter it will be used to structure the discussion about imperfections in the international foreign exchange and capital markets in which domestic and MNC firms are likely to be involved.

Table 3.1 demonstrates some examples of situations in which valuable funding and financial risk management (arbitrage and speculative) decision opportunities may arise. This is illustrated for each imperfections class suggested by Calvet. Many of these circumstances overlap into other imperfections categories, and the table is only designed to illustrate possible situations in which valuable opportunities can arise. For example, governmental interference in markets is often cited as a major cause of deviations and this source of imperfection can be extended to all other classes.

In the case of the European based enterprise a major area of governmental control lies in the actions of EC institutions in markets. For example, in the European monetary system (EMS) member countries of the EC attempt to control the value of their currency within a narrow band based around a central exchange rate with the European currency unit (ECU). Thus European nations act together to ensure that the foreign exchange markets behave in a relatively stable manner. These markets will still react very quickly to public information but profit opportunities may persist because of the concerted action of many countries in resisting equilibrium tendencies in exchange rates.

A significant area of market intervention lies in the anti-trust measures taken by the EC. Any MNC, European based or otherwise, either engaged in a cartel or exercising monopoly (or oligopoly) power in a European

**Table 3.1** Examples of market circumstances

| Classes of imperfections as a source of value to the firm | Foreign exchange markets | Offshore and domestic credit markets | Equity markets |
|---|---|---|---|
| 1 Disequilibrium hypotheses | Free float of a major currency; price shock in a major commodity, e.g. oil prices | Periodic thin offshore markets; short term government controls in domestic markets | Frequent short term disequilibria unlikely in OECD country stock markets but may occur in LDC markets |
| 2 Government imposed distortions | Managed floats; currency blocs (EMS); two tier currency markets; international monetary agreements (G7 and IMF) | Government control over transfer of ownership of domestic deposits overseas; permanent regulation of domestic credit markets | Exchange controls for domestic equity investors; controls over foreign and domestic equity stakes in local currencies |
| 3 Market structure imperfections | Oligopolistic behaviour by multinational banks and corporations in foreign exchange, offshore and domestic credit markets; permanently thin spot, forward forex, and offshore bond and credit markets | | Equity markets in developing countries with weak and semi-strong inefficiencies |
| 4 Market failure | Absence of foreign exchange markets (spot and forward) for many currencies | Absence of offshore markets | Absence of stock markets in LDCs |

market, can expect punitive and swift action under Article 86 of the Rome Treaty. This can be seen as the EC removing major imperfections from existing markets. At the same time it creates major investment opportunities for those MNCs not involved in such economic abuse. These latter companies may in fact create the opportunity by seeking help from the Commission to curb market dominance by particular firms. For example IBM's European market dominance has been challenged under EC law by other American MNCs such as Amdahl. In practice European MNCs may be dealt with less harshly than overseas MNCs in these anti-trust moves. This is because the EC is also committed to developing the industrial infrastructure of Europe via 'home grown' firms (Robinson 1983). European MNCs may therefore be in a better position than non-EC firms to exploit any new market opportunities.

Another major area of EC intervention lies in curbing market imperfections created by national governments. For example, it is possible for MNCs to play one European government off against another with respect to capital investment incentives such as concessionary loans. The 1980 ruling by the European Court against Philip Morris and the Dutch government reinforced the power of the EC in this matter.

Finally, the EC has long been committed to creating a unified, open, fair and efficient European capital market. The unification of domestic European capital markets is to be achieved by establishing certain minimum standards and the principle of equality of treatment of all security issuers and investors (Wymeersch 1983). Attempts had been made by 1993 to liberalize cross-border transactions, to improve corporate disclosure and to achieve further integration of the existing securities markets by establishing good information links between markets. Considerable work has been done in the area of disclosure and progress had been made by 1993 in the establishment of good electronic links between the major EC domestic markets. All major EC markets can now exchange data on prices of internationally traded securities. In addition, markets have developed their own trading capability, and the extensive trading of European (and US securities) on the London equity and bond markets has gone a long way towards the creation of an EC and broader European market in securities.

The scope of EC intervention, for the purpose of both controlling and freeing markets, demonstrates the critical importance of understanding the relationship between political actions and market forces. This issue will be returned to in chapter 8 when political risk and the MNC are discussed. For the present, the evidence for and against the parity relationships will be presented.

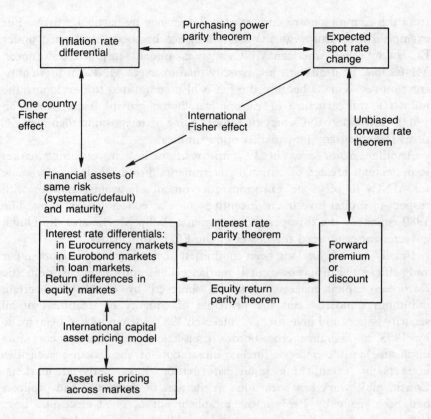

**Figure 3.4** Extended equilibrium framework

## Evidence on the parity relationships

To understand whether these deviations can occur and create genuine
profit opportunities for corporations we need to briefly consider the
evidence for and against the efficient functioning of the parity relationships
and the equilibrium model outlined in the previous section. This can best
be achieved by extending figure 3.1 to include a wider set of possible
equilibrium relationships, as in figure 3.4. The additions are the equity
return parity (ERP) theorem and the international capital asset pricing
model (ICAPM).

In the general equilibrium model outlined previously, the Fisher effect and IRP were assumed to extend over all financial assets for a given level of risk and maturity. The ICAPM encompasses the pricing mechanism for risky assets within the general model. Recent empirical research has challenged this view, and thus the evidence for these relationships will be reviewed here.

## Purchasing power parity

The empirical validity of PPP has been investigated at two levels: firstly at the level of individual commodities, and secondly by looking at broad indices of commodity prices.

In the first case and in the absence of any barriers to trade, all tradable goods are assumed to sell for the same price everywhere, i.e. the law of one price. These prices are adjusted for transportation costs, and commodity arbitrage is the process by which the prices are equalized. Evidence of PPP holding for individual goods has been mixed. The parity relationship normally holds within small transaction cost margins for homogeneous goods traded in centrally organized markets. Commodities such as gold fall into this category (Adler and Dumas 1983: 931). However, in some cases tradable goods such as automobiles have exhibited considerable deviations from PPP (Kravis and Lipsey 1978). These deviations increase considerably as one moves from well organized commodity auction markets and highly tradable commodities to non-tradable goods and services. Kravis and Lipsey concluded that commodity arbitrage works slowly and it therefore appears that violations of PPP at the level of individual goods are the norm rather than the exception.

Many studies have investigated PPP by employing aggregate price indices rather than prices of individual goods. The evidence here indicates long and prolonged deviations in purchasing parity (Krueger 1983: 63–71). Krueger comments (p. 71): 'In general, there are sound analytical reasons for skepticism about the proposition that PPP must hold, in either its absolute or relative form, without qualification. Qualification may be with respect to the time dimension, or it may be with respect to holding other factors constant.'

One of the reasons for this scepticism is the difficulties economists have encountered when conducting empirical research in this field. These include (Feiger and Jacquillat, 1982: 136–51) the difficulties in

1   Constructing identical price indices across countries. Different goods and weighting schemes used in national indices may mean that PPP holds between countries but the measurements based on the indices erroneously indicate deviations.

2   Identifying beginning and ending equilibrium exchange rate states. If measurements begin in periods when major deviations are occurring then interpretation of the ending period deviations is difficult.

3   Isolating the influence of other factors on exchange rate changes, e.g. the effects of multiple currencies.

4   Distinguishing between inflation as a cause and an effect.

Despite these difficulties, Krueger recognizes that, with some qualification, most economists will employ PPP for long term exchange rate prediction purposes especially in the case of tradable goods. Many economists will assume that despite short term violations of PPP, in the long term deviations will tend to zero for most countries. Researchers have found some evidence for a long term association between exchange rate changes and relative changes in inflation rates (Officer 1976; Edison 1987). For example, Gaillot (1970) argued, on the basis of casual observation of his results, that a positive five-year deviation in one decade was followed by a negative deviation in the next decade (Adler and Dumas 1983: 933).

A variant of this is the efficient markets perspective in which PPP should hold on an expected value basis. Roll (1979) has pointed out that within this efficient market view, short term violations of PPP can be expected. Thus the uncertainty facing the arbitrageur in buying and selling real goods and the lag in the transaction may lead to violations. However, PPP should hold on the basis of expected values, because the foreign exchange market efficiently assimilates publicly available information about future rates of inflation. Any observed deviations from PPP are random and not predictable by their very nature. PPP violations should be uncorrelated over time and so a zero serial correlation is expected in the time series of the deviations. Roll tested to see if this was the case for 23 countries between 1957 and 1976, and found positive and negative correlations for some countries.

Frenkel (1981) argued that the reasons why simple versions of PPP do not accurately forecast joint exchange rate and inflation changes is because there is a fundamental difference between exchange rate changes and national price levels. In the asset theory of exchange rate determination, exchange rates, unlike national price levels, behave like financial assets such as bonds and equities, and are very sensitive to new information and its impact on rapidly reforming expectations concerning economic events. His empirical results indicate that PPP collapsed in the 1970s. In contrast, Davutyan and Pippinger (1985) argue that no such collapse occurred and that shocks which can alter the price of non-tradables can produce biases in the standard regression of exchange rates on countries' relative prices. As a result, evidence which ignores this factor cannot be used to reject PPP. Rush and Husted (1985) have found long run support for PPP in Japan, Canada and some European countries. Meher (1990), in a novel multicountry test of purchasing power parity, does not find that PPP holds well in the short term (quarterly periods). However, his long run evidence, over five-year periods, lends considerable support to PPP.

Exchange rate models such as that proposed by Dornbusch (1976) attempt to recognize the realities of goods markets. Foreign exchange markets are assumed to respond immediately to new information on, say, government monetary or fiscal policy, but goods markets have 'sticky' prices and respond slowly to the same disturbance. The exchange rate may therefore overshoot its new equilibrium level and revert back to this as goods prices adjust. For example (Krueger 1983: 77), an increase in the money supply causes a proportionally larger exchange rate depreciation. This is followed by appreciation of the currency whilst domestic prices are increasing. In the period between the exchange rate jump and the final equilibrium, major deviations from PPP are observed and PPP only holds at long run equilibrium. Wickens (1984) respecified Dornbusch's model in discrete time and with rational expectations. He found that price stickiness was neither a necessary nor a sufficient condition for monetary policy to bring about exchange rate overshooting. Exchange rate behaviour in this model can be interpreted as a mechanism of partial adjustments. The exchange rate therefore changes from one period to the next by a certain proportion of its distance from long run equilibrium.

Bui and Pippinger (1990) point out that well organized commodity markets exhibit greater price volatility than exchange rates. Such commodity markets do not exhibit sticky prices and may have a significant and immediate interaction with foreign exchange price changes. A distinction may have to made between various goods and commodities markets and their impact on exchange rate changes. These debates on overshooting and PPP demonstrate that it is still less than clear how goods markets with sticky prices and slow adjustments interact with rapidly clearing and efficient foreign exchange and international capital markets.

These inconclusive PPP results have unfortunate implications for the neo-classical model outlined in section 3.2. The clear cut link between pricing for real goods and services in international markets and the response of foreign exchange markets has been broken. The joint assumption of this model – that foreign exchange markets react instantaneously to new information and that international prices of goods rapidly adjust – has been shown to be at odds with the evidence. The problems this creates for the MNC in the area of foreign exchange exposure, especially when changes in its input and output prices behave differently from changes in national price levels, will be discussed in chapters 4 and 5.

## The unbiased forward rate theory

In the unbiased forward rate (UBFR) theory, the forward rate or premium is assumed to continuously adjust to reflect new information, in such a way as to equal the expected rate of change of the exchange rate. In this sense, then, the foreign exchange market is considered efficient (Dufey and Giddy 1978a: 67) and the forward rate is considered an unbiased predictor of future spot rates (Cornell 1977).

Early tests of the efficiency of the foreign exchange market for floating currencies suggested that on the average the forward rate was equal to the future spot rate. However, the forward rate did seem to provide an exaggerated estimate of the likely change in the spot rate (Brealey and Myers 1981: 693). For example, sharp rises and decline in exchange rates, implied by forward rates, turned out to be more modest changes. Studies based upon more advanced econometric methods have rejected the idea that the forward rate is an unbiased predictor of the spot rate (Hansen and Hodrick 1980; Bilson 1981: Hsieh 1982; Baillie et al. 1983).

Levich (1983) has outlined the general nature of the tests designed to detect bias in forward rates. Essentially, this involves a joint test assuming both that the risk premium for the forward rate is zero, and that market participants can rationally use all available information. In formal terms, firstly,

| forward rate in period $t$ for period $t + n$ | $=$ | expected future spot rate in period $t + n$ given the information set employed by the market at period $t$ | (3.1) |
|---|---|---|---|
| $F_{t,n}$ | $=$ | $E(S_{t+n})$ | |

Thus the forward rate includes a future spot rate forecast based only on the information available to the market, and does not include a risk premium or a bias of any sort. Secondly,

| expected future spot rate in period $t + n$ | = | expected future spot rate in period $t + n$ based upon all relevant information at period $t$. | (3.2) |

In expression (3.2) market agents are able to process all relevant information efficiently and to form reasonable expectations to reflect underlying economic realities. They can therefore form rational expectations based upon their knowledge of fundamental economic variables and structural relationships. This is a market efficiency hypothesis in that forecast errors are presumed random and contain no additional information for forecasting purposes. In expression (3.1) market participants are able to set the forward rate to equal these expectations.

If this joint hypothesis is true then deviations between the forward rate and the actual future spot rate $S_{t+n}$ should have a mean of zero and should not exhibit a predictable pattern over time, i.e. a zero serial correlation should occur in the time series of deviations. In regression form,

$$S_{t+n} = A + BF_{t,n} + e_t$$

where $e$ is the average forecast error. If $A = 0$ and $B = 1$, then $F_{t,n}$ is an unbiased predictor of $S_{t+n}$. The average forecast error is not significantly different from zero, supporting a hypothesis of no bias in the forward rate.

However, two problems can occur here. Firstly, expression (3.2) may be violated because market participants cannot efficiently process information. They therefore lack knowledge of important economic variables that, for example, incorporate the effects of official interventions on exchange rates (Bailey et al. 1984: 74). Central banks will have a clear advantage over most foreign exchange market agents in this regard in that they will be privy to their own and possibly other governments' economic policies. This information may, of course, be transmitted to other market participants by the central bank's market behaviour and so violation of expression (3.2) may be shortlived.

Secondly, expression (3.1) might not hold because the forward rate reflects investors' attitudes to risk, transaction costs or other non-expectational factors (Levich 1983: 13). For example, in expression (3.1) the forward rate might now include a premium for risk, $RP_{t,n}$, as well as the prediction of the future spot rate:

$$F_{t,n} = E(S_{t+n}) + RP_{t,n}$$

This violation of the zero risk premium hypothesis in expression (3.1) does not suggest a market inefficiency since the premium may reflect the reward for the risks taken.

However, if either the zero risk premium hypothesis (3.1) or the market efficiency hypothesis (3.2) is false, the simple link between the future spot rate and the forward rate is broken and biases can occur in the relationship. It is these possibilities that cause problems in interpreting existing empirical evidence indicating bias in the forward rate. Empirical tests which reject this joint hypothesis can be interpreted either as indicating that the risk premium is non-zero, or as rejecting rational expectations, or as suggesting that both assumptions are inappropriate (Baillie et al. 1983: 553).

Baillie et al. (1983) conducted a detailed test of the unbiased forward rate hypothesis. They developed econometric models of the 30 day forward rate and spot rate for six major currencies. Observations were taken from the New York foreign exchange market for the UK, West German, Italian and French currencies for the period 1 June 1973 to 8 April 1980. In the case of Canada and Switzerland the same quality data (daily observations) was only available from 1 December 1977 to 15 May 1980. The null hypothesis that the forward exchange rate is an unbiased predictor of corresponding future spot rates was rejected for all six currencies. The authors commented:

> Our results show that the simple widespread view that the forward rates contain all relevant information necessary to forecast future spot rates is inappropriate . . . Our results based on weekly data are not incompatible with portfolio models which suggest that uncertainty about the future will induce risk premium in equilibrium, implying that the forward rate is a biased predictor of the expected spot rate. More work on the sources of uncertainty and the assimilation of new information in foreign exchanges is required.

The implication of the above and more recent tests (Hodrick 1987; Baillie 1989) is that rejection of the unbiased forward rate hypothesis is suspected to be due to risk aversion behaviour on the part of foreign exchange market participants rather than market inefficiency. This has led to an intensive search for the appropriate specification of a model of this time varying risk premium. For example, Baillie and Bollersley (1990) use standard asset pricing theory to hypothesize that the risk premium in forward foreign exchange markets is a linear function of the conditional variances and covariances of the forward market forecast error. Little support was found for a time varying premium based on the asset pricing model. However, lagged changes in the forward rate appear to be correlated with the risk premium. Thus the most appropriate means of measuring risk and uncertainty in this context is still an open question. It appears from the evidence that bias in the forward rate (i.e. a predictable pattern in the forecast error) may exist for short periods but is small and non-stationary and can be positive and negative. This creates difficulties for any forecaster in exploiting a bias.

These unresolved issues have additional implications for managers attempting to forecast the spot rate using forward rates. Levich (1978; 1979: 58) emphasized that the forward premium is still a very poor predictor of exchange rate results. He attributes this to the following:

1   Investors have great difficulty in assimilating information and forming expectations about exchange rate changes (expression (3.2)).
2   The forward rate is not 'designed' to reflect exchange rate expectations alone (expression (3.1)) and includes something else such as a risk premium.

If the first reason holds then the poor forecasting record of the forward rate may simply reflect the many unanticipated disturbances which affect exchange rates. If the poor forecasts are caused by the existence of a risk premium then investors will be mistaken in using the forward rate to predict the future spot rate. Levich concludes (p. 59) by noting that one cannot be sure which interpretation is correct. As such it is inadvisable for firms to use the forward rate as the sole exchange rate forecast input to its investment and financing decisions. This view is supported by the most recent research results reported above. In chapter 4 the forecasting of exchange rates is discussed: in particular, the possibility of producing a better forecast than the forward rate is considered.

Finally, it should be noted that there is evidence for biases in forward rates during the operation of managed systems. Several researchers have found that forward rates consistently understated actual spot rate changes (Kohlhagen 1975; Roll and Solnik 1975) and were therefore biased predictors of future spot rates.

## Interest rate parity and equity return parity

The interest rate parity relationship predicts that interest rate differentials (on assets of equal risk and maturity) will tend to equal the forward premium or discount. The IRP relationship almost always holds in the Eurocurrency markets. Empirical work regressing forward premiums against Eurocurrency interest rate differentials has produced regression coefficients very close to unity (Dufey and Giddy 1978a: 96; 1978b). This has also been the case during highly speculative periods.

As a result, IRP holds in the Eurocurrency markets *ex post* as well as *ex ante*. This is not true of PPP, Fisher and UBFR where, even in efficient markets, actual outcomes are likely to deviate from those expected. The reasons for this are not hard to find. The Eurocurrency markets contain very mobile short term capital uncontrolled by governments. Thus there is very efficient arbitrage between Eurocurrencies, and between Eurocurrencies and the foreign exchange markets. Such close integration of offshore or external markets for bank deposits are not restricted to Europe and the US. Bhoocha-oom and Stansell (1990) found a high degree of covariability between nominal interest rates in the US, Singapore, Hong Kong and Asian US dollar bank deposit markets. The close way in which US dollar interest rates on these similar risk financial assets move together suggests a high degree of integration in these Far Eastern offshore markets in US dollar bank deposits.

If we turn to the domestic credit, bond and equity markets then there is little empirical work testing IRP. However, the conditions seem to exist for IRP to hold here for some of these financial assets. In the case of domestic credit markets, which are open to arbitrage with the equivalent Eurocurrency credit markets, we would expect the Eurocurrency lending and deposit rates to fall within a band determined by the equivalent domestic rates. If this were not the case, and say the Eurodollar lending rate was above the domestic dollar lending rate, then borrowers would rapidly switch to the more familiar domestic market. In a similar fashion Eurocurrency deposit rates would have to be higher to encourage investors to move deposits out of their home country. This inevitably means a narrower margin (lending rate minus borrowing rate) in Eurocurrency markets, and profits are only achieved because of the lower transaction costs and regulatory costs of this credit market. Under conditions of no restrictions on capital movements between domestic and Eurocurrency markets, IRP should also hold between domestic markets and foreign exchange markets. The difference between US dollar domestic loan rates and UK sterling domestic loan rates should equal the forward premium or discount on the £/$ exchange rate. If capital controls exist, IRP may not hold for such domestic interest rate differences, as arbitrage between the controlled domestic credit market and its external currency credit market is restricted. However, IRP will still hold between the external credit markets and the foreign exchange market, and this will provide a strong incentive to circumvent the controls and exploit domestic interest rate deviations from parity.

In the case of bonds one would expect that, in those countries where free capital flows are permitted, the domestic term structures of interest rates would be closely joined with offshore interest rates via arbitrage in the foreign exchange, Eurobond and domestic bond markets. Hence bonds of the same maturity and risk should offer the same covered interest returns. These adjustments are more likely to occur if offshore bond markets in these currencies exist. If capital controls are employed (between domestic and offshore markets) such adjustments may be delayed and opportunities will be created for the skilled arbitrageur. Given the many alternative routes for arbitrage, it seems unlikely that any deviations from IRP would persist for domestic bonds or Eurobonds.

The interest rate and currency swaps market adds a significant new dimension to the Eurobond and international loan market. For example, bonds can be issued in one currency with say a fixed interest profile and be immediately swapped to another currency and varying interest rate profile. Loans can made in one currency or with a specific interest rate profile and these can be swapped in the same way. If interest rate swapping takes place on a regular basis between say US dollar loan and bond markets (in London, Euromarkets), then one price for interest rate risk will prevail and price differences will be illusory, probably reflecting transaction cost differences. Currency swaps between US dollar Eurobonds and Swiss franc Eurobonds will be based on long term $/Swfr forecasts. The possibility of swaps of interest rate profiles and their currencies will encourage arbitrage between capital markets and currency markets in a fashion similar to the shorter term Eurocurrency bank deposit and forward markets. Swaps allow the bank to arbitrage between Eurobond, bank loan and currency markets, exploiting any differences in the pricing of risk in these markets. Thus interest rate parity is likely to prevail in both the Eurobond market and the international loans market.

In the case of equity, a major development in the 1980s involved the emergence of offshore or Euroequity markets. These primary markets, consisting of syndicates of international banks and securities houses, have the capacity to underwrite and distribute equity securities to investors in a number of markets outside the issuing company's home market. Thus a large Swedish or Italian corporation may decide that its national equity market is too small for a major equity issue and use London instead. The banks have introduced a Eurobond style process into the area of equity issues. In particular the syndication techniques and the presence of banks large enough to absorb huge amounts of risk capital have created an important primary issues market for equity. Another development has been the rapid growth of offshore trading of foreign equities in New York. Thus the equities of major British companies are traded in New York under the system of American depository receipts (ADRs). Again one would anticipate, in the cases of Euroequity and transatlantic equity trading, that expected equity returns for the same firm denominated in different currencies would reflect expected exchange rate changes. This assumes that the firm's shares are held in globally diversified portfolios and there are no barriers between the US and the UK markets. Arbitrage between New York and London will ensure that IRP or equity return parity (ERP) will hold (after taxes and transaction costs). Similar conclusions would hold for equities that are listed on both UK and US exchanges. Some evidence for this lies in the work of Maldonado and Saunders (1981). They tested the 'law of one price' for equities traded on both sides of the Atlantic, and showed that equity prices (for the same company) were the same after adjustment for prevailing spot rates.

There may still be equity markets in which ERP is prevented from being established. These would include those where controls exist over equity purchases (by both foreigners and residents) and over the transfer of rights to equities. However, even controlled domestic equity markets may be efficient in that they may fully reflect publicly available information on expected exchange rate changes. This therefore offers an alternative mechanism for linking equity returns and exchange rates in the absence of significant arbitrage between domestic stock markets. Finally, we can note the central role of the large international banks in all of the above Eurocurrency, Eurobond, Euroequity and international loan markets. They lie at the centre of all of these markets and by carefully exploiting any price differences they bring together financial prices in many diverse financial markets.

## Fisher and asset returns

The Fisher effect predicts that in equilibrium the expected real return on capital should be the same in different countries. Thus two countries will both offer the same expected real interest rate and the differences in their nominal or actual rates will reflect the expected differences in their inflation rates. The evidence for this version of the one country Fisher effect within specific countries and across many different types of financial security is mixed and includes the following.

Fama (1975) demonstrated that the Fisher effect held for US Treasury bills in the period 1953 to 1971. He also showed that the nominal Treasury bill interest rates were very good unbiased predictors of US inflation over this period. However, since December 1980 this model has consistently overpredicted US inflation (Geske and Roll 1983: 5).

Gibson (1970; 1972) and Fama and Schwert (1977) have found empirical support for Fisher in the case of US bonds. Viren (1989) tested Fisher for 11 countries with the largest sample period being 1875 to 1984. The nominal interest rate series corresponded to long term government bond yields and inflation was measured using consumer price indices. The results indicated that nominal interest rates and inflation have only been weakly related during the past 100 years. In contrast, Moazzami's (1990) results provided strong evidence in support of Fisher as a long run proposition. In this case the 'long run' was the period 1953 to 1985. US nominal interest rate data (before and after tax) from three month US Treasury bills, six month commercial paper, and three year government bonds were employed as the dependent variable. The US consumer price index was employed to calculate the rate of US inflation. The differences in these results may be due to different model specifications and differing periods and demonstrate the difficulties in testing Fisher.

Brealey and Myers (1981: 695) provide some evidence that Fisher holds in Eurocurrency markets. One problem here is that there are some indications that differences in Eurocurrency nominal interest rates exaggerate the likely differences in inflation rates between the countries concerned. Another problem lies in interpreting whether the nominal changes are due to changes in inflationary expectations or to changes in real rates. If UK real rates rise relative to French rates and a resulting higher UK nominal rate widens nominal interest rate differences then the pound may appreciate relative to the franc. If the real rates are stable but UK inflationary expectations push up nominal UK rates and the nominal differences widen then the pound may depreciate relative to the franc (see Cornell and Shapiro 1985).

Many studies (see Gultekin 1983) have shown that US stock returns were negatively related to inflation. In particular Fama and Schwert (1977) found that US stock returns were negatively related to expected inflation, unanticipated inflation, and changes in expected inflation. These findings are clearly inconsistent with the Fisher hypothesis.

Geske and Roll (1983) suggest that the negative relationship is an empirical illusion. They argue that stock returns are negatively related to inflation because they signal a chain of events which results in higher monetary expansion. Geske and Roll provide good empirical evidence that stock returns signal changes in expected inflation, but find little evidence for a real rate effect. However, they do comment that the data suggest that a real rate effect may have been present in recent periods (p. 29)

Gultekin (1983) investigated the relationship between nominal equity returns and expected inflation across 26 countries for the period 1947–79. His regression coefficients were generally negative, and therefore did not support the Fisher hypothesis. He also found that these relationships were not stable over time and that there were differences among countries.

Solnik (1983) studied the relationship between equity returns and inflationary expectations for nine countries over the period 1971–80. His results rejected the Fisher hypothesis for each of the major stock markets of the world. In addition these results provided support for the Geske and Roll model. Solnik also found a weak relationship between stock returns and real interest rates. This suggests that in those countries with strict monetary policies and facing a deficit, investors' expectations focus more on changes in real interest rates than on inflation.

Burnie (1986) argues that inflation has two effects on the asset return generating process. Firstly, after Friedman (1977) and others, inflation has an impact on the real economy and subsequently real returns. Secondly, a Fisher effect may then be built into nominal returns. Burnie models these two effects separately in an attempt to clarify the direction for future empirical tests.

Peel and Pope (1988), in a novel use of a consensus set of public forecasts of inflation, tested for the Fisher effect using UK nominal stock returns. They rejected the hypothesis for the period 1968 to 1982. They point out that this could be due to changes in real returns or because of limitations of their proxy for inflation.

Overall, this evidence with respect to the Fisher effect raises questions about world capital market integration. It also suggests that it is possible that different inflation related return generating mechanisms come into play according to domestic economic policies.

## International capital asset pricing

The central asset risk pricing question is: how, if at all, are risky assets priced across countries? This is of interest both to shareholders and to financial managers in that conventional (domestic) capital asset pricing models underpin much of domestic corporate finance theory and capital market investment theory.

At present the evidence is organized around two hypotheses:

1   International capital markets are integrated, and thus risky assets are priced according to their undiversifiable world risk, i.e. the world or international capital asset pricing model (ICAPM) applies.
2   International capital markets are segmented and thus risky assets are priced relative to domestic assets only, i.e. domestic systematic risk is the basis of asset pricing.

Solnik (1973a) tested an ICAPM model and found that national factors were important. When these were diversified away in an international portfolio, a strong relationship existed between actual returns and international systematic risk.

Stehle (1977) found statistical problems in Solnik's approach. He tested both integrated and segmented market hypotheses by testing the hypothesis that the US capital market is completely isolated against the null hypothesis of integration. If segmentation existed then the correct market portfolio for US investors would be the US index, and under integration a world index would be required. He argued that the evidence meant that neither hypothesis could be rejected in favour of the other. However, he did conclude by noting some empirical support for ICAPM.

Other scholars have attempted to model alternative capital market equilibrium with investment barriers, notably Black (1974) and Stulz (1981a). As Stulz comments (p. 923): 'Casual empiricism suggests that models without barriers to international investment should be suspect; these models cannot explain why it appears that in every country investors on average hold more domestic securities than would be required if they held the world market portfolio.' He therefore developed a model of international asset pricing in which it is costly for domestic investors to hold foreign assets. Stulz represented the complex range of barriers to international investment as taxes on the absolute value of investors' holdings of risky foreign assets. This constituted a continuous measure of imperfections ranging from full segmentation to full integration. He concluded (p. 924) that with international barriers some risky foreign assets with low betas are likely to be non-traded. In each country all investors will hold the same portfolio of risky assets; there is one security market line for domestic assets, and this lies between two lines for risky foreign assets (those held short and those held long). Non-traded risky foreign assets plot between the two lines for traded risky foreign assets. These conclusions can, Stulz argued, form the basis for more sophisticated testing of international asset pricing models.

Stulz (1981b) has also extended Breeden's (1979) work on consumption based asset pricing models to the international arena. In these models, pricing of an asset depends on covariances with aggregate consumption rather than with surrogates of market indices. Hansen and Hodrick (1983) proposed a series of empirical tests along these lines. Cumby (1990), drawing from this literature, tested whether real stock returns are consistent with consumption based models of international asset pricing. Four major equity markets were investigated, with the data coming from returns on market indices of the USA, Japan, the UK and Germany. A particular focus of his paper is a separate analysis of equity returns during the 1980s when international capital movements were liberalized. The tests of integration require that the conditional covariance of real stock returns and the rate of change of real consumption move together over time for all assets. This was rejected for the 1970s but could not be rejected for the 1980s. These results do not conclusively demonstrate integration in these four key equity markets. They are, however, consistent with increasing integration of international capital markets during the 1980s.

These consumption models have yet to be extended to the wider set of domestic and international equity markets. Empirical work on the integration and segmentation hypotheses is therefore inconclusive. Furthermore, theoretical models of asset pricing designed to cope with the unique features of international capital markets are still at an early stage of development. Feiger and Jacquillat (1982: 282) identify the major areas of difficulty of extending this concept of CAPM from domestic to world context:

• There is a potential difference between the motivations of individual investors and those of institutional investors.

- The assumption of a representative investor across countries may be inappropriate. This undermines the concept of a universally optimal market portfolio.
- There are possible limitations on market efficiency and availability of tradable assets outside the United States.

In addition, Solnik (1977), following Roll (1977), has pointed out major problems in testing the ICAPM. Firstly, it suffers from all of the problems identified by Roll (1977) for domestic CAPMs. Secondly, given that covariances between national stock market indices are quite low, portfolios constructed by researchers will always be well diversified internationally, and this is independent of segmentation or integration. If these efficient mean–variance portfolios are used as proxies for the world portfolio then an ICAPM will, despite segmentation, fit the available data on international returns. This of course does not provide any further insight into asset pricing.

It appears from this evidence that all of the major world equity markets are neither fully integrated nor segmented. However, the large open markets of the USA and the UK, and possibly the markets in France, Germany and Japan, are likely to have a common asset pricing mechanism. In addition, the listing of equities of major MNCs on several exchanges, the emergence of an offshore market in Euroequities, the harmonization of EC domestic equity market practices and the growth of SDRs for overseas equities in New York are clear indications that a common international pricing mechanism exists for internationally traded bonds and equities. Some indirect evidence for integration can be gleaned from these developments. For example, Howe and Madura (1990) demonstrate that international listings of US companies do not produce significant shifts in a variety of risk related measures. Domestic US betas do not seem to be affected by an international listing. There was no evidence that the overseas listing affected a security's sensitivity (foreign country beta) to the overseas security market. This implies that these markets are integrated and that listing has no risk related effects on the companies' securities.

The growing sophistication of investors and the continued evolution of financial institutions in these international markets would also suggest emerging integration. Yet as Stulz (1981a) remarks, investors still seem to bias their portfolios towards their domestic equities. The pricing mechanism appears to be fairly complex and may include some of the elements identified by the authors above. Until more is known about these problem areas, caution should be exercised in interpreting the evidence for world capital market integration.

Regardless of these problems one can draw some implications for investors from current research. Covariances between national stock market returns are generally positive and moderate and therefore there will be diversification benefits with international portfolio construction. Kaplanis (1988) provides evidence that the correlation matrix of stock returns in ten major equity markets was stable over the period 1967 to 1982. The covariance matrix exhibits less stability over this period, but still indicates that diversification benefits exist. Meric and Meric (1989) demonstrate that seasonality exists in international stock markets. International stock market co-movements were stable in the September to May periods and relatively unstable in the May to September periods. Raymond and Weil (1989) demonstrate that in a period of floating exchange rate systems (1976 to 1979) US investors would have found that international diversification was superior to purely domestic diversification. Meric and Meric (1989) find empirical evidence that diversification across countries (given industrial diversification within each country) resulted in greater diversification benefits than diversifying across world industries (given diversification across countries).

Lessard (1980: 368) remarks:

> If national stock markets are segmented an international portfolio will have superior risk adjusted performance because securities are priced in terms of their domestic systematic risk, some of which is diversifiable. If national markets are integrated, holding a solely domestic portfolio will imply inferior risk adjusted performance because the securities are priced to reflect only their global systematic risk. Thus the purely domestic component of risk which is not diversified away will not be offset by any risk premium.

Thus under either circumstances, there are advantages to the investor in international diversification. A similar approach to the above analysis will be adapted to IFM problems in this text. Given the inconclusive nature of the integration versus segmentation debate, implications will be drawn both for segmented and for integrated capital markets. The latter analysis has already been performed in the previous chapter and so chapter 4 will also assume the possibility of segmentation when discussing IFM decisions.

## 3.4 Conclusion

The findings of the previous section may be summarized as follows:

1 IRP and ERP appear to hold for a wide range of financial assets. The reasons for this are not hard to find. The Eurocurrency markets and major national bond and equity markets contain very mobile capital, relatively uncontrolled by governments. Thus there is very efficient arbitrage between these capital markets and the foreign exchange markets.

2 The implication of existing research is that the unbiased forward rate hypothesis is rejected in its simplest form. Biases exist but foreign exchange markets are still considered to be efficient. The biases are suspected to be due to risk aversion behaviour on the part of foreign exchange market participants rather than market inefficiency. This suspicion is not yet based on sound empirical evidence and the most appropriate means of measuring risk and uncertainty is problematic.

3 The empirical evidence does not support PPP in the short run and casts some doubt on the long run validity of PPP. It indicates that PPP is frequently violated in the short run and can be expected to be violated for longer periods when little international trade in real goods occurs between the countries concerned.

4 Fisher has held in some domestic Treasury bill and bond markets and in Eurocurrency markets but has been decisively rejected for all major world stock markets. Thus the relative version of Fisher is also rejected for equities across countries.

5 The evidence indicates that the international Fisher effect holds for Eurocurrency bank deposits. However, the evidence with respect to equities is less than clear. National stock markets, and differences in equity returns, are likely to fully reflect publicly available information about expected exchange rate changes. However, given that domestic equity returns do not reflect Fisher, differences in equity returns are unlikely to reflect international Fisher.

6 Empirical work on the integration and segmentation hypotheses is inconclusive and so the debate about domestic versus international CAPMs is unresolved. Furthermore, theoretical models of asset pricing designed to cope with the unique features of international capital markets are still being developed and tested.

The following conclusions may be drawn. Firstly, the evidence generally favours the existence of financial price equilibrium in the financial sectors of those Western countries with floating exchange rates, sophisticated domestic markets, offshore markets in their domestic credit, and common listings of major equities. This is of course a significant part of the world economy, and it suggests that under these circumstances there exists the kernel of a world capital market. In this situation the disequilibrium hypothesis appears weak and any profit opportunities are likely to be small and short lived, if they exist at all. Unfortunately PPP does not appear to hold in these circumstances and this suggests that a clear cut link between pricing in international markets for real goods and the response of foreign exchange markets does not exist. A pricing link may exist between centrally organized international commodity markets and international financial markets. However, changing prices of less well traded goods appear to have a much weaker link with exchange rate changes. The assumption of the neo-classical model that foreign exchange markets, international capital markets, and markets for goods and services react instantaneously to new information on economic disturbances has been shown to be at odds with the evidence.

Secondly, the evidence for a major equilibrium in the financial parity relationships in all the Western and associated economies is problematic. This is because of the rejection of Fisher for equity markets, the problems in interpreting the evidence regarding biases in the forward rate, and the inconclusive debate about integration. Clearly, the evidence regarding PPP increases the likelihood of major disequilibrium states occurring at frequent intervals. However, it is possible that a unique equilibrium relationship does hold for major world equity markets. For example if, as Solnik suggests, the Geske-Roll effect is common across these countries and a common asset risk pricing mechanism exists, then such an equilibrium is likely. This is a non-Fisherian framework and, if it prevails across many countries, it points to the need for the development of an alternative to the parity relationships. Until this issue is clarified IFM managers should analyse investment and financing problems using a range of assumptions stretching from well functioning markets through to various imperfections in these markets.

Thirdly, as we move away from these integrated economies towards those with increasing governmental control of exchange and capital markets, and with decreasing sophistication of these markets, including the absence of some markets, imperfection types 2, 3 and 4 in table 3.1 and related deviations from parity become increasingly likely. The presence of imperfections alone is necessary but not sufficient evidence for the corporate treasurer to assume that profit opportunities exist. However, the association of obvious imperfections such as government controls over exchange rates with recent evidence of biased forward rates gives an indication of the likelihood of valuable profit opportunities. Other examples might include the association between government controls over capital flows and a large gap appearing between domestic and offshore rates.

The possibility of such deviations from parity conditions has the following broad implications for financial managers. Firstly, IFM issues are no longer illusions but create real problems and opportunities for companies. Managers therefore need to actively respond to these conditions. Secondly, the significance of these issues will vary across firms depending upon two factors. One is the strength and persistence of deviations from parity. Thus countries or groups of countries that continuously attempt to maintain exchange rates against equilibrium pressures will make these issues more important to the companies exposed to these policies. The other factor is the degree of corporate involvement in the environment in which the deviation occurs. The significance of IFM issues increases with the increased spread of the firm's activities across countries with high degrees of capital and currency market regulation or across regional trading blocs with high degrees of co-operation on these matters. This is likely to be accentuated as we move from wholly domestic firms through to MNCs with a global spread and as we move from Western economies through to developing economies.

Thus if these deviations occur there is much for financial managers to do with respect to IFM issues. This will be demonstrated by looking again at the three decision areas discussed in section 3.2, i.e. foreign exchange risk management, capital budgeting decisions and financing decisions. These will be analysed as separate issues in chapters 4 to 13. However, they are strongly related to each other and to other major IFM decisions such as capital structure, working capital management, and the transfer of funds within a large multinational. Such issues of integrated decision making will be addressed in chapter 8 on direct foreign investment and strategic analysis and in chapter 14 on financial planning.

# 4

# The Foreign Exchange Risk Management Problem

In section 3.2 it was argued that if the equilibrium relationships hold then corporate management of foreign exchange risk is of no value to shareholders. The evidence for the equilibrium relationships suggested that deviations from parity can occur, in particular when governments interfere in the foreign exchange and capital markets and when markets are underdeveloped or non-existent. In section 4.1 major deviations from the parity relationships are shown to make corporate foreign exchange risk management (FERM) relevant to both managers and investors. This section will also outline an active opportunistic strategy for foreign exchange risk management consistent with the pursuit of shareholder wealth maximization. Section 4.2 will be concerned with outlining the general nature of the foreign exchange risk management problem. This problem will then be explored in some detail.

The next three chapters will look in detail at examples of some of the major techniques of foreign exchange risk management. These will include strategic and operational responses (chapter 5), various internal financial techniques (chapter 6) and forward market hedges, money market hedges and currency options (chapter 7).

## 4.1 Identifying the Foreign Exchange Risk Management Problem

The relevance of corporate management of foreign exchange risks

Dufey and Srinivasulu (1983) have outlined the detailed case for the corporate management of foreign exchange risk. They began by noting that the case against could be summarized as follows: 'Foreign exchange risk does not exist; even if it exists, it need not be hedged; even if it is to be hedged, corporations need not hedge it.'

Many of the arguments associated with this position have been discussed in chapter 3 and will not be repeated here. However, it is useful to summarize the arguments for exposure management around the following questions:

1 Does foreign exchange risk exist?
2 If it exists, does it have to be hedged?
3 Even if it has to be hedged, do corporations have to do this?

We have seen in chapter 3 that major deviations have occurred in purchasing power parity. If inflation changes and exchange rate changes do not completely offset each other over the short term then firms may be exposed to exchange rate risk. In a second case, exchange rate and inflation changes may fully offset each other, but the input and output prices of a particular firm do not adjust in line with these general (relative) price movements. If this firm faces unanticipated exchange rate changes then it will be further exposed to exchange rate risk. The concept of such 'real' changes in exchange rates will be outlined later in this chapter and will be used to explore further these risky circumstances facing the firm.

The hedging of exchange risk is considered irrelevant from an efficient market perspective. In this situation any unsystematic component to risk can be diversified away and the systematic risk component in forward exchange rate contracts is priced according to CAPM. There is no addition of value to the firm by entering into forward contracts. All the firm achieves is to move to a new risk/return position in capital markets. The firm could therefore 'self-insure' by allowing gains and losses on uncovered positions to cancel each other out in the long run.

Adler and Dumas (1983) disagree with this view and identify conditions in which hedging may be of value to shareholders, creditors and managers, even when foreign exchange markets are efficient. They argue that the above advice ignores the possibility that the distribution of unanticipated exchange rate gains and losses (relative to the anticipated change expressed in the forward rate) may have very wide variances. If large adverse changes in exchange rates coincide with the timing of the receipt of a large foreign currency receivable, this currency change could lead to liquidity problems for the firm. It would be little consolation for the managers, creditors and owners to know that this would correct itself in the long run. Corporate hedging under these circumstances may be valuable if the subsequent reduction in the variability of cash flows reduces perceived default risk. This demonstrates the general principle that hedging known or expected exchange rate changes already embodied in forward premiums or discounts is of no value. However, hedging against the unexpected may reduce the costs of financial distress.

Corporate hedging of currency risk may still be considered wasteful of managerial resources if investors can hedge as efficiently as firms. However, Dufey and Srinivasulu (1983) identify several obstacles to investor hedging. Firstly, there are size barriers in forward exchange, Eurocurrency and currency option markets. For example, there are minimum size requirements for transacting in the bank dominated forward exchange and Eurocurrency markets. Investors can use fixed size futures and options contracts available from futures exchanges. However, these may be unsuitable for tailoring to the size of their exposures and have high transaction costs for the small investor. Secondly, structural barriers exist. Large MNCs can alter their exposures by internal cross-border transactions such as accelerating and delaying inter-company payments, adjusting transfer pricing, and borrowing and lending internally. These options are not open to individuals and so it is not possible for investors to hedge in exactly the same way as firms. Other structural barriers include corporations having preferential access to special hedging facilities. These might include special forward rates which are only offered by government banks to corporations trading locally in real goods and services. Finally, information on the firm's exposure is not symmetrically distributed between managers and shareholders. It is unlikely that shareholders will obtain or receive full information on the foreign exchange position of all companies in their portfolios. Thus individuals cannot make optimal portfolio hedging decisions. Managers are likely to have this information for their firm and, as a result, hedging of currency risk by the firm seems best.

Given the evidence presented in chapter 3 for and against the parity relationships there are other possible market imperfections which make exposure management relevant. In the first case, the equilibrium or parity relationships may hold between economies, but not at the level of a particular firm. For example, differences in national tax systems, taxation of nominal returns, and the existence of contractually denominated cash flows, may mean that home country (and currency) cash flows will be changed in real terms.

Secondly, major imperfections are possible including segmentation of world capital markets and major deviations in the parity relationships. Segmentation of world capital markets may create considerable difficulties for the investor seeking to diversify exchange rate risk. In addition, investors may not be able to efficiently price the systematic risk associated with the overseas cash flows. Under these conditions the treasurer of the company has a responsibility to act in the best interests of shareholders. She or he has to consider if the firm can manage its exposure in such a way as to achieve diversification benefits for the investor constrained by segmented markets. Major deviations may also occur in the parity relationships. Deviations in purchasing parity have already been mentioned. Another possibility is where IFE may not hold and so interest rate changes and exchange rate changes will not counterbalance each other. As a result, assets and liabilities of equal risk will have different values and different real interest rates will be observed for these securities across the countries concerned.

Thus under any one of the above circumstances or various combinations of minor or major imperfections, there will be risk attached to the company's exposure, be it translation, transaction or economic.

## The goal of FERM

It is clear that there are many circumstances in which the firm is exposed to foreign exchange risk. Furthermore the firm's managers are likely to be in a better position than investors and creditors to deal with this risk. Thus investors are unlikely to be able to diversify exchange risk as efficiently as corporations. The reasons for this include the inferior information available to the investor and the possible segmentation of sectors of the international capital market. Managers' planning horizons are also likely to be much shorter than the period required for the impact of exchange rate changes on profits to net to zero. Finally, MNCs have, through their legal status in many countries, a unique internal ability to circumvent barriers to hedging.

However, given that the corporation should manage foreign exchange risk, it is less than clear what foreign exchange management goal the corporate treasurer should pursue. If we assume that investors are interested in maximizing their wealth for the purpose of eventual consumption, then changes in shareholder nominal wealth are irrelevant if they are counterbalanced by price changes in the investors' consumption bundle. This is only true if there is a perfect correspondence between the shareholders' consumption bundle and the firm's exposure (Dufey and Srinivasulu 1983: 60). Thus if the firm was exposed only in Japanese yen and its British shareholders only consumed Japanese goods, then corporate exchange rate gains and losses due to sterling/yen changes would be offset by corresponding changes in the shareholder's sterling wealth and ability to purchase goods in yen. As Dufey and Srinivasulu remark (p. 60):

> At this point the question arises, who should hedge the consumption bundle? If a firm has only a few shareholders, it may be feasible for it to hedge the consumption bundle of its shareholders. But for a widely held firm with a diverse shareholder group, it would not be feasible to do so. Not only would the costs of collecting information about shareholders' consumption bundles as well as their investment positions be prohibitive, but for a group of heterogeneous consumers–investors an 'optimal hedge' cannot be found.

Given these imperfections, managers should, as a practical alternative, aim to minimize the impact of unexpected real exchange rate variations on the cash flows and earnings of the firm as measured in some relevant currency, and individual shareholders should hedge their own consumption bundles. This will be employed as the goal of FERM for the purposes of this text. It is therefore assumed, given the above arguments for active corporate hedging, that the corporate pursuit of this goal is generally in the best interest of shareholders and creditors in that it minimizes the costs of financial distress arising from currency risk. It is also assumed to be a feasible managerial goal in that it is conventionally interpreted as minimizing the effects of unanticipated real exchange rate changes on home currency returns. Thus in the case of a large US MNC the effects on US dollar returns are minimized. However, a large British oil based MNC with many US investors and a US stock market quote, dealing mainly in commodities priced in US dollars, may feel that the significance of this currency for the company also justifies its choice as their relevant *numéraire*.

It should however be noted that this goal has some limitations. Firstly, corporate hedging of foreign currency exposures does not, in general, remove currency risk. The firm has substituted existing exposure to currency risk with corporate exposure to domestic purchasing parity risk (Adler and Dumas 1984: 47). Secondly, this goal assumes that shareholders can diversify away currency risks. If investors cannot do this because of imperfections such as segmented markets, the priority goal of FERM should be to exploit currency diversification opportunities unavailable to shareholders. Once these benefits have been exploited, management can then pursue the home currency cash flow and earnings stabilization goal.

## Economic circumstances and overall strategies for FERM

In this section we explore how the overall FERM strategy may vary with specific changes in the economic circumstances facing the firm. This section links the discussion in the previous chapter on the functioning of the parity relationships at the economy level to FERM decisions at the level of the firm.

Table 4.1 summarizes the general economic conditions or circumstances under which various deviations from parity may occur. It also includes details of the appropriate strategies and tactics to be employed under these conditions. The contents of this table will therefore form the focus of discussion for this section. The economic conditions begin with idealized market conditions and progress through a range of changing corporate circumstances, parity deviations and market imperfections. It should be noted that some of these circumstances appear unlikely given the efficiency of world capital and foreign exchange markets. Thus it is unlikely that a firm will have superior forecasts of financial prices, will face segmented capital markets, or will be able to exploit major imperfections in foreign exchange markets. These contingencies are included for completeness. In addition it should be noted that, if such circumstances occur, firms are more likely to face combinations of them than a single set.

Two overall FERM strategies can be identified depending on the circumstances in the firm's economic environment:

1   a passive strategy
2   an active opportunistic strategy, either with real response a priority and financial decisions in support, or with the treasury as an arbitrageur.

In both variants of FERM strategies, the enterprise is assumed to be attempting to minimize the impact of unexpected real exchange rate variations on its home country (currency) cash flows and earnings. The corporate pursuit of this goal is intended to minimize the costs of financial distress arising from currency risk and thus avoid any shareholder value penalty associated with management ignoring the currency risk problem.

The passive strategy is suitable when a firm believes that it is operating in circumstances 1 in the table, i.e. in integrated and efficient foreign exchange and world capital markets, and when all of the parity relationships hold. If we assume that investors are not concerned about

**Table 4.1** Strategies for foreign exchange risk management

| | Efficient | | Efficient but unique corporate advantages or circumstances | Major imperfections | | |
|---|---|---|---|---|---|---|
| | 1 | 2 | 3 | 4 | 5 | 6 |
| Economic circumstances | Efficient integrated world markets. Parity relationships working | Efficient and integrated markets but firm has superior forecasts. Firm has default risks: very large losses possible as well as gains | PPP, IRP and other economic forces functioning well but may not at the level of specific firms. PPP does not work for firm | PPP deviations creating real exchange rate changes between economies | Segmented capital markets | Other major imperfections in world capital and foreign exchange markets |
| Tactics | Match assets and liabilities, and allow gains and losses to cancel out over time: self-insurance | Create exposed positions to exploit forecasting skills. Match assets and liabilities, and/or hedge to reduce variability of HC returns and default risk | Hedge to reduce unique risks faced by the firm. Exploit after-tax opportunities unique to firm | Reactive and proactive response via real strategic and operational changes | Strategy to diversify into assets that are unavailable to investors | Use whole range of financial FERM methods to exploit deviations in financial markets |
| | | | Focus on response via real decisions: financial decisions in support | | Treasury as speculator and arbitrageur | |
| | | | Circumstances 3 to 6 are the major conditions for currency risk. Use full range of FERM methods to deal with currency risks | | | |
| Strategy | Passive | | Active opportunistic | | | |

the variability of forward rate forecast errors, then exposure management is of no value to shareholders. Managers can assume that after adjusting for unanticipated changes (by matching asset and liability cash flows as far as is possible) a policy of doing nothing is acceptable to shareholders. This policy of self-insurance therefore assumes that any gains and losses on unhedged positions will cancel each other out over a long period. Conventional decisions to insure against unexpected losses by using forward or money market hedges are wasteful of managerial time and effort, in addition to the firm incurring unnecessary transaction costs.

Managers may take the view that hedging is of value to them in reducing the variability of cash and income flows, even though the same level of cash flows is expected to occur under hedge and no hedge strategies. This may allow them to concentrate their decision energies on real decisions and boost shareholder wealth in this decision area. If managers can, through their production, marketing and other strategic and operational decisions, reduce the systematic risk for the same expected cash flows, or increase the expected cash flows for the same systematic risk, then these actions would clearly be of value to shareholders.

The active opportunistic strategy is appropriate under various sets of economic conditions, especially circumstances 2 to 6 in the table, occurring either alone or in combination.

In circumstances 2 and 3, world capital markets are assumed to be integrated and efficient and the parity relationships are assumed to hold. However, the firm may find itself in a unique position relative to these well functioning markets, as in the following examples:

2(a) If the firm has superior forecasting skills relative to the foreign exchange market, then it can create exposed foreign currency positions and exploit its unique skills. It must be noted that the evidence suggests that it is very difficult for a firm to acquire such knowledge. Furthermore its acts of arbitrage when exploiting this skill are likely to quickly erode this advantage.

2(b) The specific nature of the firm's business may mean that its overseas cash flows are expected to be subject to many unanticipated exchange rate changes. As such managers, creditors and shareholders may perceive that exchange rate gains and losses may be very large relative to corporate cash flows and thus the firm has a very high default risk. Corporate matching and hedging to reduce the high variability expected in the home currency cash flows is justified in this case.

3(a) The input and output prices of the firm may not move in line with purchasing power parity across countries. The firm needs to combat this risky exposure by selective hedging of deviations from real prices. This involves a real (strategic and operational) response as well as the use of financial methods.

3(b) If international Fisher holds, then the before-tax costs of debt will be the same between countries. However, asymmetries in national tax systems and the unique ability of an MNC to exploit these differences may mean that the after-tax costs of debt will vary between some countries. Depending upon the tax difference this will favour one mode of financial hedging over another. For example, if countries differ on their tax treatment of interest expense then money market hedges may be preferable to internal transfers or forward market hedges.

In circumstances 4 in the table, major deviations are expected to occur in purchasing power parity. If PPP deviations exist and real changes in exchange rates have occurred or are likely to occur then the firm has a whole host of real (strategic and operational) responses at its disposal. Under these circumstances, changes in real decisions are a priority with financial decisions playing a supporting role. This emphasis on real decisions assumes that problems of managing foreign exchange exposures and risk permeate all aspects of a firm's operations (Dufey and Srinivasulu 1983).

More specifically, the origin of 'natural' economic and transaction exposures generally lies in strategic and operational decisions. Strategic and operational decisions are central to the survival and growth of the firm and are made with the aim of maximizing shareholder wealth. However, real decisions have inevitable exposure and risk consequences. If these natural business exposures can be managed by prior changes to strategy and operational policy (such that the shareholder wealth objective is not compromised), then the firm may be able to reduce the scale of subsequent foreign exchange risk management problems. This in turn will reduce the need for extensive use of internal and external financial techniques.

Imperfections in financial markets may also prompt a real strategic and operational response. For example, in circumstances 5 in the table, international capital markets may be considered to be segmented and investors may not be able to fully diversify against currency risks. The MNC may be able to identify opportunities for currency risk diversification that are not available to investors. It may therefore exploit the opportunities by diversifying operations overseas, such as sales, location of production facilities, and raw material sources. Diversifying operations is a strategic decision and is more appropriate for dealing with economic exposure issues, and presents little opportunity to combat risk associated with transaction and translation exposures. Diversification of the company's financing base by financing in more than one currency and in more than one capital market is another policy option that can provide these benefits irrespective of segmentation. Diversifying financing sources is also more likely to be reversible and can therefore be used to hedge aspects of economic, transaction and translation exposures.

A variant of this active opportunistic strategy is when the firm or its treasury takes the view that there are many exploitable opportunities in world capital and foreign exchange markets, i.e. circumstances 6 in the table. Treasury then begins to act as a bank, exploiting perceived mispricing in financial markets. Treasury may be very wrong in this view of markets and it may also lose sight of its primary role in providing financial services and advice to the rest of the enterprise. The danger here is that treasury will pursue profits in this role as a speculator and arbitrageur to the detriment of its other roles in the firm. As a result, real responses and financial responses to currency risk may be uncoordinated or the treasury may see financial responses as the only means to deal with currency risk.

This chapter presumes that the major foreign exchange risk problems facing firms are best dealt with by using combinations of real and financial responses set within an active opportunistic FERM policy. This policy is also assumed to be dominated by strategic and shareholder wealth concerns. The likely efficiency of world capital and foreign exchange markets, the potential for real PPP deviations, and the origin of many FERM problems in exposures created by strategic and operational decisions, suggest that most firms have a major FERM advantage by first focusing on real decisions and then using internal financial decisions followed by external markets when seeking to manage currency risk. Treasury therefore plays a major role in providing currency forecasts and financial advice to those managers taking strategic and operational decisions. It acts as the specialist corporate function designed to buffer the firm against uncertainty in financial markets. As we move from economic circumstances 1 to 6 in table 4.1 the FERM problem becomes increasingly complex. As a result the information provision, advisory and active hedging roles of treasury are likely to increase in complexity. As we have seen in chapters 1 and 2, the emergence of floating rate systems since the early 1970s and the occurrence of many of these economic circumstances have played a major part in stimulating these roles of treasury in the MNC over this period.

## 4.2   The Elements of the Foreign Exchange Risk Management Problem

The discussion and analysis in section 4.1 makes it clear that the firm faces a complex decision problem with respect to foreign exchange risk and that the significance of this problem will change with economic circumstances and corporate specific factors. Furthermore, managers will have many options open to them in combating the problem of FERM in order to minimize the effects of currency changes on home currency returns. The central elements of this decision problem will be explored in this section by considering the following elements of the FERM decision problem:

- defining exposure and collecting information on the exposure
- defining currency risk: real versus nominal exchange rates and deviations from PPP
- understanding the dynamic nature of the FERM problem: the time structure of exposure, simultaneous management of all exposure types, and recent real changes and potential real changes
- forecasting inflation rates and foreign exchange rates.

These elements of the problem will be linked together in chapter 5 in a model in which the firm chooses its specific set of FERM methods from the whole available set. This overall model seeks to aid the selection of the appropriate set of methods for a firm based on the implications of this choice for shareholder wealth.

### Defining and measuring exposure

'Exposure' is conventionally seen as those elements of a firm's physical and financial position which are generally located outside the relatively safe home base and which are denominated in 'foreign' currencies. As a result, the beginning point in exposure management is to identify exactly which assets, liabilities, income flows and cash flows are denominated in currencies other than that of the parent, and where these are located.

In section 3.2 three conventional classes of exposure were briefly defined according to the period in which they occurred, whether they reflected accounting or economic events, and the degree of uncertainty associated with these events. These types of exposure were

- economic exposure
- transaction exposure
- translation or accounting exposure.

Economic exposure is the fundamental currency exposure facing the firm and is concerned with the impact of exchange rate changes on the uncertain foreign currency stream of corporate cash flows and ultimately with the impact on the value of the firm. Wihlborg (1980) defines transaction exposure as an uncertain domestic currency value of an open position denominated in a foreign currency with respect to a known transaction. This can be seen as the known, relatively short term subset of economic exposure. Translation exposure is the uncertain domestic value of a net accounting position denominated in a foreign currency at a certain future date (Wihlborg 1980).

These concepts can be best demonstrated by considering various types of firm according to their degree of international involvement. If we consider a domestic firm actively engaged in exporting and importing then this introduces the possibility of foreign currency receipts and payments of known size and timing, and therefore exposure of these transactions to currency risk, i.e. the risk that these known receipts and payments will be adversely affected by relative changes in currency values.

In the case of a firm changing from domestic to multinational status, the decision to invest overseas in a new subsidiary may mark a dramatic change. Exposure and currency risk problems associated with the overseas investment decision include the effect of exchange rate changes on unknown long term overseas cash flows (economic exposure), on known transactions (transaction exposure) and on accounting measurements of events before and during the exchange rate changes (accounting or translation exposure).

As a firm becomes increasingly internationally involved by entering a range of overseas domestic debt markets and unregulated offshore debt markets and seeks equity funds in several overseas stock exchanges, then we see equivalent changes in its exposure. The firm now faces exchange rate risk on its sources of capital as well as its uses of capital. Economic, transaction and translation exposure issues are now intimately related to financing and capital structure decisions, as well as the capital budgeting and other real decisions.

Adler and Dumas (1984) point out that the wholly domestic firm with little importing or exporting business can also be exposed to currency risk. If a company's customer base is dominated by importing and exporting firms whose activities are influenced by exchange rate changes, then the firm's operations will be exposed to exchange rate risk. As a result, we can see that very few firms are free of currency risk.

The conventional categories of exposure may be a useful starting point in designing an exposure information system. This can consist of a series of exposure reports for each balance sheet translation, income statement translation, and cash flow exposure (McRae and Walker 1980: 73). These reports should be by currency and by unit, and by country of operations. Periodic summary reports aggregating group exposure by exposure type and currency are also essential (p. 79).

*Exposure as vulnerability to exchange rate changes*
In contrast to this conventional view of exposure, Adler and Dumas (1984) argue that exposure to risk is a correlation coefficient. If home currency (HC) returns are regressed on foreign exchange rates, then the correlation coefficient measures the sensitivity of these returns to foreign exchange rate changes. The sensitivity of these cash flows and returns to exchange rate changes therefore reflects the 'exposure' of the firm to this variable. This concept of exposure applies equally to the wholly domestic firm, the exporter or importer, and the full MNC. In all of these cases, including domestic firms and MNCs, multiple regression can reveal the sensitivity of HC returns to many exchange rates. Hedging the correlation coefficient foreign currency (FC) amount eliminates all variation in the HC return derived from exchange rate changes and leaves residual non–exchange-rate variations in the HC amount. This of course assumes that the correlation coefficient, derived from historical data, accurately estimates future exposures of the firm's cash flows. The multiple regression can be extended to analyse how the economic exposure (HC returns) of the firm alters with a host of macroeconomic variables such as interest rates, exchange rates, inflation rates, commodity prices and wages (Oxelheim and Wihlborg 1989).

These arguments with respect to the definition and measurement of exposure also suggest some design guidelines for an exposure information system. From Adler and Dumas's (1984) perspective, exposure is seen as a statistical quantity rather than a projected accounting number or cash flow. The key information required is the sensitivity of home currency cash flows to exchange rate changes. The problem here is that this concept may be difficult to operationalize owing to non-stationarity of the distributions underlying the exchange rate changes or because of problems of multicollinearity. The major value of their arguments may lie in focusing treasurers' attention on the statistical nature of exposure (p. 48). Thus a combination of the conventional categories of exposure and an acknowledgement of its statistical nature seems to be the best guideline for the design of an exposure information system.

A practical approach to dealing with the statistical nature of exposure is for the firm to forecast its foreign currency cash flows under various real exchange rate (see next section) scenarios and associated changes in competitors' positions. This can help the firm assess the pessimistic and optimistic range of its future FC exposures. The firm can use this to identify the scale of relatively certain FC cash flows over the planning period arising from contractual arrangements and stable sales and prices. It must also assess the scale of uncertain FC cash flows possible from its existing businesses. This cash flow exposure data will be invaluable in estimating the level of flexibility it must build into real decisions now and the potential role of financial methods in insuring against currency risk.

Given basic information on exposures at both subsidiary and group level, managers have to decide whether they constitute a risk for the firm and its shareholders. This involves using forecasts of real exchange rate changes to analyse the circumstances under which these exposures can be deemed risky. It should be noted at this stage that all of these exposures have risk attached to them: thus receivables face the risk of not being paid. The concern here is with the possibility of additional risk due to unanticipated real exchange rate movements.

## Defining currency risk: Real versus nominal changes in the exchange rate

It is important to distinguish between real and nominal (actual) changes in the exchange rate: 'bad weather' in terms of exchange rate volatility is an illusion if exchange rate changes fully reflect relative price changes in two countries.

Using UK indirect quotes (i.e. $\$/\pounds$ or $DM/\pounds$) in the purchasing power parity relationship,

$$\text{nominal exchange rate in period } t = \text{nominal (actual) exchange rate in period } 0 \times \frac{1 + \text{expected foreign inflation rate in period } t}{1 + \text{expected domestic inflation rate in period } t}$$

$$S_t = S_0 \frac{1 + FI_t}{1 + DI_t}$$

For example, if US inflation over a year is expected to be 5 per cent and UK inflation over the same period is is expected to be 10 per cent, purchasing power parity would predict that the pound would depreciate by approximately 5 per cent relative to the dollar. If the nominal exchange rate was 2\$/£ at the start of the year, then the nominal rate at the end of the year would be 2 (1 + 0.05)/(1 + 0.10 ) = 1.909\$/£. Thus the pound is only expected to buy \$1.909 at the end of the year compared with \$2 at the start of the year, and it appears from these nominal (actual) changes in the exchange rate that the purchasing power of the pound has declined relative to the dollar.

The real rate can be expressed as

$$\begin{array}{c} \text{real exchange rate} \\ \text{in period } t \end{array} = \begin{array}{c} \text{nominal (actual)} \\ \text{exchange rate in} \\ \text{period } t \end{array} \times \frac{1 + \text{domestic inflation rate in period } t}{1 + \text{foreign inflation rate in period } t}$$

$$RS_t = S_t \frac{1 + DI_t}{1 + FI_t}$$

If the nominal rate of 1.909\$/£ occurred at the end of the year, and the inflation rates turned out as expected, then no change would have occurred in the real rate because the real rate would be 1.909 (1 + 0.10)/(1 + 0.05) = 2\$/£. Thus prices in both countries would have increased with local inflation changes and the exchange rate change fully reflected this. As a result, there had been no change in the relative purchasing power of the two currencies.

We can see that the concept of the real rate takes into account the joint effects of inflation changes and nominal exchange rate changes. The observable nominal or actual exchange rate change may conceal these effects. The real rate and its changes cannot be observed but have to be calculated using nominal rates and inflation rates from some base period. In the above example, the change in the nominal rate is of no significance because the effect of inflation in the two countries is offset by the equivalent exchange rate change. Purchasing power parity holds and unanticipated nominal exchange rate changes are compensated for by unanticipated relative inflation rate changes. A UK firm with non-contractual dollar cash flows will probably find that these inflate at 5 per cent; when the dollars are changed back into pounds at the end of the year, these pounds will have a reduced purchasing power of 10 per cent in the

UK. The exchange rate will reflect this inflation differential of 5 per cent and so the expanded number of year end pounds will have the same power to purchase goods as the equivalent number of year start pounds.

However, if the pound actually appreciated to a new nominal rate of say 2.05$/£, and the inflation rates turned out as expected, then the real exchange rate at the end of the year would have changed to 2.05 (1 + 0.10) / (1 + 0.05) = 2.148$/£. Thus despite US inflation rates being much lower than UK rates, the nominal rate change had increased the ability of the pound to buy dollars at the end of the year. In real terms, we can see that the increase in purchasing power of the pound was much higher than this nominal increase. This is fine for a UK firm using pounds to buy goods in US dollars as the real price of these goods falls. However, if the UK firm sells many goods in dollars then its sterling revenue cash flows experience a severe fall not compensated for by purchasing power parity. Thus the dollars it receives have a much reduced real ability to purchase goods in pounds compared with the year before. In addition, it probably faces a double blow because its domestic costs may rise much faster than US competitors owing to higher UK inflation. The situation could be even worse if inflation for the UK firm's own costs turns out to be even higher than domestic UK inflation. This two-way impact of real exchange rate changes on dollar revenues and on sterling operating costs and the subsequent squeeze on net sterling income can be quite severe for the UK exporter to the US. Thus unanticipated changes in real exchange rates are the central source of currency risk for the firm. These risks are particularly acute for firms trading in a narrow range of say one or two major currencies which are subject to real changes. If a firm could diversify across say six to eight currencies then some of this real exchange risk could be diversified. This may prove difficult even for internationally involved UK firms because of customer preferences for the use of dollars, marks and pounds in the vast bulk of transactions.

## Case study: Rolls-Royce: economic exposure and risk from real exchange rate changes

Such real $/£ changes occurred in the late 1970s. In this period, a real change in the $/£ exchange rate had a major impact on the sterling revenues of UK exporters to the US. For example, Rolls-Royce, the UK aero engine manufacturer, experienced a loss of £58 million in 1979 because of a real change in the $/£ exchange rate. UK inflation in 1979 was higher than US inflation, suggesting (via PPP) that the pound would depreciate relative to the US dollar. In fact the pound appreciated against the dollar. Given that aero engines are priced in dollars, Rolls–Royce received a much lower sterling cash flow from its dollar receivables (Rolls–Royce *Annual Report* 1979). This problem stemmed from Rolls–Royce having entered into several large contracts to supply aero engines at fixed dollar terms. In contrast, most of RR production and financing costs were in sterling. This large and long term dollar transaction exposure was not hedged in the forward markets, as RR had made a mistaken and expensive bet against the $/£ exchange rate by assuming that PPP would hold.

The 1979 experience alerted RR to the need for an extensive hedging policy for transaction exposures arising from known (contractually fixed) engine orders. It also encouraged senior management to take currency risk into account when strategic decisions created new economic exposures. In particular, new engine orders and their pricing, sourcing decisions and location of production have become very important in this respect. This experience has also alerted RR to the need to fully understand the nature of its exposure to currency risk and to develop a range of responses to its currency risk management problem.

## The dynamic nature of the foreign exchange risk management problem

The concepts of exposure and risk discussed in the previous section are invaluable in structuring our thoughts on the nature of the foreign exchange risk management problem. However, the Rolls–Royce case and many other publicly discussed cases indicate that managers face a dynamic, ever changing problem. This can be explored, in part, by considering

- the time structure of exposure
- the need to simultaneously manage all exposure types
- the need to respond to recent real changes and to potential real changes in the exchange rate.

*The origin of economic exposure: elapsed time structure*
In the case of Rolls–Royce, the elapsed or historic time structure of the firm's economic exposure is likely to consist of the following (see Betts 1992; Flexl 1985; Rolls–Royce *Annual Reports* 1989, 1990):

1   A competitive or operating exposure component consisting of
    (a) unknown and uncertain foreign currency cash flows arising from future unknown engine sales and maintenance contracts, unknown new

overseas production, supply and maintenance facilities and unknown actions by competitors

(b) planned direct foreign investment (DFI) in overseas assets such as new engine maintenance facilities, and including a planned sterling economic exposure based on expected levels of research and development costs and production costs, plus similar plans by competitors.

This competitive exposure component eventually leads to

2  Contingent foreign currency (expected to be dollar) cash flows arising from engines sales currently being negotiated, and maintenance contracts associated with these ongoing engine sales.

This finally leads to

3  A transaction exposure component consisting of foreign currency (normally dollar) cash flows arising from known or agreed aero engine sales and known engine maintenance contracts from previous sales, as well as some long term FC debt arranged under fixed terms.

These 'natural' foreign currency exposures arise from a wide range of historic and recent overseas investment decisions, recently negotiated contracts and potential new contracts. At any time, the firm faces both transaction and competitive aspects of economic exposure and must deal with them all on a continuous basis.

*The simultaneous occurrence of all exposures and the need to manage them together in the same period*

Thus in practice a firm such as Rolls-Royce will experience transaction exposure and competitive exposure problems simultaneously. Transaction exposure is the immediate problem and stems from previous DFI decisions and engine sales agreements in previous periods. Economic exposure is further into the future and arises from historic and recent strategic and operating decisions. In most cases action has to be taken now to deal with these exposures to currency risk and so the firm has to simultaneously manage all elements of currency exposure on a continuing basis.

In RR's case this may involve the firm in simultaneously managing the two forms of exposure. The first is its medium or long term competitive exposure to recent or potential new changes in the real $/£ exchange rate. In the first exchange rate case RR may have to take action now to alter its strategy or its operating policies in order to avoid the adverse value consequences of a recent real change in the exchange rate. In the second case the firm may have to build its view of potentially new adverse real exchange rate changes into strategy and operating decisions to ensure that it has the flexibility to take compensating or avoiding actions if the real exchange rate change occurs.

The second of RR's exposures is its immediate, known transaction exposure to unanticipated changes in the exchange rate over the duration of contractually agreed FC (normally dollars for RR) cash flows. This transaction exposure is often unavoidable in the sense that it cannot be changed without changing some fundamental and valuable aspect of the current business. In RR's case this is the size and attraction of the US market and the use of dollars as a global medium for aero engine purchases. Thus creating flexibility or responsiveness to potential real currency changes by altering strategic and operational decisions has its limits in its possible negative impact on shareholder value. RR cannot avoid the US market for aero engines and cannot substantially alter the payment practices of the global power unit and aviation market. In practice, many firms face this problem and their treasuries have to manage this large scale, residual (or unavoidable) currency exposure problem through a mixture of internal financial transfer and external financial hedging methods. This known transaction exposure can also be managed to give time for strategic and operational changes (responses to recent real changes) to take effect. For example, the firm may decide to exploit this extra time to reduce competitive exposure by changing suppliers or reducing production costs.

In this sense we can see that financial hedging using markets and internal financial exposure adjustment has two primary aims: firstly, to deal with the unavoidable residual currency risk problems of the firm; and secondly, to buy time for strategic and operational changes to take effect relative to the currency risk problem.

*Corporate decision problems arising from the period of real exchange rate changes: recent historic and new potential changes*

The Rolls-Royce example indicates that a further dimension to the foreign exchange risk management problem is the period over which the real exchange rate change has occurred. Table 4.2 breaks this up this into two periods, one in the recent past and one in the near future (one to three years ahead), and illustrates general responses to these related problems.

In both kinds of decision problem illustrated in the table, FERM decisions begin with real strategic or operational decisions and are supported by a host of financial methods. The first case involves immediate

**Table 4.2** FERM decisions in two periods

| Real changes | Measured by | Possible FERM decisions |
|---|---|---|
| Historic: last year | Last year's nominal exchange rate changes and relative inflation changes | If a real change has occurred and this has affected competitiveness then a reactive response is required in strategic, operational or financial decisions |
| | The risk here is that the known real exchange rate changes will stimulate unknown FC cash flow changes through, say, competitors' actions | Initiate long term and medium term changes in strategic and operating decisions to reduce existing effects of real changes. Use financial methods, internal and external, to buy time for these to take effect |
| Future: a world in which real changes can occur unexpectedly | Forecasts of nominal exchange rates and inflation | If real changes are possible then a proactive response is required. The firm must also develop flexibility or responsiveness to unexpected change possibilities |
| | The risk here is that unknown real changes could promote unanticipated changes in FC cash flows and competitors' actions | If real strategic/operational changes can be made quickly, a firm has the means to deal with some real changes as they occur. Use financial techniques to deal with residual or unfavourable FERM problems |

changes in these decision variables to respond to recent changes in corporate circumstances. The second refers to creating resources and plans for change should such adverse circumstances occur. Both involve manipulating the same set of decision variables probably in the same direction in response to similar actual or expected changes in real exchange rates. They are closely related in that historic decisions to boost responsiveness to currency risk may create or limit the current response capacity of the firm. Immediate reactive decisions in response to recent real exchange rate changes may also enhance or constrain the future responsiveness of the firm.

**Table 4.3** Reactive and proactive options in FERM decision taking

|  | *Strategic* | *Operational* | *Internal* | *External* |
|---|---|---|---|---|
| Response decisions (reactive) | React to recent real change by exploiting strategic flexibility | Alter marketing, production, sourcing and other operational decisions | Exploit internal system to avoid currency risk or to arbritrage or speculate | Use external market to buy insurance or arbritrage/ speculate. Buy time for real decisions |
| Responsiveness decisions (proactive) | Build in capacity to make real changes in strategy | Develop flexibility in operational decisions | Build internal financial system. Develop treasury skills in FERM | Establish close stable links with bank suppliers of currency risk management products |

Table 4.3 expands on table 4.2 and identifies specific reactive and proactive actions that a firm can take across a wide range of strategic, operational and financial decisions. In the table it is clear that some proactive responses such as treasury development are akin to an investment outlay in a capability to respond to real changes. Reactive responses exploit such a capability.

Thus a firm can react to recent real exchange rate changes by initiating long term and medium term changes in strategic and operating decisions and hence reduce the impact of the real change. Financial methods, internal and external, can be used

- to buy time for these real changes to take effect
- to deal with those parts of the currency risk problem that cannot be tackled using strategic change
- to deal with those problems that prove too costly in terms of strategic or operational value penalty losses.

In the case of responsiveness or proactive decisions, the firm should also act now to incorporate the impact of potential real exchange rate changes into strategic and operational decisions. If the decisions are taken early enough then the firm may have the means to deal with some of the real changes as they occur. This will hopefully make HC currency cash flows less vulnerable to exchange rate changes and thus reduce the need for the firm to use internal financial methods or financial market methods to further reduce the impact of exchange rate changes on shareholder wealth. Thus the firm may be able to reduce the scale of the foreign exchange risk management problem faced by treasury and the finance function. The role of treasury here is to use financial methods to deal with the residual problems of FERM that either cannot be dealt with using changes in real decisions or are considered too costly in terms of strategic value losses.

## Economic exposure and risk: a summary

The previous sections have provided some insight into the complex nature of exposure and risk. We can summarize the main features of a concept of economic exposure as follows:

1  Exposure is created by placing (or denominating) assets/liabilities and cash flows (purchasing power) in a risky (volatile currency) environment.
2  Exposure is about varying vulnerability to risk, or the sensitivity of cash flows to exchange rate changes.
3  Exposure is about competitiveness – the varying ability of competing firms to respond to adverse or advantageous exchange rate changes.
4  Exposure is about value – the impact of real exchange rate changes on exposure and hence firm value.

Risk in this context is the uncertain nature of real exchange rate changes (or relative purchasing power change) and their impact on the exposed FC and HC cash flows and ultimately on the value of the firm. Thus unanticipated real exchange rate changes may threaten home currency profits, increase tax bills by altering profitability in an unpredictable way, or threaten financial health or corporate survival by increasing the risks of financial distress. In addition, currency changes may alter the exposure of the company. A (weakly competitive) firm can be hurt by real exchange rate change which can exacerbate the currency risk vulnerability of the firm and strengthen competitors. The Rolls-Royce 1979 example earlier is a case where the competitive positions of US aero engine manufacturers were much strengthened relative to Rolls-Royce.

We will see in chapter 5 that a firm can actively manage its exposure to currency risk. Thus a firm can alter its economic exposure by strategic changes such as changing the location/denomination of its cash flows, assets and liabilities, changing the vulnerability or sensitivity of its cash flows to real exchange rate changes, and changing its competitiveness. In chapters 6 and 7 we will see that the firm can alter some of its known transaction exposures by using a range of internal financial techniques, and that it can also externally insure against risk by using market supplied currency hedges or options.

## Forecasting inflation rates and foreign exchange rates

Sources of information such as forecasts of spot rate changes, of relative inflation rates and of corporate FC exposures are vital to strategic, operational and internal/external responses (active and proactive) to currency risk. Once these forecasts have been developed they can be applied to corporate measurement of exposure to produce estimates of likely real gains and losses. Whether the exposed positions are 'risky' depends on the likelihood of deviations from anticipated values of real exchange rates. The economic circumstances outlined in section 4.1 and illustrated in table 4.1 identify such possibilities of risk. The extent and scale of risk facing the firm will in turn determine the choice of strategy and operational changes as well as financial tactics for FERM.

### Forecasting inflation rates

Peel and Pope (1988) point out that there are many publicly available forecasts of inflation for use by corporate finance staff. Thus in the UK the five key forecasting groups are the National Institute, the London Business School, the Cambridge Economic Policy Group, the Treasury and the OECD. Similar forecasts are available from public bodies in the major Western nations, and so a basis exists for forecasting inflation differences expected between countries. If these can be combined with forecasts of changes in the nominal exchange rate then a basis exists to forecast changes expected in real rates. It is difficult to avoid using inflation forecasts in nominal exchange rate forecasts. However, if the firm uses nominal spot rate forecasts that do not use the same inflation rate forecasts then an opportunity for identifying real exchange rate changes may exist. Given the difficulties here, it is more likely that an enterprise has an advantage in forecasting cost and price inflation unique to its industry. This can allow it to forecast corporate specific deviations from purchasing power parity for itself and key competitors.

*Forecasting foreign exchange rates*

Forecasting the likely path of foreign exchange movements is a very complex task in a world of floating, managed floating and fixed exchange rate systems.

If we firstly consider the case of floating systems with efficient foreign exchange markets, the orthodox view is that forecasting becomes unnecessary (Dufey and Giddy 1978a: 80). The market forecast of future spot rates, expressed in forward rates or in Eurocurrency interest rate differentials, will fully reflect all public information. Unless the corporation is privy to inside information concerning exchange rate changes, it will find it difficult to out-forecast the market. The freely available market forecast should therefore be acquired and compared with any internal forecast or forecasting service the company is using. In the former case the market forecast can be used as a benchmark against which to judge the firm's own ability to forecast or to exploit market imperfections. In the latter case discrepancies can indicate whether the external forecasting service has unique capabilities or whether it is merely selling the firm publicly available knowledge.

In contrast to the orthodox view, Levich (1983) has reviewed studies on the performance of forecasting services for floating currencies. He noted that a major corollary of the asset view of exchange rates (i.e. where currencies are seen as financial assets) and the efficient market principle is that exchange rate changes are the result of unanticipated economic events, that is 'news' (p. 4). By definition it is impossible to forecast news. However, it can be modelled in a variety of ways using proxy variables such as unanticipated changes in the term structure of interest rates, as well as unanticipated current account balances and cyclical income movements. The evidence here confirms that these important variables are significantly related to forecast errors in the forward rate (p. 22). Levich concluded that 'Recent models focusing on the role of news suggest that superior forecasts of a few important variables could significantly improve forecasts relative to the forward rate' (p. 28). However, he strikes a cautionary note by commenting that whilst the empirical studies indicate that forecasts can lead to profits, the profits are not risk free and may be fair compensation for the extra risks of open foreign exchange positions (p. 29). Furthermore, forecasting models that worked in the past may not work in the future. An efficient foreign exchange market will incorporate information from these models, making the forward market even more difficult to out-forecast.

If we turn to the case of managed or fixed exchange rates, the movement towards equilibrium in spot and forward exchange rates, interest rates and inflation rates is artificially prevented from happening. The European monetary system (EMS) is a good example of a managed currency system. Government intervention in the foreign exchange markets is seen by many observers to be the major source of deviations from equilibrium conditions. Thus the focus of attention in forecasting generally turns to analysing likely actions together or singly by EC national central banks and their interplay with the equilibrium forces. The tendency to equilibrium is still assumed to exist but, because of government intervention, it is difficult to predict when and by how much the EC governments would bow to market forces. Under these conditions, forecasters attempt to analyse the politics of devaluation within the EMS, as well as various economic indicators of pressure on the exchange rate position being defended. The mark, its relationship to other EC currencies, and central bank statements and behaviour are often the focus of such calculations. These indicators include growth in the money supply, balance of payments, size of central bank currency reserves and government spending. Examples of such an approach can be found in Jacque (1978: 83).

A good example of a government exercising control over its exchange rate system is provided by Australia in 1983. At the end of October 1983 Australia's foreign exchange system underwent a series of important changes. Prior to this time the Australian Reserve Bank had announced at 9.30 a.m. eastern time each day an index number for the Australian dollar against a trade weighted basket of currencies. This variable link to a basket of major currencies was announced at the same time as a fixed daily exchange rate against the US dollar. The change from the end of October was to announce the trade weighted index (TWI) as before, but to set the Reserve Bank's daily exchange rate for the US dollar at the end of the day. An indicative US$/A$ rate was announced with the TWI but the banks were free to deal with their customers during the day at mutually acceptable rates. In addition the Reserve Bank considerably reduced its controls over forward contracts for foreign exchange.

Three months later saw an even more dramatic move on the part of the Australian government. The Australian dollar was floated and a major part of the existing exchange controls were abolished from 12 December 1983. The TWI and the indicative US dollar rate were no longer published by the Reserve Bank each morning and the spot and forward rates were determined by market forces on a moment by moment basis. The Reserve Bank retained its discretion to intervene in these markets, and its consent was required for certain transactions by Australians and non-residents. For example, in the former case the main areas affected were foreign borrowing, direct foreign investment abroad, repayments of overseas borrowings, and overseas futures transactions. In the latter case the key areas were portfolio investment, futures deals in Australia, and direct investment.

Thus in the space of three months Australia experienced three different sets of foreign exchange arrangements. This level of governmental intervention in the exchange rate system is unusual and is more generally confined to the exchange rate itself. However, it does demonstrate the uncertainty associated with forecasting changes in exchange rates and exchange rate systems. The EMS crisis of September 1992 provides a further example of unexpected system changes as the pound was suspended from the EMS and allowed to float freely against all EC currencies as well as the yen and the US dollar. Further realignments were forced on the EMS in January 1993 as the Irish pound was devalued after intense speculative activity in the foreign exchange markets.

A simple example of forecasting procedures for a fixed system is demonstrated by the following four stage model (see Jacque 1978: 83):

1   The nation's balance of payments is forecast and periods of deficit are identified.
2   Market forces as expressed via the conventional variables of interest rates, inflation etc., as well as indicators such as forward market rates, are used to predict the general direction in which exchange rates are expected to move.
3   The deficits from stage 1 (if they exist) are compared with the country's reserves. This provides some estimate of the pressure on the currency, and the period for which the country can maintain its current policies.
4   This in turn gives some indication of the government's economic policy choices in these circumstances. If this is compared with the political goals and constraints of the current government, then a forecast can be made of likely government action on exchange rates.

Stages 3 and 4 can be adapted to the EMS managed system. Thus the forecaster can assess when the aggregate reserves of the group of EC central banks are likely to be exceeded by the collective transactions of firms and banks trying to sell a currency. When this point is reached, the EC collective effort to support the currency (or group of weaker currencies) is likely to fail and the currency will have to find its market level. In the period 1979 to 1993 this has meant periodic devalation of currencies such as the franc, the lira, the Irish pound and the pound relative to the mark.

Forecasting changes in managed and fixed rate systems can be quite profitable for arbitrageurs and speculators (corporate and others). This is partly because the direction and possibly the size of change of the currency is generally known through the use of forecasting procedures similar to the above four steps. In addition, governments are often prepared to lose on foreign exchange in order to achieve other political goals.

In the case of the managed EMS it appears that firms, banks and other financial institutions can readily develop accurate forecasts of realignments. Thus the political negotiations that generally surround changes in the internal bands of the EMS are difficult to conceal and provide an opportunity for firms, banks and others to successfully 'bet against' European central bankers. The foreign exchange markets may still be informationally efficient under these circumstances but the set of EC central banks, by resisting the market forces, may be providing speculators with a free bonus. The EMS crisis of September 1992 is an important reminder that this problem, which plagued the Bretton Woods system, is still present in world currency arrangements.

Forecasting foreign exchange rate changes becomes increasingly difficult and less profitable as we move from fixed to managed to floating systems. Government action becomes more unpredictable, and the forces for equilibrium become more influential in necessitating frequent adjustments. Developing forecasts superior to forward rates becomes very difficult when the firm is operating in efficient markets for floating exchange rates. The exception to this latter case is the forecasting models referred to by Levich (1983).

It is clear from the above that firms operating within floating exchange regimes will not generally be able to purchase or develop forecasts superior to the forward rate. This would not prove a problem for such firms if the other parity relationships also held. However, because of purchasing parity deviations, the firm may still be exposed to foreign exchange risk even when the foreign exchange market is informationally efficient. If the firm is in a better position to hedge this risk than investors, then an active exposure management policy is required.

An important ingredient in the forecasting of changes in fixed rate and managed systems is the MNC's unique knowledge of local conditions. Corporate foreign exchange forecasting is generally done internally at group level with some forecasts purchased externally for head office. However, the local (subsidiary) input to forecasting can be important as an additional source of information based upon intimate local knowledge. A regular two way flow of information between local managers and the central treasury on exchange rates can also be valuable in influencing decisions at both levels (McRae and Walker 1980: 80).

The firm is likely to have a comparative advantage over other forecasters in forecasting relative price changes in its industry or relative price changes specific to itself. These advantages, allied with knowledge of local conditions, may give the firm an advantage in assessing the impact of real exchange rate changes on the firm. It is unlikely that the firm can gain such an advantage in forecasting changes in general price levels between the countries concerned. This would give it novel insight into a major determinant of exchange rate changes and thus the possibility of out-forecasting the forward rate.

## 4.3 Summary

In this chapter we have seen that:

1   Firms experience complex foreign exchange risk management (FERM) problems.
2   It is in shareholders' interests that managers seek to deal with this problem.
3   The aim of FERM is to minimize the impact of unanticipated exchange rate changes on home currency returns.
4   Currency risk should be assessed relative to the possibility of unanticipated real changes in exchange rates.
5   A firm can have considerable discretion concerning the nature and scale of its exposure to risk despite having little or no control over currency changes.
6   Competitive aspects of exposure can be altered by real exchange rate changes.
7   There is a wide choice of strategic, operational, internal financial and external financial methods for the firm to choose from when dealing with currency risk.
8   Managerial problems differ according to whether they arise from recent real changes or the possibility of further unexpected changes in real exchange rates.

9   FERM policies will differ according to the economic circumstances surrounding the firm and unique factors affecting the firm.
10  New information on real rate changes and on changes in corporate exposures can change decisions. Thus the forecasting of inflation and exchange rate changes is a central element of the management of currency risk.

The purpose of the following chapters is to clarify the specific role of each primary class of FERM methods in dealing with the currency risk problem. These FERM methods include adaptations to strategic and operational decisions (chapter 5), the use of internal financial techniques (chapter 6) and the use of external financial techniques (chapter 7). The presumption in these chapters is that:

1   Management have estimated their currency exposures and assessed risk. They believe, on the basis of this evidence, that the firm has a foreign exchange risk management problem.
2   Management understand the possibilities of each major FERM method.
3   FERM is very active in the company and this policy is understood throughout the organization.
4   The company has clarified its goals for FERM and these are consistent with its strategic aims.

# 5
# FERM, Economic Exposure and Adapting Strategic and Operational Decisions

This chapter considers how a firm can fashion its strategic and operational decisions as part of a set of responses to currency risk. In section 5.1 we consider how adaptations to strategy can alter economic exposure to currency risk. Section 5.2 looks at operational responses. In section 5.3 we consider how a firm can choose between a wide variety of real and financial FERM methods. Section 5.4 summarizes the chapter.

## 5.1 Adapting Strategic Decisions

The currency climate in the 1990s is too volatile for any firm to use currency forecasts as the major reference point for its long term mission and strategy. Thus a firm should not structure or change its strategic decisions solely on the basis of foreign exchange risk management (FERM) considerations. Strategic decisions should not be seen as subsumed by or captive to FERM needs. However, currency risk may have major strategic implications for the firm and strategic decisions can play a significant role in FERM. As a result, the goals of FERM relative to strategy include the following:

- to take currency volatility into account at an early stage in strategic decision making
- to identify existing strategic flexibility relative to potential new changes in the real exchange rate
- to create new levels of strategic flexibility relative to such changes.

Thus some thought will have to be given at the planning stage to increasing the responsiveness of strategic and operational decisions to unknown changes in the real exchange rate.

The underlying aim shared by the above set of goals is to enhance or protect shareholder value 'threatened' by currency risk. At this level of decision making the firm must compare the net present value of existing and prospective investment decisions before and after adapting strategic decisions for currency risk. These adaptive actions should only be considered if value is conserved or added.

Actions at the strategic level normally take the form of alterations to known levels of exposure or to potentially new levels of exposure to currency risk, as well as attempts to alter the sensitivity of exposures to exchange rate changes. One reason for doing this is to combat those competitor actions which may have an indirect and unanticipated effect on the firm's long term foreign currency cash flows. Another reason is to deal with the general vulnerability of the firm to volatile exchange rates in the 1990s.

The pursuit of the value maximization mission of the enterprise can lead to a host of decisions which alter exposures or reduce sensitivities to currency risk. These include:

- the location of production or sales in the same countries as major competitors
- the location of production and sales in many currency zones
- the creation of flexible manufacturing systems that allow rapid product differentiation
- entering new market niches that have lower price sensitivity
- the investment of large sums in research and development.

For example, an MNC might decide for long term strategic reasons to diversify across countries with its sales, its production facilities and the location of its raw material resources. These strategic aims take priority and the currency risk issue provides one of many inputs into such decisions. However, the firm should consider if it can use its strategic moves to avoid currency zones that create currency inflexibility, or to locate in currency zones with high currency risk diversification benefits.

In the case of ICI, this large UK based chemical industries MNC has restructured its strategy to reduce currency risk. ICI's exposure stems from doing business in about 40 currencies, of which only 20 are actively managed for currency risk. The US dollar, the Deutschmark and the pound dominate these exposures. It has reduced currency risk by focusing on technology which is applicable world-wide (*Financial Weekly*, 21 December 1989). It has sold its Canadian waste management company because it believes that the technology is not transferable. Such transferability creates the flexibility of choice desired in the production location decision and allows the company to build currency considerations into this strategic decision. ICI has also diversified its currency base by emphasizing the fast growing Asia/Pacific market. These strategic moves will reduce ICI's dependence on the dollar, the mark and the pound (ICI *Annual Report* 1988).

Altering the sensitivity of foreign currency (FC) cash flows to exchange rate changes is also possible. For example, if an MNC can rapidly differentiate its products this may lead to greater control over FC prices and speedier introduction of new products to overseas markets. Such differentiation is at the heart of MNC activity. The MNC exploits its unique knowledge and technological advantage to innovate in products and to reduce the duration of product life cycle. This is advantageous for the MNC regardless of exchange rate changes. However, if it also means that the responsiveness of both strategic and operational marketing and production variables can be increased in the face of currency change, then the MNC has created a further advantage for itself. This may manifest itself in products being less sensitive to FC price changes (smaller price elasticity of demand). As a result, the MNC may be able to quickly raise FC prices when the FC depreciates.

Other means of altering the sensitivity of FC cash flows to exchange rate changes include developing production systems that have prompt response times to product changes and can be used to tailor products to unique niches in the marketplace. This may also reduce the sensitivity of products to FC price changes as well as provide the means to exploit exchange rate changes. A decision to locate production in many currency zones may combine with production flexibility advantages to allow rapid shifts of production volumes from site to site and thus the capacity to quickly change the currencies of cost cash flows.

As can be seen, much of the above depends on heavy investment in R&D designed to create unique knowledge and technological advantages for the firm. In this way we can see that currency risk is intimately tied up with the knowledge advantage sought by MNCs.

Finally, some firms can turn their long term economic exposure into a competitive advantage. Firm A may seek a trading partner B with a long term exposure in A's currency. Firm A has a similar long term exposure in

B's currency. Thus the basis for a long term swap exists with B, which may also place business with A as part of the deal.

Exploiting existing degrees of freedom with these strategic decisions or creating additional strategic flexibility can therefore be an invaluable tool in dealing with currency risks. We will explore these ideas in detail in the following section by pursuing the Rolls-Royce case (see chapter 4) in greater depth. The sources for this case are public comment and articles. (see Betts 1992; Flexl 1985; Rolls-Royce *Annual Reports* 1989, 1990).

## Case study: Rolls-Royce: economic exposure

Rolls-Royce is one of only three manufacturers in the Western world with the proven ability to design, develop and produce large gas turbine aero engines. The business of the Rolls-Royce group is international, with approximately 70 per cent of its sales over the late 1980s being to airframe manufacturers or other customers outside the UK. The company is operating in two major aviation markets: civil and military. The company's strategy is to achieve strong representation in each of the principal sectors of the market, e.g. from executive jets to the largest Boeing 747s on the civil aviation side). The Rolls-Royce group maintains manufacturing, repair and overhaul facilities in Canada, manufacturing engineering and design facilities in the US and repair and overhaul facilities in Brazil, in addition to maintaining marketing or product support representatives in 30 other countries.

We have seen in chapter 4 that the complex nature of RR exposure to risk creates a major FERM problem for the company. Rolls-Royce's experience of exchange rate changes has led the company to develop a sophisticated set of real and financial responses to currency risk. In particular Rolls-Royce has to consider the following:

1   The location of major competitors in the aero engine industry and the currency composition of their revenues and costs. GE and Pratt & Whitney are the major competitors. They are both US based and have a major advantage over RR in that their major costs and revenues are in dollars and they therefore have a higher degree of currency matching than RR.
2   The location and working currencies of potential new engine manufacturers, say from Germany or Japan.
3   The degree of price flexibility RR has when selling engines and that of its two major competitors.

4   Related to point 3, the degree of product innovation and the ability to generate differentiated products. The very high R&D budget in these aero engine firms is an essential basis for this capability.
5   The degree of matching/mismatching of revenue/cost cash flows in terms of their currency structure for both RR and its major competitors.

We can identify some of the major elements of RR's strategy in the late 1980s and assess whether this strategy creates a greater flexibility relative to economic exposure to currency risk. It should be noted that much of this strategy was developed for fundamental business considerations as well as for currency risk reasons. However, it has also created the capacity to deal with economic and transaction exposures to currency risk problems.

*Group strategy and proactive responsiveness*
Considerable effort is placed at the strategic planning stage to consider the probable impact of exchange rate changes on the value of the company. Specifically, when long term strategic decisions are taken, the probable impact of foreign exchange rate changes on the underlying decisions are considered. These might involve expansions by existing subsidiaries, acquisitions of existing foreign companies, new wholly owned investments abroad or any collaborative new projects. In the 1990s Rolls-Royce has diversified out of the aero engine business into the wider power generation business. This involves the use of existing aero engines and their technology in a wide range of power unit applications such as electricity generation in gas burning stations and the propulsion of large ships. The acquisition of NEI was an attempt to diversify the high technology aero engine risks with counter-cyclical power station business. The power station market provides further opportunities for Rolls-Royce to transfer its power unit technology to industrial uses as well as to sell the power units in a wider range of markets and currencies.

*Location of facilities and currency matching*
The group therefore uses its strategic and operational decisions to reduce economic exposure in the first place and to improve the responsiveness or resilience of the firm to adverse exchange rate changes. For example, because of the pre-eminence of the US as a market for both civil and military engines the company has a major American subsidiary, Rolls-Royce Inc., based in Greenwich, Connecticut. In addition to its primary function of providing customer support services and marketing backup in the US it has an engineering base in Atlanta which keeps abreast of current

US engineering technology and tenders for US government research contracts. Another major strategic decision taken by the group was the building of plant in Perth in Australia. Rolls-Royce spent up to A$15 million on this new factory in Perth, to build jet engine turbine blades in a joint venture with three Australian companies. The venture was part of an offset deal with the Australian government following the purchase by Quantas of Rolls-Royce engines for its Boeing jumbo jets.

*Competition and exposure*

Economic exposure and currency risk are exacerbated by the complex nature of global competition facing an MNC. The MNC should therefore analyse likely changes in its competitive position as a result of recent real changes or various future scenarios of real exchange rate changes. This can be conducted as part of a general analysis of competitive changes and can directly feed into formulation of FERM policy.

Rolls-Royce's capacity to adapt strategic and operational decisions depends crucially on the nature of its competitive environment and its competitive strategy. In figure 5.1 we adapt Porter's (1980) model of competitive strategy to reflect the impact of real exchange rate changes on competitive strategy. The US competition in the form of Pratt & Whitney and GE remains strong and new business will only be won against this competition with excellent new products backed up by impeccable

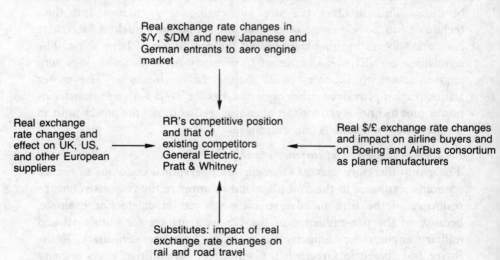

**Figure 5.1** Effects of exchange rate changes on Rolls-Royce's competitive strategy

customer service. The US base and production location of these two major competitors in the aero engine industry and the US dollar currency composition of their revenues and costs places RR at a major currency mismatch disadvantage. There is also the possibility of new engine manufacturers emerging from Germany or Japan. Real changes in the purchasing power of the yen or the mark relative to the dollar as the key sales currency or the pound as the production costs currency could exacerbate or ease these competitive threats.

With this in mind, throughout the late 1980s and the 1990s RR established a major programme to improve production cost efficiency in the UK. The aim was to reduce the competitive disadvantage of the sterling cost exposure and to hopefully maintain a large net margin between eventual sterling revenue (after going through the exchange market) and sterling costs. The global recession of the early 1990s reinforced the strategic thrust here.

We can see from figure 5.1 that real exchange rate changes can alter economic exposures for RR and its existing competitors. However, such changes can also change the exposed position of its suppliers, buyers, potential new entrants and substitutes. The way in which this occurs is crucial to its own decisions on how to alter exposures via real changes and how to exploit external markets for currency risk insurance.

This analysis of changes in economic exposure focuses on the industry in which RR operates. This has to be allied with the approach in chapter 4, in which economic exposure is also measured as a function of key macroeconomic variables such as exchange rates and interest rate changes (Oxelheim and Wihlborg 1989). Such an analysis may provide the information to predict how competitors' exposure will change and thus their likely strategic moves in response to currency risk and opportunities.

*R&D, innovation, and product differentiation*

The company devotes substantial resources to investment in advanced technology for both manufacturing and research and development. Since the mid 1970s, it has aimed to reduce the technological risk and high cost of engine design and development by proving technologies in advance of the high expenditure phase of an engine project and by making technologies transferable between engines. Thus the long term strategy of the firm emphasizes the development of advanced technology ahead of its requirement by the market. The strategy has given RR a lower cost of entry to the market with increased market opportunities at a lower risk. RR expect a higher profitability as a result.

The firm has a very high (approximately 8 per cent of turnover) R&D expenditure. This expenditure increased throughout the 1980s and 1990s and has been carefully managed to exploit the knowledge advantage acquired in new engine development and manufacturing. The key themes in R&D are value for money and the need for the firm to maintain a major competitive advantage. This knowledge advantage is very important to RR in developing and differentiating aero engine products. It allows RR to reduce the elasticity of demand for its new or improved aero engines and thus improve its capacity to alter prices in the face of real exchange rate changes.

The company has historically operated in a relatively inelastic market in its two major product divisions, civil and military aviation. It has maintained this inelastic price (insensitivity) advantage by continuous investment in and differentiation of new engines. By increasing its market share it has offset any losses in profitability caused by adverse exchange rate changes. For example, the knowledge and technological advantage has allowed the company to offer engines for a wide range of airframes and this has given it an edge over its competitors when entering new market niches. The latter have become very important with the end of the Cold War and the downturn in military expenditure in the early 1990s. The global recession of the early 1990s made this advantage doubly important in the civil power unit and aero engine market.

*Collaboration and sharing of economic exposure risks*
Collaboration is an integral part of the company's marketing and product strategy. It reduces the cost to Rolls-Royce of developing new engines as well as the attendant currency risks and offers new opportunities in additional market sectors.

A primary strategic aim has been to maintain the independence of the firm but also to achieve the benefits of collaboration with others. In this business, long term relationships with other engine manufacturers, suppliers of components, mainframe manufacturers and buyers are inevitable. Thus collaboration with many parties is a central strategic theme and takes many contractual and non-contractual forms. Collaboration is about sharing the risks of engine and aircraft supply and production, the technological and currency risks, and many other fundamental business risks. It is also about sharing the political risks arising from government funding of the development or purchasing of high technology products from their own domestic firms or from those overseas firms in collaboration with their domestic firms. A climate of business co-operation is created in which the partners recognize their need for each other and the need to share some risks. This allows the technological risk to be spread across many partners. It also ensures that some of the R&D costs are spread across several currencies. As a result, part of each partner's economic exposure to currency risk is shared with others. In this way the co-operative group gains some of the diversification advantages of the vertically integrated MNC (i.e. an aero engine manufacturer, an aircraft mainframe manufacturer, an airline, and a travel service group). One example of this for RR is its joint venture with BMW to develop the BR700 engine for medium range regional aeroplanes.

Another collaborative possibility is to swap foreign currency exposures as part of a large production and sales deal. Rolls-Royce will normally have long term US dollar economic exposures from existing and likely new sales. As a hypothetical example, we could see that Rolls-Royce could swap these dollars with a dollar hungry company such as British Airways. BA probably needs dollars for its many US dollar purchases, including planes and aero engines. Thus Rolls-Royce could do a swap with BA at a good rate to 'sweeten' an engine purchase deal. BA could then use the dollars to pay Boeing for the completed planes, and Boeing could then subsequently pay Rolls-Royce for their engines in the planes. In this way, existing dollar exposures could be moved forward into the future, new sales could be secured for all parties, and they all could share part of the currency and business risks involved.

*Integrating finance and other business functions to reduce currency risk*
The above example demonstrates that finance and marketing are intimately related in sales negotiation. Rolls-Royce seeks to establish a first class world-wide sales network by exploiting close relations with airframe manufacturers, financial institutions, governments and airlines, to boost engine sales and to secure follow-on spares and maintenance business. RR is skilled at constructing billion dollar packages to support engine sales. The negotiation skills of its sales teams with governments and with large airline purchasers are critical to this success. These organizational factors are important in ensuring that exchange rate considerations are taken fully into account when securing new engine orders.

The finance and treasury function can also be used to 'buy time' for strategic and operational changes to take effect and to manage the very significant net dollar transaction exposures remaining after all real responses to currency risk have been taken. The finance function, through its active trading capacity in currency markets and its ability to buy a wide range of forward and other currency hedges, provides a continuous insurance scheme against currency risk. RR treasury does not use this capacity to speculate. Thus firm engine orders generate known dollar transaction exposures and up to 80 per cent of the net dollar revenues are sold immediately. In the case of spares business the dollar cash flows are sold forward as they become well known or certain. Updated currency forecasts are provided to commercial negotiators. Currency options are also used to provide a stable future exchange rate umbrella during the negotiation process.

The finance function can offer many other means for firms such as Rolls-Royce to alter exposure to financial risks. For example, the long term funding of an asset with loans denominated in the same currency can reduce exposure, especially if the timing of the asset revenue and loan repayment cash flows is matched. If the asset cash flows change their currency or variability characteristics, the firm can swap out of the prior funding arrangement to a new currency and interest rate profile. Thus the emergence of sophisticated currency and interest rate swap markets adds a new dimension of flexibility to the long term financing decision and enhances the responsiveness of the firm to foreign exchange risk.

A major constraint on the use of long term funding for matching purposes is the overall capital structure of an MNC such as RR and the flexibility each subsidiary has in varying its local capital structure. For example, if national regulations insist on minimum equity levels and this has to be supplied wholly by the parent in its home currency, the role of local currency denominated debt and of currency matching will be diminished. Thus group financial policy and the constraints under which it operates can place a major limit on FERM policy.

## 5.2 Adapting and Modifying Operational Policies

Operational decisions are a further means by which a firm can alter exposure to risk and adjust its internal demand for foreign exchange risk management services (Aggarwal and Soenen 1989; Booth and Rotenberg 1990). Decisions on production levels, pricing, sourcing etc. can have a marked effect on the economic exposure position of the firm. They may also be flexible enough to help reduce the scale of economic exposure.

Marketing, production, sourcing and other real decisions may be made at a strategic or at an operational level. Operational decisions are distinguishable from strategic decisions by their shorter time horizon and generally lower degree of significance for the firm. In some cases, strategic marketing decisions on, say, market niche may enhance the operational flexibility of other marketing decisions such as pricing. It should also be noted that some decisions in areas such as product differentiation or the sourcing of semi-finished goods could be strategic in one firm and operational or tactical in another. Factors such as the degree of reversibility, overall shareholder value significance for the firm, and longevity of the effects of the decision can be used to distinguish strategic decisions from operational decisions. These two categories of decisions will hopefully overlap in a firm in terms of the periods in which they can be used to deal with currency risk.

Dufey (1983: 7) has outlined the three major questions to be asked when analysing the relationship between exchange risk and operational policies:

1   How much pricing flexibility does the firm have? That is, can the change in margins offset the effect of the exchange rate change?
2   How diversified are markets for inputs and outputs? Or, to add the time element, when can the firm shift markets for its outputs and sources of supply?
3   Are there any volume effects that could compensate for changes in profit margins?

Answers to these questions are required if the firm wishes to neutralize the influence of unanticipated real exchange rate changes on net home currency cash flows arising from overseas subsidiaries.

## Domestic importing and exporting companies

Figures 5.2 and 5.3 outline the positions of two UK companies which are importing from one country and exporting to another. In both cases production takes place in the UK and both domestic firms have extensive but different exposures to currency risk concerning their inputs and outputs. The first firm sources its inputs in France and the UK and sells its products in Germany and the UK. The second firm sources its inputs in the US and the UK and sells its products in Eire and the UK. We will initially consider the relationship between operational policies and FERM for these two domestic importing and exporting companies. The two firms will then be combined to form a single MNC and extended to include overseas operations.

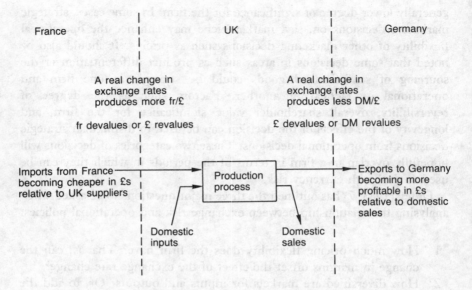

**Figure 5.2** Operations of first example UK firm

In all cases the firm faces changes in real exchange rates as opposed to a situation in which nominal exchange rate changes are fully offset by relative price changes. Thus PPP is not expected to hold and a substantial delay is expected in the adjustment of prices to exchange rates.

In figure 5.2 the firm is expected to experience favourable real exchange rate changes in both its input and its output prices. The fr/£ rate is expected to increase (franc depreciate) over a one to two year period, and the DM/£ rate to decline (Deutschmark appreciate) over this period. The fr/DM rate is therefore expected to depreciate at a faster rate than the fr/£ rate. If we assume that this is a recent real exchange rate change (or one probable in the immediate future) and the change is expected to remain in effect over say a one year period ahead, then we can analyse this situation by looking at the input (sourcing), output (pricing, promotion, product timing and volume decisions) and production decisions separately.

If the costs of imports denominated in francs remains constant then the sterling costs of inputs to the UK production process will fall. The firm can exploit this situation by replacing UK sources with increased French sources. Alternatively, it may be possible to exploit the greater price competition for domestic suppliers and secure a lower UK price. There may be a limit to this policy if long lasting and valuable supply relationships are disrupted by price being the only consideration in formulating the supply policy. The firm must therefore trade off the short term cost reduction benefits of the exchange rate change against the long term value benefits of the stable supply relationship. This is likely to be more important for the firm sourcing high value, complex, semi-finished goods, with long production times, from close industrial partners.

The appreciation of the mark relative to the pound means that exports to Germany will be worth more pounds at current mark prices. The UK firm can exploit its price advantage in a variety of ways. Firstly, it can charge the same price in pounds and therefore significantly drop the mark price. A large increase in demand is likely, unless competitors do the same or the product is price insensitive. The volume change may therefore produce the required increase in revenue. If the product is price insensitive then the firm may leave the mark price unchanged and receive the benefits of German revaluation in this way. We have seen in section 5.1 how a firm can invest in innovation, in product differentiation and in price insensitivity advantages. These strategic decisions will create the pricing flexibility for the firm to exploit such a real mark appreciation. The location of competitors is also crucial to such exploitation. If competitors are located in the UK then they may also be in a position to exploit cheap French sourcing and higher mark revenues. Such competition will quickly erode any advantage. The firm must also take care that the short term exploitation of this price advantage does not erode valuable long term advantages based on customer perception of product quality or on reliable product distributors or retailers.

The improved profitability position in the German market may also give the UK firm a promotional benefit. The sharing of higher margins with distributors in the German market may provide the firm with greater influence over them and thus give it a profit incentive to push its UK products in Germany much harder than its German domestic competitors can. A combined policy of price reduction and heavy advertising may produce a long term gain in German market share. Another component of marketing policy is the timing of new product introduction to the German market. A real change (mark appreciation) boosting sterling revenues on existing products may delay the introduction of a new version of the product. This may be held in reserve to allow for the flexibility to alter prices and boost sales if a German devaluation occurs and this leads to reduced German sales and/or reduced sterling revenues on existing products. Alternatively, if the firm is just beginning to enter the German market, the strong mark may allow the firm to sell its new products at a very competitive price in Germany. It seems unlikely that a firm could bear the costs of such new product introduction as well as reduced profits if the mark weakened and sterling revenues fell.

A German firm also faces a price disadvantage when exporting to the UK. Thus a UK firm facing German competition may be able to raise its UK prices to reflect the increased cost of German imports, or it can leave its prices unchanged so that the hoped-for volume increase produces an increase in domestic revenue. Again this is assuming price sensitive goods and no reaction by other domestic competitors.

In figure 5.2, the UK production volume decision would probably reflect lower input costs stemming from a higher proportion of cheaper French supplies, and higher sterling output prices and revenues stemming from German sales. Thus the UK firm could, if it had spare capacity, expand UK production levels to satisfy the likely increase in German and possibly UK sales, especially if there has been a price reduction for price sensitive goods.

In figure 5.3, the UK firm faces detrimental real exchange rate changes in its input and output prices. Thus it exports to Eire, where the punt (Irish pound) is expected to devalue relative to the pound sterling over the next one to two years. It also imports from the US where the dollar is expected to appreciate against the pound sterling over this period. Its imports, priced in dollars, are expected to cost more in pounds and so it should try to substitute imports from the US with UK (or even better

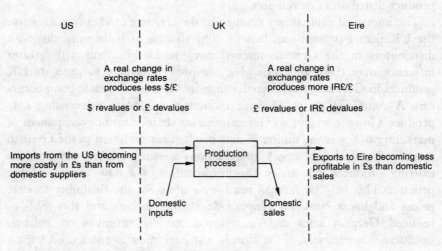

**Figure 5.3** Operations of second example UK firm

Irish) inputs. If it can do this then it may also be able to negotiate lower real prices from its US import sources. Exports to Eire priced in punts will be worth less in sterling unless the UK firm can increase its Irish prices. If competition is weak, both from domestic Irish companies and from other exporters, and demand for the product is relatively insensitive to price changes, this may be feasible. However, this seems unlikely except for luxury goods or high technology items with few close substitutes. In contrast, Irish firms may have a price advantage when exporting to the UK. This could lead to domestic price reductions for the UK firm. These problems may mean that the UK firm cannot compete because product sales revenue cannot be recouped through price rises and costs cannot be kept down by changing the source of inputs. This would lead the firm to question its UK production costs or even its UK location for production. Driving down UK costs through productivity gains may be the most immediate response possible. Relocation may be feasible in a country which has cheap source inputs both in the form of local labour and in replacements for US inputs to the production process.

## MNCs and operational responses to currency risk

If we combine these two UK domestic companies together we have a domestic company with a fairly complex importing and exporting pattern (figure 5.4). This firm has all of the currency exposure problems of the two independent firms and all of the supplier and product market choices. It can thus select the supply source with the greatest real reduction in sterling prices and switch sales and promotion efforts to the markets with the increase in real sterling prices. If we further assume that the joint company has subsidiaries with production facilities in France and Germany then we have formed a simple integrated MNC. This MNC still faces the same problems faced by the constituent companies outlined above. It thus has the full set of mark, dollar, punt, franc and pound exposures faced by the two combined domestic companies, but these may now have offsetting or currency risk diversification benefits compared with the three currency exposures of each of the domestic firms. In addition, the multinational production capacity will broaden the currency base of production costs and is likely to increase the range of international supplier relationships and cross-border selling possibilities for the MNC. The MNC may further add to its decision flexibility by being able to source some semi-finished products from within the group and this leads to internal trade in many currencies.

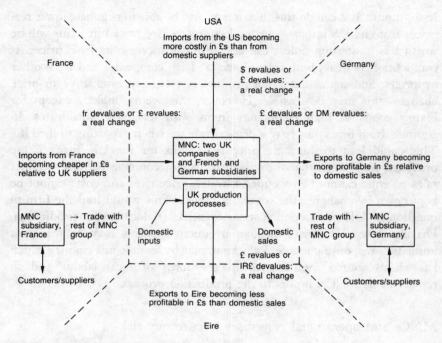

**Figure 5.4** Operations of combined firm

The MNC now faces sourcing, pricing, promotion, new product introduction and production decisions in many currencies. Its subsidiaries may face exchange rate circumstances and problems similar to the above domestic companies and may in part adopt similar strategies. Fortunately for the integrated MNC, it also has some advantages over domestic companies when exploiting flexibility of operational decisions. For example, it can exploit its many input and output currencies by seeking a balanced or offsetting currency mix of cash flows between the sales revenue side and the sourcing cost side. If the currencies adopted or required for purchasing source inputs can be balanced by a similar mix and scale of currencies for (the expected levels of) sales revenue, then changes in the costs of inputs (due to unexpected real exchange rate changes) will be offset by compensating changes in sales revenues.

In practice, few MNCs are likely to have complete control over the choice of currencies used to pay for inputs, or over the choice of currencies preferred by customers paying for finished goods or services. Few firms can, in the short term, radically reduce domestic production costs at the same capacity level or change the locations of their production processes, their raw material supply policies, and the national location of their markets without incurring major costs and therefore unfavourable impacts on cash flows and shareholder values. A firm will choose this relatively inflexible exposed position precisely because it believes it can profitably exploit real product and factor market imperfections.

As a result, the major responsibility for coping with these economic exposure problems within an MNC will fall upon production and marketing managers and not upon financial managers. Non-financial managers will have specialized knowledge of the imperfect product and factor markets in which the firm operates and this may allow the firm to minimize exchange rate risk by exploiting flexibility in many of the operational decision areas discussed above. The strategic changes discussed in section 5.1 provide the key degrees of freedom and flexibility when the time comes to alter operational decisions. For example, an MNC might diversify across countries with its sales, its production facilities and the location of its raw material resources. It might also invest in R&D, production flexibility, and a strong capability to rapidly differentiate its products and their price sensitivity.

Strategic decisions therefore take priority, with operational decisions providing an important support capability when responding to currency risk. Any remaining lack of currency flexibility in the real business of the firm can be compensated for by imaginative manipulation of the internal financial system, the currency mix for financing and various risk management products supplied by financial markets.

Treasury has an important role in adapting strategic and operational decisions to currency risk. Its information provision and liaison role, outlined in chapter 1, is central to such an adaptive response to currency risk. Thus treasury will provide the all important spot rate forecasts and assess the financial implications of exchange rate changes for senior managers of the group, subsidiaries and operating units.

## 5.3 Choosing a Corporate Portfolio of FERM Methods

In sections 5.1 and 5.2 we have seen how firms can alter their strategic and operational decisions in response to currency risk. Strategy as the key determinant of both wealth and economic exposure was assumed to be the priority response point compared with adaptations to operational decisions. In this section, we extend these concepts of priority to the whole range of FERM methods involving both real and financial responses to currency risk and explore how firms can choose between these FERM methods. The emphasis here is on the shareholder wealth impact of the methods chosen, on the periods of effective and feasible use of real and financial methods, on corporate specific and industry factors influencing the choice of FERM methods, and on various constraints faced by the firm when employing specific methods.

This section therefore identifies the factors influencing and constraining the corporate choice of strategic, operational and financial FERM methods. Within these influences and constraints firms still have considerable room for manoeuvre. The ultimate measure of these choices and the effectiveness of the portfolio of strategic, operational and financial FERM methods is their contribution to shareholder wealth. This can arise through boosts to value by extensive managerial efforts devoted to the currency risk protection of strategic investment decisions. This may also be due to reduced value penalties derived from increased stability of home country cash flows or from increased levels of expected cash flows.

The following five steps illustrate a simple decision sequence in which modifications to strategy, long term financial policy, operational decisions and internal/external financial techniques are employed together to deal with foreign exchange risk management problems:

1   Currency risk arises from unanticipated events in the firm's financial and real business environment. This is primarily manifest through recent real changes or potential real changes in exchange rates. The firm may react to such events as they occur or the treasury function may act as a continuous scanning mechanism to identify potential real changes.

2   This risk is interpreted through the firm's FERM goals and policy and leads to a set of corporate responses. The decision making unit here may be a currency committee with a brief to consider the impact of currency risk on all aspects of the firm's operations and to recommend a comprehensive response.

3   The firm makes alterations to strategy and operational policy as a priority response and then uses internal and external financial techniques to deal with the remaining elements of its currency risk management problem.

4   The firm is constrained in taking these decisions by a unique set of corporate and environmentally determined constraints which limit its choice to a subset of the wider set of FERM methods. The constraints include unique corporate or industry characteristics which restrict the

choice of methods and limit the periods of feasibility and usefulness of real and financial methods.

5   The overall value impact of all major FERM methods is the ultimate guiding criterion for choice. Each FERM method will have a different impact on corporate value, but it is the overall impact of all methods chosen that must be used to assess the effectiveness of the FERM methods mix.

The decision sequence assumes that problems of managing foreign exchange exposures and risk permeate all aspects of a firm's operations (Dufey and Srinivasulu 1983). As such the response to these foreign exchange management problems involves all major classes of decisions facing the firm.

The priority in FERM decision making outlined above requires that managers incorporate existing forecasts of exchange rate changes, of changes in exposure and of demands for financial services into the development of strategy and into operational decision making. Alterations can therefore be made to strategy and operational policy to reflect these expected changes. The adaptations to real decisions should be made in such a way as to ensure that strategy and operational policy are not 'hostages to (foreign exchange rate) fortune'. Thus some thought should be given at the planning stage to increasing the responsiveness of strategic and operational decisions to unknown changes in exchange rate.

The real responses are followed by a set of financial responses to currency risk. The (normally shorter term) transaction risk associated with known or easier to predict foreign currency cash flows can be seen as the unavoidable currency risk problem remaining after adaptations to real decisions. Financial responses therefore serve the joint purpose of dealing with residual or unavoidable currency risk problems that cannot be dealt with using real responses and of creating time for real responses to take effect.

The priority between real and financial FERM methods can be bypassed by the flexibility of some methods. Firms very active in mergers and acquisitions find it relatively easy to make rapid strategic decisions which dramatically alter economic exposures. In addition, the availability of long term currency swaps in major currencies means that external financial techniques can be used in certain circumstances to alter long term asset or liability foreign currency exposures.

The aim in employing this range of FERM methods is to protect real decisions as the basic source of wealth or to adjust them to enhance this wealth. The financial policy aim is to protect or increase the expected cash flows resulting from real decisions or to stabilize or decrease the variability of these cash flows (or both). In a currency risk context this can be interpreted as aiming to reduce the impact of unanticipated (real) exchange rate changes on the firm's expected home currency cash flows. The more stable these home currency cash flows and the higher their expected value then the more valuable they become.

Table 5.1 illustrates how the shareholder wealth question can be posed for the real and financial responses to currency risk. The value impact of each of these selected FERM methods will depend on the economic circumstances surrounding the firm. For example the scale of tax imperfections and a firm's tax paying position will affect the mixture of forward versus money market hedges according to the individual ability of each of these financial FERM methods to exploit the imperfection. As a result, we can expect to see considerable variety amongst firms in terms of the choice of methods.

In practice the firm must simultaneously employ a set of these real and financial responses to currency risk in the same period. It must therefore develop a clear policy on its preferred set of FERM methods and the relationships between the major classes of real and financial methods. The problem can be seen as one of constrained optimization in which the firm has to choose the set of FERM methods that maximize shareholder wealth (reduce penalty costs of not managing) subject to a set of firm specific constraints.

Thus a firm can inspect the whole set of FERM methods theoretically available to it. It can then reduce the list by applying obvious constraints. The later section on constraints indicates that these can dramatically limit the number of options facing a firm. However, even here the remaining set of potential FERM methods can still form many feasible combinations.

At this point the firm should choose the combination that makes the maximum contribution to shareholder wealth. Thus the firm must assess the collective impact of the methods on the value of the MNC group and at subsidiary or plant level. In these cases the questions are:

- What is the incremental impact of the use of the chosen set of FERM methods on the scale of the home currency cash flows of the MNC group or subsidiary?
- What is the impact of the use of the chosen set of FERM methods on the riskiness of the home currency cash flows of the MNC group or subsidiary?

**Table 5.1** Shareholders wealth or value questions in relation to FERM decisions

| | Real and financial responses to currency risk | | |
|---|---|---|---|
| Strategic | Operational | Internal | External |
| Is basic value protected or enhanced by relocation, R&D, new product and market niche decisions to reduce impact of currency risk? | Are pricing, sourcing, production changes for currency risk etc. a short term source of profit? At the expense of long term source of value from strategic decisions? | Does use of the internal system reduce transacting costs relative to external markets? Does use of this system reduce currency risk, variability of HC cash flows and risk of default at the expense of reduced shareholder value? | What is the least cost market method of providing the same required insurance or hedging scheme? Forward versus future versus money markets? To what extent do these methods reduce currency risk and thus the costs of financial distress and the associated penalty to shareholder wealth? Can treasury exploit major imperfections to make profit and add value? |
| Compare NPV of new or existing projects before and after managing currency risk through real changes Has the penalty loss of not managing risk been reduced? | | Does investment outlay on treasury and internal financial systems produce returns or added value that are otherwise unavailable to the firm? | |

The group, subsidiary or plant can each be seen as an ongoing investment project and the above information can be used to compare the net present value of the project before and after the use of the set of FERM methods. Thus the firm wishes to know if the NPV penalty loss of not managing currency risk has been reduced. In other words, have the costs of attempting to reduce the impact of unanticipated exchange rate changes been exceeded by the benefits? The costs here are the cost of managerial time, the transaction costs of using money market hedges etc. This use of the NPV rule and the capital budgeting decision to investigate FERM and economic exposure will be explored further in chapter 10 where an extensive capital budgeting case study is outlined.

The idea of the costs of managing FERM can be further extended by considering the costs of setting up and maintaining treasury functions to deal with currency risk. The question to be answered here is: does the investment outlay on treasury functions and internal financial systems produce returns or added value that are otherwise unavailable to the firm? Thus the firm must assess the impact of new treasury functions on the incremental cash flows of the firm and on their riskiness. In chapter 1, we have seen that FERM functions in the MNC treasury have expanded rapidly over the 1970s and 1980s. This indicates that many MNCs have found investment in treasury of considerable value in dealing with currency risk and in reducing the losses faced by shareholders due to ignorance or lack of managerial capability.

## Case study: ICI

ICI provides some insight into the kind of choices one large MNC makes in terms of its set of FERM methods.

The ICI group treasury considers itself exposed on a transaction basis to all future currency cash flows up to the time where each business unit is capable of responding to exchange rate changes via pricing adjustments. Richard Savage (1990), the Corporate Treasurer, comments:

> The time horizon on our managed exposures is capped at one year and this therefore represents the borderline where the mantle of economic risk is passed from the central treasury to the business unit. This cap also probably represents the limit of our ability to forecast currency cash flows with any degree of accuracy.

ICI group treasury therefore deals with known transaction exposures up to one year ahead. For periods beyond one year, Savage indicates that the business units must take strategic and operational decisions now to deal with serious currency risk problems that might arise in the years ahead. He thus indicates that a horizon or boundary is identified within ICI to distinguish the periods of effectiveness of real and financial decisions and to match a significant part of the FERM decision to the origin of the exposure. Treasury can transcend this when the opportunity arises but it will not create exposures to currency risk that do not naturally arise in the business.

Savage also points out that ICI's financial hedging levels for transaction exposures are controlled and guided by a periodic strategic overview. This hedging policy is further modified by tactical positions as market conditions dictate. Thus strategy dominates the use of external financial instruments, and conditions in the foreign exchange market further influence the use of market based risk management instruments. ICI also has a sophisticated internal system in which netting and asset/liability management are major internal FERM techniques.

## Corporate or industry factors constraining the choice of FERM methods

The ability of a firm to use various real and financial responses to currency risk can be dependent on corporate specific or industry factors. Firms with long term contracts or stable product demand are able to predict foreign currency cash flows with some accuracy over long horizons. For example, Rolls-Royce has long term aero engine sales and maintenance contracts and Jaguar has long term US car sales. In both cases, the firms can sell dollars forward for periods of one to two years ahead.

The time taken for operational or strategic decisions to adjust and respond to currency uncertainty also varies across firms. Firms with long R&D and production cycles, or committed to large projects or restricted to certain production locations, have major problems in making short to medium term adjustments to real decision variables. These adjustments can be achieved, but the inflexibility of real decisions means that a firm will have to make extensive use of external and internal financial techniques until the real responses begin to take effect.

Thus each firm faces its own unique set of constraints when choosing specific FERM methods. Table 5.2 provides some more examples of the constraining factors for each major class of FERM method. The constraints

**Table 5.2 Constraints in relation to FERM decisions**

| Strategic | Operational | Internal | External |
|---|---|---|---|
| Constraints on location of production | High price competition | No internal financial transfer system | Poor access to capital and foreign exchange markets |
| R&D at HQ to protect know-how | Limited sourcing possibilities | Autonomous decentralized subsidiary treasuries | |
| Slow changing product range | Price sensitive goods | | |
| Home limits on group capital structure | Close supplier and distributor relationships | | |
| Low flexibility of strategic and operational decisions | | Limited treasury capacity to search, deal etc. internally and externally | |
| Small change has high negative impact on shareholder value | | | |

on employing strategic and operational methods will be explored through the case study in the next section. Constraints on using internal and external financial techniques will be discussed in more detail in chapters 6 and 7.

The unique nature of a firm's economic exposure also depends on the nature of competition in its industry. Firms in highly competitive industries may have to focus on price adjustments caused by advantageous real changes experienced by their competitors. In contrast, firms operating in industries dominated by a few large companies may have to deal with competitive variables such as the role of R&D expenditure in product differentiation and in responding to currency risk. Firms in industries with long product development times may find that real decisions can have long lead times and this can mean little flexibility in adapting these to deal with currency risk.

Factors such as regulation can also modify the character of economic exposure in some industries. For example, Lewent and Kearney (1990), treasurers at Merck, the US pharmaceutical MNC, argue that in a competitive global pharmaceutical industry the use of pricing to alter economic exposure is not significant. Price controls are common in their industry throughout the world and this generally reduces price flexibility to manipulate or react to economic exposure.

These corporate specific and industry factors and constraints play a key role in the variety of FERM practices observed, and indicate why the overall balance struck between strategic, operational, internal and external techniques is often quite specific to a firm and its unique circumstances. In chapters 6 and 7 we will investigate the variety of internal and external FERM methods. These methods and real responses offer firms a wide variety of FERM choices. The availability of this wide range of FERM tools, ranging from strategic through operational decisions to the use of internal and external financial techniques, can enhance responsiveness to currency risk by dramatically increasing choices open to the firm. It can also create a time overlap between available methods and offer unique solutions to unique problems. In some cases market based methods may create time or flexibility for strategic and operational responses to take effect. In contrast, strategic methods such as currency risk sharing amongst project partners may be the means to counteract lack of availability or flexibility of financial risk instruments. Strategic decisions may also create the conditions for operational flexibility. Finally, the sophistication of internal financial transfer systems can have a strong impact on the need for external financial risk instruments. We can therefore see that the beneficial interactions possible within the whole portfolio of methods may be of considerable value to an enterprise and can greatly enhance corporate flexibility relative to currency risk. These benefits are only available if the firm can employ a large proportion of the full set of FERM methods open to it.

## Case study: Jaguar: constraints facing a firm adapting strategic and operational decisions for currency risk

The Jaguar car company (in the period before its November 1989 takeover by Ford) provides a good example of constraints on the use of strategic decisions to alter exposures. An important indirect exposure for Jaguar arose from the Deutschmark base of the German competition in the USA, particularly as one of these producers (Mercedes-Benz) was the price setter for the USA market (Scott 1987). This alerted Jaguar top management to the strategic impact of exchange rate changes on production cost structures in the UK. This was the major area where Jaguar felt it could compete against the German quality car manufacturers and decrease its costs. Jaguar could have relocated part of its production in the US. However, in practice one of the main selling points of Jaguar cars is their British craftsmanship. In addition, Britain is a much lower cost country to produce in than the USA. The group had considered alternative markets in an attempt to reduce its dependence on the US market. This market however is still of primary importance for the company as the USA is the world's top market for luxury cars.

In the constrained circumstances faced by a company like Jaguar, extensive use of financial risk management instruments may be the only means to deal with currency risk. This can create the time for the firm to make the required orderly realignment of its strategic and operational exposures. Adjustments to strategy and operational variables are the long term priority and are dominant, but are actually achieved via the initial and continuing purchase of short term insurance in financial markets.

Altering operational decision variables to modify exposure to currency risk has its limits. Jaguar could have sourced its components from outside the UK in those foreign currencies in which it had a long exposure, and to a certain extent this happened, particularly with mark based components. However, it was a group policy that components were sourced near to the Jaguar factories in the UK (Scott 1987). This allowed speedy replenishment of inventory levels and closer controls over quality. Foreign sourced components were only bought if they had superior quality and, hopefully, lower cost than UK sourced components. Raising prices was another solution, but there is a limit to how much prices can be increased without losing market share.

In practice many multinational firms choose relatively inflexible operational or financial positions precisely because they believe they can profitably exploit real product and factor market imperfections. As a result the major responsibility for coping with these currency exposure problems within an MNC will fall upon production and marketing managers with their specialized knowledge of the firm's imperfect product and factor markets.

## 5.4 Summary

In this chapter we have seen that strategic and operational decisions create the corporate exposures to currency risk. Modifying these decisions first is the most direct way of tackling the currency risk management problems. Attempting to deal with the problem in this way ensures that strategic and operational decision makers have a proactive stance to currency risk and are able to concentrate on its impact on the central wealth producing decisions of the firm.

Dealing with FERM problems at these decision points also means that the firm focuses on its overall economic exposures. All major exposures can be considered and any 'natural' offsetting possibilities can be identified. This prevents a narrow financial perspective dominating FERM.

A high degree of flexibility in strategic and operational decisions is essential for FERM. As indicated above, this flexibility often depends on corporate or industry specific factors and manifests itself as unique corporate advantages. The widely diversified MNC is likely to have major advantages here, especially when its marketing and production managers can exploit their specialized knowledge of the firm's imperfect product and factor markets to support currency risk management. Finally, the chapter considered how a firm could choose between a wide variety of real and financial FERM methods.

# 6

# FERM and Internal Financial Techniques

In chapters 4 and 5 we have seen that the firm has many financial and real means to respond to problems of currency risk. In this chapter, internal financial methods for FERM are discussed. Internal financial techniques include methods such as netting, matching, currency of invoicing, asset and liability management (Prindl 1976; McRae and Walker 1980). Internal techniques are distinguishable from external financial techniques (chapter 7) by their use of a variety of internal corporate means to alter financial exposures to currency risk. External financial techniques normally embody the purchase, in foreign exchange and credit markets, of contracts designed to insure the firm against risk. Both types of FERM method are primarily used to alter the company's exposure to currency risk but they may also be used to create profit opportunities by allowing the firm to make informed bets against exchange rate movements.

The firm's capability to employ many of these internal techniques depends on the existence of a sophisticated internal financial system in the MNC. The nature of this system is the topic for section 6.1. Section 6.2 considers the combined use of a set of internal (and some external) techniques in FERM. Section 6.3 is concerned with the individual use of the internal financial techniques in currency risk management, and section 6.4 describes one of these techniques in more detail by means of an example. Section 6.5 summarizes the discussion.

## 6.1 The Internal Financial System of an MNC: Financial and Real Flows

Many large multinational corporations have developed a considerable internal financial system as part of their group treasury capabilities. These systems have arisen because MNCs have extensive internal cross-currency and cross-border trade and associated financial flows. This has in many cases stimulated the development of a sophisticated internal financial transfer and transacting system. As a result, the MNC has a considerable capacity to transfer funds and profits through a myriad of internal channels and to use this system to manage a variety of financial risks including currency risk.

This system can be vital to a currency risk management policy as well as providing essential support to funding, liquidity management, and tax arbitrage decisions. The internal financial system can be used to help management maximize global after-tax profits received from a wide range of subsidiaries, as well as playing a central role in all of the above decisions areas. Its general role will be described in this section and its more specific FERM role will be outlined in sections 6.2 and 6.3. Its role in financing decisions will be considered in this chapter.

Rutenberg (1970), Robbins and Stobaugh (1973) and Lessard (1979) have all made important contributions in describing the MNC's internal financial system (MIFS). Figure 6.1 has been adapted from Lessard (p. 103) and illustrates the nature of the internal links of the MIFS. The real flows include goods, technology and materials, and the financial flows include dividends, interest and capital repayments, loans, equity investment, and credit on goods and services. Certain financial flows such as equity investment and dividends are unlikely to occur between subsidiaries. Real flows can give rise to much of the internal financial

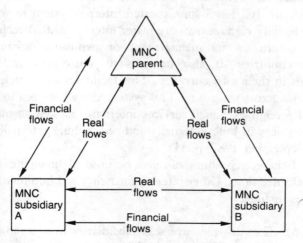

**Figure 6.1** Internal financial system of an MNC (adapted from Lessard 1979)

transfers. As a result the greater the internal real flows, the greater the capacity of the MNC to control internal financial transfers, and the greater the complexity of the MIFS. These linkages do exist between independent firms, but the MNC exercises considerable internal control over the choice of channels through which financial transfers are made, and in the timing of transactions within the MIFS (Lessard 1979: 103).

In the case of the currency risk management decision the channel choice and timing possibilities find expression in a range of internal currency risk management techniques. The following techniques can be used to substantially alter the overall exposed position of a firm and the liquidity position of each subsidiary:

1  Speeding up (leading) and delaying (lagging) the payments of accounts between subsidiaries. Modifying the credit terms between subsidiaries can substantially alter their exposed position and that of the MNC group as a whole.
2  Lending and borrowing between subsidiaries can have a similar effect.
3  The choice of invoicing currency between operating units can also be invaluable in altering exposure to currency risk.
4  Payments and receipts within the MNC can be netted off to reduce exposure and transaction costs in currency markets.

The company can also conduct its own internal financial engineering by exploiting internal suppliers and designing and producing its own spot deals, forward rate contracts, options and swaps for internal needs.

For example, ICI has a sophisticated internal system in which netting and asset/liability management are major internal FERM techniques. The company centralizes its management of exposures arising in major exporting countries. It also invoices its customers and purchasing subsidiaries in their own currency. This facilitates the matching of assets and liabilities across the group. This system also allows ICI to source some funds and foreign exchange services internally as well as purchase such financial services in bulk externally and redistribute internally (*Corporate Finance*, September 1987, p. 11).

Many of these techniques can also be used in financing and liquidity management decisions. Other internal financing and liquidity management possibilities include:

1  The MNC can finance overseas subsidiaries from a range of internal corporate funds. These can be labelled debt or equity according to

whether the type of funds have specific advantages or disadvantages in certain countries. These could include tax advantages of debt over equity, or a greater (or lesser) ability to repatriate debt funds. The internal system can also be used to circumvent difficult problems such as funds blocked by domestic legislation.

2 The dividend paid to the parent company can be adjusted according to the subsidiary's financing requirements.

3 Transfer prices on shipments between subsidiaries can be adjusted and the new prices used as a means of financing for a subsidiary.

4 Managerial and legal fees and royalties charged between subsidiaries can be varied according to their short term liquidity and financing requirements.

All of these channels can also be used by the parent to influence the transaction, translation or operating currency exposures of subsidiaries. This demonstrates the wide capability of the MIFS and the extra degrees of freedom it can bestow upon an MNC dealing with exposure, financing and liquidity decisions. The development of such a group treasury capability creates the information system and the managerial means to tackle exposure, financing and liquidity management decisions.

## The internal financial system as an interface with external financial markets and with customers and suppliers

The internal financial system of the MNC also serves as an important link with a wide range of external markets for funds, risk management services and payments services as well as with customers and suppliers.

In figure 6.2 we expand figure 6.1 to include both internal and external (market) cross-border financial transactions open to an MNC. In the figure we illustrate this for a British MNC with a French and a German subsidiary. Four major types of financial flow or transaction are described:

1 Internal financial flows within the MNC (as in figure 6.1): dividends, loans, fees, licences, transfer prices etc.

2 Financial transactions in offshore markets: Eurobonds, Euroloans, currency/interest risk management instruments, international payments and money transmission etc. These are normally with or through banks, but they can be with other MNCs or with governments.

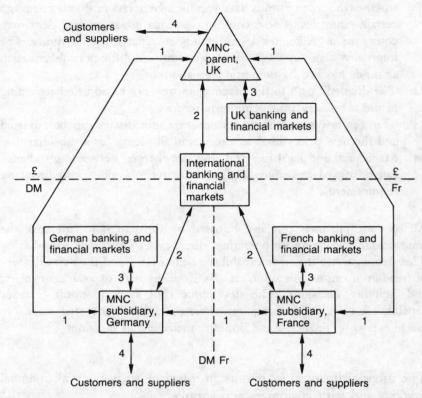

**Figure 6.2** Cross-border financial transactions for an MNC: internal and external

3   Financial transactions in domestic capital and banking markets: equity
    funds, dividends, bonds, loans, repayments etc.
4   Payments to suppliers and receipts from customers: both cash and
    credit terms.

Given these possibilities this firm has four major choices in implementing
an active opportunistic currency risk management and funding strategy.
Firstly, it can transfer funds internally between parent and subsidiary, and
between subsidiary and subsidiary. Secondly, all of its units can transact in
the offshore or Eurocurrency markets. These transactions can be money
market or forward market hedges, or a whole range of variations on these
themes. Thirdly, all units can transact in their locally based capital and
foreign exchange markets. This might involve local borrowing/lending or
currency purchases/sales. In addition, each unit may have access to

overseas domestic markets via another unit's domestic borrowing arrangements. The funds borrowed by one unit in its domestic market then become an internal transfer. As a result the MNC can become a fully fledged financial intermediary, arbitraging between domestic markets and between offshore markets and domestic markets. However, not all of these facilities are continuously available. Their availability depends upon factors such as the level of governmental controls over market access and limitations on internal transfers within MNCs. One exception to this rule is the Eurocurrency market which exists outside the control of any sovereign government. Finally, it should be noted that payments to suppliers and receipts from customers will be important sources of domestic and foreign currency, and adjustment of payment terms will play a significant part in FERM. In financial flows 2, 3 and 4 the domestic and international banking system is likely to play a central role in supporting the MNC's internal financial system. Thus the banking markets for credit, bank underwriting services, and bank money transmission and payments systems can provide financial inputs to the MNC at its various locations and can also provide the means by which many of the financial transfers can take effect within the MNC and with its customers and suppliers.

These possibilities demonstrate the significance of the internal financial system as an important part of the firm's interface with external financial markets as well as with customers and suppliers. They also indicate the importance of stable global and domestic relationships between an MNC and its core group of bankers. The combination of many internal decision variables and external accessibility, greatly increases the degrees of decision freedom open to the MNC group treasurer and the significance of close co-ordination by group treasury as a means to deal with environmental (financial price risk and supply risk) uncertainty.

## The internal financial system and market imperfections

We can gain further insight into the nature and function of the MNC's internal financial system by considering a series of potential imperfections in international financial markets.

We have seen in chapter 3 the possibility of an extensive series of market imperfections. These may seriously restrict access to market opportunities and may raise the cost of transacting in markets to such a level that internal transacting via the internal financial system of the firm is preferred. The major imperfections that create barriers to transacting across and within national and offshore markets include the following (Lessard 1979: 107):

- government restrictions on foreign exchange markets and corporate foreign exchange transactions, on funds flows in and out of a country, on domestic interest rate levels, and on allocations in domestic credit markets
- imperfections in domestic and offshore markets, such as thin markets creating low market liquidity, and structural imperfections (Samuels 1981) (see chapters 3 and 11) creating poor publicly available information sets and low informational efficiencies in markets.

These imperfections may contribute to the creation of obstacles to trade in markets for some financial services. For example, sellers of foreign exchange may not be able to establish contact with potential purchasers. Parties to a trade will therefore have to incur search transaction costs to overcome these obstacles to trade (Coase 1937; Casson 1982: 26). Table 6.1 summarizes potential obstacles to trade, and the costs required to transact in markets for foreign exchange and credit. Transaction costs are further classified using Dahlman's (1979) phases of the exchange process, i.e. the

**Table 6.1** Obstacles to trade and transaction costs in financial services markets

| Obstacles to trade in market for financial services | Specific transaction cost incurred in market | Transaction cost class |
|---|---|---|
| Limited or poor contact between buyers and sellers of foreign exchange or credit | Contract making via search or advertisement | Search phase costs |
| No knowledge of reciprocal wants with respect to credit or foreign exchange | Specification of the trade and communication of the details to each party | Bargaining and contracting phase costs |
| No agreement over price | Negotiation | |
| Need to exchange custody of credit or foreign exchange | Transfer of funds or foreign exchange | |
| No confidence that foreign exchange or credit corresponds to specification (e.g. payment date) | Monitoring of the quality and/or quantity | Policing and enforcement costs |

*Sources*: adapted from Casson 1982: 26; Dahlman 1979

research, bargaining (control), and policing and monitoring phases. High transaction costs such as these are unlikely in the credit and foreign exchange markets located in OECD countries. Imperfections such as these are particularly evident in Russia and other countries in the former Soviet Union as they struggle to create currency convertibility and effective consumer and corporate banking systems.

These imperfections and associated obstacles to trade in capital and foreign exchange markets are also likely to be relatively common for the wide ranging MNC operating in less developed countries (LDCs). As the breadth and complexity of these imperfections increase, then so also do the external transaction costs of the MNC. As a result, such an MNC is likely to have a strong incentive as well as a capacity to internalize parts of its foreign exchange and capital markets and therefore to set up an MIFS.

Other key factors and restrictions which create major incentives for the creation of an MIFS include differences in national tax systems, and the need to shift profits internally where profits are subject to governmental regulation.

Once established, the MIFS provides a unique means to exploit imperfections in global financial markets and from cross-border national regulatory differences. Lessard (1979: 107) identifies three types of gain to be made by MNCs through the use of their MIFS to circumvent barriers to transactions. These are financial market arbitrage, tax system arbitrage, and regulatory system arbitrage. The latter two forms of arbitrage are very important uses of the MIFS. The key activity for financing and FERM decisions is clearly financial market arbitrage. If major imperfections exist in external markets then MNCs can exploit the boundary between their internal system and external markets. Thus sophisticated internal transfer of funds can be of major importance when governments intervene in foreign exchange or domestic capital markets. Where exchange rates are not freely floating, and there are restrictions on foreign exchange movements, and where the MNC can, through its MIFS channels, speed up or delay payment in various currencies, there will be opportunities for gain on the part of the MNC. Other examples include the use of the MIFS to avoid domestic controls over the availability of local funds or the transfer of subsidiary dividends. The MNC with its multiple national locations should be able to borrow funds in unrestricted markets and transfer them to countries where its subsidiaries face capital market controls. In the case of restricted dividends it may be able to use debt repayment as a more acceptable way of repatriating its capital from subsidiaries.

Lessard (1979) highlights the significance of these internal financial systems of MNCs by pointing out that such a system is largely irrelevant in a domestic multidivisional firm. He puts forward two reasons for the irrelevance of the domestic internal financial system (DIFS). Firstly, domestic capital markets in countries such as the US are efficient. It is extremely difficult to achieve positive NPVs by trying to manipulate these capital markets, and transaction costs for transfers by way of these markets will not exceed the costs of the equivalent internal transfers of funds. In this situation, the DIFS offers no advantages over external markets and the parent and subsidiaries will be best served by raising capital externally rather than through any internal transfer of surplus funds. Secondly, a single corporate tax rate is generally applied to the domestic parent and its (domestic) subsidiaries. There is therefore little to be gained with respect to the overall tax bill by adjusting profits (and losses) between units of the firm. We can add to this argument the self-evident point that wholly domestic firms do not have multicurrency problems, and as such the DIFS is irrelevant with respect to transaction, translation and economic exposure issues.

## 6.2 The Combined Use of Internal and External Financial Techniques and an Active Opportunistic Policy for FERM

In this section, we consider the empirical evidence for the combined use of a large set of internal and external financial techniques in dealing with currency risk. An internal financial system and an external market transacting capability are necessary requirements for such a combined use of many internal and external techniques. Detailed descriptions of these individual techniques will be covered in the next section (internal methods) and the next chapter (external methods).

Specifically, the use of an active opportunistic strategy for internal and external financial techniques is considered in some detail and the results of a major empirical research project are briefly discussed.

If managers assume that deviations are occurring in UBFR, IRP etc. then Rodriguez (1981: 431) comments that it would be rational for managers to take the following actions:

1   holding assets in appreciating currencies rather than in depreciating currencies

2   increasing holdings of assets in appreciating currencies while decreasing debts in those currencies, and the reverse for depreciating currencies.

In the case of an appreciating currency subsidiary, Rodriguez would expect the parent managerial actions to result in the following flows:

1   increase in the holdings of cash and marketable securities, accounts receivable, and inventory; purchases of forward foreign exchange contracts
2   decrease in short term debt, accounts payable, and long term debt; sales of forward exchange contracts
3   movement towards a more positive or less negative net asset exposure position in the appreciating currency.

In the case of depreciating currencies, parent managerial actions and therefore flows in the asset and liability accounts would be the reverse of the above.

Tables 6.2 and 6.3 demonstrate what this active opportunistic strategy would mean for our British MNC example. In this case the firm can observe spot and three month forward rates for francs, pounds and marks. They indicate that there may be pressure in the exchange rate mechanism (ERM) for realignment with the mark being strengthened relative to the pound and the franc. The franc is likely to be depreciated more than the pound relative to the mark. The firm believes that realignment is imminent and this will lead to greater real exchange rate changes than those indicated by the forward rates. It therefore decides to alter its short to medium term exposures in these currencies. Such actions within MNCs' internal financial systems were likely to have been a key source of speculative pressure against the ERM during 1992 and 1993.

Rodriguez (1981) tested to see if managers of large US MNCs employed these and similar strategies and tactics when deviations from parity conditions were expected. She chose five crisis periods in the foreign exchange markets between June 1971 and June 1973 as being situations in which major parity deviations were thought to have occurred, and found the following (p. 434):

1   The companies in every crisis period were accumulating liquid (cash) holdings of strong currencies at a faster rate than holdings of weak currencies.

**Table 6.2** Active opportunistic strategy for subsidiary in appreciating currency country: German subsidiary of UK company

---

*Market conditions*
Spot rate is 2.45DM/£; three month forward rate is 2.44DM/£. Thus market expects more pounds to the mark in three months, or market expects fewer marks to the pound in three months. But firm expects larger real appreciation of the mark relative to the pound than that reflected in forward rate.

*Strategy*

| | |
|---|---|
| Increase LC assets (DM) | Decrease LC liabilities |
| Decrease FC assets (e.g. £, fr) | Increase FC liabilities |

*Tactics: external*

| | |
|---|---|
| Buy LC forward (M) | Reduce LC borrowings (M) |
| Increase LC cash and marketable securities (M) | Accelerate payment of LC accounts payable (CS) |
| Loosen LC credit terms | Reduce imports of goods paid for in LC (CS) |
| Tighten credit given in depreciating FC (CS) | Invoice imports in FC (CS) |
| Invoice exports in LC (to depreciating FC countries) (CS) | |

*Tactics: internal*

| | |
|---|---|
| Delay dividends and fees to parent | Delay payments to other (foreign) subsidiaries (lag) |
| Accelerate collection of receivables from other subsidiaries (in depreciating currency) (lead) | |

---

LC, local currency; FC, foreign currency
M, financial and forex market actions; CS, customer and supplier actions

2  They maintained long positions in forward contracts in strong currencies to a much larger degree than in weak currencies.
3  In the other current asset accounts studied, accounts receivable and inventory, the opposite behaviour appeared. The levels of weak currencies in these accounts were significantly higher than the levels of strong currencies (p. 435). Rodriguez suggested that this was due to the inflexibility of the business operations of the firms.
4  On the liability side, three accounts were studied: accounts payable, short term debt and long term debt. In all of these, there was a tendency for the average level of weak currencies to be higher than the average level of strong currencies. However, in some periods these

**Table 6.3** Active opportunistic strategy for subsidiary in depreciating currency country: French subsidiary of UK company

*Market conditions*
Spot rate is 8.3fr/£; three month forward rate is 8.6fr/£. Thus market expects more francs to the pound in three months, or market expects fewer pounds to the franc in three months. But firm expects greater real appreciation of the pound relative to the franc than that reflected in forward rate.

*Strategy*

| | |
|---|---|
| Decrease LC assets (fr) | Increase LC liabilities |
| Increase FC assets (e.g. £, DM) | Decrease FC liabilities |

*Tactics: external*

| | |
|---|---|
| Sell LC forward (M) | Increase LC borrowings (M) |
| Reduce LC cash and marketable securities (M) | Delay accounts payable in LC (CS) |
| Tighten credit in appreciating FC (CS) | Invoice imports in depreciating LC (CS) |
| Loosen credit in depreciating FC (CS) | |
| Invoice exports in appreciating FC (CS) | |

*Tactics: internal*

| | |
|---|---|
| Accelerate payments of dividends and fees to parent | Slow down collections from other subsidiaries (lag) |
| Accelerate payments to other (appreciating FC) subsidiaries (lead) | |

LC, local currency; FC, foreign currency
M, financial and forex market actions; CS, customer and supplier actions

relationships were reversed for long and short term debt. This could have been due to a preference on the part of lenders for lending in these strong currencies. Thus perceived profit opportunities were mainly exploited through the accounts payable route rather than through borrowings.

5   Given the significance of the cash account in exploiting perceived parity deviations in foreign exchange markets, Rodriguez investigated how this was done. She discovered that the major means were (p. 437): (a) internal funds initially generated in weak currencies were converted into strong currencies; (b) internal funds initially generated in strong currencies were allowed to remain in those currencies.

The companies were not increasing their short term borrowings in weak currencies to exchange into strong currency holdings. Thus the money market was not being used to alter the net exposure position. Hawkins (1981: 443), in the discussion on Rodriguez (1981), suggested that this reflected the different transaction costs (defined to include search costs) of the external market and internal corporate transfer alternatives.

Rodriguez's massive piece of empirical work provides some concrete evidence for managerial behaviour expected under deviations from UBFR, IRP etc. By and large, managers behaved as expected but with some biases in the foreign currency assets and liabilities they actually changed. Furthermore, this work provided two important insights into managerial behaviour. Firstly, it suggests that in practice managers had a high concern for avoiding transaction risk. Managers stressed the importance of translation exposure, but the account movements measured did not create positions which produced reported exchange gains or avoided reported exchange losses (Rodriguez 1981: 436). Secondly, managers tended to hedge only when they expected losses, rather than when they expected gains. Their control over account movements left accounts exposed only when the exposures were expected to generate reported exchange gains. Thus corporate treasurers were seen to be asymmetrically risk averse, hedging against any expected loss, but not actively exploiting the opportunity of gain.

The study focused on short term foreign exchange risk management decisions during a period of exchange rate crises. The primary FERM techniques employed were medium and short term internal and external financial techniques. The study gives little insight into managerial practice with respect to dealing with economic exposure and the links between internal/external techniques and real responses to currency risk.

The imperfections identified above and the transaction costs incurred in external markets provide some insight into the rationale for internal financial systems in the MNC and for their opportunistic use by treasurers. It is clear that one major rationale for a corporate preference to use the internal financial transfer system in this way is to gain from perceived market imperfections. However, other related factors appear to be at work here.

Holland (1992b), in a study of corporate use of internal and external FERM techniques, noted a corporate preference for the use of internal financial techniques compared with external financial techniques. In the cases studied, the preferences were applied to the supply of foreign exchange risk management services and many other related financial services. Thus internal FERM methods and internal sourcing of currency services and risk management services were the first priority, followed by relationship bank sources for these financial services, followed by market (transaction oriented bank) sources. This priority of internal over external financial techniques is similar to a 'funding policy of least resistance' identified by Donaldson (1969). In these cases, corporate desire for control and predictability in association with perceived low internal transaction costs (i.e. lower than market transaction costs) led to the preference for internal over external financial techniques.

There appear to be several size and complexity related factors at work when establishing this priority of internal over external financial techniques. For example, ICI has a preference for the use of some internal techniques over external techniques. Thus the complexity of the business, with over 200 manufacturing locations in over 40 countries, has created much internal cross-border cross-currency transactions between subsidiaries. This has created many internal opportunities to manage foreign exchange risk and has provided the incentive for ICI to look here first for FERM responses rather than in the external financial markets.

## Problems in using the internal financial system in an active opportunistic way

Despite the clear advantages open to an MNC by using its MIFS in an active opportunistic way, some caution should be expressed here.

In tables 6.2 and 6.3, the actions at the level of the German and French subsidiaries were designed to exploit managerial perceptions of political pressures for a realignment in the ERM. The forward markets indicated pressure here but none of the rates were at the boundaries for the bilateral ERM exchange rates. If management are wrong in their forecast of 'weak' and 'strong' currencies, then many of the actions in tables 6.2 and 6.3 will not produce a gain and may well produce costs for the firm. Using the internal financial system to bet against the foreign exchange markets is an unwise policy unless the firm has access to inside information on the likely actions of EC governments.

Another problem may arise if the German and French treasurers have high degrees of autonomy from the group treasury in the UK. The actions of these two treasurers to optimize their short term financial positions relative to their views of ERM changes may lead to a less than optimum position for the parent. The German subsidiary may be tempted to radically change its short term sterling assets and liabilities in such a way that values of group assets and liabilities and associated cash flows become less predictable and more volatile. Thus the overall aim of the group – to minimize the impact of unanticipated exchange rate changes on home currency cash flows and earnings – may be confounded by fragmented FERM across the group.

Thus group control over internal financial flows or transactions is essential to co-ordinate an active opportunistic FERM policy and to ensure that the firm can avoid a fragmented approach to FERM. Centralized netting and invoicing techniques are means to avoid the costs of fragmentation associated with each subsidiary making its own decisions (*Corporate Finance*, September 1987, p. 11). The existence of this system may also lead to reduced use of external risk management techniques and possibly improved economies of scale in markets.

It should be noted that there can be constraints on the use of internal techniques. Not all internationally involved firms can make full use of these techniques. An adequate number of subsidiaries is required for such internal financial transfers, and a high degree of centralization of treasury is essential. Thus low internal sophistication of treasury can act as a major constraint as the firm relies on the international banking system to co-ordinate its internal financial flows. Political control over transfer prices, netting and tax avoidance can further reduce such flexibility. Finally, adverse customer and supplier reaction to manipulation of payment or credit terms may limit the usefulness of these approaches.

## 6.3 Internal Financial Techniques for Currency Risk Management

In this section we consider in more detail the (individual) use of three examples of internal financial techniques. These are netting, leading and lagging, and matching as an asset/liability management technique.

### Netting

Netting refers to the parent company and its subsidiaries periodically 'settling up' the net amounts owed or owing as a result of trade within the firm. The objective of a centralized netting centre within an MNC is to reduce transfer costs and to speed up payments out of depreciating currencies. In the case of the British MNC in figure 6.2, the central treasury will estimate the overall payments and receipts due in a period within the group. These will then be 'netted out' for each unit and its net payments or receipts position assessed. The basic idea behind netting is to transfer only these net amounts, usually within a short period. The problem then is to establish which unit should transfer what amount to satisfy each unit's net expected position. Many transfer options will be feasible and treasurers will have to identify the least cost combination, in particular one that reduces transfer costs and minimizes the number of foreign exchange conversions. A detailed example of netting, in which a British MNC nets out across its world-wide organization, will be outlined in the following section.

Netting is often controlled by host governments and a firm may have to request permission to net. This may only be given if it is based on real (as opposed to purely financial) transactions or if it is restricted to netting within the firm. In some cases netting is not permitted at all, unless the MNC is home based, or it can demonstrate that its imports and exports net out and do not have a negative impact on the country's balance of payments position or foreign exchange reserves.

## Leading and lagging

Leading and lagging occur when an MNC makes adjustments to the credit terms allowed between its units. In the case of the appreciating Deutschmark, earlier repayment (leading) of mark denominated debt financing may avoid higher payments when the marks are subsequently exchanged for home currency. In a similar fashion, mark denominated accounts payable would be speeded up and receivables slowed down. Internally the German subsidiary would slow down (lag) the payment of dividends, fees and royalties to the parent in Britain and generally increase its non-mark liabilities to the other (depreciating currency) units. The French and British units could also speed up their payments to the German unit and therefore reduce their exposure in marks. The effect of these joint internal and external actions should be designed to reduce the overall exposure of the whole MNC. The total set of these leads and lags should be assessed relative to the effects on the home currency cash flows of the parent. A subsidiary should not be allowed to make leading and lagging decisions that increase the uncertainty of home currency cash flows with respect to unanticipated exchange rate changes.

The company's forecasts of the expected path of exchange rates over a 12 month period are a key ingredient in developing a leading/lagging policy. If the central treasury can appraise the relative strengths and weaknesses of particular currencies, it can develop guidelines for subsidiaries on leading and lagging. This is essential to prevent suboptimal leads and lags at the subsidiary level and to provide a basis from which to predict weekly or monthly netting positions. This activity presumes that the firm can out-forecast the foreign exchange market, or that imperfections exist that are worth exploiting. Given the efficiency of currency markets in major currencies, the treasurer should be cautious here and remain sceptical of such claims.

Governments also exercise considerable control over leading and lagging. This may be based on the belief that a large number of MNCs leading and lagging against a particular currency may cause destabilization of the currency. MNCs may, of course, be reflecting the forces for equilibrium affecting a currency rather than be the cause of the change. The evidence on this matter is inconclusive (Hawkins 1981) but MNCs are still considered by many governments to be the source of their currency's instability. Generally, weak currency countries will attempt to constrain exporting MNCs from delaying or lagging collections of appreciating currency receipts. The same countries will attempt to restrict the ability of MNC importers to speed up payment for the imported goods in the local currency. The reverse considerations would apply to an appreciating currency country. The resulting controls normally take the form of limits on the credit terms allowed for imports and exports. In some cases export terms may be lagged by 180 days but imports into the same country may only be allowed 30 days' leading terms. Certain industries will have standard credit terms and these may be used by governments to question the leading and lagging practices of a firm. Not all countries impose these controls and the UK and certain other developed countries (with their own home grown MNCs) do not interfere in leading and lagging.

## Matching

Matching is an asset and liability management technique in which a company matches say its dollar outflows with its dollar inflows, such that they correspond in size and the period in which they occur. This particular strategy is valuable if the firm wishes to minimize the impact of unanticipated exchange rate changes on its net cash flows. If the matching is complete in terms of currency, size and timing, then changes in values of outflows will be offset by equivalent changes in values of inflows.

Mismatching in terms of currency, size and timing of cash inflows and outflows will create an exposed position. The use of, say, the Canadian dollar as a partial matching substitute for the US dollar may work if parallel movements are expected to occur in these currencies. This form of matching is only sensible when there are strong reasons to believe that a particular pair of currencies will move together. If they do not, then the firm will be doubly hit by adverse unanticipated exchange rate changes in both currencies.

Mismatching in this way may be forced upon the firm by the way in which its operations generate foreign currency cash flows. A major constraint on matching is the lack of availability of internal (or external) inflows and outflows in the same or 'parallel' currencies. The firm may be forced to trade in many different currencies that are unsuitable for matching or it may not be able to find a suitable external partner to swap currencies. These net mismatched positions may be hedged or the firm may wish to use this open position to exploit a perceived opportunity in foreign exchange or Eurocurrency markets. The latter policy is risky in a world of efficient currency markets. This exposed mismatched policy may be feasible for the firm that trades in many different currencies and experiences a 'portfolio' effect in which unanticipated movements in one currency are cancelled out by opposite changes in another currency. In these circumstances matching may become irrelevant as a technique to combat foreign exchange risk.

## 6.4 Netting as an Example of the Use of Internal Techniques

Netting has been briefly discussed in the previous section and is a significant problem area in the management of foreign exchange risks. It is also a problem area that lends itself well to analysis using formal model building techniques. Netting will therefore be used here as a convenient means to demonstrate the benefits of model building in the FERM decision area. Netting will also be used to show how the internal FERM techniques can involve considerable interaction between the subsidiaries and the MNC parent.

An MNC with many overseas subsidiaries and considerable internal trade will generate a large number of multicurrency payments and receipts between its units. These internal payments and receipts are expected to go through the foreign exchange markets *en route* to the relevant subsidiary. However, the costs of transferring funds between these units can be very high, depending upon transaction costs in foreign exchange markets (i.e. the buy/sell spread), the opportunity cost of unused or delayed funds and various other transfer costs.

If a firm can centralize its information gathering on inter-unit transfers and can also centrally direct financial transfers, there may be opportunities to reduce the total funds transferred, the number of transfers and hopefully the cost of transfer. If the firm cannot centralize its information gathering it may still be able to acquire the necessary information from the banking system. Several of the major international commercial banks can provide a treasurer with information on the state of his or her company's balances world-wide. These are usually the previous day's balances and can include information from all of the MNC's banks (Bickerstaffe 1984). In the following detailed example of the netting technique and model building in FERM, it is assumed that comprehensive information on inter-unit transfer options is available. It is also assumed that netting takes place within the context of a financial planning and liquidity planning process.

In table 6.4 our UK MNC has collected data on the residual payments and receipts expected within its world-wide operations over the next three days. All payments and receipts are expressed in pounds. The exchange rates for conversion to pounds are based upon forecasts for the target transfer time which is common to all units. In fact, each payment is in the subsidiary's domestic currency and has to go through the foreign exchange market to be converted into the receipt currency. Given the number of transactions in the table, this will be very expensive for the firm.

Twenty-two payments totalling £441 million are to be made between the subsidiaries. If we assume that the costs of transfer are approximately 0.1 per cent of the volume transferred then the total cost of transfers will be £441,000. As this is for a three-day horizon only it is clear that the annual costs of transfer would be a very large sum.

**Table 6.4** Payments and receipts within a multinational enterprise (£ million)

| Receiving unit | UK | France | Germany | Australia | Hong Kong | US | Total |
|---|---|---|---|---|---|---|---|
| UK | 0 | 32 | 6 | 0 | 31 | 3 | 72 |
| France | 11 | 0 | 12 | 0 | 2 | 0 | 25 |
| Germany | 22 | 10 | 0 | 14 | 0 | 0 | 46 |
| Australia | 14 | 0 | 22 | 0 | 36 | 30 | 102 |
| Hong Kong | 67 | 0 | 14 | 50 | 0 | 11 | 142 |
| US | 12 | 0 | 2 | 19 | 21 | 0 | 54 |
| Total | 126 | 42 | 56 | 83 | 90 | 44 | 441 |

*Paying unit* (column header spanning UK through US)

Bilateral netting between units is possible. Thus the Australian subsidiary is expecting £22m from Germany, and the German subsidiary is expecting £14m from Australia. If the Australian subsidiary receives net £8m from Germany then the two transactions will be completed. This reduces the scale of each inter-subsidiary payment, but unless they net to zero between some subsidiaries, the global number of payments between subsidiaries remains unchanged.

The data in table 6.4 can be used to calculate the overall net payments or receipts position of each unit relative to the rest of the MNC. For example, the Australian subsidiary will pay out £83 million and will receive £102 million and it therefore expects a net payment of £19 million. As long as it receives this net payment from the central treasury and this is used to settle all of its payments and receipts outlined in table 6.4, it will be unconcerned about the origin of the net payment within the firm. Table 6.5 summarizes the net payments/receipts positions of all units.

This information is very valuable in that it demonstrates how the number of payments and the overall volume of transfers can be reduced by settling the net positions between units. However, the netting problem still remains and the firm must decide which unit transfers which amount to other units, such that the net payments/receipts position for each unit is satisfied. Table 6.6 illustrates the problem. In table 6.6, the paying units are those with a negative net position in table 6.5, and the receiving units those with a positive net position. $X_1$ to $X_9$ are the unknown sums to be transferred between units. Thus $X_1$ is the amount to be transferred from the UK to Australia, and $X_5$ is the amount to be transferred from France to Hong Kong. Transfers from a country must equal the net payment position for each unit. Thus in the case of Germany,

$$X_3 + X_6 + X_9 = 10$$

In a similar fashion, transfers to a country must equal the net receipt position of that unit. Thus in the case of Hong Kong,

$$X_4 + X_5 + X_6 = 52$$

Also included above and left of each unknown sum in table 6.6 are transfer costs as a percentage of the quantity transferred. These are estimates of the transfer costs and they are assumed to be a linear function of the volume transferred. This is likely to be a robust assumption if the volume range is

**Table 6.5** Net receipts and payments within MNC (£ million)

|              | Out | In  | Net |
|--------------|-----|-----|-----|
| UK           | 126 | 72  | −54 |
| France       | 42  | 25  | −17 |
| West Germany | 56  | 46  | −10 |
| Australia    | 83  | 102 | 19  |
| Hong Kong    | 90  | 142 | 52  |
| US           | 44  | 54  | 10  |

**Table 6.6** Netting transfer requirements (£ million) and transfer costs (%)

| Receiving units | | Paying units | | |
| | UK | France | Germany | Total |
|-----------------|-------|--------|---------|-------|
| Australia       | 0.10  | 0.10   | 0.11    |       |
|                 | $X_1$ | $X_2$  | $X_3$   | 19    |
| Hong Kong       | 0.08  | 0.075  | 0.088   |       |
|                 | $X_4$ | $X_5$  | $X_6$   | 52    |
| US              | 0.11  | 0.11   | 0.12    |       |
|                 | $X_7$ | $X_8$  | $X_9$   | 10    |
| Total           | 54    | 17     | 10      | 81    |

narrow. This assumption much simplifies the netting problem in that the goal of minimizing transfer costs can be simply expressed as follows:

$$\text{Minimize} \quad 0.001X_1 + 0.001X_2 + 0.0011X_3 + 0.0008X_4 + 0.00075X_5 \\ + 0.00088X_6 + 0.0011X_7 + 0.0011X_8 + 0.0012X_9$$

Many solutions are possible which satisfy the payment and receipt requirements of each unit. For example, a manager could inspect table 6.6 and come up with solution in table 6.7. This is a feasible solution in that the treasurer can transfer these funds and the payment and receipt position of

**Table 6.7** Possible netting solution (£ million)

| Receiving units | Paying units | | | |
| | UK | France | Germany | Total |
| --- | --- | --- | --- | --- |
| Australia | $X_1 = 10$ | $X_2 = 4$ | $X_3 = 5$ | 19 |
| Hong Kong | $X_4 = 40$ | $X_5 = 9$ | $X_6 = 3$ | 52 |
| US | $X_7 = 4$ | $X_8 = 4$ | $X_9 = 2$ | 10 |
| Total | 54 | 17 | 10 | 81 |

each unit will be satisfied. The cost of this solution to the netting problem is

$$(10 \times 0.001) + (4 \times 0.001) + (5 \times 0.0011) + (40 \times 0.0008) + (9 \times 0.00075)$$
$$+ (3 \times 0.00088) + (4 \times 0.0011) + (4 \times 0.0011) + (2 \times 0.0012) = £72,090$$

However, the manager cannot be sure that he has found the least cost solution to this problem. One way to find this optimum solution is to formulate the problem as a linear programming (LP) problem. Shapiro (1978a) has demonstrated the feasibility of the linear programming approach to the netting problem and this section draws from his work by developing an example for a British MNC. Some of the large international banks also offer computer based linear programming models to allow customers to minimize the cost of netting (Bickerstaffe 1984). This operations research technique can be used to search through all feasible solutions (i.e. those that satisfy the payment and receipt requirements for each unit) to find the least cost solution for the transfer of funds between units. Much of the formulation of this problem in the LP format has been demonstrated above, and the full formulation is as follows:

Minimize    $0.001X_1 + 0.001X_2 + 0.0011X_3 + 0.0008X_4 + 0.00075X_5$
$+ 0.00088X_6 + 0.0011X_7 + 0.0011X_8 + 0.0012X_9$

subject to    $X_1 + X_2 + X_3 = 19$
$X_4 + X_5 + X_6 = 52$
$X_7 + X_8 + X_9 = 10$
$X_1 + X_4 + X_7 = 54$
$X_2 + X_5 + X_8 = 17$
$X_3 + X_6 + X_9 = 10$

$X_1$ to $X_9$ are $\geqslant 0$

**Table 6.8** Results of linear programming run for
netting problem

| Variable | Value | Object |
|---|---|---|
| $X_1$ | 19 | 10 |
| $X_4$ | 25 | 8 |
| $X_5$ | 17 | 7.5 |
| $X_6$ | 10 | 8.8 |
| $X_7$ | 10 | 11 |

Value of objective: 715.5

**Table 6.9** Interpretation of linear programming run: netting solution ($£$ million)

| Receiving units | | Paying units | | |
| | UK | France | Germany | Total |
|---|---|---|---|---|
| Australia | $X_1 = 19$ | $X_2 = 0$ | $X_3 = 0$ | 19 |
| Hong Kong | $X_4 = 25$ | $X_5 = 17$ | $X_6 = 10$ | 52 |
| US | $X_7 = 10$ | $X_8 = 0$ | $X_9 = 0$ | 10 |
| Total | 54 | 17 | 10 | 81 |

The optimal solution to this problem has been found by running a linear programming model. Any standard LP program that allows sensitivity analysis of the results will suffice for this purpose. The details of the run are shown in appendix 1 and the final results are as in table 6.8. In terms of table 6.6, this solution can be interpreted as in table 6.9.

Only five relatively small transfers are required to satisfy the payments and receipts outlined in table 6.4. Total payments are reduced from £441 million to £81 million and the costs of transfer are now £71,550. Much of the cost savings in this example have actually been achieved by the calculation of net positions in table 6.5, and at first sight the LP solution (tables 6.8, 6.9) does not seem to add much to the solution arrived at by managerial inspection (table 6.7). However, the treasurer does at least know that this is the best solution and that there may be many occasions when the LP solution produces dramatic savings over the inspection solution.

**Table 6.10** Sensitivity of payments and receipts
constraints in netting problems

| Net values | Range (£ million) |
|---|---|
| UK payments | 54 to 64 |
| French payments | 17 to 27 |
| German payments | 0 to 10 |
| Australian receipts | 9 to 19 |
| Hong Kong receipts | 42 to 52 |
| US receipts | 10 to infinity |

Furthermore, the LP model provides some very valuable additional information:

- an analysis of the sensitivity of the solution to changes in the net amounts to be paid/received by each unit
- an analysis of the sensitivity of the solution to changes in the costs of transfer

Tables 6.10 and 6.11 summarize the results of sensitivity analysis using the computer program. Full details are shown in appendix 1.

From table 6.10 it is clear that UK, French and German net payments do not affect the least cost solution until they move outside their limits.

**Table 6.11** Sensitivity of costs to transfer in netting problem

| Variable | Lower limit | Current value | Upper limit |
|---|---|---|---|
| $X_1$ | NB | 0.0010 | 0.00112 |
| $X_2$ | 0.00095 | 0.0010 | NB |
| $X_3$ | 0.001088 | 0.0011 | NB |
| $X_4$ | 0.000788 | 0.0008 | NB |
| $X_5$ | NB | 0.00075 | 0.0008 |
| $X_6$ | NB | 0.00088 | 0.000892 |
| $X_7$ | NB | 0.0011 | 0.001112 |
| $X_8$ | 0.00105 | 0.0011 | NB |
| $X_9$ | 0.00108 | 0.0012 | NB |

NB, not bounded.

Any increase in these net payments above the upper limits, will mean that another optimum solution is possible. Australian and Hong Kong net receipts can also be varied within a £10 million range of decreases from existing values without affecting the solution. US net receipts can take any increase without changing the optimum.

From table 6.11 it can be seen that the current solution is particularly insensitive to the costs of transfer. In many cases there is no boundary (NB) to the increase in costs and these can take any value without changing the least cost solution. In other cases small changes in transfer costs will begin the search for a new optimum. In the case of transfers from the UK to Australia a small increase in costs on $X_1$ will do this. In a similar manner, small decreases in the cost of transfer on $X_8$ from France to the US will affect the current solution.

The use of the linear programming method and sensitivity analysis of the netting problem gives a valuable demonstration of the benefits of model building in foreign exchange risk management. Many other model building possibilities exist: for example, treasurers may find that a combination of a simulation and optimization models provides the most suitable decision aid for the netting problem. Such a model could have the design features shown in figure 6.3. An existing LP computer program could form the core of this model. Some relatively minor adaptations could be employed to calculate tables 6.5, 6.6 and 6.8 to 6.11 and also to output solutions 'near to' the current optimum. This model could form a valuable netting information system for the treasurer, especially if supported by an adequate system for collecting data on inter-unit payments and transfer

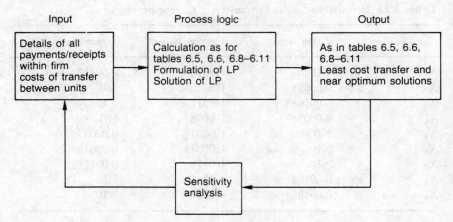

**Figure 6.3** Possible model for netting problem

costs. In practice, some large international banks offer such services with respect to payments netting information and computer based optimization models. Given the general availability of financial modelling packages with some kind of optimization facility, it seems that the above model building exercise is well within the capacity of most large MNCs (see Rutenberg 1982). An adapted simulation/optimization model will not be demonstrated in this book but the wider benefits of model building for the international financial manager will be discussed in chapters 10 and 12, where computer based capital budgeting and financing models will be discussed.

Finally, it should be noted that similarly sophisticated information systems and analytical techniques are required for other internal FERM techniques. For example, simulation methods appear to be particularly suitable for investigating the implications of matching and leading and lagging decisions.

## 6.5 Summary

Corporate planning can provide a key context for the rational use of a set of internal FERM techniques. Planners can provide treasury with essential currency exposure management information from long term plans for expansion and growth in the business in overseas territories. In the case of ICI, the large British chemical MNC, the planners and treasury teams critically review aggregate cash forecasts from these plans (Hodgson 1980). This in turn is used to identify the overall division expected between internal and external funds, as well as the long term operating strategies to deal with economic exposure. From this assessment, the treasury should have a clear view on long term transfer pricing policy between subsidiaries, and other long term policies on fees for internal legal services, managerial services and technical knowledge. General policy on inter-subsidiary lending and dividends to the parent can also be established at this point.

The successful development of a corporate plan and guidelines on internal flows can clarify the usage of internal techniques by group treasury and local subsidiary managers. Treasury must also prepare detailed estimates of the medium term currency exposure of each overseas subsidiary. This involves each subsidiary forecasting its payments and receipts, both internal to the MNC and external to suppliers and customers, expected over monthly periods up to a year. The subsidiary can also estimate its asset and liability positions over these periods and assess its room for manoeuvre with these exposure variables. This information needs to be collated centrally so that the MNC has overall medium term forecasts for payments/receipts and its world-wide asset/liability position.

The centralized information and the foreign exchange forecasts can provide the MNC with the basis for implementing the active opportunistic policy outlined in section 6.2. Depending upon the opportunities open to it, the MNC can:

1   Adopt medium term operational policies that are consistent with overall corporate strategy, i.e. chapter 5 responses to currency risk.
2   Lead and lag payables/receivables on the basis of this information, up to a horizon of, say, six months.
3   Match some payments and receipts in common currencies.
4   Decrease LC assets and increase LC liabilities in depreciating currencies, or increase LC assets and decrease LC liabilities in appreciating currencies.
5   Identify opportunities for netting the residual payments and receipts pattern. These may exist in the week or month ahead. Clearly the netting model outlined in the previous section is an essential decision aid for corporate treasurers faced with this problem.

These actions are designed to alter the firm's exposure to currency risk. However, the firm is still likely to have a short and medium term currency transaction exposure problem in a period say 3 to 12 months ahead. These may include the remaining exposed positions in assets/liabilities and in external payments/receipts. External techniques such as money market hedges or forward market hedges may be employed to counteract these remaining exposures to currency risk. Chapter 7 will consider these external responses to currency risk.

The choice between the internal FERM techniques (listed as 2 to 5 above) depends on their availability and cost, and their impact on the volatility of home currency cash flows and ultimately shareholder value. Thus the key questions to be asked of FERM policy and the extensive use of internal techniques are:

● Does the use of these internal financial methods reduce the volatility of corporate HC cash flows?
● Does their use increase the expected level of HC cash flows?
● Does their use protect fundamental value arising from the real business?

- Does their use create extra value by allowing the firm to exploit market imperfections?
- Does their use produce overall additions to value which exceed the cost of the internal financial system and other treasury operations? Thus staff salaries and internal financial system technology costs must be considered in such an appraisal.

Positive answers to these questions will encourage extensive use of internal financial techniques. However, the sceptical treasurer should be wary of their role in adding value by exploiting imperfections or market inefficiencies. The active use of internal techniques and the development of internal financial systems should be justified in terms of their collective ability to minimize the impact of unanticipated exchange rate changes in home currency cash flows. This reduction in home country cash flow volatility may enable the firm to avoid financial distress and allow managers to focus their energies on real product and factor markets as the primary source of corporate value.

# 7

# FERM and the Use of External Risk Management Instruments

In chapters 5 and 6 we have seen that the MNC can deal with part of its exposure to currency risk by altering real decisions and by employing a variety of internal financial techniques. It was also noted that MNCs vary in their ability to exploit such FERM methods. As a result, even after extensive efforts in this respect the firm is likely to have a major problem of exposure to currency risk. Fortunately for the firm, foreign exchange and credit markets and other agents external to the firm offer a range of insurance services designed to deal with these risky exposures.

These external FERM methods have multiplied in form in the past decade as a wave of innovation occurred in international financial and banking markets. Major facilities here now include forward exchange contracts, currency futures, currency options, currency swaps, short term borrowing, discounting, factoring and government exchange risk guarantees. The bulk of these risk management instruments are provided in foreign exchange and credit markets with some specialist services available from governments, customers and other MNCs.

All involve the firm in some form of contractual arrangement which binds the firm to fully discharge its side of the contract. The contract may involve foreign currency transactions of the same scale as the (normally known transaction) exposure or, in the case of instruments such as an (unexercised) currency option, may only involve small cash outflows in the form of an insurance premium. Contractual terms such as maturity and amount are generally tailored by international banks to the client firm's requirements. However, some instruments are only available through exchange based markets and are inflexible as to terms. These external techniques are generally used by firms to insure against a possible loss on known transaction exposures. However, they can also be used to 'bet against' perceived deviations in real exchange rates or interest rates.

The classical external financial techniques employed by firms are the forward market hedge and the money market hedge. More recently, currency options and currency swaps have become an important part of treasury's defence against currency risk. In section 7.1 we explore the use of three major currency risk instruments: the forward hedge, the money market hedge and currency option. The currency swap is described in chapter 11. This is followed by an analysis in sections 7.2 and 7.3 of the continuous covering or hedging problem facing firms, and their constraints in using hedging techniques.

## 7.1 Market Supplied Risk Management Instruments

### Case data

The following case data will be used to explore the forward hedge, money market hedge and currency option decision choice. Hero Books, a British publisher, exports books to Berlin Book Stores, a German customer, and expects to receive a DM1,000,000 payment in 90 days. The current prices in the currency, eurocurrency and currency option markets are as follows:

- spot rate is 2.95DM/£
- forward rate for three months or 90 days is 2.93 DM/£
- German annual interest rate is 5.40 per cent
- UK annual interest rate is 8.11 per cent
- strike price of (US style) put option on Deutschmark is 2.94DM/£; premium is £0.0025/DM; duration is 90 days.

The treasurer of Hero Books, Susan Barclay, pays for a regular exchange rate forecasting service, and the most recent forecast leads her to believe that the spot rate will be 2.935DM/£ in three months. We will consider the decision alternatives open to Susan Barclay as treasurer and explain the limitations of each approach. The above data will be used in calculations for a forward hedge, a money market hedge and a put currency option.

### Remaining exposed: the 'do nothing' alternative

If Susan Barclay has a high degree of confidence in her forecasting service then she may decide to leave the DM1,000,000 exposed to changes in the

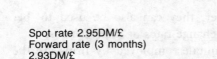
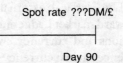

Spot rate 2.95DM/£
Forward rate (3 months)
2.93DM/£                                                        Spot rate ???DM/£

Day 1                                                          Day 90
1 August                                                       31 October

Leave the DM receivable                    Receive DM1,000,000 from customer
exposed to exchange rate                   Sell the DM1,000,000 in the spot market
changes

**Figure 7.1** Hero Books: no cover of transaction exposure

DM/£ rate and wait and see what the DM/£ rate turns out to be (figure 7.1). If the forecast turns out to be correct, Hero would sell the DM1,000,000 in the spot market in 90 days and receive 1,000,000/2.935 = £340,715.5.

If the forecast turns out to be incorrect, and the spot rate turns out to be 2.96DM/£ in 90 days, then Barclay would have to sell the DM1,000,000 in the spot market at this poor rate and receive 1,000,000/2.96 = £337,837.8. Thus the more the mark depreciates, the lower the sterling returns from the sale to Berlin Book Stores. However, if the mark were to strengthen relative to the pound, the sterling receipts would be boosted. This highlights the double sided nature of the risk of gains and losses from unanticipated exchange rate changes. Barclay has 90 days to reconsider this decision, and may decide to hedge if her forecasting service changes its view or if other information emerges to suggest that the exchange rate will be very volatile towards the end of the 90 day period.

## Forward market hedge

In figure 7.2 we see that Hero Books can avoid the transaction exposure by selling the marks forward at 2.93DM/£ for delivery on 31 October. Hero receives DM1,000,000 from the customer on that date and then immediately delivers this mark sum to a bank handling the deal. It therefore receives 1,000,000/2.93 = £341,297.

If Berlin Book Stores pays up on time, the marks receivable and the forward contract for sale of marks are matched and Hero Books does not face any currency risk.

If Berlin Book Stores does not pay for the book order on day 90 and delays payment by ten days then Hero must still discharge the forward sale

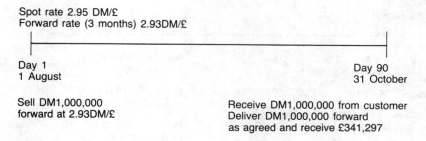

Spot rate 2.95 DM/£
Forward rate (3 months) 2.93DM/£

Day 1
1 August

Day 90
31 October

Sell DM1,000,000
forward at 2.93DM/£

Receive DM1,000,000 from customer
Deliver DM1,000,000 forward
as agreed and receive £341,297

**Figure 7.2** Hero Books: forward cover of transaction exposure

of marks with the bank. This may mean that it has to go into the spot market on day 90 to buy the marks for delivery to the bank. If it has to buy DM1,000,000 in the spot market at a lower rate per pound (e.g. at 2.92DM/£, pay £342,465) than it sells them to the bank (at 2.93DM/£, receive £341,296) then it will make a loss (£1169) on the forward contract. When the marks are eventually received from Berlin Books, Hero is still exposed and may make further exchange losses when selling the marks through the spot market on day 100.

Because of this, Hero Books may decide to arrange varying forward dates for its forward contract to correspond with varying settlement rates of FC receivables or payables. The bank providing this service will charge Hero Books the least favourable forward rate over the uncertain settlement period. (For a detailed analysis of these variations the reader is recommended specialist books on foreign exchange risk management such as McRae and Walker 1980.)

## Money market hedge

In this example, illustrated in figure 7.3, Hero Books immediately borrows DM1,000,000 at an annual interest rate of 5.4 per cent. This deal can be done in London in the Euromark markets or in Frankfurt in the domestic German bank deposit market. Hero will therefore owe $5.4\% \times (3/12) \times 1,000,000 = DM13,500$ in interest at the end of the 90 days. This can be purchased forward three months for payment to the lender.

The DM1,000,000 is converted to sterling on 1 August at a spot rate of 2.95DM/£, yielding £338,983. This is immediately invested in the UK in a three month sterling bank deposit at 8.11 per cent per annum and will earn interest of $£338,983 \times (8.11/100) \times (3/12) = £6873$.

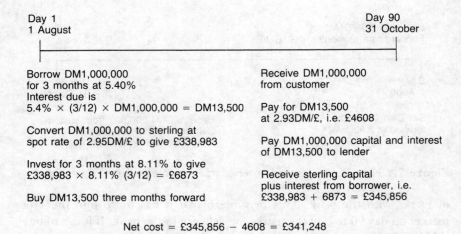

Day 1
1 August

Day 90
31 October

Borrow DM1,000,000
for 3 months at 5.40%
Interest due is
5.4% × (3/12) × DM1,000,000 = DM13,500

Convert DM1,000,000 to sterling at
spot rate of 2.95DM/£ to give £338,983

Invest for 3 months at 8.11% to give
£338,983 × 8.11% (3/12) = £6873

Buy DM13,500 three months forward

Receive DM1,000,000
from customer

Pay for DM13,500
at 2.93DM/£, i.e. £4608

Pay DM1,000,000 capital and interest
of DM13,500 to lender

Receive sterling capital
plus interest from borrower, i.e.
£338,983 + 6873 = £345,856

Net cost = £345,856 − 4608 = £341,248

**Figure 7.3** Hero Books: money market cover of transaction exposure

On 31 October the British firm will receive its DM1,000,000 payment. It will use this to pay off the capital of its mark loan and use the forward contract to pay off the interest. The forward contract costs 13,500/2.93 = £4608.

In the UK on 31 October the bank repays the British firm its deposit plus interest, i.e. £345,856. The net cost is therefore £345,856 − 4608 = £341,248.

The small sterling difference between the forward and money market hedging transactions reflects the interest rate parity holding between the UK and Germany. If this were not the case then arbitrage between the two domestic markets via the foreign exchange market would, in the absence of capital markets, quickly re-establish IRP.

## Currency options

As before, Hero Books exports books to a German customer and the DM1,000,000 receivable is due 90 days from 1 August. However, Barclay now decides to deal with this mark exposure by buying a put option on the DM1,000,000 (figure 7.4).

This contract gives Hero the right to sell (or put) marks for pounds at an agreed exercise or strike price. When the marks are received from the client, Hero can exercise the contract and sell the marks to the bank for pounds at the agreed exercise price. Hero is not obliged to make this sale of

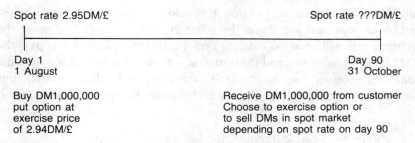

**Figure 7.4** Hero Books: option cover of transaction exposure

marks via the option contract if the marks are not paid on time by the German customer or if Hero believes it can get a better rate in the spot market.

This particular contract would not be directly sold in exchange based option markets. In markets such as the Philadelphia Stock Exchange, the dollar is the medium of exchange and the mark and the pound are employed as the underlying or 'foreign' currencies of options. However, a bank could construct a tailored 'over the counter' (OTC) contract such as this for its customer. In this case, the bank offers Hero Books a contract with a strike or exercise price of 2.94DM/£ and a premium of £0.0025/DM. The premium cost will be £0.0025 × DM1,000,000 = £2500. If exercised the option will produce 1,000,000/2.94 = £340,136 less £2500, i.e. = £337,636

If the mark depreciates to say 3DM/£ and the option is exercised then £337,636 would be received by Hero Books. However, if Barclay used the spot market she would receive DM1,000,000/3 = £333,333 less the £2500 premium, i.e. £330,833. At this spot rate the option is therefore a better deal and will be exercised. In fact, in the whole of the depreciating mark exchange range above the break-even rate of DM1,000,000/£337,636 = 2.96177DM/£, the mark put is in profit and will be exercised in preference to the spot market. Throughout this range the option is 'in the money'.

If the mark appreciates to say 2.75DM/£, then selling the marks in the spot market will produce DM1,000,000/2.75 = £363,636 less the £2500 for the unexercised put premium, i.e. £361,136. This will be the best means to change the marks into pounds because exercising the option at its exercise price of 2.94DM/£ only produces (1,000,000/2.94) − 2500 = £337,636. The spot market is therefore a better deal at this spot rate and the option will not be exercised. In this appreciating mark exchange rate range the put contract is 'out of the money' compared with the spot market price.

If Barclay is concerned that Berlin Book Stores will delay payment, then a purchase of a 120 day mark put option should be considered. This will allow Barclay to wait and see when the payment will be made and what the exchange rate will be at the date of payment. If Berlin Book Stores pays the DM1,000,000 on day 90 and the option is not exercised the remaining 'time value' in the option may be retrievable from the bank seller or writer. For more information on the valuation of exchange traded options, see chapter 2.

## The choice between currency risk hedge techniques

We can now compare the consequences of adopting each of the above policies for Hero Book's problem:

*Do nothing*    We saw that the unhedged alternative may be profitable or it may produce large losses. The latter may be very significant for the occasional exporter dealing with a single large overseas sales.

*Forward hedge*    The firm sells DM1,000,000 forward on day 1 at 2.93DM/£ and receives a certain £341,297 on day 90.

*Money market hedge*    The firm borrows DM1,000,000 at an annual interest rate of 5.4 per cent. This is converted into sterling in the spot market on day 1 and invested in UK bank deposits for 90 days at 8.11 per cent. On day 90 the British firm receives its DM1,000,000 payment and pays off the mark loan. In the UK it receives the receipts of its UK sterling investment and ends up with £341,248.

*Currency option*    The use of a currency option for this transaction allows the firm to speculate on the mark appreciating whilst protecting itself against a sudden drop in its value relative to the pound. If exercised the option produces £337,636.

It is difficult to compare the above techniques because they are serving different decision purposes. The forward and money market hedging techniques have a clear advantage over the no hedging choice because they remove the possibility of loss at day 90. However, the price they pay for this is the lost opportunity to gain from exchange rate changes.

The forward and money market hedging techniques are easiest to compare with each other because they share the same aim of insuring against any change in the full HC value of the FC transaction exposure. These techniques can be compared by determining which produces the higher home currency (sterling) receipts for providing the same reduction in exchange variability in home currency cash flows and thus the same reduction in the likelihood of financial distress. On this basis the forward market hedge produces slightly more sterling cash flow than the money market hedge.

*(mm adv)*

However, we can see that the money market hedge does offer some added flexibility compared with the forward hedge. It offers immediate liquidity for the firm because the firm has borrowed marks from a bank on the strength of its marks receivable and immediately changed these marks into pounds. This capital could be used to gain a higher return than that offered by the three month sterling bank deposit. The firm may make better internal use of the capital by paying off a bank overdraft with an interest rate of, say, 14 per cent per annum.

In the case of the currency option, in the appreciating mark range below 2.94DM/£ the potential for gain by not exercising the option has no upper limit. This is also true for the no hedge choice at this exchange rate range. The no hedge alternative would produce the higher return under these circumstances because of the absence of a premium and is therefore the superior alternative. In the depreciating mark zone above 2.94DM/£, the put will be exercised. The premium has served its purpose and the firm will prefer to use the option rather than the more expensive spot market. In this case the no hedge policy is inferior to the option because increasing losses from mark depreciation cannot be avoided.

The currency option, when exercised, produces £337,636. This is not as good a sterling outcome as the money market hedge (£341,248) or the forward hedge (£341,297). However, this is a certain sterling cash inflow if the day 90 spot rate turns out to offer a poor rate of exchange. If the day 90 spot rate offers a good rate of exchange and can boost sterling cash inflows, the firm with the option can decide to exploit this in a way it could not with one of the 100 per cent covered hedges. If management is very risk averse, the forward and money market hedges offer the means to simplify an uncertain world and to focus managerial energies on non-financial decisions. However, if managers are prepared to pay a premium they can create an extra degree of decision freedom relative to exchange rate changes.

The currency option, when used with the known mark exposure in the above example, offers the opportunity to speculate, at a price, on the future spot rate. However, the size of option premiums suggests that the currency option is an expensive way of making this bet. The currency option and its high insurance cost seem best suited to the problem of dealing with uncertain FC cash flow exposures. If Hero Books is facing an uncertain sales negotiation with Berlin Book Stores, the contingent mark exposure can be insured against exchange risk by buying the right to sell the marks if they arise. The premium is still expensive but it allows Hero's sales staff to negotiate the deal in marks knowing that mark sales yet to be negotiated will, if agreed, produce certain sterling cash flows. This removes a key source of exchange rate risk for the firm.

## Hedging translation exposures

In the above example, money market and forward hedges and currency options have been used to hedge cash flow or transaction exposures. However, the MNC can also hedge balance sheet items measured in foreign currencies. It may wish to do this because a particular overseas asset or liability, as measured by accounting conventions, is considered to be particularly sensitive to exchange rate changes. Thus a dramatic change in the HC value of the overseas asset or liability, due to unanticipated changes in the relevant exchange rate, may have a significant and adverse effect on the company's consolidated balance sheet and profit and loss account. It is this contingency that provides the incentive for managers to hedge balance sheet items. However, if a forward market hedge is taken out against this undesirable accounting event, this hedge could result in an accounting gain or loss against the exposure and a cash flow loss or gain on the forward contract. If the home capital market is informationally efficient, in the semi-strong sense (see chapter 13), then such hedging of accounting or translation exposure is of no value to shareholders. Indeed, if the forward contract shows a loss then the capital market will recognize this cash flow loss in its valuation of the firm. In general, hedging to avoid translation exposure risk and to reduce the variability of HC balance sheet and profit and loss items is wasteful of managerial resources. In practice, many MNCs do manage translation exposure to currency risk (Belk and Glaum 1990; Collier and Davis 1985; Collier et al. 1990). This may be due to managers ignoring or being ignorant of the precepts of efficient market theory. However, it may also be because they are faced with situations where hedging can reduce the variability of profits and this means that the firm can avoid a higher tax bill. This may be the case in some countries where profits in excess of a certain percentage of equity are subject to additional taxes (Dufey and Srinivasulu 1983: 59). In such cases, reducing tax cash outflows by hedging profit and loss or balance sheet items is of value to the shareholders of the firm.

## 7.2 Cases in the Hedging of Transaction Exposures

In this section, two cases of corporate hedging are briefly described before we turn to corporate policy in this field.

### Case study: Rolls-Royce

Rolls-Royce has a substantial net US dollar cash inflow. For example, in the period 1982 to 1986 this inflow was equivalent to between 17 and 22 per cent of group turnover in each year. This dollar net cash flow exposure is particularly important because Rolls-Royce's contracts for civil aero engines are long term, with final payment frequently up to five years after the firm engine order is placed. In addition the company is exposed in the short run on individual sales over the period when final sale negotiations are concluded. It has therefore been important for the company to develop a foreign exchange management policy to reduce its exposure to currency movements. The existence of UK exchange controls until the late 1970s limited the company's ability to undertake forward currency sales. Apart from the constraints imposed by the exchange control regulations, the market for medium or long foreign exchange contracts was extremely limited, so almost all forward sales of US dollars had to be confined to the short term.

In 1979, the company's exports constituted 41 per cent of its sales. As discussed in chapters 4 and 5, the firm made a large exchange loss of £58 million in 1979 owing to an unexpected real change in the $/£ exchange rate. This has led to an active analysis and management of economic exposure in the firm and these policies have been outlined in chapters 4 and 5.

This experience and the considerable $/£ volatility over the 1980s and into the 1990s have also led to more active management of the large known dollar transaction exposures. The company has developed a hedging policy which reduces the impact of exchange rate movements in any one year. Firm engine orders are substantially covered when contracts are secured; about 80 per cent of the net US dollar revenue arising from an order is generally sold immediately and the balance is covered selectively as the delivery date approaches. Net US dollar cash inflow from sales of spare parts is forecast for each year over a five year period and is sold forward progressively on a five year rolling programme, so that the total proportion sold in respect of a particular year is increased as the period covered becomes closer and the forecast therefore becomes more certain.

The company considers itself risk averse but this does not prevent RR from using all currently available instruments for managing its exposure. Options, currency swaps, cylinder options and other techniques currently available are all used for hedging risk. However, forward exchange contracts, normally dollar sales, are the technique most extensively used by the company, with currency options added where appropriate.

The tender to contract risk is reduced by providing the company's commercial negotiators with updated forward exchange rates for use in the preparation of sales contract proposals and in the evaluation of order profitability. This policy results in greater predictability of sterling cash flow and profits, minimizing exchange rate exposure risk and providing a more certain base from which the company can plan its future.

Thus the Rolls-Royce group makes extensive use of financial hedging as a means of managing its transaction exposure in addition to the strategic and operational changes mentioned in chapters 4 and 5.

## Case study: Jaguar

Jaguar, when independent of Ford, had very little strategic flexibility, some operational flexibility and little or no internal financial flexibility in dealing with currency risk. As a result the residual exposure and risk remaining after the use of strategic and operational approaches were very significant. These were managed by the extensive use of currency risk management instruments available through banks and other suppliers. Jaguar made extensive use of the forward market when managing this currency exposure. This policy required very careful handling and relied considerably on company forecasting skills concerning company dollar cash flows (see Edwards 1988; Lane 1988; 1989).

Within a two year hedging horizon period, Jaguar had a base-case hedging policy for its US dollar exposure. The exact hedging percentage for each subperiod within the hedging horizon was decided on an opportunistic basis, with particular emphasis on forecast exchange rates and the target rates derived from the overall business objectives of the group.

The target $/£ rates were those at which the firm could make a profit on car sales in the US. The rule here was to attempt to engage in forward contracts if they could be achieved at £/$ levels which were profitable relative to these target rates. This timing issue appeared to be the only opportunistic element of the hedging policy. Clearly there were some dangers here in that if hedging was delayed for too long or was done at a low percentage of dollar receivables then the inevitable forward contract rate could involve a poor exchange rate.

Much of this hedging policy became redundant on the Ford takeover. The net dollar cash flows from the Jaguar subsidiary were not seen as the central FERM problem of a US based parent with large scale cash flows in many other major world currencies. In this sense, Jaguar's much publicized currency problems of the 1980s were finally solved.

## 7.3 Continuous Covering Policies and the Mix of Financial Hedge Techniques

In section 7.1, the uses of market supplied currency risk management instruments were compared for a single transaction exposure. In the cases in section 7.2 we note that, in practice, MNCs and other internationally involved firms have a continuous stream of known and partially known FC transaction exposures for periods from one day to, say, 18 months. In these cases forward hedging is a continuous activity over the exposure management period.

A firm which generates continuous transaction exposure in one volatile exchange rate such as the $/£ may find that uncovered gains and losses on individual transactions are small, and of the same scale. As a result the cumulative loss or gain over a year is not much larger than zero. This view flows from the idea that the forward rate is unbiased or, if it is biased, the error (forward rate less spot rate at maturity) is too small for most large MNCs to exploit. If a firm trades in five or six currencies, then diversification effects will further reduce the destabilizing impact of uncovered gains and losses on home currency returns. This raises the question as to whether FERM is required in many enterprises.

Despite this, firms such as Jaguar, Rolls–Royce, ICI and many others can be observed to continuously hedge when they have regular exposures in one major currency or a group of major currencies. In these cases, continuous hedging of transaction exposures can be seen as a low cost insurance scheme for conservative treasurers and their firms. Within a decision period such as one year, it helps remove the unanticipated effects of exchange rate changes on home currency cash flows. If there is a bias in the forward rate and it works against the firm, this can be seen as a small cost to allow managers to focus on the real business rather than the vagaries of financial markets. A similar comment can be made concerning money market hedges. If IRP holds then this hedging should have similar effects to forward hedging. Continuous hedging in this way can be very important for the firm with 'lumpy' FC exposures. A foreign exchange loss on one very large FC exposure, or on a stream of large exposures over say one month, may create financial distress for the firm. The firm cannot wait for these losses to be compensated by subsequent gains from exchange rate changes.

In chapters 5 and 6, the possibility of real exchange rate changes was discussed. Purchasing power parity may not hold between two economies or it may not hold at the level of the firm's input and output prices. If the firm has exhausted its real and internal financial capability to respond to this risk, then the systematic use of financial market instruments to hedge the remaining, continuing exposure is justified.

Continuous covering policies are the result of much learning as firms have experienced volatile exchange rates and the impact of real exchange rate changes on the business over time. As a result treasurers have learnt to identify

1   the acceptable level of risk taking in the management of transaction exposures, and have therefore clarified the aims of their financial hedging
2   the unique nature of their firm's transaction exposures
3   how to co-ordinate external suppliers and internal users of currency risk management instruments
4   the special set of factors promoting and constraining the use of financial hedging techniques
5   the strategic and operational flexibility available for FERM
6   the internal capacity to transact in financial hedges and to transfer or source currency risk management instruments internally.

Given the varied learning experiences of firms concerning the nature of their transaction exposures problem and of currency risk, it is no surprise to observe much diversity in the management of transaction exposures (Belk and Glaum 1990; Canaday and Feenstra 1991; Collier et al. 1990). Issues 5 and 6 have been dealt with in previous chapters. The focus in the rest of this chapter will be on issues 1 to 4.

## Attitudes to risk and diversity of practice

Managerial attitudes to currency risk can manifest themselves in a variety of ways in practice. These include the way in which natural transaction exposures (remaining after real and internal financial methods) are dealt with through financial hedges, and the way in which the firm uses its currency trading function (if it exists) (see Belk and Glaum 1990 for some empirical evidence here).

1 In the case of natural transaction exposures, managerial attitudes to currency risk can be expressed through the following hedging policies:

(a) A conservative policy, such as: 'close out' or hedge 100 per cent of all expected foreign currency cash flows using the forward market, future market and money market as soon as the cash flows arise and are known. Use options to hedge the maximum value of uncertain cash flows. Thus options could be used to cover possible cash flows two standard deviations above the expected cash flows levels.

(b) Proportional or partial hedging of transaction exposure, such as: use forward and money market hedges to actively manage or hedge a specific percentage of the known FC exposures. Thus it is at the senior managers' and treasurers' discretion to vary the hedge percentage with the maturity of the exposure; the percentage hedged will decrease with increasing maturity, reflecting less information about future exposures. Options are used to hedge part of the range of uncertain cash flows, e.g. 40 per cent of two standard deviations above the expected cash flows. Thus a low risk policy for partial hedging of natural exposures could be: hedge 100 per cent of three month and 70 per cent of six month known FC exposures; hedge a high percentage of uncertain FC exposures with options, e.g. 65 per cent of two standard deviations above the expected cash flows. A higher risk policy for partial hedging of natural exposures could be: hedge 50 per cent of three month and 25 per cent of twelve month known transaction exposures above say $10,000; hedge a low percentage of uncertain FC exposures with options, e.g. 25 per cent of two standard deviations above the expected cash flows.

(c) Speculative risk taking policies, such as one of the following. Firstly, alter the high risk policy in 1(b) to reduce the hedge percentage per maturity period, because treasury believes it has a better than market forecast of future spot rates. Secondly, adopt a no hedge policy in which all certain/uncertain FC cash flows are left fully exposed and the firm effectively speculates over all possible future spot rates and cash flow states. Thirdly, use options to cover known cash flows and await developments in markets to see if the options will be exercised or the spot market will be used. Thus options are used to speculate over a range of future exchange rates.

2   If the firm has currency trading capabilities it can adopt trading policies to reflect the policies in 1. Thus trading policies could take the following forms:

(a) A policy of only trading in the 'natural' currencies of business. This is done subject to the real needs of the business. Trading skills are used to secure ready access to markets so that the firm can rapidly deal with its own exposure problems. Dealers are not allowed to take uncovered currency exposures at all, or are limited to a maximum of say $50,000 for a short period. Thus the firm is likely to choose variants of policy 1(a) or a low risk version of 1(b) and to use currency trading to support these policies..

(b) A decision to trade in all major currencies in the forward, spot and option markets irrespective of existing corporate exposures. Thus the firm may pursue a risky version of 1(b) and may create exposures in currencies which do not naturally arise in the business. Dealers limits may be very high and their performance measures linked to profitable trading. The primary aim is to make a profit from this trading activity.

Some large MNCs such as BP or ICI are heavily involved in foreign exchange dealing. Firms such as these are likely to have a high degree of internal and external cross-border and cross-currency transactions. The high volume of foreign currency dealing in the currencies which naturally arise in the business can lead to the development of skills that are similar to those of banks. An MNC may also have a wide global scope and this provides it with special access to some currencies. Both advantages may be a source of profit. These factors may lead the MNC to trade in other currencies and with other MNCs and behave like conventional bank dealers.

If a firm does not have this trading capacity, then some combination of 1(a), (b) and (c) is open to it depending on its attitudes to risk and the availability of hedging instruments. In the case of the firm with the trading capability, its natural exposures can be exacerbated by risky trading and new exposures can be created in currencies not normally used in the business.

Belk and Glaum (1990) found considerable variation in the risk taking behaviour of managers of 17 UK MNCs and in their hedging policies for transaction exposure. In 16 MNCs where transaction exposures were managed there was considerable diversity, ranging from hedging all exposures to large scale trading in currencies. The hedging practices identified in their study covered much of the range in 1 and 2 above and it is clear that in practice managerial risk preferences may vary from very risky or speculative policies to conservative hedging policies, with the latter dominating in this study. In the Collier et al. study (1990) involving 11 UK MNCs and 12 comparable US firms, 8 out of 19 firms that perceived themselves as having low currency risk preferred to 'close out' transaction exposure to risk. The majority (11 out of 19) of the firms perceiving themselves to be of low risk did actively manage their transaction exposure to risk. Where transaction risk was perceived to be high, the case firms adopted a close out policy.

In chapter 4 we have seen that, given imperfections in world financial and banking markets, managers should, as a practical alternative, aim to minimize the impact of unexpected real exchange rate variations on the home currency cash flows and earnings of the firm. Corporate pursuit of this goal is considered to be in the best interests of shareholders and creditors in that it minimizes the costs of financial distress arising from currency risk. An active corporate hedging policy using financial markets should always bear this goal in mind.

Thus the risk attitudes of managers and the combination of financial hedging methods chosen must be assessed in shareholder value terms. The questions here are:

- Do they reduce the volatility of corporate HC cash flows?
- Do they increase the expected level of HC cash flows, and thus increase value?
- Do they protect fundamental value arising from the real business?
- Do they create extra value from this financial hedging activity?

The trading functions of treasury must also be assessed in these terms. The questions to be posed here are:

- Does the investment outlay on treasury functions and external transactional systems produce returns or added value that are otherwise unavailable to the firm?
- Can treasury exploit major imperfections in currency markets to make profit and add value?

The firm must therefore assess the impact of new treasury functions on the incremental cash flows of the firm and on their riskiness. The ability of treasury to 'beat' these markets and make profits should be seen as secondary to the aims of the real business of the firm.

High risk policies as in 1(c) and 2(b) should be carefully monitored by senior managers to ensure that treasury is serving the real needs of the business and has not become disconnected from the firm as it pursues trading and speculative profits. There is considerable danger in policy 2(b) that treasury will create new exposures to currency risk that do not naturally arise in the business. This risk taking can increase the volatility of corporate HC cash flows and can increase the likelihood of financial distress for the firm and reduce shareholder value. The March 1991 Allied Lyons case described in the next section, involving speculative trading by treasury in $/£ currency options, provides a signal lesson for those firms that do not ask such questions of treasury. Treasurers who insist on pursuing such policies should justify them in terms of the economic circumstances facing the firm in currency markets and their ability to out-forecast the market. They must also demonstrate that this activity does not distract their attention from their main role in directly supporting and advising the real business.

The conservative and low risk hedging policies must also be justified in terms of these questions and the shareholder wealth maximization goal. Extensive and possibly costly blanket hedging in this way can be questioned if it has no impact on the level and the stability of home currency cash flows within the decision period chosen. This may be because the parity relationships are working across economies and at the level of the firm, or because of currency diversification effects across the firm's cash flows, or because real responses to currency risk such as sourcing decisions or internal methods such as matching of assets and liabilities have dramatically reduced corporate exposure to currency risk. If these factors are at work or these corporate decisions have taken effect then 'close out' or active hedging is costly and serves no real purpose for the firm.

## Case study: Allied Lyons

Allied Lyons, a large British food and drink multinational, had an active international growth strategy in the period 1988–91 (*Financial Times*, 20 March 1991, pp. 16, 37; *The Guardian*, 20 March 1991, p. 15). By 1991, half of Allied Lyons's profits came from overseas, with US subsidiaries and exports to the US being important contributors to group profits. Sales of Beefeater gin and Ballantine's, Teacher's and Long John Scotch whisky, as well as sales from subsidiaries such as Dunkin' Donut, create a large US dollar inflow to the group. These were obvious targets for the use of forward $/£ deals to sell the known dollar cash flows, and for the purchase of pound call (buy pounds, sell dollars) currency options to cope with the exchange of more volatile dollar cash flows.

However, the treasury at Allied Lyons, acting with a high degree of autonomy, decided to take a bet on the path of the US dollar. During 1990 and early 1991 it appears to have sold some very large dollar call options (pound puts), as well as employing some complex strategies to trade in $/£ volatility. This was based on the view that the US dollar would continue to fall against sterling. Indeed by the end of February 1991 it had fallen to 2$/£. However, the dollar turned sharply at this point and rapidly appreciated relative to the pound: by 20 March 1991 it had reached 1.78$/£. Allied's reporting year ended in March 1991, and so the news broke of its very large losses (£150 million) in the foreign exchange markets. The treasury could therefore not hold on in the hope that the dollar would weaken against the pound and thus bring the dollar call options back into profit for Allied Lyons.

The sale or writing of such a large number of call options on the dollar appears to have left the Allied Lyons treasury with a very much larger exposure in dollars than that expected to arise in the food and drink business. It could satisfy only a small proportion of the call on it for dollars from its own dollar cash flows. The latter had been depleted by dollar sales in foreign exchange markets. The rise of the dollar meant that call options sold at 2$/£ were valuable to holders (buyers) when the actual rate turned out to be 1.78$/£. As a result the option holders were highly likely to exercise their option to buy dollars at a cheaper rate (50p each) than existing market prices (56p each). Clearly, the reverse loss conditions applied to Allied Lyons as the seller of the call contracts. It was relying on the dollar depreciating against the pound: it expected that all of the call contracts sold would be 'out of the money' as far as purchasers were concerned. They were not expected to be exercised with a falling dollar, and so Allied Lyons expected to pocket the call premiums. However, given the actual spot rate of 1.78$/£, Allied Lyons had to spend many more pounds than it initially envisaged to buy dollars for their call option holders. The scale of the losses on these contracts suggested that Allied Lyons had become a significant player in the dollar call options market.

This was an unusual role for such a conservative enterprise. It was clearly inconsistent with the need of the firm to sell its known dollar cash inflow exposures in the forward dollar market, to sell dollar call options and to speculate on $/£ volatility. The speculative policy went badly wrong and had an immediate impact on the company share price and probably dented the confidence of its bankers. The aim may have been to boost profits hit by the UK recession. However, treasury appeared to have a high degree of autonomy here, with loss limits and exposures levels very loosely controlled. The apparent lack of control by senior executives over treasury objectives and activities was one of the more worrying features of this case.

## Corporate factors and market constraints in the choice of a hedging policy

Clearly a firm must establish the broad aims of its continuous hedging policy consistent with shareholder wealth maximization. However, the extent of the firm's hedging in terms of percentage transaction exposures covered over each maturity period will also depend on

- the key corporate factors creating its transaction exposure
- how it can improve its access to markets for currency risk management instruments
- how it can co-ordinate information, sourcing and decision making and hedging within the MNC
- the constraints it faces in using market hedging techniques
- the factors promoting their use within the firm.

Understanding these corporate factors and external constraints can provide a basis for an informed hedging policy. However, they must be married with corporate forecasts of transaction exposures and exchange rate changes. The combination of these forecasts with the factors and constraints will play a central role in clarifying the currency risk problem facing the firm and in designing a continuous hedging policy consistent with shareholder wealth maximization.

MNCs can be observed to use a mixture of forward, money market, futures, currency swaps, option and no hedge methods within a continuous transaction exposure hedging policy (Soenen and Aggarwal 1989; Millar 1990; Canaday and Feenstra 1991). Assuming that the aims of FERM, the attitudes to risk, the perceptions of risk and the economic circumstances are constants, the mix of forward and money market hedges depend on many corporate factors. If the firm's need for liquidity is high this will encourage the use of money market hedges. If corporate access to overseas domestic forward or credit markets in the required currencies is poor and this affects the availability of forward or money market hedges in specific currencies and in certain periods, then this will limit the use of either method. If both hedges are unavailable, this should encourage the use of swaps and possibly a no hedge policy.

The use of options compared with money market and forward hedging techniques depends on the degree of certainty of corporate FC cash flows. High certainty encourages the use of the hedging techniques. A high proportion of contingent cash flows encourages the use of options. Thus if a large portion of the FC cash flows are known with a high degree of certainty, these can be fully matched on a continuing basis. If they can only be partially matched, forward contracts can be used for the unmatched FC cash flows to provide a certain HC cash flow over the hedging horizon. The uncertain portion of the FC cash flows can only be guessed. However, a conservative (high) estimate here can provide guidance for the scale of use of currency options.

Many other corporate factors will come into play here, including the range of foreign currencies faced by the firm, the 'lumpiness' and scale of its foreign currency cash flows, and the level of expertise of treasury staff.

MNCs can use a wide range of currency risk management instruments in order to develop experience in their use and to understand what is possible with these instruments. This knowledge will allow the firm to rapidly alter its hedging policies as the nature of corporate FC cash flows changes (e.g. they become more contingent and less certain), as corporate financial problems change (increased need for liquidity, FERM more important because of more FC cash flows) and as market conditions alter (new types of hedging contracts emerge, more currencies become available with forward markets, or deviations from parity occur).

## Improving access to markets and co-ordinating internal supply and use of currency risk management instruments

MNCs can expand and diversify their access to sources of hedging instruments by co-ordinating their use of a core set of relationship banks (Holland 1992a). These banks will be the primary source of tailored money market, forward hedging and currency option contracts designed to match the firm's specific transaction exposure management needs. This group of banks provides the firm with a stable supply of risk management instruments, and access to new innovations.

Canaday and Feenstra (1991) point out that these relationships vary with the nature of the firm's hedging policy and the scale of currency trading business involved. The firm that covers all of its transaction exposures may only generate a low level of foreign exchange transactions. The volumes of trading are likely to be modest, unless the firm is very large. Thus a modest foreign exchange supply relationship is likely to be set within a more significant overall banking relationship for the supply of a wide set of financial services. The role of the bank is to provide advice on alternative risk management instruments and to supply these at market prices. The bank gains some of its profits here from the overall supply relationship. If the firm has a more active stance on managing its exposures, then currency trading volumes may be boosted. From the bank's position, the increased volumes, the increased variety of instruments required and the possibility of advising this active policy can all make the relationship more profitable and viable in its own right. Thus a firm with such a hedging policy may be able to establish a small number of foreign exchange relationship banks. Finally, if the firm is an active trader in foreign exchange markets, then bank margins can become very narrow as the sophisticated client seeks inter-bank buy–sell rates in the currency markets. However, if the firm has the means to make very large scale deals then it can enter into a wholesale relationship with banks and thus act in a manner similar to banks.

MNCs will, to a lesser extent, use currency risk management instruments such as traded currency options and currency futures from exchange based markets. This further diversifies supply and provides additional price pressure and information to control the relationship banks providing the core of hedging instruments. However, the contractual terms of these instruments mean that they are difficult to tailor to the specific exposures of firms. The important point in all of these bank–corporate relationships for each type of corporate hedging/trading policy is to ensure that the bank partner understands what the policy is. If this is the case, then the close supply (and possibly trading) relationship with the bank(s) can provide the firm with an extra buffer against exchange rate uncertainty.

The increased sophistication of treasury trading and information technology in the 1980s enhanced the scope for internal transacting and stimulated the emergence in some MNCs of treasury as an 'in-house bank'. These treasury functions are seen as internal equivalents to external bank suppliers and offer the means to enhance internal co-ordination of transaction exposure management. The in-house bank can buy the currency risk management instruments in bulk from banks, sell them in portions to subsidiaries and keep part of the price difference as a 'profit'. In addition, they can exploit their centralized information on internal currency surpluses and deficits to produce these instruments from internal sources and sell them to subsidiaries. This central function can also act as the mandatory hedging decision making unit for all transaction exposures faced by subsidiaries. This would ensure that the group policy on transaction exposure management is consistent across all subsidiaries and the MNC can make best use of its internal financial system.

ICI, the large UK based chemicals MNC, has such a centralized system for the majority of hedging in the group (Henderson and Rogerson 1987). The UK is the base from which the bulk of exports are made and these UK exposures are the most significant in the group. These exposures with customers and subsidiaries (invoiced in their own currencies) are centralized at group treasury in the UK for the main exporting countries. Subsidiaries are covered from currency risk by the group treasury booking the known transactions at the forward rate appropriate for the transaction maturity and currency. Contingent exposures on say foreign currency price lists will only be covered by the group if requested by the overseas subsidiaries. This centralization means that the UK company can develop a coherent exposure management policy for the group exposures arising from the UK. It can net receivables and payables across the group to reduce overall exposure, and can use its bulk buying power to secure fine rates in the currency markets. Thus one centre of expertise is developed in the group. Outside the UK, exposures of Western European subsidiaries are centrally managed by the treasury management centre in Zurich. In other countries, the relatively small exposures are handled locally.

In practice MNCs will vary their policies on whether the subsidiary must use the central group facility as its sole supplier of hedging instruments and whether it must transfer all responsibility for its hedging decisions to the in-house bank (Belk and Glaum 1990). Too much centralization of decision making may interfere with the autonomy of the subsidiary, and so the benefits of treasury centralization may be restricted to a service role in which bulk buying in foreign exchange, money and option markets and internal production of services are the primary functions of group treasury. In essence the MNC has decided that the incremental value benefits of allowing subsidiary managers to combine their local hedging decisions with their operational decision making outweigh the value benefits of centralized decision making on hedging. This decision may also be much influenced by the ethnocentric attitudes of HQ managers and the political risks of centralizing all financial decisions.

This internal capability, whether a fully centralized hedging and service provision unit or not, when added to carefully managed external supply mechanisms such as relationship banks, transaction oriented banks and exchange based markets, further expands the corporate supply system for currency risk management instruments. This portfolio of internal and external supply mechanisms combines to improve the general capability of the firm to react quickly to changes in its FERM problems and to react to new developments in financial markets. This combined supply system can therefore be seen as an important part of any FERM policy in an MNC in that it also creates a rapid response system designed to reduce the impact of unanticipated exchange rate changes on home currency cash flows. Similar comments can be made concerning the management of interest rate risk. It is here that treasury can be seen to be performing a specialist corporate function designed to buffer the firm against uncertainty in financial markets.

## Factors limiting and promoting the use of external financial techniques

The key constraints on the use of external financial techniques include

- non-availability of domestic forward and credit markets
- non-existence of forward, spot or option markets in certain currencies
- government regulation and control over spot, forward, option and money markets.

A firm may therefore be prevented from employing these techniques for a variety of reasons. Forward or currency option markets may not exist for some currencies. For example, spot markets may exist for significant currencies such as the Brazilian cruzeiro, but the absence of a forward market (in an international financial centre or in the domestic financial centre) in this currency means that alternative forms of hedging have to be considered. Domestic markets may offer forward contracts if the domestic currency is not traded forward in the international centres, but trading may be thin and government control may be high. Major world currencies such as the dollar, the pound and the Deutschmark will have highly active forward markets offering terms from a few days to 12 months with the possibility of even longer terms of up to five years. However, the availability of longer term contracts drops off dramatically as one moves out of these currencies. Further constraints on the use of forward markets stem from governmental controls over the nature of forward deals. In some cases, the firm seeking the forward contract must persuade government officials that it is for real trade purposes as opposed to a wholly financial transaction.

Certain combinations of corporate factors and characteristics of market instruments encourage the use of externally supplied currency risk management products. Internationally involved firms differ in their use of external market based techniques according to specific corporate characteristics. Their use is likely to be much higher in those firms with

- extensive external cross-currency, cross-border trade flows and associated financial transactions
- little strategic or operational flexibility in dealing with FERM problems
- little internal capacity to make FERM decisions.

Market supplied risk management services such as forward contracts and currency options are often much more immediate and accessible for the firm with underdeveloped internal information and financial transfer systems. In addition, the shorter term well known foreign currency cash flow exposures remaining after strategic and operational adaptations to exposure to currency risk are in many firms well suited to the use of external financial techniques. As a result, the medium sized corporation with few overseas subsidiaries is likely to rely heavily on well established and generally accessible markets for currency risk management instruments.

In addition, establishing forward deals in periods, from six months to two years ahead means that the firm has a clearer idea of its financial position over this plan period. This also creates a period of relative certainty for operational and strategic decisions: the firm has time to reflect and make the longer term adjustments to strategy, and time to react and make the medium term alterations to operational decisions. This creates overlaps in the periods in which real and financial decisions can respond to currency risk and extends the overall responsiveness of the firm to currency risks. This demonstrates how the external supply system counteracts some of the inflexibilities encountered in strategic and operational decisions and possibly internal financial methods. It also illustrates the limits to the concept of balancing various real and financial techniques, and demonstrates how several FERM techniques can be combined to deal with currency risk.

This combination of factors (size, relatively large scale of FC cash flows, lack of flexibility in real decisions, absence of internal transacting systems, market accessibility, well known exposures etc.) is therefore likely to lead to a preference for external FERM techniques over internal means.

The following case provides some insight into how a firm can be constrained in its use of real responses to currency risk and how an extensive financial hedging programme can become the centrepiece of FERM.

## Case study: Merck

Merck & Co., a US pharmaceutical MNC, is an example of a company which has learnt much over the 1980s concerning the nature of its economic and transaction exposure and the role of financial hedging in FERM. Merck's treasurers Lewent and Kearney (1990) provide much detail for this policy, and this case is a brief summary of their views.

The company discovers, develops and distributes human and animal health pharmaceuticals. The global industry is very competitive with no firm holding more than 5 per cent of the world market. The industry typically invoices its customers in their local currencies. Merck has about 70 overseas subsidiaries. These typically import products in a part finished state, complete the manufacturing of the product, and market and distribute the final product. Sales are in local currencies, with input costs a mix of import costs (mainly US dollars) and local currency.

Lewent and Kearney (1990) argue that:

1 The use of pricing to alter economic exposure is not significant. Price controls are common in their industry throughout the world and this generally reduces price flexibility to manipulate or react to economic exposure.

2   Competitive responses to currency risk are more likely to play a role in more fundamental long term decisions on R&D and marketing. Thus the MNC invests to create knowledge which in turn creates many forms of flexibility including currency flexibility.

3   Merck's exposure to currency risk tends to be limited to net asset and revenue exposures, with the latter including the most significant economic and financial exposures.

The strengthening of the US dollar in the early 1980s and its potential detrimental impact on the dollar value of net revenues overseas led Merck in the mid 1980s to analyse carefully the impact of currency changes on overseas cash flows. A sales index was constructed to measure the relative strength of the dollar against a basket of Merck's trading currencies. This highlighted the vulnerability of Merck's home currency cash flows (flowing from overseas subsidiaries) to a strengthening of the dollar.

Their awareness of this exposure led them in the mid 1980s to review the firm's global allocation of resources (assets) across currencies and in so doing to determine whether the firm was matched in individual currencies. This analysis revealed that the currency distribution of assets differed from the sales mix. This was because of the heavy asset concentration of research, manufacturing and headquarter operations in the US, and because the sales exposures were in approximately 40 currencies. The analysis made clear that there was a major currency mismatch. They initially considered relocating manufacturing, research and HQ sites but soon realized that there were few obvious candidates for asset relocation (and hence changing the currency of cost cash flow exposures) and so any changes here would have a negligible effect on their net income exposures. Finally, much of their internal financial flows were already being exploited to reduce exposures to currency risk.

As a result of this assessment of the FERM problem, the firm developed an extensive financial hedging programme. They recognized that this would have to be their main response to currency risk. Shareholder requirements dominated their planning of the hedging programme. They decided that well diversified shareholders and financial analysts were not too concerned about currency volatility and its impact on earnings. However, such volatility in earnings could interfere with the firm's capacity to boost internal funds and to use these to make long term investments in R&D and in marketing. These were the source of the primary advantages of the firm in the form of unique pharmaceutical knowledge and brand names. Creating these advantages in turn created some flexibility relative to currency risk. They decided that the best they could do for their shareholders was to maximize long term dollar cash flows and to focus on the potential effect of currency movements which might prevent management from pursuing this goal. Reduction of the impact of currency volatility on cash flows became the major FERM goal. This was also expected to reduce volatility in the supply of retained earnings as the major source of investment capital. This meant that extensive hedging of overseas FC cash flows was the centrepiece of their programme, with currency options being preferred over forward contracts.

Thus the 'residual' FERM problem to be dealt with using external market risk management instruments was extensive for Merck. It was the major corporate response to currency risk, and considerable effort was expended in designing the financial hedging programme. In brief, this programme consisted of five major steps:

1   The production of exchange rate forecasts to provide a range of best guesses about the likely boundaries of dollar strengths and weaknesses.
2   An assessment of the impact of unfavourable exchange rate movements on the five year strategic plan.
3   A critical examination of whether the exposures should be hedged. The shareholder analysis above dominates these considerations.
4   The choice of the most cost effective financial instruments subject to the company's risk preferences. In a strong dollar world Merck would prefer a forward sale because the contract would produce the same gains as the option without incurring the costs of the option. In a weak dollar period both the unhedged and option positions would be preferred to hedging using forward contracts. Since volatility was common and movement either way was likely, Merck was unwilling to forgo the potential gains in a weak dollar period, and so options were the first preference. The cost of the option was accepted as a cost of ensuring a stable climate for implementing the strategic plan.
5   The construction of a hedging programme in which they varied option usage by varying the horizon period for the use of long term options, varying the strike price, and varying the amount hedged. These decisions are continuously refined by sophisticated modelling and experience.

Merck continues to actively adapt all steps in this system as it learns more about the nature of their exposure and risk.

## 7.4 Summary

This chapter began with a comparison of market supplied currency risk management instruments for use with a single transaction exposure. This section illustrated the main features of each hedging method and their limitations and strengths. In practice, MNCs and other internationally involved firms have a stream of transactions of known exposures and these are continuously hedged over the short to medium term exposure period. MNCs have learnt much about their transaction exposure problems over the past two decades and a variety of practices have emerged. This chapter has argued that firms should develop these policies in a manner consistent with shareholder wealth maximization. Thus managers should clearly understand the risks they are avoiding or perhaps exacerbating by their activities in forward, money and options markets. They should also attempt to understand the nature of their transaction exposure and the factors promoting and constraining the use of hedging techniques. Understanding these corporate factors and external constraints can provide a basis for an informed hedging policy. However, they must be married with corporate forecasts of transaction exposures and exchange rate changes. The combination of these forecasts with the factors and constraints will play a central role in clarifying the currency risk problem facing the firm and in designing a continuous hedging policy consistent with shareholder wealth maximization.

Finally, we can note that in chapters 4, 5, 6 and 7 we have explored a wide range of real and financial responses to currency risk. The availability of FERM tools ranging from strategic through operational decisions to the use of internal and external financial techniques can enhance responsiveness to currency risk by dramatically increasing the choices open to the firm. This portfolio of FERM methods can also extend or ensure a time overlap between methods and offer unique solutions to unique problems. In some cases market based methods may create time or flexibility for strategic and operational responses. In contrast, strategic methods such as currency risk sharing amongst project partners may be the means to counteract lack of availability or flexibility of market supplied risk management instruments. Strategic decisions may also create the conditions for operational flexibility. The sophistication of internal financial transfer systems can have strong impact on the need for external financial risk instruments. We can therefore see that the beneficial interactions possible within the whole portfolio of methods may be of considerable value to an enterprise. These benefits are only available if the firm can employ the full set of methods open to it. In this way we can see that the whole portfolio of FERM methods can greatly enhance corporate flexibility relative to currency risk.

# 8

# Corporate Foreign Investment Decisions

The commercial enterprise investing overseas finds its path strewn with many novel problems unique to the international arena. These include a variety of national tax systems, the availability of government grants and loans, the risks of political interference, and controls over the repatriation of overseas income. In addition the firm may face a wide range of possible market imperfections. In particular, imperfections in world product and factor markets, segmentation in world capital markets, and deviations from the parity relationships were identified in section 3.3 as likely to be significant influences on IFM decisions. These issues were ignored in section 3.2 where the analysis of the international capital budgeting decision was assumed to be identical to that of the domestic decision. These additional complexities in the international economic environment therefore stimulate a renewed look at traditional domestic capital budgeting techniques and a consideration of why firms invest overseas.

The aim of this chapter is to understand how an MNC can generate a set of investment opportunities. In section 8.1 we consider the various theories of direct foreign investment (DFI) and seek to explain the corporate rationale behind decisions, in particular the manner in which overseas projects are likely to generate additional wealth for the owners of the firm. In section 8.2 we consider the nature of political risk and its impact on the overseas investment decision. In section 8.3, we consider how these theory sources can be used together in a strategy to co-ordinate the search for and evaluation of valuable overseas investment opportunities. In section 8.4 we consider how MNCs have developed their global strategy: this insight into global strategy provides further clues and guidance in the search for overseas investment opportunities. This chapter provides an essential context for chapters 9 and 10 where detailed analysis of the international capital budgeting decision is undertaken.

## 8.1 Theories of Foreign Investment by the Firm

The major forms of international involvement open to a firm are importing and exporting, direct investment overseas in productive assets, licensing and management contracts. Direct foreign investment is therefore just one form of overseas involvement in economic activities. The broad question of which of these is most appropriate for a particular firm will be briefly addressed in this section, but the primary emphasis here will be on the overseas investment decision by the firm.

The theory of DFI emerged in the 1960s when Hymer (1960) followed by Kindleberger (1969) argued that imperfections in national and international product and factor markets were the major determinants of DFI. In the neo-classical world of perfect competition, where there are no barriers to trade, information is costless, and there are no economies of scale, exporting is the only form of international involvement possible. In this world there would be no advantages accruing to a firm locating its productive facilities abroad and so DFI should not take place. Of course DFI does occur and it is seen to be a significant and growing feature of the world economy. Given the relative permanence of this phenomenon, considerable scholarly effort has been expended since the 1970s in attempting to explain corporate DFI. Major contributors to this debate have been Caves (1971), Vernon (1966), Buckley and Casson (1976) and Dunning (1977).

Hood and Young (1979) and Calvet (1981) have provided comprehensive reviews of the various theories of DFI and these will provide a basis for much of the discussion in this section. Calvet (1981) has proposed a taxonomy of the determinants of DFI based upon varying degrees of market imperfections. As noted in chapter 3, he distinguished between the following four major classes of imperfections:

1   market disequilibrium hypotheses
2   government imposed distortions
3   market structure imperfections
4   market failure imperfections.

For example, the common feature of group 1 hypotheses can be seen as the short term nature of the disequilibrium conditions and the associated profit opportunities. The reactive response of profit seeking firms and other arbitrageurs to these opportunities will eventually bring about a return to equilibrium conditions. DFI flows would therefore only occur under disequilibrium conditions and would continue until markets adjusted and reached new equilibrium conditions. Thus DFI is considered to be of a transitory nature and is curtailed when rates of return between countries are equalized. One example from Calvet (1981) clearly illustrates this view of the DFI process:

> ... foreign direct investment would flow from high labour cost countries to low cost countries in the pursuit of cost minimization. This hypothesis is no exception to the transitory character of the DFI phenomenon, because the demand for labour in countries where wages are low will tend to hike up labour costs, while the lack of demand in source countries will drive wages down. The result: a finite life for direct investment.

However, DFI does seem to be of a more permanent nature than the above view would suggest, and market imperfection groups 2, 3 and 4 are generally thought to provide a more complete explanation of the determinants of DFI.

In group 2, governments are seen to be distorting markets and therefore creating profit opportunities. The distortions can take place in markets for real goods, raw materials, foreign exchange and domestic capital. The forms of government induced distortion are many and varied and include tariffs, import quotas and differences in national tax systems. These can create incentives to invest abroad as the net benefits of having a foreign subsidiary begin to outweigh the net benefits of exporting.

The EC is a classic case of governments combining to form a competitive internal market and at the same time erecting common external barriers to trade. This market imperfection provides two reasons for inward investment by firms external to the EC: firstly, the raising of tariffs would make their exports more expensive; and secondly, production within the EC would provide access to a large protected market. Large US MNCs found the EC an attractive prospect in the 1960s and 1970s and Japanese MNCs have reacted in a similar fashion in the 1990s . European firms have also found the large US market a very attractive base for their operations for similar reasons.

Group 3 refers to firms deviating from perfectly competitive behaviour owing to their power to interfere with market pricing mechanisms. This could be due to oligopolistic behaviour by large MNCs in markets for real goods, raw materials and foreign exchange. Oligopolistic behaviour could manifest itself in two ways: firstly, a firm may create barriers to entry by its creation of unique products in the marketplace; secondly, such firms may display their interdependence by predicting and then emulating the actions of their competitors.

Vernon (1966) made an important contribution in this respect when he developed the product life cycle theory of DFI. In this theory overseas investment is seen as part of the natural life cycle of a product from its initial launch through maturity to its eventual decline. In the first stage domestic production predominates as production teething problems are ironed out and a market presence is established. In the second stage – maturity – the well established production technology creates opportunities for long production runs. However, competition from similar products reduces profits and raises questions about production costs. When this occurs overseas production facilities are sought to exploit lower costs abroad and to ensure that positive domestic and overseas profit margins are maintained during the decline of the product. This is essentially a defensive strategy in that the MNC is reacting to the threat of losing its domestic market by moving abroad to reduce unit production costs and thereby prolong the profitable life of the product.

Knickerbocker (1974) has extended this idea of defensive DFI by describing the 'follow the leader' behaviour of some firms. When one member of an oligopolistic industry 'breaks rank' and invests abroad the other firms react quickly with similar overseas investments. This graphically demonstrates the interdependence of oligopolists as they attempt to ensure that no member of the industry group achieves competitive advantages denied to others.

Caves (1971) has also made a major contribution with respect to oligopolistic behaviour and DFI. He argued that the MNC has a considerable capacity to initially differentiate its products in its domestic market. Small changes, both physical and subjective, may prove crucial in protecting a product from imitation and may also prove essential in maintaining consumer interest in the product. This ability of the MNC to differentiate its products in this manner is based upon its typical heavy investment in research and general marketing functions. This in turn allows it to produce a steady stream of new products at lower cost than its competitors. If successful the firm can use its unique knowledge, of producing and marketing the product, at little or no extra cost in overseas markets. If such knowledge cannot be easily separated from the physical production process or marketing function then DFI may be the best means to exploit it. In some cases overseas investment may be pursued to maximize profits on the heavy research and marketing costs already incurred in the domestic market.

Calvet's group 4 deals with situations where markets fail, in particular due to departures from perfect market assumptions about production techniques and commodity properties (1981: 44). This refers to situations where it is not possible to create a market in a particular commodity or good. The commodity generally seen to be central to this debate is technical and managerial knowledge. The characteristics of knowledge, especially the 'lumpy' inventive process and the associated 'leaking' of ideas during the process, create problems for both the production and the international transfer of knowledge. As Calvet remarks:

> First, reasons of social efficiency would dictate that existing knowledge be made available as a free good. Hence the dilemma: how is the production of new knowledge to be motivated, if no property rights are to be granted? Second, the natural characteristics of knowledge would favour its transfer within a single firm, hence 'justifying' foreign direct investment over other alternatives of exploiting foreign markets.

Calvet concludes by noting that if markets for knowledge are difficult to organize, internalization within the firm achieves two objectives: firstly, to provide channels for the transfer of knowledge at lower cost than via external modes; and secondly, to slow down the dissipation of this knowledge to competitors.

## The eclectic theory of international production and the MNC

Dunning (1979) seeks to integrate many of the competing theories of DFI into an eclectic theory of international production by MNCs. He identifies industrial organization theory, the organizational failures literature and location theory as the major sources of explanation of direct foreign investment. A combination of these theories is employed to explain the international involvement of firms and their choice of modes of transacting. Industrial organization theory and location theory explain the willingness of firms to go overseas. The work of Williamson (1975), Buckley and Casson (1976) and others explains the choices made to transact in markets or within the MNC.

Industrial organization theory stresses the ability of an internationally involved firm to compete with domestic firms in their domestic market, in terms of the ownership specific advantages of the international firm. These advantages include technology and marketing skills, and other advantages not available to domestic firms. When the firm expands abroad, it creates an imperfect market for its goods in the receiving economy. Firms may possess ownership specific advantages because of home country characteristics and industry characteristics, as well as because of unique corporate attributes (Dunning 1981). Firms that originate in countries with comprehensive protection of proprietary rights and with tight controls over inward DFI will have a strong tendency to develop ownership specific advantages. At the industry level, if features such as a high degree of product or process technological intensity exist, as in the consumer products and chemical industries respectively, the emergence of ownership specific advantages seems likely. Finally, the enterprise may stimulate the development of its own ownership advantages by its attempts to be innovatory or market oriented.

Location theory isolates country specific advantages as a key variable in explaining the decision to invest overseas. If the firm cannot combine its advantages with advantages unique to a particular location, then exporting and licensing may be viable alternative forms of overseas expansion. The location specific advantages could include unique factor inputs such as cheap labour or raw materials, or access to an otherwise inaccessible (large) market. Dunning also argues that the source of location specific advantages may vary according to country, industry and firm specific considerations. For example, the Japanese government's financial aid to Japanese firms investing in South East Asian labour intensive industries may create or enhance location specific advantages in these countries. A more conventional example is a host government offering incentives to make locations within its borders more attractive. At the industry level, industry specific tariffs and non-tariff barriers can affect the attractiveness of a location. At the level of the firm, factors such as managerial perceptions of a location's characteristics can strongly influence the location decision.

Internal organization theory (organizational failure theory) stresses the transaction cost efficiency of transacting within firms as opposed to arm's length transacting in overseas markets. In this theory, markets will be internalized when the transaction costs of overcoming market imperfections exceed the costs of internal corporate trading. Buckley and Casson (1976) have employed many of the above ideas on the significance of transactions and their costs in developing the internalization rationale for the MNC. Their view is that the MNC consists of many interconnected activities such as marketing, research and development, and training of labour as well as production. The connection between these activities is a series of flows of intermediate and intangible products such as knowledge and expertise as well as the more conventional semi-processed materials and tangible goods. Markets in incomplete products are difficult to organize and these problems are compounded when one deals with intangibles such as knowledge. It is this which provides the incentive to bypass markets and internalize transactions within the firm and, in the case of the MNC, across national borders. Buckley and Casson emphasize the role of industry specific factors as the source of the imperfections which provide the incentive to internalize markets. These factors may include the nature of the product, economies of scale and the structure of the external market. Knowledge of the product, in terms of marketing skills and production technology, is seen as a very significant industry specific factor and this provides a strong incentive to internalize knowledge market imperfections.

Magee (1976) has developed a very similar argument in his appropriability theory of MNC economic behaviour. He stresses the argument that the MNC's advantage derives from its capacity to fully appropriate returns from its investment in knowledge and technology. Magee argues that a distinctive feature of these firms lies in their knowledge or information creation capacity with respect to complex technologies. These technologies and the firm's knowledge are less likely to be imitated than simple technologies. Furthermore, the MNC can transfer sophisticated technology more efficiently internally than via markets. The latter point stems from the public good nature of knowledge and the need for innovatory MNCs to protect their unique knowledge. Patent systems offer some protection but more effective control and possibly a slowing down of the diffusion of the innovation may be achieved by internalization of knowledge market imperfections via DFI. If an MNC has the capacity to internalize in this way, then it also has the incentive to invest in facilities that may generate further innovations as well as the means to maximize returns from its existing knowledge.

In both the internalization theory and the appropriability theory the possession of assets such as special technology alone does not give a firm a unique advantage. It is its ability to internalize the asset, rather than license or sell the asset to foreign firms, which gives the MNC the key advantage. Thus the combination of unique knowledge or managerial skills in tandem with the ability to exploit internalization advantages over imperfect international markets places the MNC in a very strong position.

Finally, it should be noted that the firm incurs costs when it internalizes market imperfections. These may include the costs of sophisticated control and communication systems essential for economic exchange within the MNC. The marginal costs associated with internal search, bargaining and monitoring of transactions must be less than the equivalent marginal costs in markets for internalization to be a feasible strategy. This is the case when we are considering internalizing markets for real goods and services or markets for capital and financial services. In the first case, internalizations lead to the creation of real production assets owned by the firm, and these subsidiaries may be located in the home market or overseas. In the second case, internalization leads to the setting up of a sophisticated treasury function that sources capital and financial services internally as well as exploiting world capital, currency and banking markets.

## Corporate choices for overseas involvement

The above theory of markets and hierarchies, and the associated theories of internalization and appropriability, are valuable in explaining why a firm would prefer to set up a subsidiary rather than transact directly in markets. However, they do not provide a full explanation of why a firm would wish to set up the subsidiary abroad. Industrial organization theory and location theory provide the insights to understand why a firm will invest abroad.

These theory sources taken together constitute the current orthodoxy in theorizing for MNCs. Dunning (1979) has integrated the theories into an eclectic theory of international production based around ownership, locational and internalization advantages, i.e. the OLI theory of international production. These suggest which route of overseas involvement is likely to be preferred by a firm. Dunning (1981) uses table 8.1 to clarify the alternative entry modes to servicing overseas markets. As can be seen from the table, ownership specific advantages are a necessary prerequisite for each form of international involvement by the firm. If internalization and location advantages are absent then contractual resource transfers such as licensing or management contracts are feasible. If foreign location advantages are absent then exports or contractual resource transfers are feasible, with the former being more likely since the firm would have the opportunity to exploit two sources of advantage. If all three advantages are present then all three modes of overseas involvement are feasible but overseas production is more likely given that the firm can exploit all of the advantages in this way.

**Table 8.1** Advantages of alternatives in overseas involvement

| Route of servicing market | Advantages | | |
| --- | --- | --- | --- |
| | *Ownership* | *Internalization* | *(Foreign) location* |
| Foreign direct investment | Yes | Yes | Yes |
| Exports | Yes | Yes | No |
| Contractual resource transfers | Yes | No | No |

This theory is a valuable contribution in understanding entry modes to overseas markets, but it does suffer from some limitations. For example, interactions amongst the advantages and the impact of this on choice is not clear. Agarwal and Rawaswami (1992) studied the effect of interrelationship among a firm's ownership advantages (size, multinational experience, ability to develop differentiated products), location advantages (market potential and investment risk) and internalization advantages (contractual risks) on its choice of entry mode to overseas markets. Their findings (for one industry) imply that though some firms would like to invest overseas they are constrained by their limited size and experience of multinationality. In contrast, large experienced MNCs were prepared to invest in overseas markets with relatively lower potential if their strategic needs required this. Smaller less experienced MNCs preferred to enter high potential markets by sharing the costs and risks via joint ventures. They also found that firms with a higher ability to differentiate their products were concerned about the loss of this advantage in countries with high contractual risks. This led to a preference for direct investment over exporting because this allowed greater control and protection of the advantage overseas. In markets that have high potential but exhibit high investment risks, the investment risk location disadvantage led the case firms to prefer exporting over DFI to exploit the market potential location advantage. Their results also implied a tendency to avoid exporting when the potential returns through the other entry modes are high, and to prefer exporting when the potential risks for the other modes are high. In the case of sole venture (DFI), firms did not prefer this mode when contractual and investment risks were high, even when market potential was high. However, firms may use this route, even when contractual risks are high, if they can offset these risks through a high ability to differentiate their products. This implies that differentiation, rather than size, is the important factor here in promoting the DFI route.

Another perspective on the limitations of the eclectic theory can best be demonstrated by using it to explain the economic grounds for disinvestment. Boddewyn (1983) has used Dunning's eclectic theory to consider whether foreign disinvestment theory is the reverse of DFI. He notes that the first difference between disinvestment and investment is that the former requires only that one of the ownership specific, location specific or internalization advantages be absent, whereas the latter requires that the three conditions be satisfied simultaneously. Secondly, ownership specific advantages do not sufficiently differentiate between parent company and subsidiary factors. Barriers to exit, such as production and distribution facilities linked to other parts of the firm's global operations, may therefore protect a subsidiary from disinvestment. Thirdly, if the original investment has been made by an oligopolist on a 'follow the leader' basis then it does not follow that the firm will disinvest if the leader does so. It may stay in the market precisely because the other oligopolist has left. Other major differences with the OLI investment theories include the higher divisibility of the overseas asset in disinvestment and the magnified role of the potential buyer of the asset. Boddewyn concludes that Dunning's theory is strong on explaining the initial decision to invest overseas in production facilities. However, subsequent decreases (disinvestment) in DFI will require changes in only one of the three conditions. To understand disinvestment therefore requires research on how these advantages erode over time and what forms the disinvestment takes. Thus Dunning's theory offers us the opportunity to lay the foundations of a disinvestment theory by testing his model of DFI through a 'reverse mirror image'.

Despite these limitations the eclectic framework provides some important clues as to how an MNC makes choices between overseas disinvestment and investment in production plants and sales offices as well as decisions to develop consultancy and licensing facilities. It also provides some important insights into the sources of value and the origin of incremental cash flows associated with the project (Contractor 1984). However, the entry mode decision should not be made in isolation (Kim and Hwang 1992). The choices should be placed in the broader strategic context for the MNC. Sections 8.3 and 8.4 clarify the impact of strategy on such choices. In addition, this decision area is much complicated by the range of political systems facing the MNC, in particular by the role of governments in restricting the options identified above. The concept of political risk will be investigated in section 8.2 to assess the implications of governmental interference for corporate strategy on overseas involvement. This provides some insight into how political forces constrain strategic decisions concerning the appropriate mode of overseas involvement for the MNC.

## 8.2 Political Risk and the MNC

Multinational firms operate within and across a wide range of political systems. These include:

- democratic, highly developed market economies
- underdeveloped economies with various political ideologies
- strongly nationalistic countries
- centrally directed economies
- groupings of nations into economic and political systems
- elements of previously linked states.

Figure 8.1 summarizes the conventional view of political risk in which conflict arises between the aims and purposes of international firms and those of host governments. The economic basis for this conflict is generally about the control of allocation of resources of MNCs and the distribution of the perceived surplus from the operations of the MNC within the host

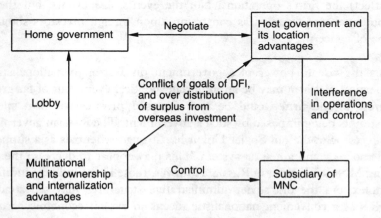

**Figure 8.1** Conventional view of political risk

country and on a global basis (Rugman et al. 1986: 268). The dispute may lie in which ownership specific or locational advantages have created the surplus, and who should receive the benefits, the firm or the host country. The literature in this field has generally focused on the 'political risks' facing direct foreign investment by MNCs in one host country. In particular, the possibility of a conflict of goals between the host country and MNCs and the risk of expropriation of overseas subsidiaries have received considerable attention. Various strategies have been suggested in which the MNC negotiates directly with the host government, or via its home government, so as to reduce the actual or expected impact of such interference. Other possibilities of governmental interference are also considered in this literature and include specific discrimination against foreign firms, or a policy of gradually forcing out overseas firms.

In practice the international firm faces the possibility of governmental interference in its whole range of financial decisions, including financing and currency risk management decisions (Vernon 1983). For example, the cross-border flow of funds to other subsidiaries of the firm may be severely restricted.

The expression 'political risk' has several meanings in the literature, ranging from unwanted governmental interference in firms to unstable political climates constraining corporate policies. Kobrin (1979: 71) has attempted to clarify what is meant by this term in the following manner:

> What we are, or should be, concerned with is the impact of events which are political in the sense that they arise from power or authority relationships and which affect (or have the potential to affect) the firm's operations. Not the events, *qua* events, but their potential manifestation as constraints upon foreign investors should be of concern.

Thus the rise to power of a government on a strongly nationalistic or ideological platform may be an important political event, but of far greater interest to the firm would be the increased prospect of firm specific constraints being imposed by such a government. The Russian government as successor to the old Soviet Union has strong credentials as a supporter of democracy and a market system. This may appear to decrease the risks facing MNCs investing in Russia. However, those in the military-industrial complex and the old soviet administrative structures may see attacking MNCs as a convenient nationalistic means to exploit economic hardship and to sabotage economic reform and thus their best route back to power.

Under these circumstances, an MNC may face higher risks in the new Russia than it did in the old Soviet Union.

Kobrin further points out that, although the same governmentally imposed constraints (e.g. restrictions on funds transfer) may be motivated by economic as well as political factors (or both), the two may be distinguished for the purposes of corporate analysis and response. For example, it may be possible to identify economic and political rationales for the imposition of certain constraints. Thus subsidiaries that are central to a country's economic development, and can be efficiently operated wholly in the host country, may face a wide range of controls, irrespective of the ideology of the particular government. Alternatively, a firm may be at risk because of a combination of host country ideology and home country origin. Hence a subsidiary of a firm originating from an old colonial power may be particularly sensitive to political changes in a newly independent nation.

Vulnerability of a firm to governmental interference is therefore a function of both the political and economic significance of the firm to a country, and its unique characteristics. Natural resource subsidiaries, based in developing countries and providing crucial overseas earnings, have been particularly exposed to expropriation. Manufacturing subsidiaries, relying on other parts of the MNC to provide key inputs and product markets, and located in countries with several alternative manufacturers, have been less susceptible to governmental interference.

Kobrin also distinguishes between the environment and the firm. Instability is seen as a property of the environment, and risk a property of the firm. The link between these depends on whether outcomes are evaluated under conditions approximating to uncertainty or certainty. The most likely situation facing the manager of the MNC is subjective uncertainty, where managers have to make their own subjective judgements about most of the important outcomes and their likelihood of occurrence. In this situation business risk can be seen as a function both of the political events and of the managers' perception of the events. This in sharp contrast to certainty where both outcomes of events and their impact on the firm are known, and so the firm does not face business risk.

The above attempt to broaden and clarify the concept of political risk can form a central part of any managerial response to potential political interference in investment, financing and exposure decisions.

Eiteman and Stonehill (1989: 501–2) outline a managerial strategy for dealing with political risks associated with the overseas investment decision:

1  forecast political risk
2  negotiate the pre-investment environment
3  develop operating strategies during the investment
4  identify compensation strategies after expropriation.

The first step is the use of various techniques to forecast political risk and identify its expected impact on the firm. Several models have been built to help assess the political stability or otherwise of various political systems. These include the business environmental risk index (BERI) and the political system stability index (PSSI). Clearly such models can be of considerable value to managers in judging likely outcomes for the firm. The major difficulty with these methods is the lack of an explicit conceptual link between their measures of political instability and the particular impact of an unstable political system on the firm. The firm and its political risk advisers must therefore assess the special vulnerabilities of the firm to specific scenarios of political events in the country concerned and thus the likelihood of an adverse impact on the firm. The Russian scenario illustrated above is one of many possible political futures for that country. The scenario of a return of absolute power in the hands of the old soviet elite may hold few fears for McDonalds fast food outlets in Moscow. However, firms such as Rolls-Royce with joint ventures on aero engine development and aircraft construction, or British Aerospace involved in a joint venture for satellite launching, may find that both new absolutists emerging in Moscow and Western governments fearing the return of the Cold War would abort high technology joint ventures with clear defence implications.

This detailed firm specific analysis cannot identify all scenarios and identify all risks with confidence. Thus a proactive move is to try and reduce the risk beforehand. Steps 2, 3 and 4 above are concerned with this approach. In the second step the firm negotiates the environment prior to investment. This includes concession agreements, adaptation to host country goals, planned divestment and investment guarantees. The third step involves developing post-investment operating strategies to increase the costs to, and decrease the benefits to, a government of political interference. Thus the firm can adapt its production, marketing, distribution and other operating policies with this in mind. Finally, when expropriation occurs, the firm can identify compensation strategies to increase the likelihood of payments from the nationalized subsidiary. Such strategies include rational negotiation, application of power tactics to bargaining, legal remedies (national and international) and management surrender in the hope of receiving salvage values.

This academic refining of the concept of political risk and appropriate managerial strategies does not seem to have its counterpart in managerial views and practices. Kobrin (1979) reviewed the existing surveys of managerial assessments and evaluations of political environments and noted (p. 75) that:

1   Managers consider political instability or political risk, typically loosely defined, to be an important factor in the foreign investment decision.
2   Rigorous and systematic assessment and evaluation of the political environment are exceptional. Most political analysis is superficial and subjective, not integrated formally into the decision making process, and assumes that instability and risk are one and the same. The response is frequently avoidance; firms do not get involved in countries that they perceive to be risky.
3   Managers appear to rely for environmental information primarily on sources internal to the firm. When they look for outside data, they are most likely to go to their banks or the general or business media.

Despite these limitations, in practice there is some evidence that MNCs are becoming more sophisticated in their analysis of political systems and their effect on the firm. Kobrin et. al. (1980), in a preliminary survey, conclude that the assessment and evaluation of non-market environments is emerging as a new management function in relatively large international firms. The development of corporate political risk assessment methods and functions is a necessity in the 1990s for any MNC considering expansion into Eastern Europe and the now independent states of the former Soviet Union. Democracy and market systems will be very fragile here over the decade. The managerial strategy proposed above may therefore be of some value to those companies aware of the complexity of the change process in these countries, the opportunities open to them, and the need to carefully manage the inevitable political risks.

This section has highlighted the role of political risk analysis in identifying constraints for corporate strategic choices. The ability of the MNC to exploit market imperfections through internalization is likely to be heavily constrained by the corporate perception of the relationship between such corporate actions and political interference. The firm therefore needs to balance the exploitation of opportunities for profits against the possibility of provoking unwanted political interference.

## Transnational co-operation and political risks

The focus of the fairly conventional analysis of political risk outlined above has been on interaction between individual host countries and MNCs. At present, one of the major threats to the unique transnational autonomy of the MNC comes from developments in the international political system. World institutions such as the United Nations, the Organization for Economic Co-operation and Development (OECD) and the European Community (EC) have become very active in developing guidelines to monitor and control MNCs' economic behaviour. These developments give a strong indication that significant and highly likely globally organized political events will impinge upon the operations of MNCs. The major institutions and vested interest groups are illustrated in figure 8.2.

For example, the OECD has developed a code of conduct, i.e. a set of guidelines for overseas corporate behaviour, and this specifically refers to issues such as disinvestment, expropriation, inter-company transfers, taxation, financing etc. (adopted by the Council of Ministers at their Paris meeting in June 1976). This and other developments in the EC and UN ensure that MNCs are becoming more aware of the need for good 'corporate citizenship' and the need to balance profit seeking actions against the social and economic goals of host countries.

In June 1992, the UN organized the Rio de Janeiro Earth Summit (the United Nations Conference on Environment and Development, UNCED) to sign a convention on climate, to establish a framework to protect the biological diversity of the globe, to outline a declaration on the protection of tropical forests, and to establish a comprehensive action plan for environmentally sensitive economic development. This summit was the culmination of much debate and conflict from the early 1970s concerning world development, global pollution and the North–South economic divide. These problems and issues moved up the world political agenda over this period and the convening of the conference was a considerable coup for the UN.

If we view the Rio Earth Summit from the narrow perspective of the MNC and the political risks it faces, then the conference and the mood it represents could constitute a major source of co-ordinated global political risk. For example, the Climate Convention sought to make massive energy savings to avoid global warming. The large US, Japanese and European car

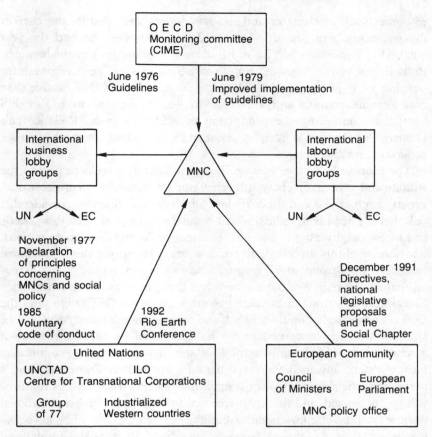

**Figure 8.2** World institutions and the MNC

manufacturing MNCs would face a heavy bill if they had to rapidly reduce the release from their cars of carbon dioxide as a warming gas or of nitrous oxides as one source of acid rain. The implementation of lean burn engines and the reduced reliance on fossil fuels would mean high costs in R&D and in production changes. High energy using nations such as the US, with their own car producing MNCs, have historically resisted target setting for pollution levels here. However, President Clinton decided in April 1993 to sign the Biodiversity Treaty and seek the most effective means to curb US pollution sources. Nations with large tropical forest areas have also argued that they need compensation for forest conservation as well as for providing the forests that absorb the warming gases from the industrialized North. The MNC is therefore embroiled in a political debate about global resources such as clean air and the rain forests and, despite the current disagreements, will probably face escalating costs here beyond the year 2000. However, some MNCs will find new opportunities in this context. Rolls-Royce provides power units (based on existing aero engines) for burning gas in power stations. These produce far less sulphur dioxide than coal burning stations and are therefore less vulnerable to EC or US legislation controlling the production of acid rain gases. Rolls-Royce's intensive R&D effort is likely to maintain this advantage over other power generation methods.

The framework Convention on Biological Diversity seeks to protect the wildlife and genetic diversity still remaining on the globe. Pharmaceutical, genetic engineering and other biologically based MNCs face considerable risks here. The bulk of industrialized countries are arguing that this genetic and biological diversity is a global resource, whilst the developing nations, where most of this diversity still remains, are arguing that this is a national resource. The group of 77 countries from the developing South is co-ordinating the policy of these nations on these matters. Equivalent policy liaison groups in the industrialized North include the OECD bloc and the G10 countries acting on their behalf and for their home based MNCs. The latter groups are concerned that a halt be called on the destruction of animal and plant life (mainly in the LDCs) so that, in part, they continue to form a genetic and medicinal seed bank for the future. From the MNC's perspective the risks are that existing or new patents based on this resource will be questioned, and that their freedom to exploit this global or national resource will be circumscribed or become very expensive. They have also expressed concern about demands on them to provide funds and equipment for LDC scientists to do their own research at home as well as to allow them a share in profits from new drugs developed from genetic banks in their countries. Again the economic basis for this conflict rotates around the technological, production and marketing advantages of the MNC in exploiting global biodiversity and the nation based location advantages in providing the diversity. Thus the roles of country or MNC advantages in creating the surplus, and in determining who should receive the benefits, the firm or the host country, is also central to this debate. Unfortunately, many members of the group of 77 are in such dire economic positions that their need for aid and for incoming investment may mean they have to make *ad hoc* deals on these matters with large MNCs. This could undermine the achievements of Rio and its inevitable successors in the 1990s. The political risk and ethical issues here will continue to plague MNCs throughout the 1990s and beyond.

At a more regional level, the EC has shown considerable interest in legislating to control MNC transfer pricing, taxation behaviour and company disclosure practices towards employees (Robinson 1983). Figure 8.3 summarizes developments here.

In the case of tax, differences between the EC member states have created incentives for the MNC to manipulate domestic European tax systems, and so tax harmonization policy on the part of the EC is seen as the long term solution to this problem. However, in the short term, national tax agencies have the 1977 Directive on taxation in transfer pricing

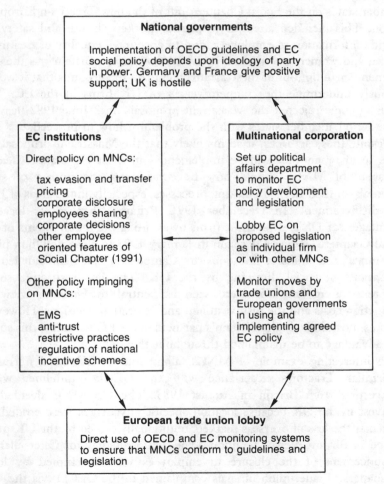

**Figure 8.3** European institutions and the MNC

for guidance. This increases co-operation between the tax agencies in transferring information and ensures that artificial transfer of profits between subsidiaries of an MNC is contained.

A second area of major interest to the EC lies in encouraging the sharing of corporate decision making powers between managers and other corporate interest groups, particularly trade unions. This level of political interference in the crucial area of managerial decision making autonomy has caused some alarm within MNCs. The 1980 Vredeling proposal was the first major attempt to establish EC standards here. The December 1991 Maastricht summit produced further agreement amongst 11 of the 12 member states on the Social Chapter draft of the new Treaty on European Union. This included attempts to protect workers' health and safety, to provide information to employees, and to encourage equality of treatment of men and women at work and in the labour market. Britain was the sole EC member to opt out of these arrangements on the grounds that it would seriously undermine the competitiveness of UK firms in the EC. The Danish people rejected the Maastricht proposals on 2 June 1992, leaving the other 11 member states with the problem of how to proceed.

Despite these setbacks, it seems likely that the Maastricht proposals in some form or another will be implemented in most EC states. Clearly, managers of MNCs should now be considering the impact of such proposals on their decision making processes, especially in the areas of DFI and disinvestment. In December 1991, Britain enhanced its location advantages for US and Japanese firms by avoiding the requirements of the Social Chapter. Hoover's decision in January 1993 to close its Dijon plant in France and transfer the jobs to Cambuslang in Scotland led to accusations of social dumping by the UK. The less restrictive social requirements in the UK were seen as central to Hoover's view of production costs and the disinvestment and relocation decisions. However, it seems most unlikely that Britain's partners in the EC will allow this social cost advantage to be maintained throughout the 1990s.

An interesting example of MNCs falling foul of EC social norms is Caterpillar Tractor's experience with the OECD guidelines when disinvesting from Britain in August 1983. The US MNC decided to disinvest in the UK because location specific advantages were eroded, in particular the loss of overseas markets traditionally served by the UK plant located in Birtley, Newcastle upon Tyne. Unfortunately for Caterpillar its announcement of the closure to employees was pre-empted by local newspapers. Trade union officials complained to the OECD, via the UK contact point, that its guidelines on consultation and disclosure to employees had been violated. Caterpillar was also accused of abusing its own corporate code of conduct as well as the Vredeling proposals. This was particularly embarrassing for a company that had argued against the Vredeling proposal on the basis that its internal code of conduct was an adequate protection for its employees (McDermott 1984). Caterpillar was exonerated on the OECD complaint but its corporate image as a concerned employer was tarnished. This in turn may make the firm a focus of attention and perhaps increase the level of governmental interference especially in other European locations.

An analysis of the likelihood of such environmental events may give a firm some indication as to the nature of future political interference in operations. However, analysis of joint political actions by governments also requires that clear cut links be identified between such concerted actions and their impact on the firm. This highlights the point that events such as Rio in 1992 and Maastricht in 1991 can produce systematic global or regional political risk for all MNCs or for those in specific industries such as car production or biotechnology firms. This contrasts with conventional views of political risk in which a firm is subject to unanticipated interference by one government. The general principles of political risk analysis identified by Kobrin are still relevant in situations involving co-operative action and legislation by many governments. Thus in scenario building the firm needs to concentrate on events which are political in the sense of power or authority relationships which affect or have the potential to affect the firm's operations (Kobrin 1979: 71). In the case of the UN, the OECD and the EC, the crucial question is whether these supranational institutions do have powers similar to sovereign states and whether this power is likely to be directed at MNCs. At present, it appears that the EC is the only supranational institution with the means, via anti-trust moves and Directives (and their incorporation in national laws), to have a significant influence on MNC decision making. However, even in the case of the EC the active use of the anti-trust clause in the Treaty of Rome is a fairly recent phenomenon, and EC Directives have historically been very slowly implemented by member states. Robinson (1983) is optimistic that these supranational institutions will have a major influence on MNCs and argues that 'soft law' emanating from institutions such as the OECD is proving influential and that the 'hard law' of the EC will have a major impact. This may well turn out to be the case but it does seem that, for some time to come, MNCs will face interference predominantly from the traditional source of individual nation states. A focus therefore on factors such as bilateral investment protection treaties between MNC home countries and host countries may give the MNC clearer indications of likely levels of political interference.

The question concerning the power of supranational institutions to control MNCs is therefore still an open one. However, it is clear that MNCs should analyse these events in the way suggested by Kobrin so as to assess for themselves the likely impact of these developments on their operations. Existing prescriptions for political risk analysis are particularly weak in linking expected environmental events to their impact on a firm. This leaves the firm somewhat in a vacuum in the analysis of political risk. One solution is for the firm to expend resources in identifying its relationships expected with specific political systems. In particular, detailed scenario building can help identify whether the firm faces certainty, objective uncertainty or subjective uncertainty in these matters. If the uncertainty is subjective, the contribution to risk will be greater because managers will be uncertain about both outcomes and the probabilities associated with them. Attitudes of managers to overseas involvement will become critical in this case as risk is now also a function of the perception of managers as well as the events themselves. An ethnocentric bias in these attitudes may severely limit the scope of analysis and dramatically reduce the perceived investment opportunity set for the firm.

Despite the limitations of existing frameworks for political risk analysis the MNC still has to take political issues into account in its international capital budgeting decision. Managers do consider political risk to be a very important aspect of this decision but apparently do little to build political risk analysis into the search for and evaluation of overseas investment opportunities. In the following section an attempt is therefore made to demonstrate how political risk analysis can play an explicit role in international capital budgeting decisions.

## 8.3 A Strategy for Co-ordinating Investment Decision Making in the MNC

In this section we draw together the various strands of thought discussed in sections 8.1 and 8.2 and use them to outline a normative strategy for co-ordinating overseas investment decision making by the MNC. This involves an active search for a set of positive NPV projects and their subsequent evaluation. The specific analytic methods for evaluation of capital budgeting projects will be outlined in chapter 9, with a detailed case example illustrated in chapter 10.

Figure 8.4 combines the DFI and political risk theory areas discussed in sections 8.1 and 8.2 and shows how they can be employed to investigate and guide the strategic investment choices faced by the firm. In the diagram, the eclectic theory of MNC behaviour isolates the three key conditions which a firm must identify if it is to embark upon direct foreign investment:

1   It must have ownership specific advantages relative to other firms in the market.
2   This market must have a location specific advantage for the investing firm.

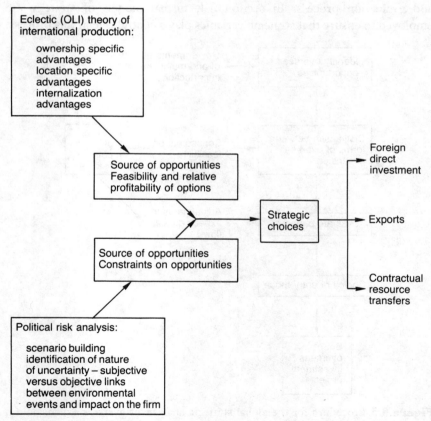

**Figure 8.4** Theoretical basis for the MNC's strategic investment choices

3    The firm must be able to fruitfully exploit its advantages internally rather than through market trading.

The eclectic theory is of particular importance to an MNC involved in the strategic analysis of perceived overseas expansion opportunities. It clearly indicates that a DFI opportunity must satisfy ownership, internalization and location conditions before it dominates exporting or licensing choices. If it does, then the strategic analysis must take into account the role of political risk as a constraint on corporate actions as well as assessing the economic viability of the project. This choice between each entry must be placed in the global strategy of the MNC (Kim and Hwang 1992). The absence of such a strategic context may lead to analysis of each opportunity in isolation and to unplanned *ad hoc* choices of overseas expansion modes. In this section, this strategic context is employed to guide the investment search and evaluation process. In section 8.4, formal models of strategy are employed to ensure that strategic variables play a central role in this process.

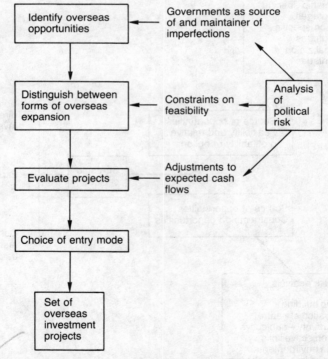

**Figure 8.5** Procedure for the global strategic analysis of overseas expansion opportunities

A simple procedure to guide a global strategic analysis of overseas expansion opportunities is outlined in figure 8.5. This figure forms the basis for the discussion in this section.

## Identifying valuable overseas investment opportunities

The initial step is to identify world-wide opportunities for overseas expansion and to assess the strength and persistence of the imperfections underlying them. Conventional finance theory suggests that the first step would be to search for specific conditions which give rise to positive NPV overseas investment opportunities. This would be consistent with the conventional goal advanced for corporate finance in which managers should seek to identify projects which achieve shareholder wealth maximization (SWM). This provides an ideal to aim for, rather than an operational search goal. This is because orthodox financial theory is less than clear on how managers might identify positive NPV projects (Brealey and Myers 1981: 736). Managers may therefore feel that search goals deemed consistent with SWM are more suitable. For example, if managers believe, on an *a priori* basis, that market growth and production cost economies are more likely in the US, the Far East and Australia, and that these offer the best prospects for improving shareholder wealth, then this can act as a guide to a much reduced global search for overseas investment opportunities.

Alternatively, the firm may have the resources to systematically scan world markets and production locations to identify investment opportunities. A systematic global search would include the following:

1 The identification of all major markets in which demand for the company's products is expected to grow.
2 The assessment of the strength and persistence of growth in these markets stemming from
   (a) Market imperfections due to governmental controls over the flow of goods or capital
   (b) Market failures, especially with respect to the firm's specific skills and knowledge. These market failures may persist because of the intrinsic difficulty of creating markets for intermediate goods and for knowledge.
3 Forecasts of the likely actions of competitors in these markets and their impact on growth expectations.

If the opportunities can be identified, the net present value rule can be used to assess whether the opportunities uncovered are expected to increase shareholder wealth.

Dunning's (1979) work on the eclectic theory of international production can be used to give further guidance on the above search. It may be particularly valuable in identifying how combinations of ownership specific, location specific and internalization advantages create valuable investment opportunities. This may be useful in combating the limitations of orthodox finance theory in identifying positive NPV opportunities.

An understanding of the firm's unique ownership specific advantages is an essential element in the investment opportunity search process. These advantages may derive from unique corporate attributes such as heavy investment in research and development and in the general marketing function. According to Dunning, they may also be attributed to industry and country characteristics. Thus factors such as home market size and extent of product differentiation in an industry may contribute to the ownership specific advantages held by a firm.

Location specific advantages can be classified into existing and emerging advantages. Again, these can be analysed on the basis of firm, industry and country attributes. Existing location specific advantages may consist of

1   those stemming from comparative costs as identified in neo-classical trade theory
2   those accruing to the firm by virtue of its multiplant economies
3   those stemming from industry characteristics such as industry specific tariffs in a particular location.

Location specific advantages may emerge in some countries because of government policy to improve the attractiveness of the location. This could include new tax benefits, expansion of the higher education system, and the availability of new 'soft' loans. Locations may also be expected to become more accessible to the multiplant economies held by some MNCs. The entry of Spain to the Common Market has made Spain more open to incoming DFI in industries such as the automobile industry which were previously protected by the Spanish government. In a similar fashion, the potential or actual removal of industry specific tariffs may make a location appear more attractive to a firm. For example, the British government was forced by the EC in the mid 1980s to open government computer contracts to all major computer manufacturers. ICL, the British based computer firm, therefore lost a major market advantage and other computer firms such as Honeywell, Hewlett-Packard and IBM may now find the UK market attractive enough to increase their current level of investment in Britain. Since the ending of the Cold War, Russia has been able to capitalize on its abundance of scientific talent and its world leads in significant high technology areas. In May 1992 the US telecommunications firm AT&T signed up 100 senior Russian scientists to do contract research in the field of fibre optic technology. Initially, this is a joint venture with a former state controlled research establishment. However, the combination of access to new locations, low costs and high corporate needs could lead to the establishment of R&D subsidiaries by MNCs in Russia.

## Distinguishing between DFI, licensing and exporting choices

In the second step of the global investment strategy (figure 8.5), managers can employ the three conditions outlined in table 8.1 to distinguish DFI opportunities from disinvestment, licensing and exporting opportunities. This requires

1   Examination of the perceived opportunity to see if location and ownership specific advantages are expected to persist.
2   Assessment of the relative costs of transacting in the firm and in the overseas market. In addition, the firm should assess its potential for achieving transaction cost economies relative to the market being considered.

If internalization and location advantages are absent but ownership specific advantages exist, then licensing or other forms of contractual resource transfer are the only feasible means to expand abroad. If locational advantages do not exist but ownership and internalization advantages do exist, then exporting is a feasible route for servicing the overseas market. If all three advantages exist, then DFI is feasible. These criteria may also be applied to existing operations overseas. If one of the ownership, locational or internalization advantages is expected to be eroded or completely lost, then disinvestment may be necessary. Licensing or exporting may therefore replace DFI as the current mode of economic involvement in a country.

DFI may also become feasible if the firm is able to reorganize and achieve internal transaction cost economies. This may be done through the introduction of new organizational structures which reduce internal research, contracting and monitoring (hierarchical control) costs. Clearly this change would also have to be associated with locational and ownership advantages for DFI to be feasible. One example of such reorganization was the change from a divisionalized structure to a global matrix structure in some MNCs. This was designed to capture the benefits of centralization and local knowledge at the same time. Unfortunately, there are some well publicized cases, such as Dow Chemical, in which this kind of reorganization has not achieved its promised benefits. Bartlett (1983) argues that the central issue is to build and maintain a complex decision process rather than to find the right formal organization structure. This may therefore be the way forward for a firm to effect substantial internal transaction cost economies.

The DFI and contractual resource transfer options both contain many sub-options. Thus DFI may vary according to ownership strategies and entry strategies. Ownership options range from minority stakes, through various forms of joint venture depending on the nature of the partner, to 100 per cent ownership. Generally, the degree of ownership choice will depend on the need for control. If the firm can exploit its ownership, locational and internalization (OLI) advantages with a less than 100 per cent stake then other degrees of ownership become feasible. In the case of entry strategies for DFI, the major options are 'green field' building of production facilities or the acquisition of existing facilities. The choice here will lie with the option which allows the firm to make best use of its OLI advantages. This choice may, however, be severely constrained by governmental interference, especially in the case of acquisitions.

## Evaluating overseas investment projects

The final steps in the global investment strategy (figure 8.5) involve evaluating each overseas expansion choice, including DFI, disinvestment, licensing and exporting options, and choosing between these projects on the basis of their positive NPV contributions to the firm. The first two steps of the global investment strategy can be used to identify the influence of the ownership, locational and internalization factors and political risk on the incremental cash flows expected by the parent from the project. This approach can therefore provide basic data for the conventional NPV analysis of alternative capital budgeting projects including DFI, licensing, contractual resource transfer and other hybrid forms of overseas involvement. These data, in turn, can be processed and analysed using a computer based capital budgeting model. The global search and analysis stages can also provide the background information or scenarios for sensitivity analysis of a particular project. The logic of international capital budgeting evaluation will be discussed in chapter 9, followed by a detailed case example in chapter 10.

## Political risk as a constraint on investment search and evaluation

Political and economic events are intertwined and are experienced together by the manager of the MNC. In the above analysis of the investment search and evaluation decision process we have used a framework derived from economics, with political events implicitly employed as constraints (figure 8.5). However, political risk analysis can be explicitly used in this decision process to assess the interaction between political and economic events and their expected impact on overseas operations. The major difficulty in this approach lies in the poor conceptual link between the analysis of political changes and the identification of events likely to impinge upon the firm. Despite this problem, an attempt to explicitly identify the possible impact of political events on the firm is a strategy superior to one in which political events are assumed away or only partially incorporated in the decision process.

Thus the simple strategic procedure outlined above can be extended to include corporate assessments of political risk in each step of the above analysis. In figure 8.5, political risk analysis is shown as providing key inputs to each step. Political risk analysis is therefore considered to have a wider area of application than its conventional use involving DFI analysis.

For example, if we take a European perspective, then in the first step, involving a search for overseas opportunities, political risk analysis can help identify both the source of many market imperfections, and the commitment of European governments and the EC to their maintenance. In the second step, information on governmental preferences for certain kinds of MNC involvement can be invaluable in assessing the political feasibility of DFI, licensing or exporting. If all three economic advantages are present, it may still not be feasible to exploit them through DFI. This may be because potential political interference is viewed as a constraint in exploiting direct investment advantages and so licensing is chosen as the preferred means for overseas expansion. One example of this is where location advantages exist at present but where there may be some doubt on their continued availability owing to uncertainty about the implementation of, say, EC Directives and anti-trust law. This may be interpreted as political interference, raising the expected corporate or internal transaction costs to a point where arm's length trading is preferred. As a result the boundary between the firm and the market is determined in part by political risk considerations. Another example of this may be where exporting is the preferred mode but growing protectionism in the EC means that direct investment is the only means to gain access to the market. In this case the market transaction costs are raised by political interference and internalization advantages make DFI feasible. Japanese MNCs may be particularly vulnerable to this possibility.

In general, the issues here can best be addressed by considering the impact of likely government actions on ownership specific, location specific and internalization advantages. Thus government or inter-government actions may enhance or reduce some or all of these advantages for a firm. Ownership advantages may be improved by a country's protective attitude to certain industries. Internalization advantages may be limited by a country's anti-trust policy. Location advantages may be improved by a government's heavy investment in infrastructure.

One major source of growing political interference stems from the tougher implementation of the EC Social Chapter and the OECD guidelines on MNCs. European trade unions have been active in identifying abuses of the OECD code of conduct, especially in the areas of the disinvestment decision and industrial relations. The EC Social Chapter as the successor to the Vredeling initiative will be important in this respect. As a result of the December 1991 Maastricht summit this is expected to be implemented in the 1990s in at least 11 out of the 12 member countries, with the UK allowed an opt-out clause. This will make MNC decision making in many areas subject to many additional costs included in the health and safety provisions and in providing information and advance consultation with the workforce. This is seen by some EC member states such as the UK as reducing their responsiveness to change precisely when the challenge from Japan is at its greatest.

The trend for increasing implementation of the EC Social Chapter and the OECD code may decrease the attractiveness of some EC locations for US and Japanese MNCs and may therefore influence the way in which these companies expand overseas. Thus a US or Japanese MNC may consider investing in the UK in preference to, say, Germany because of the competitive advantages of avoiding the costs thought to be associated with the Social Chapter of the 1991 Union Treaty. MNCs with European subsidiaries will have to be particularly aware of the effects of their disinvestment decisions on their image as good corporate citizens, especially if corporate behaviour during contraction of employment or disinvestment involves violation of either the Social Chapter or the OECD guidelines. The possibility that these new location and political costs may be incurred needs to be incorporated into the first two stages of the strategic analysis (figure 8.5) and the consequences for investment and disinvestment decisions assessed.

Finally, in the third stage, political risk assessments can be incorporated into the NPV analysis of overseas projects. Political risks considered to be unsystematic in nature (relative to a particular world or domestic portfolio) can be identified, and adjustments made to expected cash flows to reflect the risks. The discount rate remains unchanged, because these adjustments do not alter the systematic risks of the project. This issue will be considered again in chapter 9 on project evaluation.

The formal strategy outlined in figure 8.5 and described above can serve as a central co-ordinating device for capital budgeting in the MNC. Its benefits are clear:

1 It is based upon the prevailing wisdom and theories about the overseas expansion behaviour of MNCs.
2 It explicitly incorporates political risk analysis throughout the complete strategic analysis.
3 It uses well established concepts of finance in the form of the NPV rule to aid in the evaluation of projects and in making the final decision.

The major weakness of this approach stems from the availability or otherwise of resources to implement it in detail. A global search process is likely to be limited both by the cognitive and attitudinal limitations of managers and also by the organizational capacity of a firm. However, MNCs will inevitably grope towards such a strategy and devote considerable resources to the overseas investment decision. A decision to structure this key decision area based upon the best elements of theory and practice therefore seems appropriate.

## 8.4 Global Corporate Strategy and Investment Decisions

We can gain further insight into how an MNC can generate a set of investment projects by considering some of the strategic planning practices of MNCs.

F. R. Root (1977) has described one evolutionary overseas expansion strategy employed by some firms. This initially involves exporting, followed by partial overseas investment in selling and/or service facilities, possibly in parallel with some licensing agreements. The eventual establishment of full overseas production completes the overseas investment process. This can be seen as a deliberate learning strategy by the firm. The firm begins with low risk (and low return) overseas involvement and, by learning more about its specific advantages, it becomes more involved in overseas projects with higher risk and return characteristics.

Other strategies employed by MNCs include the following (Vernon and Wells 1981):

- exploiting technological leads
- exploiting a strong trade name
- exploiting other advantages, including economies of scale, shut-out pricing, vertical integration, multiple markets and sources, and follow the leader
- exploiting a scanning capability.

These strategies and Root's evolutionary strategy are based upon the unique experiences of many companies and offer rich insight into the strategic possibilities for an MNC. They are also consistent with the global investment search strategy outlined in section 8.3 in that they can provide guidelines with respect to specific opportunities. For example, Root's evolutionary strategy may be appropriate for one particular opportunity facing a firm. The firm may feel that this substrategy will allow it to gradually collect the necessary information on ownership, location and internalization advantages. Thus this strategy could be employed within the context of the capital budgeting search strategy outlined in section 8.3. Similar comments apply to the other substrategies identified above. For example, exploiting technologies and trade name advantages can be seen as part of a global search for ownership, location and internalization advantages by an MNC.

An evolutionary strategy may be of particular importance to firms new to overseas business and to those firms facing situations where the level of risk is very high. However, the more mature multinational, fully experienced in DFI, licensing and exporting, may decide that it does not have to take this traditional route. Instead a world-wide perspective, in which the firm seeks to identify its unique advantages and those of particular locations, seems most appropriate in an increasingly competitive world market.

Dymsza (1984: 170) has outlined one such model for comprehensive strategic planning for multinational corporations. The basic elements of this model include the following steps:

1  A re-evaluation of company philosophy or business mission.
2  A managerial audit of strengths and weaknesses of foreign subsidiaries and the overall MNC.
3  An assessment of competition in national markets and a projection of key political, legal, economic, cultural, regulatory, technological and business factors in major countries and regions.
4  An analysis of major opportunities and risks and a specification of key strategic issues by major units around the world.
5  The formulation of objectives and global strategies for the corporation, divisions and national subsidiaries, with contingency plans to deal with changing and unexpected developments and action programmes to achieve implementation of the strategies.
6  Given the strategic plan the units of the MNC determine the operational plans, including detailed budgets.
7  A control system monitors performance against targets in the tactical plans and budgets.
8  Periodically, the MNC revises its strategic plan to adapt to changes that have taken place.

Many variations on the above theme are possible but the model captures many features to be found in the strategic planning systems of multinational corporations. Dymsza points out that it should be seen as a dynamic model in a highly interdependent process. Thus steps 1 to 8 can be considered as iterative with much passage of information throughout the hierarchy, and managers at many levels will be involved (to varying degrees) with the global planning process. There is a growing literature on the topic of global strategy, but the detailed appraisal of this important subject area is outside the scope of this book. The interested reader may wish to consult Channon (1978), Porter (1980), Davidson (1982), Robock and Simmonds (1983), Rugman et al. (1986) and Daniels and Radebaugh (1992) for detailed variations on the global planning theme described by Dymsza.

Again, this form of global planning has much in common with the overseas investment strategy outlined in section 8.3. This can be seen as an essential component of the form of global strategy espoused by Dymsza and others, with the limitations of each of these differing but related approaches being offset by the benefits of a combined approach to planning. Thus sections 8.3 and 8.4 can be seen as providing a key link between the purely financial considerations of this book and the broader strategic concerns of the MNC as manifest in Dymsza's model.

## 8.5 Summary

In this chapter we have considered how a firm can develop a global investment strategy. To do this we have had to consider various theories of direct foreign investment (DFI) and the way in which overseas projects are likely to generate additional wealth for the owners of the firm. Political risk was seen as a key constraint in this decision area and the chapter sought to identify operational concepts of political risk and its impact on the overseas investment decision. These concepts and theory sources were combined in a simple decision procedure designed to guide the search for valuable overseas investment opportunities. This was supported by a discussion of how MNCs have developed their global strategy and the relationship between global strategy and the search for overseas investment opportunities. This chapter provides an essential context for chapters 9 and 10 where detailed analysis of the international capital budgeting decision is undertaken.

# 9

# The Analysis of the Capital Budgeting Decision

This chapter is concerned with analysis of the overseas capital budgeting decision. The global strategic investment analysis discussed in the previous chapter provides a key context for this chapter in that it aids the MNC's search for valuable overseas investment opportunities. In contrast, the assumption at this stage is that the overseas investment opportunity has been identified.

This chapter investigates how the firm can use the project to exploit identifiable imperfections and the related corporate advantages and how this can increase the wealth of the firm and its shareholders. This requires a systematic evaluation of the benefits and costs of the overseas investment decision. The chapter therefore focuses on theoretical models for the valuation of capital budgeting projects. It provides the basis in chapter 10 for a detailed case example and the development of a computer based model as a decision aid for managers involved in this complex decision area.

We begin by looking at the two central tasks in a capital budgeting exercise:

- the development of a decision model or rules to value the risky cash flows generated by a project
- the prediction of the size and risk of the incremental after-tax cash flows of the project.

The first task, concerning the appropriate decision model, has long been the focus of financial theory. In this task two major issues arise:

- What is the appropriate opportunity cost of capital for the project cash flows?
- How can value dependencies between the investment decision and the financing decision be analysed?

Clearly these two issues are related. In efficient domestic capital markets, the second issue rarely arises. However, in the case of the internationally active firm such dependencies arise frequently in the capital budgeting decision. For example, the availability both of governmental interest subsidies and of project specific funds may create dependencies between investment and financing decisions. These dependencies must therefore be explicitly analysed.

In the second major capital budgeting task, the central issue is how to create adequate high quality information on the project's expected cash flow stream. The issues of how to maximize information flows from internal sources and how to make best use of available information are amongst the most difficult practical problems faced in capital budgeting. Three approaches to this problem may be adopted:

1  Clarify what is meant by incremental. In particular, identify which of the project cash flows are incremental to
   (a) the project, irrespective of its geographic location within the MNC's world-wide operations
   (b) the subsidiary and its geographic position
   (c) other subsidiaries or affiliates of the firm
   (d) the parent or whole MNC cash flow position.
   In addition, decide what portions of these cash flows are remittable back to the parent.
2  Classify the incremental cash flows so that the effects or otherwise of real exchange rate changes can be isolated. This should allow managers to assess those parts of the cash flow stream affected by real deviations from parity and those parts remaining unaffected.
3  Develop a computer based project cash flow model. This can be used to simulate various economic conditions, and to assess the sensitivity of cash flows to possible changes. Both the systematic risk and the unsystematic risk of the cash flows may be analysed in this way. In the case of systematic risk the sensitivity of project value to changes in the discount rate(s) can be assessed. In the case of unsystematic risky events, alterations can be made to cash flows to assess their impact on project value.

The choice of a decision model and the creation of cash flow information are central to the international (and domestic) capital budgeting decision. Thus the following pages attempt to answer some of the above questions, beginning with the decision model issue in section 9.1 and continuing with the cash flow generation problem in section 9.2. This will be followed in chapter 10 by a capital budgeting case example in which a computer based model will be used to generate the cash flow information and to perform sensitivity analysis on the case problem data.

## 9.1 A Decision Model for International Capital Budgeting

The choices open to the international financial manager with respect to a decision model are limited to various forms of the NPV rule. This model is generally considered to be conceptually superior to both the internal rate of return model and the payback model (e.g. Van Horne 1980: 115). Major competing forms of the NPV model include the following:

- the net present value rule using a corporate weighted average cost of capital (WACC) as the discount rate in the NPV model
- the adjusted present value (APV) rule in which specific discount rates are identified for different risk classes in the project's cash flows.

Much of the debate on the relative merits of these decision models and their components can be found in Modigliani and Miller (1963) and in the *Journal of Finance* between 1973 and 1977, with Myers (1974; 1977) and Bar-Yosef (1977) being the contributors to this debate. Shapiro (1978b), Lessard (1981) and Booth (1982) have made major contributions, drawing on the work by Myers and others and adapting it to the IFM field. This debate will be briefly summarized here.

### The weighted average cost of capital and the NPV rule

We begin by looking at the concept of the corporate weighted average cost of capital. The WACC is the after-tax interest on debt for the company weighted by the proportion of debt in the firm's capital structure, plus the return on equity expected for the company weighted by the proportion of equity in the firm's capital structure. In formula terms it can be measured by the following:

$$\text{WACC} = r_d\,(1 - T_c)\,(D/V) + K_e\,(E/V)$$

where $T_c$ is the corporate tax rate; $D$, $E$ are the market values of corporate debt and equity respectively; $r_d$, $K_e$ are the corporate debt interest rate and required return on equity respectively; and $V = D + E$ is the total market value of the corporation.

The company's required return on equity can be measured using the capital asset pricing model as follows:

$$K_e = r_f + \beta_e + (r_m - r_f)$$

where $\beta_e$ is the company beta value, $r_m$ is the expected market return and $r_f$ is the risk free rate.

The advantage of using the WACC as the discount rate in the net present value rule is that it is simple, given that all financing effects are included in a single discount rate. The disadvantage is that it assumes that individual projects are identical to the firm as it currently exists. In other words new projects are assumed to be of identical systematic risk to the firm, and to make an identical contribution to debt. However, in the case of international capital budgeting neither of these assumptions is likely to be valid. Overseas projects are likely to be of different systematic risk and to make individual contributions to the firm's capital structure.

In addition, there are other possible sources of increased or reduced value in the financing decision as well as those created by the availability of interest tax benefits. The former include government funds being available at better than market rates and the possibility of valuable opportunities becoming available to the multinational in segmented capital markets. These additional value effects should therefore be explicitly analysed.

## The adjusted present value rule

These problems indicate that the elements of project value should be examined individually. Myers (1974) suggests that this problem can be solved by a return to the fundamental principle of value additivity. This states that the whole value of a project is equal to the sum of the values of the parts. (Brealey and Myers 1981: 400).

In this approach the value effects of the financing and investment decisions are separated as follows:

$$\text{APV} = \overset{(1)}{\sum_{t=0}^{n} \frac{E(CF_t)}{(1+k_t)^t}} + \overset{(2)}{\sum_{t=0}^{n} \frac{TS_t}{(1+r_t)^t}}$$

where term (1) is the present value of the expected operating after-tax cash flows discounted by $k_t$, the all equity discount rate reflecting the project's business risk; and term (2) is the present value of the tax benefits produced by employing debt, discounted at the cost of debt $r_t$.

This method can be widened to include all important side effects of accepting the project. The idea behind APV is to 'divide and conquer' this complex problem. No attempt is made to try and capture all effects in one calculation, especially when interactions between investment and financing decisions are expected to occur (Brealey and Myers 1981: 406). The APV rule therefore divides up the present value terms and focuses on each term to maximize the development and use of information. Thus project cash flows are classified according to their systematic risk characteristics. A present value for each risk class of cash flows is calculated by employing a unique discount rate for its level of systematic risk. These present value terms are then summed to find the increment to value derived from the investment decision.

Lessard (1981) has expanded this approach to deal with the problems of evaluating foreign investment projects. The APV equation now contains cash flow categories and present value terms that explicitly deal with the following factors:

| (1) | (2) | (3) | (4) |
|---|---|---|---|
| APV = PV of capital outlays | + PV of remittable after-tax operating cash flows | + PV of tax savings due to depreciation | + PV of financial subsidies |

| (5) | (6) | (7) | (8) |
|---|---|---|---|
| + PV of project contribution debt capacity | + PV of other tax savings | + PV of additional remittances | + PV of residual plant and equipment |

### Discount rates for capital budgeting

The cash flow and present value terms (1) to (8) above will be discussed in more detail in the case study problem to be analysed in chapter 10. In the model, each of the cash flow categories is discounted at an appropriate rate to reflect its unique systematic riskiness. Some version of the capital asset pricing model (CAPM) is used to calculate discount rates for foreign investment risks that are considered systematic in nature, i.e.

$$\begin{array}{ccc} \text{project discount} \\ \text{rate} \end{array} = \begin{array}{c} \text{risk free} \\ \text{rate} \end{array} + \text{project beta} \left( \begin{array}{cc} \text{market} & - & \text{risk free} \\ \text{rate} & & \text{rate} \end{array} \right)$$

In the present state of knowledge, management will have to decide which view of international capital markets (integrated or segmented) corresponds to the systematic relationship between the project returns and those of an economy (world or domestic). For example, if the project has input and output prices dependent on the world economy then a world capital market factor seems most appropriate. The evidence discussed in chapter 3 provides some support for the integration assumption.

A further problem in estimating discount rates lies in calculating beta values. As a first approximation, the firm can assume that the project risk is identical to that of the rest of the enterprise. Thus the company's beta derived from its reference stock market (segmented domestic or integrated international) can be used to estimate the project beta. Such betas are based on historic security and market returns. As a result, the analysis assumes the future returns generating process is the same as the historic process. In addition, historic stock market betas will have to be 'degeared' or reduced so that the effects of corporate debt financing are taken out. The joint debt and equity financed company returns will be more volatile than those of the same all equity financed company because of the effect of gearing. The tax benefits on interest charges will also boost the debt/equity measured returns $D/E$. Thus the all equity beta can be calculated from the company beta as follows:

all equity beta = company beta$/1 + [1 -$ marginal company tax rate $\times (D/E)]$

This provides an all equity beta suitable for estimating an all equity discount rate for the firm's operating cash flows. This is a valuable reference point for the firm when assessing how different (if at all) the risk characteristics of the project are from the rest of the firm. Essentially the firm has to assess how the returns from the project will move or covary with returns from its reference equity market index. This may be easier to assess if the changes in systematic risk characteristics involve a relatively small change from those of existing assets with well known risk characteristics. Clearly, if the firm has little experience of a totally new type of project it may face a major difficulty in generating the basic data for beta calculations.

Many problems arise with discount rates if the firm makes unfounded assumptions about the nature of the risk they face. For example, when estimating discount rates for overseas project, managers may initially assume that projects arising in politically unstable regimes require larger risk premiums than those recommended for comparable domestic projects. However, if capital markets are segmented the foreign project may be providing otherwise unattainable diversification benefits to home based shareholders. These are valuable to shareholders and as a result discount rates can be lowered to reflect the diversification benefits.

Alternatively, if capital markets are assumed to be integrated, the foreign project's required return measured relative to a world portfolio will generally be lower than the required domestic return. This is more likely if the project is located in a less developed country (LDC) where different economic and political risks can provide larger diversification benefits. Such benefits should however not be exaggerated, because the economies of most LDCs and the internationally attractive projects that arise within them are likely to be linked to the world economy in a significant way. Again, in this case, discount rates may be lower than initially assumed by managers.

Managers may also view some risky events (e.g. major commodity price changes) as having a unique impact on a project, whereas in practice the unanticipated commodity price change has a pervasive influence throughout the world economy. Managers may assume that this 'project specific' risk is diversifiable in a portfolio context and reduce expected returns accordingly. In so doing, they may be ignoring a risk that is globally systematic and thus important to their shareholders and other investors holding world diversified portfolios (or partially diversified portfolios) subject to a world risk pricing mechanism.

The above example demonstrates that the national origin of the firm's shareholders or the international diversification or composition of their portfolios does not matter in integrated capital markets. British shareholders holding a British only portfolio are still subject to a world asset pricing mechanism in integrated markets. A change in the firm's investor composition to overseas shareholders holding more internationally diversified portfolios will not change this.

The UK market index, risk free rates and betas will reflect this world risk pricing mechanism and will therefore provide suitable information for discount rates. Thus the use of the UK index may be seen as appropriate for UK domestic firms with assets located in the UK economy.

If the project is located overseas and has risk characteristics unusual in a UK context then its beta may be best measured relative to a broader equity market such as the US market or even better a global market index. Markets such as the US security markets provide beta data for a very wide range of assets.

Thus a portfolio consisting of companies included in the existing US market, the UK market, and in other open equity markets may be seen as the appropriate market portfolio to reflect the asset pricing mechanism in the various open national capital markets in which the MNC's shareholders and other investors are assumed to transact. This may be approximated by an index composed of stock market indices from the major world equity markets. If such a convenient international market index is not readily available, the British MNC may decide that the US market index is a reasonable surrogate source for market returns, risk free rates and project betas. The US domestic market deals in claims on cash flows derived from a wide variety of assets. Thus most of the world's industries will be represented here, as will many overseas companies and US MNCs with extensive overseas assets. In addition, this market has extensive risk measurement information services and is likely to provide an international firm with a rich data set on asset betas and associated project returns. US betas can therefore provide one basis for estimating project discount rates. Alternatively managers may prefer to use one of the world capital markets indices now being provided by international banks as the basis from which to estimate project betas and discount rates.

## Exploiting information sources on discount rates and project risk

Clearly, a firm must make full and economical use of available information on discount rates and project risks. Two methods of doing this are,

- adjusting expected project cash flows for unsystematic or diversifiable risks

- using systematic risk cash flow categories as a means to maximize information usage.

It is possible to employ both methods together as long as the analyst understands the scope and limits of each approach.

In the first case above, Shapiro (1978b: 11) has argued that the expected project cash flows can be adjusted for unsystematic risk. Those political and economic risks that are deemed unsystematic in nature (relative to say a world or domestic portfolio surrogate) are identified and expected cash flows are adjusted to reflect managerial views of these risks. As long as these adjustments do not alter the systematic risks of the project, there is no reason (from the CAPM view) to change the discount rates to reflect these risks. The practical difficulty with this approach lies in identifying, on an *a priori* basis, risks that are systematic or unsystematic. Risks that appear to be unique to a situation, and are diversifiable, may turn out to be systematic. Bank lending to LDCs in the 1970s was based on the view that the loans would not go into default together because of the relative uniqueness of each LDC economy. Despite these difficulties, adjusting cash flows for unsystematic risks is likely to be an important means for exploiting information sources and assessing the impact of risks on project value.

Overseas subsidiaries of an MNC may have access to unique information on the local political situation and political risks impinging on the project. This in turn can be used to estimate the likelihood of events which would reduce or terminate returns from the project. At one extreme this may mean expropriation of the firm's overseas assets; more likely is the use of new controls over remittances from the project back to the parent. These events may appear unique to the firm and its project. However, if they are part of a systematic political movement across the Arab world, or South American countries, the full adjustment of the cash flows for these risks would be mistaken. Clearly, the interaction between national and world politics and their impact on project returns may introduce subtle and significant systematic risk factors to the project.

In contrast to the above way of viewing unsystematic risks, the APV approach offers a method to exploit information on systematic risks. This is suitable for the international capital budgeting decision because it may be relatively easier to acquire information on discount rates for the riskless or low risk cash flow streams. Government bond markets may be a significant source of information on discount rates for low risk cash flows. Whilst it may be difficult to identify market portfolio surrogates that provide some clue as to the appropriate all equity discount rate, the APV rule allows the analyst to isolate this measurement problem to the all equity rate for the operating cash flows. The use of the APV version of the NPV rule does not solve the problem of whether systematic risk should be measured relative to the firm's home country market portfolio, or relative to a world portfolio. However, by separating out the financing effects and other sources of value it may simplify the search for information on market discount rates for the various cash flow terms and allow the maximum use of available information on each systematic risk cash flow class. This is in contrast to a simple use of the NPV method in which one overall discount rate is adjusted to reflect all information on total project systematic risk. This approach would not involve such a comprehensive analysis of the timing and scale of the risks being assessed.

However, it should be noted that it is possible to employ many features of the APV approach with the more conventional form of the NPV rule. Thus the cash flow terms could be divided up as in the APV approach and all available information on systematic risk classes fully incorporated in the analysis. The cash flows can then be added together to arrive at one overall cash flow stream. This requires only one discount rate. Again, like the pure equity rate in the APV rule, it will be difficult to measure the appropriate discount rate for this cash flow stream.

A key empirical question is: given that these two models are identical in concept, and slightly different in form, which of them allows managers to make the best use of the data available to them? Given that the NPV rule can also be used to fully employ all cash flow information it seems that the argument that APV is superior to NPV is overstated. The empirical question revolves around which of the two versions of the NPV model is more useful to financial managers estimating discount rates. If the operating cash flows form a relatively small proportion of the stream of benefits from the project, the problem in measuring the all equity rate seems to be less severe. Furthermore if a positive APV is achievable without the value benefits provided by operating cash flows then the relative ease of measuring the other discount rates makes the APV version of the NPV operationally superior. Empirical research has yet to clarify these operational issues. It may well be the case that it is equally difficult in either situation to estimate the appropriate discount rates. This seems likely, given that this is one of the central unresolved measurement issues in capital budgeting. Finally, it should be noted that the difficulties outlined here in estimating discount rates do not devalue the idea of dividing up the cash flow terms to employ all available information. This approach will be adopted here so that either the conventional NPV rule or its APV variant can be used.


## 9.2 Developing Cash Flow Information

We have seen how the APV rule is based on project cash flows being classified according to their systematic risk characteristics. This allows decision makers to focus on each present value term to maximize the development and use of market based information on discount rates. This (risk class) classification of cash flows reflects the fundamental requirement in capital budgeting to acquire a capital market or shareholder valuation of the incremental project cash flows.

The generation of cash flow information can be further improved by classifying the cash flow terms into two other categories:

- according to the source or origin of the elements of the cash flows
- according to the sensitivity of the cash flows to real exchange rate changes.

In the first case, an attempt is made to exploit multiple corporate information sources on these cash flows. Various managerial groups within the enterprise have unique information on the project and its cash flows. A co-ordinated approach to organizational information gathering can enrich the information base for capital budgeting analysis. In addition, this approach also enables the analyst to consider how ownership, locational and internalization advantages are a source of value and of positive incremental cash flows for the MNC. In other words, this is an important means to tie together the theory of direct foreign investment (DFI) with capital budgeting theory (Holland 1990).

In the second case, the cash flow categories are designed to maximize the use of information concerning the impact of changes in the external financial environment on the purchasing power of the incremental cash flows. This has clear links with the valuation problems discussed in the previous section.

All of these cash flow classification schemes converge as in figure 9.1 when their cash flow data are employed within the APV model to evaluate the capital budgeting proposal.

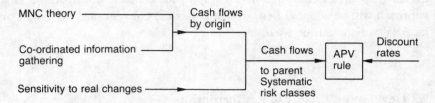

**Figure 9.1** Convergence of cash flow classification schemes on the APV model

## Identifying cash flows: the source or origin of elements of cash flow

A fundamental requirement in capital budgeting is for the firm to identify precisely which incremental cash flows arise because of the project and which of these are remittable to the parent. The portion of the incremental cash flows remittable to the parent is the funds ultimately available to the shareholders of the MNC and therefore forms the basis for evaluating the project.

Project cash flows will be influenced by many complex firm specific advantages (ownership and internalization) and by subsidiary location factors. They will arise in the firm in many different geographic and organizational sites. In this section the incremental cash flows arising from the existence of a project are identified according to their source or origin. In addition, the changes in the cash flows as they are remitted to the parent are identified.

The categories of incremental cash flow by origin are as follows:

1   Cash flows that can be estimated independently for a project (i.e. wherever it is located in the MNC and irrespective of the form of financing). These include both revenue and operating cost cash flows.
2   Cash flows derived from the subsidiary in which the project is located e.g. location cost and revenue factors such as local labour rates and local managerial skills in the subsidiary.
3   Cash flow changes arising elsewhere in the MNC global system and stemming from the existence of the project (including those cash flow changes arising at the parent HQ). These incremental system cash flows arise because of the impact of the project on those parts of the MNC outside the project itself and its location. They are therefore independent of project characteristics or project host location. These cash flow changes may therefore occur in other subsidiaries (in other locations) or in the group HQ via its global tax or funding position.

4  Those parts of cash flows 1, 2 and 3 that are transferable back to the parent (or arise at the parent because of the project).
5  These sources of incremental cash flow form the aggregate incremental cash flow back to the parent. These are the cash flows available for distribution to shareholders and thus the basis for valuing the project.

These cash flow categories are shown in figure 9.2. In the diagram, a project has been identified by a US MNC car manufacturer who wishes to set up engine plant to serve the whole Far East market. The engines are to be supplied to its three car assembly plants in Taiwan, the Philippines and Australia. All of the assembly sites are potential sites for the engine plant and this means that there are three projects to consider. However, the Philippines is the most likely site at present and is used as the first location to consider in the analysis. The cash flows originate in the engine plant project (category 1) within the Filipino subsidiary (2) or within the Taiwanese and Australian parts of the MNC (3). These are changed as they

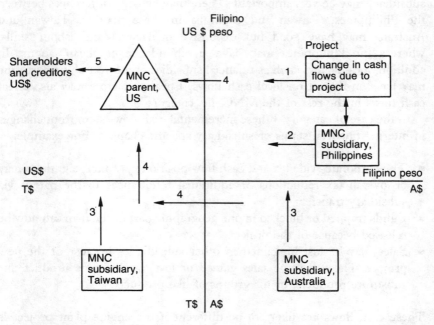

**Figure 9.2** Cash flows for example project: see text for details

are remitted (4) back to the US parent to form the aggregate incremental cash flows from the project (5).

## The origin of cash flows and the sources of advantage for the MNC

The cash flow categories 1–5 identified in the previous section correspond to the sources of advantage to the US MNC concerning the car engine plant project. These in turn can be identified from the MNC theory discussed in chapter 8 as ownership, location and internalization advantages.

Project specific cash flows arise from unique firm specific advantages such as engine production technology, engine design and market knowledge. The firm can expect to receive these cash flow benefits through car sales wherever the project is located within the MNC's Far Eastern market.

Location factors are likely to be a strong influence on category 2 cash flows. The national location of the project and the characteristics of a local subsidiary may have a major influence on the incremental project cash flows. Thus factors such as local labour costs and managerial skills in the subsidiary may be very important. There may be large differences between the Philippines, Taiwan and Australia in these matters. Taiwan and Australia may have good but expensive managerial and labour skills, whereas the Philippines may have an abundance of cheap labour. In addition, local factors such as financial subsidies or a favourable tax regime may have an impact on local cash flows. Location factors may also affect cash flows in the rest of the MNC, i.e. category 3.

In the case of category 3 these incremental cash flows stem from changes in internal financial status or subsidiary specific changes. For example:

- The corporate-wide tax and cash flow position may alter, e.g. there may be overall tax reductions or additional remittances to the parent via subsidiary transfers.
- Funds trapped or blocked in one geographic part of the firm can now be released because of the project.
- Sales may be lost or gained in other subsidiaries because of the new project. These may be sales gained or lost for the same product, for substitute products, or for groups of like products.

These cash flows are likely to be different if the engine plant project is located in Taiwan or Australia. For example, an enhanced ability to exploit bilateral tax treaties between the US and these countries may improve the global tax position of the US MNC, and this may vary by location. Sales lost by each subsidiary are also likely to differ if the location of the engine plant beside an assembly plant reduces the assembly plants costs and its capability to sell and deliver in the region.

In the case of category 4, remittable cash flows depend on many internalization advantages based on internal financial capabilities, including

- The corporate capacity to analyse and exploit such remittance possibilities, i.e. treasury capacity to adjust dividends and interest payments, to net payments, to lead and lag, and to adjust transfer prices, fees and royalties. All these financial decision variables stem from a sophisticated internal financial transfer and information system.
- Tax specialists and their knowledge within the firm, especially their ability to recognize national tax differences and double taxation treaties, and to adjust the timing of taxes and the type of cash flow they are imposed on (dividends versus interest payments) to minimize the tax liabilities facing the firm.
- The operational flexibility of managers to adjust real flows in order to maximize financial flows back to the parent, i.e. the ability to manipulate sales and production volumes, pricing and sourcing decisions within the MNC.

Treasury is a particularly important function in this respect in that it controls the internal financial transfer system. If the US car manufacturer has such a system (as described in chapter 6), then this internal advantage gives it the capability to maximize category 4 incremental cash flows by selective adjustment of many internal financial variables. The greater the sophistication of this internal financial transfer system in the US car manufacturer, then the greater the MNC's flexibility in dealing with such matters. Treasury has an important role in liaising with operational managers (whether at HQ or in autonomous subsidiaries). For example, these parties may have to jointly analyse the changes in incremental cash flows possible via changes in operational decisions.

The sophistication of the internal financial system is also likely to be very important for the tax specialists when minimizing the corporate tax bill and exploiting new tax opportunities arising from the project. Tax is a particularly important variable in the international capital budgeting decision model. This is because the nature of the tax system and the tax rate can affect most of the individual present value terms in the APV model.

For example, in March 1984 the British Chancellor of the Exchequer announced major changes in the UK tax system. This involved phasing out all capital allowances and lowering corporation tax, all over a three-year period to 1987. Both British and foreign multinationals had to assess how their capital budgeting calculations would change due to new interactions between the British tax system and other national tax systems. US MNCs were placed in a position where they could benefit from joint US/foreign-country tax treaties by averaging income from a low tax country such as the UK with income from high tax countries such as Germany and France (Brown 1984). This created an incentive for US MNCs to increase their investment in Britain in 1983–4 to take immediate advantage of the disappearing tax allowances. They could then use these to defer their tax payments at future lower UK tax rates. Similar arguments apply to those British and non-US MNCs who found that their global tax bills were deferred and reduced by investing in Britain.

## Identifying cash flows: comparative advantages of managerial groups within the MNC in generating cash flow information

The aggregate incremental cash flows to the parent (category 5) are the funds ultimately available to the shareholders of the MNC and therefore form the basis for evaluating the project. Information on these cash flows can best be generated by exploiting the relative advantages that functional managers, local subsidiary managers and parent MNC managers will have concerning cash flows. These are likely to be manifest as advantages due to the proximity or expertise of the managerial group relative to the project, the location, the subsidiaries or the parent HQ.

Project specific cash flows (category 1) generated from the MNC's 'firm specific advantages' may be best estimated from the HQ or parent's viewpoint. Specialists at the US HQ of the car manufacturer, involved in developing the engine technology or the new engine plant production methods, may be in the best position to estimate these cash flow effects of the project wherever it is located.

These cash flows will be a major source of information on the after-tax operating cash flows. Cash flows specific to the project are independent of any financing method or other valuation effects. After adjustment for home country tax rates the remittable portion of these cash flows can be discounted at the all equity discount rate in the APV model.

Project cash flows generated within the subsidiary's economic sphere of influence and activity (category 2) may best be estimated from the Filipino subsidiary's viewpoint. Thus local management, with their experience of running the car assembly plant, already know much about location advantages such as labour costs or proximity to markets. These will also make a major contribution to the operating cash flows. The location of the project may also be the primary source of financial subsidies and of some additions to corporate debt capacity as expressed in the APV model. Thus managers in the Filipino subsidiary may contribute the core data for estimating these cash flow elements in the APV equation.

It will be difficult to completely separate cash flow categories 1 and 2 given their dependence on each other. However, if the US MNC decides at some stage to perform the analysis for all three Far Eastern sites, then differences between the sites in terms of their combined (1 and 2) cash flows will reveal much about the unique nature of categories 1 and 2.

Cash flows transferable to the parent from the Filipino subsidiary (category 4) depend crucially on the sophistication of the internal financial transfer system and the flexibility of operational decision variables such as production volumes or selling prices in each national location. These cash flow changes may be best estimated by co-operative forecasting between treasury and operational staff. Not all of the project cash flows generated at the level of the subsidiary will be available for return to the parent. For example, Philippine government controls over dividends, fees and transfer pricing may mean that only a portion of the local subsidiary's cash flows can be returned to the home country of the MNC. In addition, practical constraints on exploiting operational variables such as product pricing will place a limit on their role in boosting remitted cash flows. Detailed analyses of the likely remittances and other transferred funds are clearly essential. At this point, treasury staff and operational managers can also assess the probable range over which remittances might occur. This can provide data for optimistic, expected and pessimistic views of remittances and their use in an APV based spreadsheet model to assess the sensitivity of project value to remittances.

In the same way, additional cash flows generated in other parts of the corporate system (i.e. in parts of the system other than the project and its subsidiary location: category 3) may best be estimated by a combination of those senior head office managers and subsidiary managers sharing a broad view of the overall activities and financial position of the MNC. For example, changes in the parent tax cash flows are often central to these calculations.

System dependent cash flow changes may also involve reductions in MNC parent cash flows as well as increases. For example, lost sales may occur elsewhere in the MNC's world-wide business. The MNC must take these negative incremental cash flow changes into account when valuing project returns. Again HQ staff and non-project subsidiary managers may be best placed to jointly estimate such system losses.

This co-ordinated approach maximizes the information required for the APV equation and can ensure that a corporate as opposed to a subsidiary view dominates the evaluation process. Cash flow categories 1 and 2 will clearly be the major source of information on the operating cash flows defined in the APV model. Cash flow categories 2, 3 and 4 can be the primary sources of information on the other major risk class cash flow categories adopted for the APV model, i.e.

| PV of tax savings due to depreciation | + | PV of financial subsidies | + | PV of project contribution to corporate debt capacity | + | PV of other tax savings and additional remittances |
|---|---|---|---|---|---|---|

A significant issue in exploiting comparative information advantages within the MNC is the nature of internal politics in the capital budgeting decision process. The Taiwanese and Australian subsidiaries may be competing for the engine project to ensure that they are the dominant subsidiary in the Far Eastern region. Thus subsidiary managers may bias the data to improve their chances and to undermine those of competing subsidiaries. In addition, central functions such as treasury or tax may have an incentive to bias data for their own functional purposes. Clearly, HQ managers, when assessing aggregate incremental cash flows (category 5) derived from all of these sources, will have to exercise some caution when dealing with the figures. If several project locations are considered then this may encourage subsidiaries to provide much more information. The subsidiaries competing for the project in this way may allow senior group managers to sift out some aspects of the bias.

## Identifying cash flows according to the sensitivity of cash flows to real exchange rate changes

The final cash flow category considered here concerns classifying cash flows according to their sensitivity to real exchange rate changes. All the types of cash flow identified above, including project cash flows, subsidiary cash flows, and aggregate cash flows remittable to the parent, may be further classified into

- cash flows (mainly operating and outlay flows) that are not contractually denominated in nominal terms
- contractual cash flows denominated in a particular currency, e.g. interest on debt, or tax rebates based on historic cost depreciation.

Lessard (1981) analyses some of these cash flow types under various assumptions about equilibrium and deviations from equilibrium and proposes specific analyses (real and nominal) for each situation. Figure 9.3 generalizes this approach and shows the whole range of combinations of cash flow types and environmental assumptions.

In the tree diagram the cash flows can be those that arise from the project (category 1), those from the subsidiary hosting the project (category 2), or those aggregate cash flows remittable to the parent (category 5). The first branching criterion refers to contractual versus non-contractual cash flows, and the second branch is concerned with assumptions about the economic environment. Thus in each case (project, host subsidiary, or aggregate cash flows) there will be four different possibilities. Each class of cash flow may consist of both contractually denominated and non-contractual components, as well as occurring under equilibrium and deviation conditions.

If we firstly consider cash flow type (i) on figure 9.3, and if PPP and IFE hold, then the problem of cash flows in different currencies and their

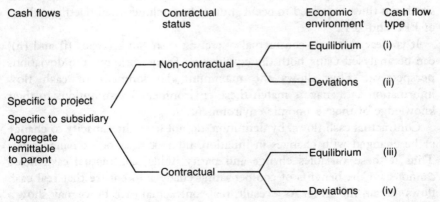

**Figure 9.3** Combinations of cash flow types and environmental assumptions

appropriate discount rates is much simplified. In equilibrium, discounting nominal cash flows using nominal discount rates is identical to discounting real cash flows using a real rate. Since many companies develop real data first, and then adjust for exchange rate and inflation rate changes, a real analysis seems simplest (Lessard 1981: 123). The current spot rate can then be used to convert the (real rate) discounted (real) foreign cash flows to a single currency base.

As discussed previously, the assumption that the parity relationships hold is likely to be fairly robust with respect to the major Western industrialized economies. Thus an analysis based upon cash flows stated in units of constant purchasing power and discounted at a real rate of interest (plus a systematic risk premium) seems most appropriate for these conditions.

This analysis can be adapted for the different (deviations) circumstances surrounding cash flow type (ii) as follows (p. 125). Firstly, PPP may hold generally between economies, but there may be significant changes expected in project specific (relative) input or output prices. These relative prices can have a large impact on the value of the project compared with deviations from PPP and they will therefore need to be considered in the (real) analysis above. Secondly, if divergences are forecast to occur between IFE and PPP then joint estimates of local cash flows and exchange rates are required. The important point is to account for the expected change in the real rate of exchange rather than absolute changes (in inflation and exchange rates) already included in the real analysis. Alternatively, absolute (inflated) cash flow values and a nominal analysis can be employed and both deviations and equilibrium effects included in the calculation. This has the advantage of dealing in cash flows and discount rates at values similar to those expected to occur, but it also includes the offsetting effects of PPP and IFE.

It is clear that non-contractual operating cash flows (types (i) and (ii)) can be analysed using both the equilibrium framework and the deviations perspective. This allows the maximum development of cash flow information as managers match these environmental assumptions to their knowledge of their economic environment.

Contractual cash flows, by definition, do not have the capacity to change or be changed with changes in inflation, interest rates or exchange rates. Thus if these variables change and parity holds, contractual cash flows cannot gain the benefits of compensating changes to ensure that real cash flows remain the same. As a result, real contractual cash flows may show a significant adverse decline in HC purchasing power. If these variables change and parity conditions are such that parity does not hold, contractual cash flows may experience dramatic adverse real changes in their HC purchasing power.

Contractual cash flows (types (iii) and (iv)) will generally have low systematic and default risks. As an approximation their discount rate can be derived from the company's nominal borrowing rate in local capital markets. If IRP and Fisher do not hold between the relevant domestic markets, then offshore rates (if they exist) can be used to calculate the present value. This can then be converted into the base currency using current spot rates.

If the firm has considerable flexibility as to the location of the project within subsidiaries and this has a major impact on the real/PPP deviation position then the real analysis should begin at the project/host subsidiary stages of cash flow generation. The MNC may have considerable flexibility when choosing which internal financial transfer mechanisms to use, or when choosing the subsidiary to host the project. Thus it may be possible to alter the extent to which the project is subject to real exchange rate changes or to change the mix of contractual or non-contractual cash flows. These changes involve adapting the economic exposure of the firm in terms of its sensitivity to real changes in exchange rate changes. This decision is closely related to the FERM decisions to create responsiveness to foreign exchange risk and should form part of a joint approach to FERM and capital budgeting.

## The capital budgeting information gathering process

The three classes of cash flow described in this section are important means to maximize the information set for capital budgeting. The optimum sequence in developing the cash flow information appears to involve three major steps.

Firstly, develop information on cash flows according to the source or origin of the elements of the cash flow. This exploits managerial expertise at subsidiary and HQ level. It provides a way of looking at cash flows and added value that is consistent with the OLI theory of multinationality. It also provides a framework for thinking about sources of incremental cash flows and added value and for maximizing the exploitation of many organizational information sources. The output of this stage of the analysis will be a detailed information set on incremental cash flows at the level of the project, the host subsidiary, other subsidiaries, the parent HQ and aggregate incremental cash flows to the parent. This information should also provide clear indications as to which cash flows are relatively certain and of low systematic risk, and which form the main ingredients of the riskier (all equity financed) operating cash flows.

Successful completion of the first step provides the raw data for the second step, involving an analysis of the sensitivity of cash flows to real exchange rate changes. This can be done at the level of the project, the host subsidiary or the parent. However, the primary focus of the capital budgeting analysis lies in the expected value of incremental funds to the parent and thus the funds ultimately available to the shareholders. It may therefore only be necessary to analyse the aggregate incremental cash flows (category 5) for the real impact of exchange rate changes. The central HQ may have an information advantage here over subsidiaries in terms of availability of several independent currency forecasts as well as the data on historic impact of exchange rates on project cash flows. The subsidiary, in turn, may have an advantage in assessing the impact of currency changes on local input and output prices and thus real changes at the level of the project. These relative information advantages concerning cash flow sensitivity to currency changes will be important in a full analysis of real exchange rate changes and project value. The output of this stage of the analysis will be an identification of real changes (if any) expected in contractual and non-contractual cash flows flowing back to the parent.

The cash flow analyses in the first and second steps provide the data necessary for the final step. This involves identifying the various risk classes of cash flow in the APV model from the aggregate incremental cash flows (category 5). Each cash flow risk class can then be discounted at its unique (systematic risk) rate. A detailed example of this and previous stages is provided in the case in chapter 10.

The principles of capital budgeting analysis discussed in this chapter will be applied in chapter 10, in which a capital budgeting example is demonstrated. This example is followed by simulation runs from a computer based capital budgeting model. These are designed to simulate the problem and to perform sensitivity analyses of the results.

## 9.3 Summary

The aim of this chapter has been to try to combine the best insights of extant financial theory with the unique problems of evaluating overseas investment projects. This has been done in such a way as to produce usable decision rules that fully employ available information. The APV rule and the wide class of cash flow categories discussed in this chapter provide clear design guidelines for a spreadsheet modelling exercise. The approach adopted therefore provides managers with both the technology and a robust conceptual framework to tackle this complex decision area. Given the complexities faced by MNC managers when investigating the many alternatives within the international capital budgeting problem, computer based corporate cash flow models become invaluable. Such a model will be described in the case in the following chapter.

# 10

# The StrathKelvin Company: A Case in International Capital Budgeting

In this chapter, the principles of capital budgeting in an international context are illustrated through an extensive case study. The case also provides the means to discuss the role of financial modelling in this key decision area.

## 10.1 Company Background and Expansion Needs

The StrathKelvin company is a British based MNC specializing in the manufacture and sale of a variety of electronic consumer goods. These products fall within a narrow price range but, because of the sophisticated production technology of StrathKelvin, they can be specially tailored to the changing needs of fashion and national preferences.

StrathKelvin is particularly successful at present with its high tech electronic diary and personal organizer. This organizer is designed to match language requirements, local commercial practices and other special aspects of national markets. StrathKelvin also produces a range of small hand held personal computers as well as a range of sophisticated financial calculators.

StrathKelvin believes it has a technological lead in production methods for such electronic consumer products, both in the lightness, compactness, versatility and high degree of accuracy of its diary/organizers, PCs and calculators, and in its ability to specially tailor its products for local markets.

For example, in France it has established a significant share for all of these goods in the business executive market. The growth in sales in

France has been supported by the capability of the diary/organizer to receive or transfer data from the national Minitel network. In Britain, it can take selected stock market data from telephone facilities and it can be used as the interface with home banking systems. The company markets the organizer through specialist quality outlets such as 'top of the market' clothes and fashion goods shops as well as business oriented retailers such as office equipment suppliers. The combination of good design, excellent technological capabilities and targeted marketing has meant that StrathKelvin has been able to create a high status, high quality product image amongst higher income groups.

StrathKelvin prides itself on its Scottish origin. It has its HQ in Glasgow, but has major group operations in London (treasury) and in Coventry (R&D). It uses the pound as its group reporting currency.

The main production facility is currently concentrated in Scotland. This produces complete electronic consumer products as well as components for these products. Electronic components produced in Scotland are also assembled in smaller assembly plants close to consumers in the main population centres. These are located in Strasbourg in France, in Milan in Northern Italy, and in Canada, Hong Kong and Australia. The proximity of the smaller assembly plants to customers was believed to be one of the key strengths of the firm. It allowed it to quickly satisfy customers' needs and to keep abreast of changing fashions in the EC, North America, and the Pacific Rim.

A small product development group existed in Luxembourg. This small group worked in close association with French, German and other EC retailers and was used to keep an eye on fashion developments in this market. StrathKelvin's wholesale, marketing and sales force were distributed worldwide.

Sales in France and Germany received a considerable boost in the past two years owing to the electronic diary becoming very fashionable with the 18 to 40 age group, especially those involved in business and commerce. This EC sector of the global market was also served by the five StrathKelvin assembly plants in Strasbourg, Milan, Canada, Australia and Hong Kong. The Strasbourg assembly plant was relatively small and much of French and German demand was satisfied by the Glasgow and Milan operations.

French and German customers had been complaining recently about delays in delivery of diary/organizers from Scotland and from overseas assembly sites. They had also expressed concern about the slow response of the Scottish operations to their need for rapid design changes to reflect a very changeable customer base. StrathKelvin felt that the German and French sectors of the EC market were developing very fast, and it had to decide quickly whether to exploit these sectors before they became dominated by emerging US and Japanese competitors. EC competitors were active in this market and StrathKelvin felt it had to act quickly to preserve its market share.

Expansion of current production facilities in Glasgow was not feasible because this factory was operating at near capacity and local planning regulations limited expansion on the existing Glasgow site. Expansion to other production facilities in Scotland was feasible, but the costs of slow response to changing market needs, of delivery delays during 'gift seasons', and of transportation of goods from Scotland to the main EC markets, were now proving to be major competitive disadvantages.

All of the assembly sites plus a site in southern England near the Channel Tunnel were possible locations for the new production plant. Theoretically there were six projects to consider. However, management believed that their major strategic option was to build a factory somewhere near the Franco–German border and to use this to fully exploit their existing EC assembly and distribution network. Southern England, France, Belgium and Germany were identified as the primary target locations. Senior management considered France as the most likely location, given that a production operation near the Luxembourg design team and the Strasbourg assembly subsidiary appeared to be the obvious means to deal with customer problems and the recent rapid growth in the EC. They therefore began the analysis by considering France as the primary location.

Discussions with French trade officials suggested that the Alsace region could provide a suitable location. This was a region with high development status as France tried to exploit the post-1992 open market in the EC. The French government was in a position to offer StrathKelvin a project loan on relatively easy terms. Factory sites and a skilled labour force were available, and cheaper assembly labour was available owing to the closedown of 'rust belt' industry in the region. The Strasbourg assembly site and the Luxembourg design office were nearby and both were expected to play a key role in the development. The region was also nearer the major EC population centres than central Scotland. A decision to invest would mean that StrathKelvin would set up a major operating subsidiary in France.

## 10.2 The Problem for Treasury and Group Management Accountants

The group management accountants and treasury staff were asked to assess this proposed project. The group management accountant James Laurie and his assistant Susan Dooley were given the task of collecting the core data for the analysis. Group treasury staff led by Patrick Campsie were asked to assess the cost of capital and financial risks associated with the project and to provide this to the management accounting team for the final evaluation of the project.

Laurie and Dooley had faced similar capital budgeting problems before whilst working in other MNCs. These experiences had taught them that before trying to estimate the cash flows, they should try to understand why the cash flows arise. This led them to try to clarify the nature of StrathKelvin's production advantage and how this matched up with the advantages of the French site.

Laurie and Dooley recognized that the aggregate incremental cash flows to the StrathKelvin parent group were the funds ultimately available to the shareholders of the firm and therefore formed the basis for evaluating the project. Their previous experience had taught them that basic information on these cash flows could best be generated by exploiting the relative advantages that group functional managers, local subsidiary managers and sales managers were likely to have when forecasting cash flows associated with their function. They were also aware that there were problems of information bias and 'politics' within the firm as each (assembly) subsidiary competed for the production plant to make it the dominant site in the EC and possibly the Pacific Rim.

Given this experience, they therefore decided to break the cash estimation and valuation problem into five constituent parts. This consisted of

1 Identifying StrathKelvin's specific advantages and those of the proposed site and using these to classify broad categories of change in corporate cash flows associated with the project. New sales and product design possibilities and productivity improvements based on joint StrathKelvin and location advantages were important here. Product design, production and R&D specialists spread around the firm were considered important specialist sources of production cost information. International sales staff with experience of France,

Germany, the rest of the EC, North America and the Pacific Rim were identified as the specialist suppliers of market information.

2   Asking managers of assembly subsidiaries to assess the impact, if any, of a French production site on their operations and cash flows. Head office staff, with prior experience of these subsidiaries, were also asked to provide independent forecasts of these changes at the level of subsidiaries.

3   Asking group staff – treasury and taxation in particular – to assess the impact, if any, of a French production site on group operations (and cash flows) located within the EC.

4   Using these data to perform a preliminary analysis of incremental cash flows to the group and to assess the net present value of the project.

5   Using the initial calculations in 4 as the basis to build a tailored spreadsheet financial model designed to perform a series of detailed sensitivity analyses on the project.

These activities reveal the central role of group treasury and management accountants in generating and collecting internal information on the project prior to the analysis stage. The tasks of liaising with production staff, sales managers and group treasury and creating this information base were considered by Laurie and Dooley to be substantially more difficult than the task of applying the logic of the net present value rule.

The five activities outlined above are described in the following sections.

## 10.3 StrathKelvin Project and Location Advantages and Cash Flow Changes

Laurie and Dooley initially discussed the project with Strasbourg managers, Luxembourg design staff and group R&D staff. These discussions were supplemented by further insights and comments by their own management accountancy staff working with production managers. It became clear from these talks that much of the project specific cash flows arose from unique StrathKelvin advantages such as its production technology, flexible product design and specialist market knowledge. StrathKelvin expected to receive the cash flow benefits associated with these advantages wherever the project was located within its global span. More specifically, StrathKelvin had developed a special expertise in the UK production site in automating production operations and in developing a production technology with a high degree of responsiveness to product design changes. Both advantages were transferable to the French site, given excellent local skill levels. These advantages when allied with responsive design staff and a flexible assembly operation were expected to provide an important boost to StrathKelvin's sales in France and Germany.

Once Laurie and Dooley had some idea of the in-house advantages, they turned to StrathKelvin's sales staff located in the EC and asked them to forecast sales levels expected there. The lack of production experience outside Scotland was a problem for them. This was because the national location of the project and the characteristics of a local subsidiary were known to have a major influence on the incremental project cash flows. Thus factors such as the nature of local competition, the existence of specialist national industries, the local labour costs, and the availability of managerial skills in the proposed subsidiary were all considered very important. In addition, local factors such as financial subsidies or a favourable tax regime would have an impact on local cash flows. These location factors would also affect cash flows in the rest of StrathKelvin. In order to circumvent these problems, Laurie and Dooley commissioned a short consultant's study of their competitors' production cost structures and the availability of skilled labour.

This report and their own sales staff's sales forecast provided the basis for StrathKelvin to forecast the joint effect of project and location factors on incremental cash flows. Combining the project specific and location advantages led Laurie and Dooley to forecast that the Alsace production site would boost sales to the equivalent of an extra 60,000 completed diary/organizer units per annum with a sales growth rate of 2 per cent per annum. The units were expected to sell for fr250 each and to cost fr210 to produce. They expected the fr/DM exchange rate to remain stable over the life of the project and so they also used francs to estimate sales revenue from sales in Germany.

These new sales were primarily based on improved access to customers in France and Germany. If the plant was located in southern England the initial additional sales would only be 45,000 units per annum. Scotland would be too far away and expansion there would not generate any extra sales. The price of a diary/organizer unit produced in any one of these three sites was expected to remain at fr250 at today's prices. Costs were expected to reduce at the proposed French plant by 2 per cent per annum. (In an initial conservative analysis these are assumed to be zero.) These productivity gains were expected to flow from the contribution of the Luxembourg based product design team located in this fashion conscious part of the world economy and from group production and R&D staff. The Italian, Australian, Canadian and Hong Kong locations were not expected to generate these productivity gains owing to limited design and production skills.

## 10.4 Changes in Cash Flows at Subsidiary Level

Laurie and Dooley were also aware of further types of incremental cash flows stemming from the release of blocked funds or arising because sales were lost or gained in other subsidiaries. Discussions with Patrick Campsie at group treasury and with managers of the French and Italian assembly subsidiaries revealed that funds previously blocked in France and not available to the group treasury in London would become available to the much enlarged French subsidiary located in this development zone in France. These were tax liabilities on French revenues that would be much reduced by the now much larger French subsidiary being able to persuade the French tax authorities to take a less stringent view of these tax liabilities. They were expected to be fr1,500,000 and available at the start of the project.

In addition, sales equivalent to 20,000 completed diary/organizer units were expected to be lost in the Italian assembly plant as the new French production site could offer tailored diary/organizers to existing customers within the EC, and could ship these at lower cost than the Milan or other non-EC sites. The Glasgow site was not expected to lose sales. These replaced sales were expected to decline by 15 per cent per annum. The home currency profits lost on these replaced sales were estimated at £3 per unit. A southern England location for the new production plant would only lead to 15,000 lost diary/organizer sales for the Italian assembly plant.

The subsidiaries assembling diary/organizers in Canada, Australia and Hong Kong were not expected to lose sales in this way. The French assembly subsidiary would gain sales and these were included in the new French production plant sales totals.

## 10.5 Changes in Remittable Cash Flows and Global Tax Payments

Group treasury and tax staff felt that the new larger French subsidiary would create many extra degrees of freedom for StrathKelvin in remitting funds and reducing the global tax bill. The possibility of exploiting bilateral tax treaties would be enhanced by the larger tax paying status of this subsidiary in France. Exploiting this advantage depended on StrathKelvin's tax specialists' ability to minimize tax liabilities facing the firm. In particular, this depended on their ability to recognize national tax differences and double taxation treaties, to adjust the timing of taxes, and to exploit differences in the types of cash flow on which taxes are imposed (e.g. dividends versus interest payments). Tax staff expected that £20,000 per annum would be generated in terms of extra tax saving. The new French subsidiary would be better placed to exploit bilateral tax treaties between these countries than the UK treasury and could then remit these back to the group treasury in London. These tax savings are ignored in the initial conservative analysis.

The final category of cash flow considered by Laurie, Dooley and group treasury was remittable cash flows. Campsie and his treasury staff argued that these depended on a range of internal financial capabilities including the corporate capacity to analyse and exploit such remittance possibilities, i.e. the treasury's capacity to adjust dividends and interest payments, to net payments, to lead and lag, and to adjust transfer prices, fees and royalties – in other words, all of the financial decision variables stemming from a sophisticated internal financial transfer and information system.

Despite the sophistication of StrathKelvin's internal financial transfer system, remittances from Italy and France direct to the UK were still facing some controls. Patrick Campsie, the treasurer, argued that the new French subsidiary would provide StrathKelvin with an important new legal jurisdiction and this would enhance the capability of the internal financial system to circumvent these controls. The incremental cash flows generated here and available to group treasury in London were expected to be £40,000 per annum over the life of the project. These are also ignored in the initial conservative analysis.

## Additional cash flow and financial data

The discussions so far also produced the following data:

1   The project has an expected life of ten years, and a capital outlay of fr18,500,000.
2   The investment is expected to add £1,000,000 to StrathKelvin's borrowing capacity. The UK risk free rate is currently 11 per cent and StrathKelvin can currently borrow pounds at 13.5 per cent per annum.

3   The French government will provide a subsidized loan of fr5,000,000 at 6 per cent per annum, and the current French borrowing rate is 20 per cent.

4   The residual value (ten years ahead) of plant, buildings and land in home currency and today's values is estimated to be 5 per cent of the initial outlay.

5   Treasury has estimated exchange rate and inflation changes as

| | |
|---|---|
| current spot rate: | 11.5 fr/£ |
| UK inflation forecast: | 5.00 per cent p.a. over project |
| French inflation forecast: | 12.00 per cent p.a. over project |

Purchasing power parity was expected to hold over the life of the project. Thus the nominal fr/£ exchange rate was expected to show a franc depreciation of approximately 7 per cent per annum relative to the pound, but the real fr/£ exchange rate was expected to remain unchanged. Treasury therefore felt that there would be periodic realignments of the nominal fr/£ exchange rate irrespective of whether the pound was within the EC exchange rate mechanism (ERM). They could not predict when this would occur and so they estimated an average rate of change over the ten year life of the project. International Fisher was also expected to hold and this was approximately reflected in the French and UK interest rate difference of 6.5 per cent.

## The adjusted present value rule

StrathKelvin used the adjusted present value (APV) variant of the net present value (NPV) rule. Project cash flows were classified according to their systematic risk characteristics. A present value for each risk class of cash flows was calculated by employing a unique discount rate for its level of systematic risk. These present value terms were then summed to find the increment to value derived from the investment decision. As indicated in chapter 9, the APV equation contains cash flow categories and present value terms that explicitly deal with the following factors (also see Lessard 1981):

APV = PV of    + PV of       + PV of                  + PV of
      capital    remittable     tax savings due         financial
      outlays    after tax      to depreciation         subsidies
                 operating
                 cash flows

+ PV of project   + PV of other   + PV of additional   + PV of residual
  contribution      tax savings     remittances      plant and
  to corporate                                      equipment
  debt capacity

The capital asset pricing model (CAPM) is used to calculate discount rates for foreign investment risks that are considered systematic in nature, i.e.

discount rate  =  risk free  +  beta for   $\left(\begin{array}{l} \text{market} \;-\; \text{risk free} \\ \text{return} \qquad \text{rate} \end{array}\right)$
for each risk      rate           risk class
class.

Patrick Campsie at the group treasury has assumed global stock market integration and used betas (from international stock markets) to assess the riskiness of these cash flow categories. He has estimated discount rates as follows:

risky cash flows (in £s):
    discount rate for operating cash flows (all equity rate)  18.00%
    discount rate for residual values                  18.00%
    discount rate for extra tax savings              18.00%
    discount rate for remittances                     18.00%
low risk cash flows (in £s):
    discount rate for depreciation tax allowances        11.00%
other financial data for the problem:
    UK corporate tax rate                       52.00%
    UK capital gains tax rate                 30.00%
    French corporate tax rate               50.00%
    extra tax savings p.a. from deferrals and
          transfer pricing                    £0.00
    additional remittances p.a. home currency     £0.00

## 10.6 Initial Calculation of Present Values

The above data provided Laurie and Dooley with the basis for an initial crude calculation of each PV element in the APV equation. These example or test calculations will be outlined in this section. The detailed calculations will be illustrated in the following section where a financial spreadsheet model will be used to simulate StrathKelvin's problem.

1    Capital outlay = 18,500,000 francs, i.e. 18,500,000/11.5
     = £1,608,696.

2    Released funds = 1,500,000 francs = £130,434.
     These are funds accumulated in France to pay for tax liabilities. The
     new larger French subsidiary can be used to reduce this tax liability
     by transferring some costs from the new project to the existing
     assembly operations. Thus these funds are released for use in the
     project. These reduce the capital costs in France by this increment of
     1.5 million francs.

3    Assuming that purchasing parity holds between France and Britain:

     $$\text{Exchange rate per year} = 11.5 \times \frac{(1+0.12)^t}{(1+0.05)^t}$$

     Exchange rate year 1 = 11.5 × 1.12/1.05 = 12.2667fr/£
     i.e. pound appreciates, it can buy more francs over time; or franc
     depreciates, it can buy fewer pounds over time.

4
$$\begin{aligned}\text{Operating cash} \\ \text{flows per year}\end{aligned} = \left[ \left( \begin{aligned}\text{exchange} \\ \text{rate}\end{aligned} \right) \left( \begin{aligned}\text{net cash} \\ \text{flows} \\ \text{from} \\ \text{sales}\end{aligned} \right) - \left( \begin{aligned}\text{profit} \\ \text{from} \\ \text{replaced} \\ \text{sales}\end{aligned} \right) \right] \left( \begin{aligned}1 - \text{tax} \\ \text{rate}\end{aligned} \right)$$

Sales are increased by 2 per cent p.a.
French inflation is 12 per cent p.a.
Replaced sales decline by 15 per cent p.a. and their profit contribution
    increases with UK inflation of 5 per cent.
The goods initially ($t = 0$) sell for fr250 and cost fr210, leaving a
    contribution margin of fr40.
If productivity gains of say 2 per cent are considered then the costs of
    fr210 would be reduced by 2 per cent p.a. These are ignored in the
    calculation below, but are incorporated in the spreadsheet model in
    section 10.7.
Thus for year 1 the operating cash flow is:

[(1/12.2667)(60,000 × 1.02 × (250 − 210) × 1.12) − (20,000 ×
(1 − 0.15) × 3 × 1.05)](1 − 0.52) = £81,582.22

For the ten year period:

| Year | Cash flows | Year | Cash flows |
|------|-----------|------|-----------|
| 1 | 81,582.22 | 6 | 136,622.8 |
| 2 | 91,962.71 | 7 | 148,921.1 |
| 3 | 102,586.9 | 8 | 161,813.6 |
| 4 | 113,525.4 | 9 | 175,371.8 |
| 5 | 124,847.4 | 10 | 189,670.5 |

These operating cash flows are discounted at the all equity rate of 18 per cent and summed over the life of the project (ten years) as follows:

$$\text{PV of operating cash flows} = \sum_{t=1}^{10} \frac{(\text{operating cash flow})_t}{(1+0.18)^t}$$

$$= £526.934.1$$

5   Residual value (after tax) $= \dfrac{(0.05)(18,500,000)(1+0.05)^{10}(1-0.3)}{(11.5)(1+0.18)^{10}}$

$$= \frac{(0.05)(18,500,000)(1.6288944)(0.7)}{(11.5)(5.2338351)}$$

$$= £17,523$$

$$\text{Annual depreciation} = \frac{18,500,000}{11.5 \times 10 \text{ years}} = £160,896.6$$

Hence tax allowances $= 160,896.6 \times 0.52 = £83,652.18$.
These are discounted over the ten-year period at the low risk rate of 11 per cent to produce the PV of tax allowances, i.e. £492,647.1.

7   Project's contribution to corporate debt capacity, in period 1:

$$\frac{0.135 \times £1,000,000 \times 0.52}{(1+0.11)^1} = £63,243$$

These discounted tax benefits are summed over the life of the project to find the additional PV created by the project's contribution to corporate debt capacity. In this example it is £413,424.1.

8   Governmental loan:
   Capital repayments per year = 5,000,000/10        = fr500,000
   Interest per year                    = balance × government loan rate
   Interest year 1                       = 5,000,000 × 0.06   = fr300,000
   Total repayments year 1      = 500,000 + 300,000 = fr800,000

$$\text{HC NPV of loan} = (1/11.5) \left[ \text{face value} - \sum_{t=1}^{10} \frac{\text{total repayments}}{(1 + 0.2)^t} \right]$$

$$= (1/11.5) \, [5,000,000 - 2,967,365] = £176,750.9$$

9   Extra tax savings over period $t = 1$ to 10: = £0.
   Discounted over ten years at 18 per cent:   £0.

10  Additional remittances over period $t = 1$ to 10: £0.
   Discounted over ten years at 18 per cent: £0.

11  The final APV was the sum of these PV elements:
   APV = − 1,608,696 + 130,434 + 526,934 + 17,523 + 492,647 +
                413,424 + 176,751 + 0.0 + 0.0 = £149,019

Thus the initial indications were that this was a worthwhile project. It has a positive APV and should therefore be accepted. It is interesting to note that large proportions of the PV arise from non-operating cash flows. Thus in this case, tax allowances, increases in corporate borrowing capacity and the governmental loan have all made substantial contributions to the overall APV.

## 10.7 The Need for a Spreadsheet Model

At this point the management accountants, Laurie and Dooley, felt that they needed to transfer the problem to a spreadsheet. They recognized the problem involved considerable computation. The initial set of data and calculations were very tentative and required much more analysis. Thus in order to investigate this problem further, Dooley, as the Lotus 1-2-3 specialist, developed a financial spreadsheet for sensitivity analysis of key input variables. She used the above calculations as the basis to develop the Lotus 1-2-3 model. The use of this model forms the focus of analysis in the following sections.

Figure 10.1 outlines the structure of their spreadsheet model. It indicates the input, calculations and output of the model, together with some general examples of sensitivity questions that Laurie and Dooley thought were likely to be investigated.

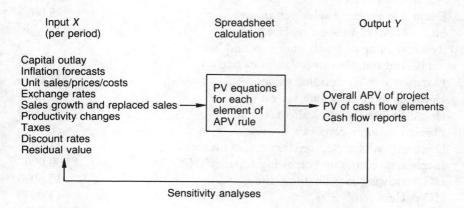

**Figure 10.1** Structure of spreadsheet model

## Spreadsheet input

Laurie and Dooley began their analysis with conservative assumptions and then added likely present value gains to StrathKelvin's ability to circumvent tax and remittance restrictions or to make productivity gains. This conservative analysis assumed expected values for annual product sales, sales growth, prices, costs and residual values, with zero additional remittances, tax savings and productivity gains.

| | |
|---|---:|
| Life of project | 10 years |
| Capital outlay | fr18,500,000 |
| Additional and restricted funds released by project | fr1,500,000 |
| Spot rate | 11.50fr/£ |
| Home country (UK) inflation forecast | 5.00% |
| Foreign country (France) inflation forecast | 12.00% |
| Degree nominal exchange rate reflects PPP | 100.00% |
| No. of sales units per annum | 60,000 |
| Price per unit in year 1 (FC) | fr250 |
| Annual growth rate of sales | 2.00% |
| Cost per unit in year 1 (FC) | fr210 |
| Productivity gain p.a. as $-\%$ of cost per unit | 0% |
| Discount rate for operating cash flows (HC) | 18.00% |
| No. of sales units replaced due to project | 20,000 |
| Decline in replaced sales per annum | 15.00% |
| HC profits per unit on replaced sales | £3 |
| Residual value of plant, buildings and land in HC and today's values (as % of outlay) | 5.00% |
| Discount rate for residual values | 18.00% |
| Home country corporate tax rate | 52.00% |
| Home country capital gains tax rate | 30.00% |
| Foreign country corporate tax rate | 50.00% |
| Discount rate for depreciation tax allowances | 11.00% |
| Increase in corporate borrowing capacity (HC) | 1,000,000 |
| HC borrowing rate for these funds | 13.50% |
| HC riskless rate | 11.00% |
| FC government subsidized loan | fr5,000,000 |
| FC borrowing rate | 20.00% |
| Government loan rate | 6.00% |
| Extra tax savings p.a. from deferrals and transfer pricing (HC) | £0 |
| Discount rate for extra tax savings | 18.00% |
| Additional remittances p.a. (HC) | £0 |
| Discount rate | 18.00% |

## Spreadsheet output

*Present value of capital outlay*
Given as £1,608,695.

*Present value of released funds*
Given as £130,434.


*Exchange rates and operating cash flows*

| Period (year) | Nom. exch. rate if PPP = 100% (fr/£) | Cost/unit, t = 0 prices (fr) | Operating cash flows (£) | Discounted cash flows (£) |
|---|---|---|---|---|
| 1 | 12.26667 | 210 | 81,582 | 69,137.51 |
| 2 | 13.08444 | 210 | 91,963 | 66,046.23 |
| 3 | 13.95674 | 210 | 102,587 | 62,437.65 |
| 4 | 14.88719 | 210 | 113,525 | 58,555.17 |
| 5 | 15.87967 | 210 | 124,848 | 54,572.05 |
| 6 | 16.93831 | 210 | 136,623 | 50,609.47 |
| 7 | 18.06754 | 210 | 148,921 | 46,750.18 |
| 8 | 19.27204 | 210 | 161,814 | 43,048.66 |
| 9 | 20.55684 | 210 | 175,372 | 39,538.74 |
| 10 | 21.92730 | 210 | 189,671 | 36,239.36 |

Hence NPV of operating cash flows is £526,935.

*Residual value*
PV of residual plant, buildings and land after CGT is calculated as
£17,523.3.

*Tax allowances for depreciation*

| Period (year) | Depreciation (£) | Tax allowances (£) | Discounted allowances (£) |
|---|---|---|---|
| 1 | 160,870 | 83,652 | 75,362 |
| 2 | 160,870 | 83,652 | 67,894 |
| 3 | 160,870 | 83,652 | 61,166 |
| 4 | 160,870 | 83,652 | 55,104 |
| 5 | 160,870 | 83,652 | 49,643 |
| 6 | 160,870 | 83,652 | 44,724 |
| 7 | 160,870 | 83,652 | 40,292 |
| 8 | 160,870 | 83,652 | 36,299 |
| 9 | 160,870 | 83,652 | 32,702 |
| 10 | 160,870 | 83,652 | 29,461 |

Hence present value of depreciation tax allowances is £492,646.9.

*Increases in borrowing capacity*

| Period (year) | Tax benefits (£) | Discounted benefits (£) |
|---|---|---|
| 1 | 70,200 | 63,243 |
| 2 | 70,200 | 56,976 |
| 3 | 70,200 | 51,330 |
| 4 | 70,200 | 46,243 |
| 5 | 70,200 | 41,660 |
| 6 | 70,200 | 37,532 |
| 7 | 70,200 | 33,812 |
| 8 | 70,200 | 30,462 |
| 9 | 70,200 | 27,443 |
| 10 | 70,200 | 24,723 |

Hence PV of increase in borrowing capacity is £413,424.09.

*Government loans*

| Balance due (fr) | Capital repaid (fr) | Interest paid (fr) | Total payments (fr) | Discounted payments (fr) |
|---|---|---|---|---|
| 5,000,000 | 500,000 | 300,000 | 800,000 | 666,667 |
| 4,500,000 | 500,000 | 270,000 | 770,000 | 534,722 |
| 4,000,000 | 500,000 | 240,000 | 740,000 | 428,241 |
| 3,500,000 | 500,000 | 210,000 | 710,000 | 342,400 |
| 3,000,000 | 500,000 | 180,000 | 680,000 | 273,277 |
| 2,500,000 | 500,000 | 150,000 | 650,000 | 217,684 |
| 2,000,000 | 500,000 | 120,000 | 620,000 | 173,031 |
| 1,500,000 | 500,000 | 90,000 | 590,000 | 137,215 |
| 1,000,000 | 500,000 | 60,000 | 560,000 | 108,532 |
| 500,000 | 500,000 | 30,000 | 530,000 | 85,598 |

Hence PV of loan interest and capital repayment is fr2,967,365.
Net present value of loan is fr2,032,635 or £176,750.8.

*Extra tax savings due to deferrals and transfer pricing*
In this run the savings are nil.

*Additional remittances*
In this run the additional remittances are nil.

*Present value summary*

| | |
|---|---|
| PV of capital outlay | 1,608,695 |
| PV of released funds | 130,434 |
| NPV of operating cash flows | 526,935 |
| PV of residual plant, buildings and land after CGT | 17,523 |
| HC PV of depreciation tax allowances | 492,647 |
| HC PV of increase in borrowing capacity | 413,424 |
| HC NPV of loan | 176,751 |
| HC PV of extra tax savings due to deferrals and transfer pricing | 0 |
| PV of additional remittances | 0 |
| | |
| Total of net present values | £149,019 |

## Sensitivity analysis of the project

Laurie and Dooley and their management accounting team decided to investigate this problem further by using the spreadsheet model to estimate the impact of the changes in key variables on the value of the project. As a result they have posed the following questions.

### Question 1

Laurie and Dooley have produced the following results from a spreadsheet analysis:

*Run A* is a pessimistic view and assumes: a 2 per cent decline in productivity; no extra tax savings or remittances; a residual value of zero; and that the firm has to pay 10 per cent of the outlay in year 10 as clean-up costs ( − 10 per cent residual value in spreadsheet model).
*Expected* results are as in the previous section.
*Run B* is an optimistic view and assumes: a 2 per cent increase in productivity; an extra £20,000 tax saved per annum; extra remittances of £40,000 per annum; and a residual value increased to 20 per cent of capital outlay.

To which of these variables does the APV appear most sensitive?

*Present value summary*

|  | Run A | Expected | Run B |
|---|---|---|---|
| PV of capital outlay | 1,608,695 | 1,608,695 | 1,608,695 |
| PV of released funds | 130,434 | 130,434 | 130,434 |
| NPV of operating cash flows | 207,757 | 526,935 | 813,536 |
| PV of residual plant, buildings and land after CGT | (35,047) | 17,523 | 70,093 |
| HC PV of depreciation tax allowances | 492,647 | 492,647 | 492,647 |
| HC PV of increase in borrowing capacity | 413,424 | 413,424 | 413,424 |
| HC NPV of loan | 176,751 | 176,751 | 176,751 |
| HC PV of extra tax savings due to deferrals and transfer pricing | 0 | 0 | 105,966 |
| PV of additional remittances | 0 | 0 | 211,931 |
| Total of net present values | £(222,729) | £149,019 | £806,086 |

*Answer*

The value additivity principle states that the whole value of a project is equal to the sum of the values of the parts. This principle is very useful in international capital budgeting because many sources of project value can be investigated separately. Thus the present value of the expected operating after-tax cash flows can be found by discounting them at the all equity discount rate reflecting the project's business risk. The present value of the tax benefits produced by employing debt can be discounted at the cost of debt. Both sources of value can be added together to find the total value increase and to assess whether it exceeds the capital outlay for the project.

Given value additivity we can look at each value term separately in terms of its impact on APV.

It is clear that productivity gains or losses are very important to the project. Small variations here have a large impact on the PV of the operating cash flows and thus on the APV. Changes in residual values or clean-up costs have little relative impact on the final APV. Changes in remittances and extra tax savings can produce major benefits for the final APV.

## Question 2

Laurie and Dooley believe that treasury and tax staff have deliberately underestimated additional remittances and tax savings. It appears that they intend to use the new project location to boost their functional performance relative to low initial expectations. Laurie and Dooley estimate that additional remittances and tax savings could both be as high as £100,000 per annum. What would the impact on APV be if these cash flows were generated?

*Answer*

Again assume value additivity, and discount these cash flow streams separately as follows: that is, discount extra remittances of £100,000 per annum at 18 per cent and tax savings of £100,000 at 18 per cent, and add these extra PV elements to the expected values above. Thus:

| | |
|---|---:|
| HC PV of extra tax savings due to deferrals and transfer pricing | 529,828 |
| PV of additional remittances | 529,828 |
| | 1,059,656 |
| Total of net present values | 1,208,675 |

Thus an extra £1,059,656 would provide a considerable boost to the expected APV by increasing it to £1,208,675. This seems a most unlikely increase.

### Question 3
What if group profits are much lower than expected over the life of the project, such that StrathKelvin can only exploit 50 per cent of its tax allowances?

*Answer*
Again assume value additivity and adjust the tax allowance benefit. Thus multiply the PV of this tax factor by 0.5 and reduce the overall APV by this amount. Tax savings fall from £492,647 to £246,326 with the same incremental reduction in expected APV.

Questions 2 and 3 demonstrate that it is possible to assess many changes in APV without running the spreadsheet again.

### Question 4
If the project was located in southern England, the only significant change was expected to be the 25 per cent reduction in sales from 60,000 to 45,000 and in lost sales from 20,000 to 15,000: no extra remittances, no extra tax savings, no cheap loans, no released funds. Francs would still be used as the foreign currency because the diary/organizers would be sold in francs and Deutschmarks. What is the APV?

*Answer*
Given that the same percentage reduction in sales (45,000/60,000) and lost sales (15,000/20,000) is expected, we can recalculate the PV changes very quickly by multiplying the operating cash flows PV by 0.75 to arrive at the new operating cash flows PV, and setting the other relevant PV elements to zero. Thus there is no need for a spreadsheet recalculation. As we can see from the following summary, the southern England location produces a negative APV and does not look as attractive as the French site.

*Present value summary*

| | |
|---|---|
| PV of capital outlay | 1,608,695 |
| PV of released funds | 0 |
| NPV of operating cash flows | 395,201 |
| PV of residual plant, buildings | |
|    and land after CGT | 17,523 |
| HC PV of depreciation tax allowances | 492,647 |
| HC PVof increase in borrowing capacity | 413,424 |
| HC NPV of loan | 0 |
| HC PV of extra tax savings due to deferrals | |
|    and transfer pricing | 0 |
| PV of additional remittances | 0 |
| | |
| Total of net present values | £(289,900) |

## Question 5

Real and nominal exchange rate changes and PPP holds. Patrick Campsie asked Dooley and Laurie to explain why the real rate and nominal rate are different.

## Answer

Dooley and Laurie explained that if for example French inflation over a year is 12 per cent and UK inflation over the same period is 5 per cent, purchasing power parity would predict that the franc would depreciate by approximately 7 per cent relative to the pound. If the nominal exchange rate was 11.5fr/£ at the start of the year, then the nominal rate at the end of the year would be $11.5 \times (1 + 0.12)/(1 + 0.05) = 12.267$fr/£. If these inflation differences continue for another year, then the nominal rate at the end of year 2 would be (using year 0 as the base) $11.5 \times (1 + 0.12)^2/ (1 + 0.05)^2 = 13.084$fr/£. Thus the pound buys 12.267 francs at the end of the first year compared with 11.5 francs at the start of the year, and it appears from these nominal (actual) changes in the exchange rate that the purchasing power of the pound has increased relative to the franc.

The real rate can be expressed as

$$
\begin{pmatrix} \text{Real exchange} \\ \text{rate in} \\ \text{period } t \end{pmatrix} = \begin{pmatrix} \text{nominal (actual)} \\ \text{exchange rate} \\ \text{in period } t \end{pmatrix} \frac{1 + \text{ change in domestic inflation rate in period } t}{1 + \text{ change in foreign inflation rate in period } t}
$$

$$
RS_t = S_t \frac{1 + DI_t}{1 + FI_t}
$$

If the nominal rate of 12.667fr/£ occurred in period 1 then no change would have occurred in the real rate, because the real rate in period 1 is $12.667(1 + 0.05)/(1 + 0.12) = 11.5$ fr/£. In the same way for period 2 (using year 0 as the base period), the real rate is $13.084(1 + 0.05)^2/(1 + 0.12)^2 = 11.5$fr/£. Thus prices in both countries would have increased with local inflation changes and the exchange rate change fully reflected this. As a result, there had been no change in the relative purchasing power of the two currencies.

We can see that the concept of the real rate takes into account the joint effects of inflation changes and nominal exchange rate changes. In the above example, the change in the nominal or actual exchange rate is of no significance because the effect of inflation in the two countries is offset by the equivalent exchange rate change, i.e. purchasing power parity holds. A UK firm with non-contractual franc cash flows will probably find that these inflate at 12 per cent and, when they are changed back into pounds at the end of the year, these pounds will have a reduced purchasing power of 5 per cent in the UK. The exchange rate at the end of the year will reflect this inflation differential of 7 per cent and so the expanded number of year end pounds will have the same power to purchase goods as the equivalent number of pounds at the start of the year.

*Question 6: real and nominal exchange rate changes: PPP does not hold*
Susan Dooley agrees that if French inflation is 12 per cent and UK inflation is 5 per cent, and if PPP holds, she would expect to see the pound appreciate by approximately 7 per cent per annum relative to the franc. However, she argues that the exchange rate mechanism will constrain PPP and so the nominal rate change is only likely to reflect 60 per cent of the inflation difference. She therefore expects the pound to appreciate by only 4.2 per cent per annum relative to the franc.

What impact would these changes have on the real exchange rate? How would they affect sterling APV? How can we interpret the results?

*Answer*

If purchasing power parity only reflected say 60 per cent of the inflation differences, then the nominal fr/£ would increase (pound appreciate) at a lower rate (pound appreciates at a lower rate) but the real purchasing power of the pound would decrease from 11.5 to say 11.4fr/£: the pound buys less real franc purchasing power, or the franc buy more real pound purchasing power. Thus the sterling APV increases because of real increase in franc revenue.

Thus, if PPP held, the exchange rate change over year 1 would be 11.5 − 12.2667 = 0.76667. If PPP only reflected 60 per cent of interest rate differences, then the exchange rate change would be 0.6 × 0.76667 = 0.46002, and the nominal rate at the end of the year would be 11.5 + 0.46002 = 11.96fr/£. If the pound actually appreciated to this nominal rate of say 11.96 fr/£, then the real exchange rate would have changed over this period to become 11.96 × (1 + 0.05)/(1 + 0.12) = 11.2125 fr/£ at the end of the year.

Thus despite UK inflation rates being lower than French rates, the nominal rate change had increased the ability of the franc to buy pounds at the end of the year. In real terms, we can see that a real decrease in purchasing power of the pound occurred in tandem with a nominal increase in the number of francs purchased for £1.

This is fine for a UK firm such as StrathKelvin which sells many goods in francs, as its franc revenue cash flows can purchase more goods in the UK because of their increased purchasing power relative to the pound. Thus the francs it receives have an increased real ability to purchase goods in pounds compared with the year before. The impact of this PPP deviation is shown in the following summary of PVs. The operating cash flows PV and thus the overall APV have been increased by the real franc appreciation.

*Present value summary*

| | |
|---|---:|
| PV of capital outlay | 1,608,695 |
| PV of released funds | 130,434 |
| NPV of operating cash flows | 597,255 |
| PV of residual plant, buildings and land after CGT | 17,523 |
| HC PV of depreciation tax allowances | 492,647 |
| HC PV of increase in borrowing capacity | 413,424 |
| HC NPV of loan | 176,751 |
| HC PV of extra tax savings due to deferrals and transfer pricing | 0 |
| PV of additional remittances | 0 |
| | |
| Total of net present values | £219,339 |

*Question 7: productivity gains, and product cost and price inflation*

Laurie and Dooley are interested in the impact of changes in product costs brought about by expected productivity gains of 2 per cent per annum in the new French production site and the impact of (firm specific) product cost inflation and price inflation on APV values. They assume that PPP holds between the two economies but that their (firm specific) inflation for franc prices and costs at 10 per cent is lower than French (national) inflation of 12 per cent. What will be the new operating cash flows and APV?

*Answer*

The new variables can be introduced to the analysis by making some small adjustments to the equation for operating cash flows (section 10.6, step 4):

(a) Costs are first adjusted for a productivity gain of 2 per cent. At $t = 0$ prices, the cost in period 1 is $210(1 - 0.02) = 205.8$, and the cost in period 2 is $205.8\,(0.98) = 201.7$.

(b) Cost inflation is then included:

cost in period $t$ = (cost after productivity gain) × $(1 + \text{cost inflation})^t$

For example, with 10 per cent cost inflation, the cost in period 1 is $205.8(1 + 0.1) = 226.38$, and the cost in period 2 is $201.7(1.1)^2 = 244.037$.

(c) Prices are also inflated for price inflation:

price in period $t$ = (price at $t$ = 0)(1 + price inflation)$^t$

For example, with 10 per cent price inflation, the price in period 1 is 250(1 + 0.1)$^1$ = 275, and the price in period 2 is 250(1.1)$^2$ = 302.5.

(d) Thus the contribution margin per unit can be deduced: the margin in period 1 is 275 − 226.38 = 48.62, and the margin in period 2 is 302.5 − 244.04 = 58.46.

(e) Thus sales revenue can be obtained:

$$\begin{array}{c}\text{sales revenue}\\\text{in}\\\text{period } t\end{array} = \left(\begin{array}{c}\text{sales}\\\text{volume}\end{array}\right)\left(\begin{array}{c}\text{sales}\\\text{growth}\\\text{rate}\end{array}\right)(\text{contribution margin in period } t)$$

Sales at $t$ = 0 are 60,000 units per annum, and sales increase by 2 per cent p.a. Thus the sales revenue in period 1 is 60,000(1.02)$^1$ 48.62 = fr2,975,544, and the sales revenue in period 2 is 60,000(1.02)$^2$ 58.46 = fr3,649,307.

(f) French inflation is 12 per cent p.a.

(g) Replaced sales decline by 15 per cent p.a. and their profit contribution increases with UK inflation of 5 per cent.

(h) As PPP holds the real rate remains at 11.5fr/£ over the 10 years.

Thus the operating cash flow for year 1 is:

$$[(£/12.2667)(\text{fr2,975,544}) - (20,000 \times (1-0.15) \times 3 \times 1.05)](1-0.52) = £90,730$$
and for year 2:

| Period (year) | Nominal exchange rate (fr/£) | Unit cost at $t$ = 0 price (fr) | Contribution margin (fr) | Operating cash flows (£) | Discounted cash flows (£) |
|---|---|---|---|---|---|
| 1 | 12.26667 | 206 | 48.62 | 90,730 | 76,890.11 |
| 2 | 13.08444 | 202 | 58.46 | 110,939 | 79,674.39 |
| 3 | 13.95674 | 198 | 69.68 | 132,107 | 80,404.12 |
| 4 | 14.88719 | 194 | 82.43 | 154,342 | 79,607.91 |
| 5 | 15.87967 | 190 | 96.92 | 177,754 | 77,697.90 |
| 6 | 16.93831 | 186 | 113.33 | 202,453 | 74,994.81 |
| 7 | 18.06754 | 182 | 131.92 | 228,550 | 71,747.60 |
| 8 | 19.27204 | 179 | 152.92 | 256,161 | 68,148.72 |
| 9 | 20.55684 | 175 | 176.64 | 285,405 | 64,346.19 |
| 10 | 21.92730 | 172 | 203.39 | 316,401 | 60,452.99 |

$$(1/13.0844)(\text{fr}3,649,307) - (20,000 \times (1-0.15)^2 \times 3 \times 1.05^2)](1-0.52) = £110,939$$

The changes in productivity (cost reductions), the contribution margin per period and the operating cash flows are calculated over the life of the project as follows:

Thus the operating cash flows are discounted at the all equity rate of 18 per cent and summed over the life of the project (ten years) to give a total NPV of £733,965.

*Present value summary*

| | |
|---|---:|
| PV of capital outlay | 1,608,695 |
| PV of released funds | 130,434 |
| NPV of operating cash flows | 733,965 |
| PV of residual plant, buildings and land after CGT | 17,523 |
| HC PV of depreciation tax allowances | 492,647 |
| HC PV of increase in borrowing capacity | 413,424 |
| HC NPV of loan | 176,751 |
| HC PV of extra tax savings due to deferrals and transfer pricing | 0 |
| PV of additional remittances | 0 |
| | |
| Total of net present values | £356,049 |

As we can see, the productivity gains and the lower cost and price inflation at firm level have boosted operating cash flows and APV by £207,030.

## 10.8 The Role of Financial Modelling in Decision Making

In the previous sections we saw how Laurie, Dooley and Campsie liaised when identifying data and calculation logic for a spreadsheet model. The logic of their spreadsheet model was derived directly from the APV rule. A simplified version of this has also been written in the BASIC programming language: a listing of the BASIC program is shown in appendix 2.

The major design considerations employed in building this model include

- choice of relevant input variables
- level of detail of input and mode of input
- complexity of calculation sequence

- choice of relevant output
- range of sensitivity analysis to be included.

In this case many of these choices were simplified by restricting the model to the terms used in the APV model. The model discussed here has been specifically designed for teaching and learning purposes rather than as a practical decision aid. It therefore illustrates the APV (or NPV) rule and assumes very simple tax systems, nominal operating cash flow calculations, nominal discount rates, one type of loan repayment schedule, and nine elements in the APV equation.

In practice, financial managers will have to adapt their model to their unique and probably more complex circumstances. For example, managers may feel that market based foreign exchange forecasts are a more important input variable than inflation rates. Alternatively, inflation forecasts at the level of the firm and the economy may be seen as a crucial input. In part, the answer to these problems of model design lie in the economic circumstances surrounding the project. If major deviations from parity are expected then both real and nominal analysis will be required, and the model will have to cope with this more complex situation.

In addition a global tax model may be required to optimize corporate world tax payments. Further extensions to the model (and program) might include extra APV elements, a more sophisticated analysis of the operating cash flows, a wide range of loan calculations and many other features unique to a particular decision. For a more complete analysis of such design considerations in financial modelling, see Holland (1981).

In the case, we saw that Dooley and Laurie used the model to explore a variety of 'what if?' questions concerning the impact of changed assumptions about remittances, tax savings, lost sales etc., and combinations of changes in these input variables, on the APV of the overseas investment project. If they wished they could have defined an output APV and looked at the suitable groups of input variables or scenarios to achieve this objective. They also modelled additional variables such as productivity changes, product cost inflation, product price inflation, and real versus nominal exchange rate changes. They considered adding further variables such as a detailed cost structure, including labour, raw material and other costs. They decided that the model should be kept as a simple and low cost way of exploring key relationships in the capital budgeting decision.

Dooley and Laurie also recognized that the model could be used both for new capital budgeting decisions and for evaluating existing overseas operations. They saw that the model could be used to explore economic exposure issues for both new assets and existing assets. Capital budgeting is the logical point to address currency risk and economic exposure issues arising from new overseas projects. The capital budgeting framework, based on the NPV rule, is also the appropriate basis to consider the value implications of currency risk for existing overseas assets.

For example, in the case, investment in R&D and product design skills was expected to lead to innovative new products. This investment was expected to lead to higher flexibility and responsiveness relative to foreign exchange risk. As a result they expected to be able to rapidly alter prices and reduce costs in the face of adverse real exchange rate changes. These decisions on R&D and product design were seen as a means to protect basic value created by the investment decision. This case provides a link with the discussions on managing economic exposure in chapters 4 and 5. In the Rolls-Royce case, we can see that RR could use such a model to investigate economic exposure decisions with existing assets and new investment decisions.

## 10.9 Summary

The StrathKelvin case has allowed us to explore a detailed problem in international capital budgeting. In particular, the case has provided some insight into

- the analysis of the ownership advantages of MNCs and the location advantages of various overseas production sites
- the variety of cash flows arising in international capital budgeting and how they relate to ownership and location advantages
- how many different types of project cash flow arise in various locations in the global enterprise and how these can be transferred back to the parent group in its home country base
- the need for a systematic approach to the generation of project information and to the evaluation of the project
- the complex analytical problems in this decision area and the role of financial spreadsheets in supporting the analysis.

The case illustrates how the marriage of orthodox theory with the appropriate technology can allow managers to grapple efficiently with a very difficult decision area. This financial modelling approach will not remove or solve the fundamental difficulty of making long term strategic decisions in a climate of high uncertainty. It does, however, provide managers with a clearer perception of this problem area, and the means to efficiently develop and employ any available data. More specifically, the use of a capital budgeting model is an essential ingredient in generating the necessary cash flow information. The APV rule and the wide class of cash flow categories used within it are ideal for computer based model building. The model also allows managers to explore the sources of competitive advantage created by the firm and their role in boosting shareholder wealth. The approach provides managers with both the technology and a robust conceptual framework to tackle this complex subject. The chapter has therefore been used to illustrate how managers can employ the insights of financial theory and the theory of the MNC to deal with the unique problems of overseas corporate investment.

# 11

# International Sources of Finance for the Firm

In this chapter we consider the wide variety of sources of funds for the international enterprise. We begin in section 11.1 by describing the main characteristics of international financial centres. These centres are important sources of many different kinds of finance. In the case of the very large centres such as London and New York they are the dominant locations for raising syndicated Euroloans, Eurobonds and commercial paper.

In section 11.2 we investigate the typical funding vehicles employed in these markets. The focus here is on the way in which firms raise syndicated Euroloans, Eurobonds and commercial paper as well as the central role of the international bank in these markets.

In section 11.3 we describe the use of interest rate and currency swaps in risk management in the MNC treasury. The swap market allows corporate treasury to divide the funding decision into two clear divisions: firstly, the sourcing decision; and secondly, the choice of the appropriate risk profile for interest payments. Thus the use of these risk management instruments is intimately related to the raising of funds in international financial markets and has become a central feature of liability management in the 1990s.

This chapter therefore provides an essential context for chapters 12 and 13 in which debt valuation and the global financing decision are investigated.


## 11.1 Characteristics of Financial Centres

The large international financial centres are to be found in London, New York and other key industrial and commercial nations such as Germany

(Frankfurt), Japan (Tokyo) and France (Paris). Other locations such as Amsterdam (Holland), Zurich (Switzerland), Milan (Italy), Edinburgh and Glasgow (Scotland), Singapore and Hong Kong have extensive links both with the largest financial centres and with their own local regional and domestic financial markets. However, London and New York are premier centres in terms of the variety of funding and financial services and the scale of financial business conducted. Tokyo is emerging fast as the Asian/ Oceanic equivalent, especially in banking services and funding. The three are the top centres for international lending, stock market activity and foreign exchange business (*Economist*, 27 June 1992).

These centres are very important for the financing and foreign exchange risk management decisions taken by the MNC's treasurer. They are the operational location of many key international markets for loans, bonds, equity, interest rate swaps, currency swaps, debt for equity swaps, and a host of foreign exchange services and products. The unique ability of these centres, particularly London and New York, to combine all of these markets in one place makes them very attractive to the corporate treasurer. International banks are central participants in all of these financial markets as they compete for corporate custom.

Centres such as London and New York are complex institutions: it is difficult to provide a coherent explanation and description of their origin and their full set of functions. As we move to the regional and domestic financial centres this problem becomes more acute. Numerous descriptive criteria are commonly employed to help distinguish a full international financial centre from the regional centres. These criteria overlap in many respects but do not provide a clear model or theory of financial centre origin and function.

With this problem in mind, various commonly used criteria have been linked together in a simple wheel in figure 11.1. The labels around the wheel indicate measures of centre location advantages that make a financial centre attractive to many individual, corporate, banking and sovereign state users. Thus London is near the edge of the wheel for most advantages except, for the scale of the UK domestic economy, the significance of the pound as a global currency, and the absence of extensive secrecy laws. New York is also close to the edge except for the limitations it faces on types of banking allowed, on bank secrecy, and on duty free non-resident banking (except for the dollar based international banking facilities, IBFs): New York also has a much more formal regulatory system than London (self-regulating) both for commercial banking and for its security markets. Other centres such as Paris, Frankfurt, Hong Kong and Singapore have a much

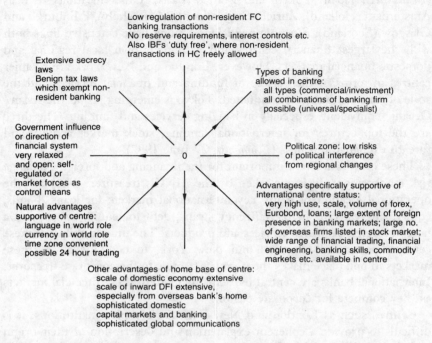

Low regulation of non-resident FC
banking transactions
No reserve requirements, interest controls etc.
Also IBFs 'duty free', where non-resident
transactions in HC freely allowed

Extensive secrecy
laws
Benign tax laws
which exempt non-
resident banking

Types of banking
allowed in centre:
    all types (commercial/investment)
    all combinations of banking firm
    possible (universal/specialist)

Government influence
or direction of
financial system
very relaxed
and open: self-
regulated or
market forces as
control means

Political zone: low risks
of political interference
from regional changes

Natural advantages
supportive of centre:
    language in world role
    currency in world role
    time zone convenient
    possible 24 hour trading

Advantages specifically supportive of
international centre status:
    very high use, scale, volume of forex,
    Eurobond, loans; large extent of foreign
    presence in banking markets; large no.
    of overseas firms listed in stock market;
    wide range of financial trading, financial
    engineering, banking skills, commodity
    markets etc. available in centre

Other advantages of home base of centre:
    scale of domestic economy extensive
    scale of inward DFI extensive,
    especially from overseas bank's home
    sophisticated domestic
    capital markets and banking
    sophisticated global communications

**Figure 11.1** Wheel model of financial centre advantages

more limited set of the above location advantages, scoring highly on only
some criteria. However, the Japanese, German and French governments
are very supportive of the development of Tokyo, Frankfurt and Paris as
full international centres with similar capabilities as London and New
York. Tokyo seems the most promising candidate for this elevated status,
given the significance of the Japanese economy and the time zone location
of Tokyo. Germany and Frankfurt also offer such possibilities. The
advantage of the Deutschmark currency and German economic strength
are certainly helping Frankfurt in this respect. However, Paris, Frankfurt
and other European centres are hampered by the existing capabilities of the
nearby City of London. The abundance of many location advantages
explains the continuing attraction of London to multinational banks and
firms. As a result, centres such as Milan are unlikely to offer the wide range
of services available in London. Other centres such as Edinburgh and

Glasgow in Scotland continue to prosper by pursuing a niche strategy as a regional financial centre.

In the case of the multinational bank, London offers the opportunity to fully exploit all forms of banking, to achieve major economies of scale in transacting, and to provide a full range of services to their multinational corporate clients. As a result, the international enterprise, when seeking funds or currency risk management services, will inevitably find that significant calls on multicurrency funds or financial services will be dealt with by the multinational bank operating in the extensive international financial markets located in London and other global centres. The specific function of these markets and of international banks operating in these centres has been dealt with in chapter 2. We therefore now turn to the methods of raising funds in these markets.

## 11.2 Raising Loans and Issuing Securities in the Euromarkets

In chapter 2 we have noted that the two major sectors of the Euromarkets are the syndicated Euroloans markets and the Eurobond markets. The former refers to lending by large international banks to international borrowers. The Eurobond market is the means for direct transacting between borrowers and lenders, with the banks providing broking, underwriting and selling services. The large multinational banks dominate this financing business and have played a major role in the development and growth of these offshore loan and bond markets.

### The Euroloan market

The Euroloan markets provide short term, medium term (three years) and long term (ten years and beyond) loans required by banks, corporate customers and government borrowers. The sources of these funds are domestic bank deposits whose ownership is transferred to banks outside the controlled domestic monetary systems. Thus US dollar deposits originally held in US banks are placed on deposit in London or Paris to become Eurodollars. The 'Euro' prefix refers to the high volume of these funds circulating in Europe, mainly through London. However, this market is world-wide and sectors of the market exist in financial centres in the Middle East and the Far East (Asiadollar market).

The market operates at two levels. Firstly, there is the very competitive inter-bank wholesale market centred in London, in which banks with top credit ratings and the highest quality assets lend their funds to each other at the London inter-bank offering rate (LIBOR). Secondly, smaller banks, corporate borrowers and national governments (in the late 1970s from Eastern Europe or developing countries, and now primarily from the Western industrialized countries) can acquire loans from the 'retail' end of this market.

Figure 11.2 illustrates the main features of the Eurolending process in the retail market. It also highlights the pivotal role of international banks in the whole lending process. In step 1 the corporate borrower may make its initial approach to the syndicated loan market via well established relationships with its 'house' or 'lead' banks. This relationship bank or banks will be mandated to raise the funds on behalf of the firm and will establish the broad interest that other banks may have in participating in the loan. The relationship banks will form the core of the syndicate or lending consortium, with other interested banks co-opted into the arrangements. Steps 2 to 5 in figure 11.2 illustrate the subsequent loan syndication process and the monitoring of the loans.

The availability of loans will depend, in part, on the deposit position in the banks approached. Generally, the large international banks such as Citibank or Deutsche Bank have considerable capacity to command deposits in the Euro inter-bank market when required. However, a surplus of deposits in a group of smaller banks will mean that the borrower should

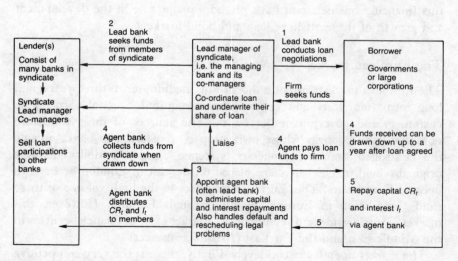

**Figure 11.2** The Eurolending process in the retail market

be able to negotiate better terms. Thus 'shopping around' a core group of relationship banks and possibly new banks should pay dividends.

In this loan market the large international banks only lend after detailed credit investigation of the borrowers. This can be simplified and short-circuited if the lead bank and co-managers have a long standing credit relationship with the corporate borrower. This will give them privileged access to information and thus allow them to quickly assess likely loan performance and the likelihood of default (Holland 1994).

Thus the lead banks play a major role in negotiating the terms of the loan with borrowers, taking part of the loan risk, identifying other banks to participate in the loan syndicate, selling participation certificates for some loans, and managing the repayment of interest and capital to lenders. Lead banks will receive a major portion of the initial and continuing fees for these services. Co-managers of the loan will receive a smaller portion of the fees commensurate with the scale and breadth of these services rendered to the borrower. This fee structure, especially the initial expenses and management fees, may be seen by the bank as an important means of boosting its effective return from the loan. Borrowers will have to include these costs with the nominal interest rate when assessing the effective interest rate cost of the funds. An example of such calculation is presented in chapter 12.

Loans in a particular currency are commonly priced according to a 'LIBOR plus' basis. The bank's cost of funding is covered by LIBOR and its administrative costs are covered by the fee structure discussed above. The bank must add a profit margin to these costs to achieve its expected return in this corporate client default risk class. The gross margin over LIBOR thus depends on the bank's view of funding cost risks (for the rollover period of deposits secured to fund the loans) over the life of the loan as well as the credit quality standing or riskiness of the borrower. The funds concerned may be committed to the borrower on a medium term (e.g. three years) or a long term (e.g. ten to fifteen years) basis, ensuring availability of funds for some time. However, interest rates are adjusted frequently depending on changing deposit interest rates and the bank's maturity structure of deposits. Revision of interest rates takes place every three or six months and borrowers bear considerable risk from one interest adjustment or rollover period to the next.

The bank in turn must find these funds from the short term deposit markets every three to six months and can face a funding risk if it allows the quality of its assets (especially its loans portfolio) to deteriorate. Funds are likely to be available in the Euro inter-bank market to the high credit rated bank at all times. The funding costs may vary considerably if deposit rates fluctuate from period to period. If the bank's credit rating slips and it moves out of an inner circle of top class banks it may find its own funding costs rising and its previously secure access to mobile funds in the inter-bank market somewhat reduced. These risks ensure that international banks in the 1990s only lend to the highest quality corporate and sovereign state borrowers.

Capital may be repaid in a variety of ways and can be matched according to the way in which the funded project generates cash flows. Regular semi-annual capital repayments after a two to three year period of grace, a few large payments towards the end of the loan, or a final single lump sum or 'bullet' payment are all possible. Fixed rate Eurocurrency loans are also available. This has the advantage to the borrower of knowing at the outset the exact amount of interest to be paid, but the rate charged will be higher to reflect the risk now borne by the bank lender.

The loans are generally raised by a syndicate of banks in which the risks of a particular borrower are distributed across several banks. The hope here is that, in the case of default, no single bank is placed in a risky position. Of course, simultaneous default by several large sovereign states or a set of large property companies would negate these diversification benefits and seriously affect the position of certain banks. This former possibility was at the heart of the LDC based world banking crisis of the 1980s and is still present in the 1990s with the demise of the Soviet Union and its Eastern European empire.

Euroloans are primarily raised in US dollars, but Deutschmark and yen loans are available. The amounts can vary from $5 million to $5 billion, but in practice a more typical loan would be in the $50m to $250m range. In principle, the loans could be denominated in any of the major world currencies. The close proximity and working relationship with the foreign exchange markets means that considerable flexibility is possible in terms of currency of denomination. For example, the borrower may negotiate a clause in the loan contract which allows a switch of currency in any rollover period. This switch should not lead to a change in real borrowing costs because the parity relationships are likely to hold in these markets. Thus different nominal interest rates in dollar and mark loans for the same borrower should reflect differences in $/DM forward rates and exchange rate expectations over the life of the loan (see chapter 3). This currency switching facility may be useful as a means to hedge a change in the currency of revenue cash flows arising in the funded project. The firm can therefore match the currency of debt payments with its changing capacity to pay.

In the 1990s, EC banks and US banks emphasized higher quality lending to Western governments and companies and turned away from the heavily indebted countries. International firms began to make more sophisticated use of the Eurolending market by employing more flexible financing arrangements such as multi-option facilities. In addition the Euroloan syndication facilities became very important in funding the surge of takeovers and management buyouts in the latter half of the 1980s. These loan markets also provided competitive funding facilities to those firms with limited access (relatively lower credit rating) to the Eurobond and other Eurosecurity markets. These firms could then use the swaps markets to gain indirect access to the Eurosecurity markets. As a result the composition of syndicated borrowers has changed significantly since the early 1980s (*Bank of England Quarterly Bulletin*, February 1990, pp. 71–2).

In 1991 and 1992, a key change in corporate borrowing practices involved a switch from syndicated lending to bilateral lending (Coggan 1991). This might explain the depressed state of the market in 1991 and 1992 (see chapter 2). The motives for this are unclear. In part, the change may be due to the difficulties that syndicates of banks have faced with major corporate borrowers such as Polly Peck or the Robert Maxwell owned enterprises. This behaviour may also reflect a reduced confidence that lead banks can control borrowers in distress and that high quality credit information is being released by their relationship customers. It may also reflect reduced confidence on the part of bankers in the risk spreading benefits of syndication. In the case of large MNCs such as BP this has been an opportunity to simplify their lending relationships. In August 1991, BP announced that it had replaced a number of syndicated loans with a series of bilateral loans. This reduced the number of banks concerned from 67 to 27 with consequent savings in the costs of managing such a large number of banks.

Corporations seem to have recognized that to have a large number of banks involved in syndicated lending can dilute close banking relationships and thus the commitment of their bankers when times become harder. The banks have also recognized that some syndicated lending practices, such as the sale of loan participations combined with an agent bank collecting repayments, can impair credit control, and that more intensive contact with borrowers is required. These factors can combine to exacerbate problems of loan renegotiation during downturns in the economy. In the syndicate a few banks, probably with their own difficulties, can cause problems for the corporate borrower and the other banks by holding up agreements on rescheduling or altering the terms of the syndicated loan. Bilateral lending or syndicated lending with a very small syndicate (club) of relationship banks can ease some of these problems. These agreements are likely to lead to better flows of information amongst the parties to the loan and, given the reduced number of banks, may also mean lower transaction costs and speedier access to funds for the borrower. However, if the loans are very large and banks wish to spread their lending risks, the syndicated loan continues to look an attractive medium for all parties.

*Securitization and corporate borrowing opportunities*
We have seen in chapter 2 how the international banks are now subject to the effects of securitization. A major example relates to the securitization of the Euromarkets. It appears that the shift from the indirect financing (financial intermediation or internal bank transacting role) to direct financing (external market transacting) via the security markets has been led by changes in transaction costs both in the Euromarkets and within the international bank. Changes in investor preference and in technology are key factors in changing transaction costs and encouraging this shift in the financing mechanism. Thus in the mid 1980s, as the Eurosecurity markets developed, there was a movement away from syndicated bank euroloans to a greater use of note issuance facilities (NIFs), and Eurocommercial paper, as well as a growing use of the existing Eurobond market.

Securitization in the Euromarkets has created a major set of new opportunities for large MNC treasuries as they exploit the funding capabilities of securities houses and investment banks. The availability of large amounts of money to lend, once the commercial banker's primary competitive advantage, no longer dominates funding choices for (high credit rating) corporate treasuries when they can raise cheaper funds elsewhere. The strength of the security houses and investment banks lies in their highly developed ability to provide these corporate funds and services and also to satisfy the needs of the new breed of investor. Thus they securitize debt and in so doing make it negotiable and saleable direct to investors, bypassing the traditional financial intermediation performed by commercial banks. This can often be done at rates lower than those at which the banks can afford to lend. This switch from financial intermediation to an agency or brokerage role posed a major problem for the large commercial banks. However, as discussed above, the syndicated loan market still has a clear role for corporate treasurers in the 1990s. In addition, many large international banks have responded to these changes by offering both lending and security issue facilities from new integrated commercial and investment bank arms. Thus all of these sources of funds are expected to continue to play a major part in funding international firms, with the international bank playing a central role in this funds provision.

## The Eurobond market as a source of corporate funds

The second major source of corporate financing in the unregulated international capital market is the Eurobond market. This market permits lenders to lend directly to borrowers across national borders, without the financial intermediation of a bank. Banks do however play a major role in the Eurobond market as brokers, underwriters, sellers of paper and managers of bond issues.

Eurobonds differ from foreign bonds in that the latter are issued in one country in its currency by a foreign borrower. By contrast, the Eurobond is issued in one currency (or a currency basket such as the ECU or the SDR) for sale in many capital markets, with the sale managed by an international syndicate of underwriters. The borrowers or issuers of the bonds include MNCs, public sector organizations, sovereign states and commercial banks. The lenders or purchasers of the bond securities are individual and institutional investors, with the latter group dominating.

Generally, purchasers buy Eurobonds in currencies other than their own, and a major attraction of these bonds for investors is that in most currencies they are anonymous bearer bonds that exempt individuals from capital gains and withholding taxes in their own domestic tax system. In contrast, foreign bonds are identifiable by investor name, are subject to domestic regulation, and have in some cases been subject to withholding taxes on non-residents. There have been attempts by national governments to place overseas investors in foreign bonds on an equal footing with domestic investors. Thus the US has removed withholding taxes on US dollar bonds raised by foreign firms (Yankee bonds) or by US companies' overseas subsidiaries in New York. These changes are likely to erode some of the advantages of Eurobonds. However, the unregulated nature of the Eurobond market means that its costs are lower and its issuing process is much faster than its domestic or foreign bond counterparts. This speed of issue is very important for rapid mobilization of funds for the firm. It is also very important if the firm and its bankers are exploiting a short lived tax loophole.

Banks play a major role in the Eurobond market by bringing together lenders and borrowers, underwriting the bond issue, selling or placing the bonds, supporting the secondary market in bonds, and managing the repayment of interest and capital to investors. The participating banks will receive a fee for each of these services rendered to the borrower or investor.

Eurobonds can be arranged via established domestic banking channels. Thus a Japanese firm can use its close Japanese relationship bank as a lead bank to sell or distribute its bonds issued in London. These could be yen Eurobonds and end up as part of a Japanese individual's or institution's portfolios.

The key to the market is an established and high quality credit rating with an internationally recognised rating agency such as Moody's or Standard Poors. The credit rating agencies can economize on the processing of public information and translate it into an easily understood measure of bond default risk. This is unlikely to do any more than mirror an efficient bond markets' view of this risk. However, the agencies add their reputation to this risk assessment and this is likely to inspire confidence in bond purchasers. A close relationship bank may be very important in supporting the first major corporate issue in this market and in establishing a high quality credit rating. The relationship bank supplements the credit rating by demonstrating, via its in-depth knowledge of the firm, a willingness to underwrite and place the bonds. Once the firm has established 'name recognition' in the Eurobond market through these signalling mechanisms, it may have a much greater degree of freedom in choosing lead bankers for its Eurobond issues.

Figure 11.3 illustrates the bank role in the issue of a Eurobond. The following activities are indicated in the figure and described in the sections below:

1    negotiating terms
2    selling bonds
3    agent banking
4    stimulating the secondary market.

*Negotiating terms*

The offshore bond markets provide medium to long term funds of three to fifteen year's maturity for high quality corporate, bank and sovereign state borrowers. Fixed coupons or interest rates are common but floating rate notes are also important. The floating rate is usually LIBOR or some other market base plus a risk premium depending on the quality of the issuer, and this rate is generally set semi-anually. As with the Eurocurrency

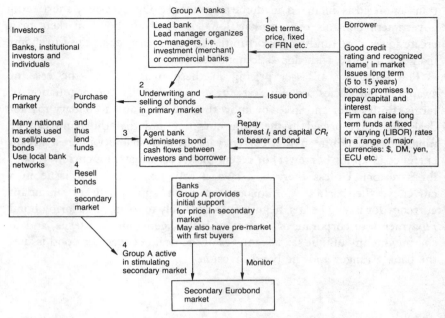

**Figure 11.3** The bank role in the issue of a Eurobond

market, the major denomination is in dollars, with marks, pounds, yen and ECUs also available.

Asset pricing in this market is also likely to be dominated by parity relationships, albeit with securities of longer maturity and greater risk. The yield to maturity of bonds (internal rate of return) calculated on the basis of the market price of bonds and the stream of capital and interest repayments is a weighted average of future spot interest rates. If interest rate parity and international Fisher hold, the term structure of interest rates in, say, dollars and marks would reflect expected \$/DM changes over the life of the bonds. Eurobonds of different currency but the same maturity and risk should therefore offer the same covered interest returns. However, short-lived tax differences between countries may alter this balance and create a window of opportunity for the corporate treasury. In the case of domestic bonds, in countries where free capital flows are permitted, the domestic and European term structures of interest rates would be closely joined together via arbitrage in the foreign exchange, Eurobond and domestic bond markets. Hence Eurobonds of the same currency, maturity and risk should offer the same returns as domestic bonds except for additional transaction costs incurred in domestic markets. On occasion, short term government controls over capital flows or domestic bond markets may create lower cost funding opportunities for the treasurer in the Eurobond market compared with domestic bond funding.

The efficiency of asset pricing in these markets, and the ease of swapping currencies and interest rate terms, simplify the negotiation of terms. Both issuer and investor know that the issue and secondary market deals are fairly priced in the issue currency and that the bond can be rapidly swapped into another currency of payment (liability interest stream currency swap for borrower) or receipt (asset return stream currency swap for investor). Unless there is a special (say tax) reason for issue in a currency, the parties can choose the most appropriate or abundant currency for issue. Terms' negotiations are likely to focus on tailoring bond repayments to corporate or project cash flow generation patterns, and to sharing out any unique tax advantages of the deal between the bond issuer, the bank arranger and the bond investor.

*Selling the bonds*

The lead bank and the rest of the issue managers (group A) as well as some specialist selling banks place the bonds in the primary market. This may involve selling to many small investors via extensive branch networks or to large institutional investors via more direct methods.

The 'bought deal' in which one bank (or a small number of banks) buys the whole issue is becoming popular. The bank(s) subsequently sells large blocks of the issues to large institutional investors. This practice has emerged from the US equity and bond domestic market and has begun to find favour in the Eurobond market. Under this method the bank handles the whole deal, including corporate advice, new issue and trading functions. By buying the whole issue and distributing the bonds to large investors it hopes to makes a further 'turn' on the price and reduce selling costs. Corporate treasurers see the 'one stop banking' approach, in which they are offered the full fund raising service from one institution, as being less costly in terms of fees than a multibank syndicated approach. Only the very largest Eurobond lead managers can provide this kind of service. Thus Nomura, Daiwa, CSFB, Deutsche and a few more very large international banks are capable of providing this service. This capability, in turn, is likely to reinforce the large Eurobond market shares held by these banks.

*Agent banking*

The agent bank plays a major role in administering the bond cash flows over their life. Thus the collection of investors' funds, the transfer of a large capital sum to the borrower, and the repayment of capital and interest to the investors are carefully managed by this bank. .

*Stimulating the secondary market*

A secondary market for Eurobonds has grown rapidly as these financial institutions continuously seek to adjust their portfolios. As a result the original investors are not committed to a borrower until the final maturity of the bond issue. The lead bank in the issue and the co-managers (group A) will generally support the secondary market for up to a year after the issue, by acting as a market maker (buyer and seller) in the bonds. This imparts liquidity to the bonds and provides a further incentive for investors to purchase the bonds.

## Euronote and Eurocommercial paper: the role of medium and short term securities in funding the firm

The medium and short term Europaper market emerged in the 1980s as an important new source of funds for the MNC. Two examples are briefly described here: firstly, bank underwritten note issuance facilities (NIFs); and secondly, Eurocommercial paper.

In the case of NIFs the corporate borrower issues negotiable short term (three to six month) notes. These are reissued every three to six months. Thus the firm can raise medium term (five to seven years) funds at rates linked to varying rates in short term Euro or domestic credit markets. Note issuance facilities (NIFs) are important because they provide the corporate treasurer with the option of when to sell his short/medium term paper. The banks offer to buy this paper at an agreed premium over a floating base rate such as LIBOR. This insurance scheme allows the corporate treasurer (for a fee) to choose to issue the paper when alternative market interest rates are considered excessive.

Figure 11.4 illustrates the role of international banks as part of a medium term security underwriting syndicate in which the banks either provide the insurance scheme in primary paper markets or, if the corporate paper does not sell, provide the firm with an equivalent credit.

The period 1985–90 saw a rapid process of evolution within the Europaper market as insured note facilities increasingly gave way to the

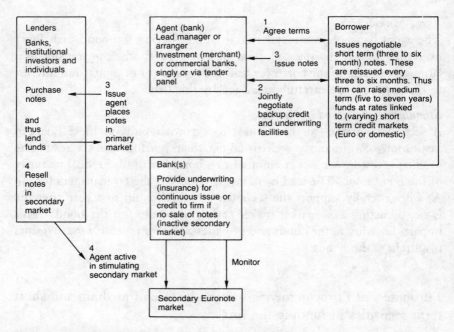

**Figure 11.4** The role of banks in the Euronote market

launch by top rated borrowers of pure Eurocommercial paper programmes that did not require any backup in the form of standby credit. The Eurocommercial paper market acquired some depth and there has been a growing tendency for rates in the Euro and US commercial paper markets to converge. This has opened up opportunities for US borrowers to raise funds in Europe, particularly at the longer maturity end of the commercial paper market range. The issue process is similar to that illustrated in figure 11.4 for NIFs, with banks playing a central role in placing the paper and stimulating the secondary Eurocommercial paper market. However, they do not provide the underwriting or replacement credit facilities of NIFs and thus this issue is made at much lower cost to the firm.

## 11.3 The Use of Interest Rate and Currency Swaps

A major development in international capital markets in the 1980s was the emergence of the swaps markets.

An interest rate swap is a means to transform an interest payment cash flow stream from floating to fixed or vice versa, or from floating against a certain market index such as LIBOR to floating against another such as the US banks' inter-bank base rate. No principal changes hands in this swap and the exchanges of interest cash flow can be done on a net basis. This transformation can be done both for the payer and for the receiver of the interest cash flow stream. It therefore alters the cash flow characteristics of an existing or new asset or liability. In some cases this swap can be used to reduce liability costs or to improve asset returns. This is only likely if the parties to the exchange are exploiting different risk/return trade-offs in two capital markets, or tax and/or regulatory differences between markets. The swap can also be used to alter the exposure of the firm to unanticipated interest rate changes. This mechanism can also be used to swap interest rate exposures between currencies, say floating mark payments for fixed sterling payments. In this case the (counter) parties to the exchange would also exchange principals at an agreed exchange rate. This currency and interest rate swap can possibly reduce the cost of funding and alter exposure to interest rate risk and currency risks. It also allows the firm to separate out the decision on where to source funds from the decision as to the interest rate or currency risk characteristics of funding.

Thus in swaps markets borrowers can swap borrowings from one currency to another (currency swaps) and from fixed to floating rates or vice versa (interest rate swaps). Borrowers do not have to tap the floating rate market directly in order to obtain floating funds. Nor do they have to make an issue in dollars if they want dollars. Swaps, both interest rate and Eurocurrency, are now a major part of the primary Eurobond market, with many new issues being immediately involved in a currency or interest rate swap. The ability of a bank to swap in this way is often the principal reason, after price, why a corporate treasurer would choose the bank for the deal.

## Interest rate swaps

Interest rate swaps are a novel means for banks to satisfy customers' changing needs as to terms of funding. They also allow the bank to arbitrage between Eurobond and bank loan markets, exploiting any differences in the pricing of risk in either market. If this arbitrage is successful and part of the benefit is passed on to the client, the firm concerned may be able to reduce its costs of funds and reduce its exposure to unanticipated interest rate changes by providing a closer match between its asset and liability cash size and timing characteristics.

However, treasurers should be sceptical of cheap funding opportunities offered here by their bankers. The perceived benefit of such an interest rate swap is that it allows the borrower to tap the market where it can raise funds most easily and cheaply, but then to pass the liability to another borrower and obtain the interest rate structure it prefers. Cheaper funding can arise if each counterparty has special access to certain markets, or has a higher credit rating (better credit risk) in certain markets which is unavailable to the other counterparty. The swap is the means for the counterparties to share their funding advantages. If swapping takes place on a regular basis between such markets then one price for risk will prevail: price differences will be illusory, probably reflecting transaction cost differences. Thus the firm is swapping interest repayment cash flow streams of the same value and this alone does not add value for shareholders. The main advantages of interest rate swaps are that they open a much wider range of global financing possibilities to companies and countries and they offer a flexible means to alter exposures to interest rate risks. The latter may reduce loss of shareholder value owing to lower risk of financial distress, and this is a potentially important role for such swaps.

In figure 11.5, counterparty A is a first class AAA rated borrower that

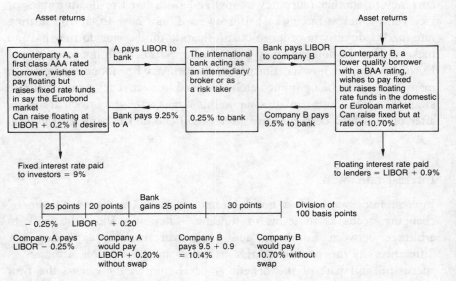

**Figure 11.5** Principles of an interest rate swap

wishes to pay a floating rate but raises fixed rate funds in say the Eurobond market. It has good access to this market and can raise floating rate funds at LIBOR + 0.2 per cent if it desires. Counterparty B is a lower quality borrower with a BAA rating. Party B wishes to pay a fixed rate but raises floating rate funds in the domestic or Euroloan market. It can raise fixed rate funding but at a rate of 10.70 per cent. In this situation the international bank, acting as an information intermediary, brings together the two parties and arranges the swap as in the upper part of the figure. In terms of 100 basis points (1 per cent), the benefits of the swap are divided as in the lower part of the figure.

Many variations are possible on this theme.

- The AAA borrower may pay the bank part of its interest reduction benefits for the swap service rendered.
- Company B may have fixed asset returns, say 10.8 per cent, on financial assets of the same amount. It is therefore 'locked in' to a fixed spread of 0.4 per cent.
- Company A may have floating asset returns, floating on the same base rate of say LIBOR + 1 per cent. It has therefore matched its floating interest rate repayments with similar income cash flows, and is locked into a certain net return of 1.25 per cent.

Banks can act as brokers to bring together firms with these matching needs. They could also take a risk by accepting one half of a deal until a suitable partner emerged, i.e. the bank replaces counterparty A in the deal.

## Currency swaps

Currency swaps are a key means for a bank to provide a corporate client with funds in one currency and then immediately swap into the customer's desired funding currency and thus alter its exposure to currency risk. They also allow the bank to manage its own currency exposures or to arbitrage perceived differences in future currency prices and in interest rates in the same currencies. In both of these cases the bank is using its unique position and information advantages to maximize its income and to shift, share or reduce its risk position stemming from contracts with other customers.

In the example in figure 11.6 the fixed interest rate streams and repayments of principal are exchanged at an agreed exchange rate over the life of the swap. Firstly, the interest rates are set at the beginning of the contract and are assumed to be equal in real terms at that time, i.e. interest

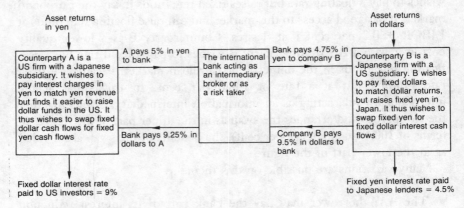

**Figure 11.6** Principles of a currency swap

rate parity prevails. Both streams have an equal present value at $t = 0$ in a common currency. Secondly, the interest rate difference (9.5 − 5.0 per cent) implies that the dollar is expected to depreciate by 4.5 per cent per annum over this period. As a result, this depreciated annual exchange rate is used throughout the life of the swap as the basis for the currency exchange.

Many other variations in currency swaps are possible. Thus fixed interest rate profiles in one currency can be swapped with varying interest rate profiles in another currency. Floating interest rate profiles in one currency can be swapped with floating interest rate profiles in another currency.

The perceived benefit of such a currency swap is that it allows the borrower to tap the market where it can raise funds most easily and cheaply, but then pass the liability to another borrower and obtain money in the currency and with the interest rate structure it prefers. If swapping takes place on a regular basis between dollar and yen loans (or bonds) of equivalent risk, then interest rate parity will prevail and nominal interest rate differences will be illusory, reflecting exchange rate change expectations and possibly transaction cost differences. The main advantages of currency swaps are that they open a much wider range of currency of denomination financing possibilities to companies and countries, and they offer a flexible means to alter exposures to currency risks. Clearly, a joint currency and interest rate swap can simultaneously deal with both types of financial price risks.

Swaps of interest rate profiles in different currencies will arbitrage between capital markets and currency markets in a fashion similar to the shorter term Eurocurrency bank deposit and forward markets. As a result, interest rate parity and international Fisher are likely to prevail in the Eurobond market and the international loans market via swaps arbitrage.

## Debt for equity swaps

Debt for equity swaps are another variant on the swapping theme. They allow the firm flexible funding for its subsidiary in a less developed country (LDC) or for the acquisition of assets in a debt laden LDC, and they can also provide cheap access to local currency funding.

In the example in figure 11.7 a UK bank, owed $100 million debt by an LDC, exchanges it with a US MNC firm requiring the means to expand its operations in the LDC. The debt is worth much less than its face value and so the MNC only pays $50 million in cash to the UK bank. The MNC cancels the debt with the LDC government in exchange for $70 million local currency or domestic purchasing power equivalent. This $70 million equivalent is exchanged with local enterprise owners (could be the government) to purchase the local enterprise.

These steps are taken simultaneously so that all four parties achieve their aims. The bank reduces its LDC debt and probably realizes a better price for the debt than is available in secondary markets for LDC debts. The LDC country reduces its debt burden by $100 million. The MNC acquires

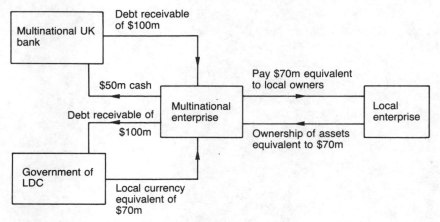

**Figure 11.7** Principles of a debt for equity swap

an asset that is otherwise unavailable or is only available at a price higher than $50 million. Local investors sell the asset at a local price equivalent of $70 million. Thus the presumption is that this deal is the best available to the MNC, the local investors, the LDC and the bank.

## 11.4 Summary

In this chapter we have considered the main characteristics of international financial centres and the wide variety of sources of funds available for the international enterprise. A selection of key funding vehicles, including syndicated Euroloans, Eurobonds and commercial paper, was investigated as well as the central role of the international bank in these markets. Finally, the potential use of interest rate and currency swaps in risk management in the MNC treasury was investigated. This chapter therefore provides an essential context for chapters 11 and 12 in which debt valuation and the global financing decision are investigated.

# 12

# The Debt Financing Decision

## 12.1 Valuing Risky Debt

The overseas debt financing decision is a complex decision problem in its own right. For example, in the case of the MNC financing overseas subsidiaries it involves choices (for the parent company) between home currency (HC) financing, local currency (LC) financing for subsidiaries, foreign currency (FC) financing (foreign to home and subsidiary), and internal mobilization and transfer of funds from units in surplus to those in deficit.

As we have seen in chapter 11, overseas foreign currency denominated debt can also take many different forms including bank loans, market issued bonds and commercial paper. These all involve the firm in cash inflows from lenders, to be followed by cash outflows in repayment to the lenders. They all comprise the common ingredients of risky cash flows occurring over time. As a result the basic decision model for evaluating debt financing choices and their associated corporate cash flows is the conventional NPV model. The goal is therefore to identify the incremental cash flows created by the debt financing decision and to maximize the net present value of the loan, the bond sale, or debt security issues. The model can be expressed as follows:

NPV of borrowed funds = PV of cash inflows − PV of cash outflows

or

$$\text{NPV} = B_0 - \sum_{t=0}^{t=\text{debt maturity}} \frac{RP_t}{(1 + r_t)^t}$$

All of these financial variables are expressed in nominal home currency terms: $B_0$ is the amount borrowed (period 0); $RP_t$ are the overall repayments per period, where $RP_t = CR_t + I_t$; $CR_t$ are the capital repayments per period; and $I_t$ are the interest payments per period, where $I_t =$ (interest rate × balance outstanding) per period. If we are employing the conventional NPV model to value the debt, then $r_t$ is the opportunity cost of funds per period for this corporate funding risk class. This discount rate has to be identified from market interest rates for debt of the same maturity and in the same default and systematic risk class. This may be possible if the debt type has many similar market equivalents and if an abundance of periodic (yearly) interest rate data can be estimated from market prices for debt.

Treasurers conventionally prefer to calculate interest rate costs rather than the NPVs of financing opportunities (Folks and Advani 1980). They therefore set the above NPV equation to zero and calculate the internal rate of return (IRR) for a debt financing opportunity. This internal rate of return can be interpreted as the effective cost of debt or an average of the multiperiod market interest rates expected to prevail over the life of the debt. The IRR can be compared with prevailing market interest rates for debt of the same maturity and risk to assess whether the debt is 'cheap'. If the effective (calculated IRR) cost of debt is approximately the same as market interest rates on debt of similar risk and duration, then the assumption of zero NPV debt can be seen as reflecting fair pricing of debt in an efficient capital market. If it is higher than market rates then lenders or bond investors are probably overcharging compared with the international price for such debt. This may be acceptable to the borrower if bank loan interest rates are also covering other implied bank costs for supplying or making available a range of non-loan services. If the effective cost of debt is lower than equivalent market rates, and this form of debt is normally priced in an efficient market, then this cheaper than market source may reflect a transient tax or interest rate subsidy – a 'window of opportunity'. The possibility of such market imperfections or unique corporate circumstances has been discussed in chapter 3.

The terms of various types of debt can vary considerably. In the case of a simple bond, the capital balance outstanding is generally constant over the term of the contract and interest is calculated either on a fixed (coupon) or a varying percentage of the constant balance. As a result, capital repayments ($CR$ per period $t$) are zero for every period except the final period when the total capital (bullet) is repaid. In the case of a simple term loan, the capital balance declines each period by a known sum. This may be a constant figure calculated as the total capital divided by the number of periods, or the balance outstanding may be reduced using other standard methods such as double declining digits. Interest will be calculated on the balance outstanding and may be based on a fixed or floating interest rate. In this case capital repayments ($CR$ per period $t$) will be positive each period and will progressively reduce the balance to zero by the end of the term. The cash flow repayment terms of the debt are normally tailored to the ability of the firm to repay the debt. In the case of asset specific funding, the way in which the asset generates surplus after-tax cash flows will determine the design of these repayment terms in the financing package. It may also determine the way in which the debt capital is distributed to the borrower over time to reflect the periodic financing needs of the project.

Tax is a significant variable in the financing decision. For example, tax deductions may be allowed for interest charges and for bond flotation costs or loan administration costs. In the following equation, only interest costs are considered as a 'tax shelter':

$$RP_t = CR_t + (1 - T_t)I_t$$

where $T_t$ is the marginal corporate tax rate per period. This equation assumes that the firm has taxable profits and that the debt is raised in a jurisdiction where the firm can use interest payments to reduce its tax bill by a cash flow increment equal to (tax rate × interest payments) in any period of debt maturity. The identification of such taxable profits and the raising of the debt in the currency and jurisdiction which maximizes tax benefits are central concerns of MNC treasurers and their advisory bankers.

If interest payment subsidies exist then

$$RP_t = CR_t + (1 - T_t)(I_t - U_t)$$

where $U_t$ is the interest rate subsidy per period. This may also be expressed as a lower than market interest rate $LI_t = I_t - U_t$.

## Foreign currency loans and cash flows

If borrowing and repayments occur in a foreign currency then

$$B_0 = B_{f0}/s_0$$

where $B_{f0}$ are foreign currency borrowings and $s_0$ is the spot rate in period 0 (FC per unit HC , e.g. 2.5 DM/£). In addition,

$$RP_t = RP_{ft}/s_t$$

$$\text{where } RP_{ft} = CR_{ft} + (1 - T_{ft})I_{ft}$$

where $s_t$ is the spot exchange rate expected in period $t$, and the subscript $ft$ refers to FC values per period.

Thus if multiperiod spot exchange rate forecasts are available, these foreign currency debt cash flows can be converted to home currency cash flows and the home currency discount rate can be used in the home currency version of the NPV model to value the debt.

If gains or losses on exchange rate changes are taxable or deductible, the tax effects will depend on the capital repayment pattern of the type of debt employed. In the case of a bullet bond the capital gain or loss will occur at the end of the term when the total capital borrowed is repaid. In the case of a term loan, gains and losses can occur throughout the life of the loan. In general, the tax due or avoided can be calculated as follows:

$$\begin{pmatrix} \text{tax deduction} \\ \text{or reduction} \\ \text{per period} \end{pmatrix} = \left[ CR_{ft} \Big/ \begin{pmatrix} \text{exchange rate} \\ \text{change from; } s_0 \end{pmatrix} \right] \begin{pmatrix} \text{tax} \\ \text{rate} \end{pmatrix}$$

$$= (\text{exchange gain or loss}) \begin{pmatrix} \text{tax} \\ \text{rate} \end{pmatrix}$$

$$TT_t = [CR_{ft}/(s_0 - s_t)]T_t$$

$TT_t$ includes the exchange gains or losses on capital repayments and thus on additional or reduced tax cash flows (in home currency). It can therefore be included in the home currency NPV formula above to either increase or reduce $RP_t$.

In assessing the financing cost in this way the corporate treasurer will have to forecast the expected path of exchange rates and interest rates, as well as changes in other key variables (e.g. tax rates), over the lives of FC loans. A spreadsheet model will be an essential decision aid here.

## Alternative uses of the NPV model

An alternative calculation to the above would be to discount the nominal FC total repayments at the nominal FC opportunity cost of funds and then to use the spot rate to convert the FC net present values to HC terms. This

HC NPV can be used to compare the FC debt with the home currency alternatives:

$$\text{NPV} = \frac{B_{f0}}{s_0} - \frac{1}{s_0} \sum_{t=0}^{t=\text{debt maturity}} \frac{RP_{ft}}{(1 + r_{ft})^t}$$

where, $RP_{ft}$ is the nominal FC total after tax repayments and $r_{ft}$ is the nominal FC opportunity cost of funds.

This has the advantage of avoiding forecasting exchange rates over the life of the foreign currency debt. However, this is likely to be one of the most significant variables in valuing risky FC debt. If we ignore tax and if the international Fisher effect (IFE) holds over the life of the debt then the firm will be indifferent as to the currency of funding. However, exchange rate considerations will be very important if deviations in IFE are considered probable and thus real differences in interest rates are considered likely between debt denominated in different currencies. The timing of the exchange rate and interest rate changes will also be an important factor. In the case of debt with contractually fixed capital and interest repayments, early appreciation of the foreign currency of borrowing will reduce the HC value of the debt (increase cost) more than a later appreciation. This is because the greater amount of HC required to service the fixed but appreciating FC payments will be paid earlier and thus have a higher cost per unit of HC. The time profile of the debt cash flows will also be important here. In the case of a single FC appreciation early in the life of the debt, a bullet repayment of FC capital at the end of the debt life will be less costly in HC than level capital FC repayments spread over the life of the debt. The further out in time the FC appreciation and the further out in time the FC debt repayments, the less costly or more valuable the debt becomes.

As a result the treasurer may decide that despite the difficulties involved, currency forecasting is worthwhile because it allows the treasurer to assess the sensitivity of debt value (financing cost) to a range of exchange rate scenarios. Understanding this problem, and identifying which debt funding opportunities are most valuable (least costly) and remain so under many exchange rate scenarios, will require considerable computational support. This issue will be considered in sections 12.2, 12.3 and 12.4.

As indicated earlier, the FC denominated use of the NPV debt valuation model can be further 'simplified' by using it to calculate the home currency internal rate of return or effective home currency cost of funds. This has the apparent advantage of removing the need to estimate interest (discount) rates over the life of the foreign currency debt. Folks and Advani (1980) advocate the use of this IRR criterion (or yield to maturity or effective cost of funds) for this analysis. This equates the present value (HC) of these interest and principal payments with the (HC) value of the financing proceeds. The firm then chooses the source of funds with the lowest effective interest cost. Treasurers employ such methods because of the estimation difficulties and because of their familiarity with interest rates in this context. However, this approach suffers from the conventional problems of IRR in that it is a single internal statistic of the debt cash flows and does not reflect the multiperiod financing opportunities open to the firm. The market price for funds of this risk class must play a role in the funding decision and should, as a minimum requirement, be used as a benchmark by the rational treasurer.

If data on the term structure of interest rates for the HC funds of similar risk are available, NPVs can be calculated. This ensures that investment and financing decisions are made using the same criteria and that value interactions between projects and their funding can be assessed on the same terms. The adjusted present value rule was employed in chapters 9 and 10 to consider these issues in the capital budgeting decision.

Finally, it is important in this funding context to identify the additional NPV (financing cost reduction) derived from the international dimensions of the financing decision. The reference point for this comparison is the domestic home country market of the MNC. In this case, if the (HC) capital market is efficient, then the HC funds will have a zero NPV, and the firm should therefore only consider those alternative funds that have positive NPVs (less than market interest costs). Interest rates for HC Eurocurrency funding would be preferable here as a more accurate reflection of the HC opportunity cost of financing for the firm. Any difference in the NPVs (or financing costs) of the domestic and the equivalent offshore alternative, both assumed to be efficiently priced, should only reflect the difference in transaction costs between these (common currency funding) markets. A similar conclusion can be arrived at for two domestic capital markets that are both integrated and efficient. Thus when IFE and IRP hold between markets it should be difficult for the firm to issue positive NPV (lower than market interest costs) debt securities in these markets.

## The significance of taxes

When taxes enter the domestic scene and taxable profits exist, there may be positive NPVs (cheap funding) when the firm borrows in efficient domestic markets. As the capital structure debate has demonstrated, these benefits are only likely to exist if the firm has unused debt capacity and if investors cannot obtain the tax benefits through personal borrowing. In addition, Miller (1977) has argued that these benefits are exaggerated if the corporate demand for debt increases and interest rates rise to offset the advantages of debt over equity. Masulis (1980) has however presented some empirical evidence for the tax benefits of domestic debt and it seems likely that, as there are international differences in tax rates and systems (personal and corporate), the MNC may be in a position to increase its tax advantages by borrowing in the country with the most favourable tax system. Major differences between national tax systems can include:

1  different corporate tax rates and systems which affect the size of the tax relief or allowances on interest charges on the debt
2  differential treatment of foreign exchange gains and losses on the capital repayments or on interest payments: some countries tax gains and disallow losses and vice versa
3  whether the tax system recognizes the gains and losses on the interest or capital repayments when the exchange change occurs or when an actual interest or capital repayment is made.

These differences in tax rates and systems, and in the treatment of gains and losses and when they are recognized, will greatly complicate the calculation of after-tax debt cash flows. These tax complexities will interact with financial market pricing issues to further exacerbate the computational and analytical problem.

For example, if IFE and IRP hold between two capital markets there may be differences in their after-tax interest rates, adjusted for the exchange rate forward premium or discount. As a result the firm's choice of the currency of denomination of borrowing may have a significant effect on the NPV calculation. This may be accentuated if IRP and IFE do not hold between certain capital markets. If systematic deviations are assumed to exist in IRP and IFE, further additions to NPV (reductions in financing cost) may be gained. The classification scheme for deviations outlined in table 3.1 will be useful in identifying these situations. Other major imperfections such as governmental subsidies may also be identified using this scheme.

If the financing opportunities open to the firm are analysed in the above way they can be ranked on an NPV basis and the highest NPV financing source chosen. Some important caveats have to be mentioned. Firstly, only external sources of funds have been considered here. The internal financing sources must also be analysed on the same basis and a choice made using the same NPV criterion. Secondly, the valuation of the debt financing decision has been assessed in isolation from other IFM decisions. Political risks of financing have been ignored. If the highest NPV (least interest cost) financing opportunity also exposes the firm to increased political risks then the MNC may prefer to raise debt locally to counteract the risk of asset expropriation. Currency risk, and the benefits of currency matching of assets and liabilities or of hedging the currency risks of FC financing, have also been ignored. Both political risk and currency risk management will affect the choice of funds. The value interactions between all of these IFM decisions will be explored in chapter 13 on financing strategy and in chapter 14 on the development of financial plans.

## 12.2 Choices in the Financing Decision

Figure 12.1 illustrates a simplified view of the many choices facing a firm in its overseas debt financing decision. It is assumed that the financing problem has been identified in this simple form within the context of an explicit financing strategy and that simple heuristics have been employed to screen out unlikely sources of funds. In the diagram, the firm has three major choices:

*Choice of debt issuing unit*   This is assumed to be the parent, a subsidiary, or an affiliated company that needs the funds. This choice determines the jurisdiction within which the firm may face taxes on capital gains and tax deductions on interest expenses or capital losses. An MNC may decide to issue debt via a subsidiary located in a favourable tax jurisdiction and then indirectly transfer the funds internally to the unit in need of the funds. Exploitation of a domestic tax system in this way for a non-domestically based subsidiary will be frowned upon by most tax authorities, who will generally demand that any tax benefits accrue only to debt employed within their jurisdiction.

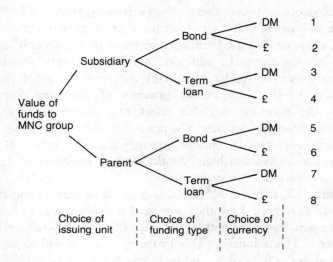

**Figure 12.1** Choices in overseas debt financing

*Choice of funding type* Two different types of debt are illustrated in the diagram, bonds and term loans. Many variations are possible on each of these themes. For example, a Eurocurrency term loan may have a fixed or floating interest rate, and capital may be repaid in equal increments or on some reducing balance basis. The choice between these debt forms will depend upon their relative availability, costs and perceived level of subordination in the firm's debt structure. This choice issue should of course be clarified within the context of the financing strategy to be discussed in chapter 13. Taxes may play a role in the choice of debt types and terms because of the way in which they affect the size and timing of the tax bill. Bullet bonds will have deferred tax on capital gains (if they occur) and thus deferred tax bills, whereas term loans may have annual capital gains and therefore tax liabilities throughout the life of the loan.

*Choice of currency* The choice of currency of financing is crucial, especially with respect to tax. Clearly, home currency (HC) financing within the home tax jurisdiction will mean that there will be no currency capital gains or losses to consider. Foreign currency (FC) financing considerably complicates the tax issues involved, in that HC gains and losses due to exchange rate changes have to be considered.

The precedence between these choices is only shown for illustrative purposes and may not represent the natural precedence of choices facing a firm. All three choices are interdependent and all are strongly influenced by tax considerations. In addition, the diagram only illustrates the endogenous variables under control by the firm. As noted previously, exogenous variables such as the presence of deviations from parity, especially the international Fisher effect, may also give rise to positive NPVs in the financing decision. The possibility of deviations from parity as well as tax considerations considerably complicate the analysis of the debt financing alternatives and highlight the need to construct models to aid financial managers in this area.

In figure 12.1, a British MNC issues debt via its parent company or via its German subsidiary. Both the parent and the subsidiary can issue bonds or acquire term loans and both of these debt forms can be denominated in sterling or in Deutschmarks. This financing problem will be explored in more detail in the following example in which the parent MNC considers choices 5, 6, 7 and 8 in a range of exchange rate circumstances. This problem has been simplified in that it ignores the debt issuing unit problem and tax considerations when dealing with exchange gains and losses.

## 12.3 A Financing Decision Problem

Exco, a large UK MNC, has been advised by its bankers, Norbank, that it can raise its required funds as £25,000 or, given the current spot rate of 4DM/£, as DM100,000. This debt can be raised as a bond issue or as a term loan. Norbank can offer both commercial and investment banking services in London and so can provide both bond issuing services and term loan facilities in either marks or pounds.

In all cases, the debt will be for eight years. The mark debt has a fixed bond coupon or nominal loan interest rate of 3 per cent. The sterling debt has a fixed bond coupon or nominal loan interest rate of 7 per cent. In the case of the bond, the capital will be repaid in one bullet payment at the end of the bond life, whilst in the case of the loan, the capital will be repaid in equal annual increments. The bond issue and underwriting costs amount to 5 per cent of the bond face value and are paid to the bank at the start of the bond life. A similar 5 per cent arrangement and administrative fee has to be paid for the loan.

Exco and Norbank recognize that exchange rate considerations are likely to have a large effect on the value of either type of DM debt. Three DM/£

exchange rate scenarios are identified for the eight year duration of the DM debt:

*Scenario 1*   Inflation in both countries is expected to be constant at 6 per cent and purchasing power parity is expected to hold. In this scenario, German nominal interest rates are being controlled by the government.

*Scenario 2*   UK inflation is expected to be 6 per cent, but German inflation is expected to be lower at 2 per cent, over the eight year duration of the debt. Purchasing power parity and international Fisher are expected to hold.

*Scenario 3*   UK inflation is expected to be 6 per cent, and German inflation is expected to be lower at 2 per cent, both over the eight year duration of the debt. However, at the start of year 4, the European exchange rate mechanism (ERM) is expected to evolve to fixed exchange rates based on a 3.5DM/£ nominal rate in that year. Thus purchasing power parity is not expected to hold after this year. International Fisher is expected to hold over the duration of the debt.

The likelihood of each exchange rate scenario is estimated as

- scenario 1: 0.25
- scenario 2: 0.35
- scenario 3: 0.40.

The spot rate today is 4DM/£, and the corporate tax rate in Germany and the UK is 50 per cent.

Exco is an AA rated company and expects to pay low effective interest rates given its high quality credit rating and thus low risk of default on the bond or loan. Exco estimates that its effective market interest rate is approximately 8 per cent. This rate is employed to discount the after-tax sterling debt cash flows and to value the sterling debt. The sterling after-tax debt cash flows are calculated for the mark debt, and are discounted at this rate to find the value of the mark debt to the firm.

Exco and Norbank use the above data to choose between the mark or pound bullet bond and the mark or pound term loan by calculating the net present values of each debt type under each exchange rate scenario. The expected value of each debt type is calculated, and the largest expected value indicates the most valuable or least costly debt under this range of exchange rate scenarios.

Detailed calculations are shown for the sterling financing choices and for the mark bond and the mark term loan under each exchange rate scenario. Note that the + sign in year 0 refers to cash inflows to Exco from the net proceeds of the debt after paying initial costs of 5 per cent of capital borrowed. Other cash flows of capital and interest repayment are cash outflows from Exco.

## Sterling debt

The bond or loan is for £25,000, and the UK interest rate is 7 per cent.

*Bullet bond*
The cash flows are as follows:

| Period (year) | Capital repaid (£) | Interest paid (£) | Total repayments (£) | After-tax cash flows (£) |
|---|---|---|---|---|
| 0 | +23,750 | 0 | +23,750 | +24,375 |
| 1 | 0 | 1,750 | 1,750 | 875 |
| 2 | 0 | 1,750 | 1,750 | 875 |
| 3 | 0 | 1,750 | 1,750 | 875 |
| 4 | 0 | 1,750 | 1,750 | 875 |
| 5 | 0 | 1,750 | 1,750 | 875 |
| 6 | 0 | 1,750 | 1,750 | 875 |
| 7 | 0 | 1,750 | 1,750 | 875 |
| 8 | 25,000 | 1,750 | 26,750 | 25,875 |

In this sterling bond the initial costs are £25,000 × 5% = £1250. Thus the effective bond capital received is £25,000 − 1250 = £23,750 (or £24,375 after tax).

Interest is charged per year on the total bond value, i.e. £25,000 × 7% = £1750 p.a. The only capital payment is the full face value of the bond: thus £25,000 is repaid at the end of year 8.

The after-tax interest payments are £1750(1 − 0.5) = £875 p.a.

The after-tax cash flows are discounted at 8 per cent to arrive at a *debt value of £5840*.

*Varying balance loan*
The cash flows are as follows:

| Period (year) | Balance due (£) | Capital repaid (£) | Interest paid (£) | Before-tax cash flows (£) | After-tax cash flows (£) |
|---|---|---|---|---|---|
| 0 | 25,000 | +23,750 | 0 | +23,750 | +24,375 |
| 1 | 21,875 | 3,125 | 1,750 | 4,875 | 4,000 |
| 2 | 18,750 | 3,125 | 1,531 | 4,656 | 3,891 |
| 3 | 15,625 | 3,125 | 1,313 | 4,438 | 3,781 |
| 4 | 12,500 | 3,125 | 1,094 | 4,219 | 3,672 |
| 5 | 9,375 | 3,125 | 875 | 4,000 | 3,563 |
| 6 | 6,250 | 3,125 | 656 | 3,781 | 3,453 |
| 7 | 3,125 | 3,125 | 438 | 3,563 | 3,344 |
| 8 | 0 | 3,125 | 219 | 3,344 | 3,234 |

In this sterling term loan the initial costs are £25,000 × 5% = £1250. Thus the effective loan capital received £25,000 − 1250 = £23,750 (after tax, £24,375).

The capital is repaid in equal instalments over the eight years, i.e. 25,000/8 = £3125 p.a.

The initial debt balance in period 0 is £25,000; the balance in period 1 is £25,000 − 3125 = £21,875; that in period 2 is £21,875 − 3125 = £18,750; and so on.

The interest paid in period 1 is £25,000 × 7% = £1750; that paid in period 2 is £21,875 × 7% = £1531; that paid in period 3 is £18,750 × 7% = £1313; and so on.

The cash flow is reduced by the effect of the after-tax factor of (1 − 0.5).

The after-tax cash flows are discounted at 8 per cent to arrive at a *debt value of £3336.*

## Deutschmark debt, scenario 1: equal inflation 6%

*Bullet bond*
The cash flows are as follows:

| Period (year) | Nominal exchange rate (DM/£) | Real exchange rate (DM/£) | Capital repaid (DM) | Interest paid (DM) | Total re-payments (DM) | After-tax cash flows (DM) | Total re-payments (£) | After-tax cash flows (£) |
|---|---|---|---|---|---|---|---|---|
| 0 | 4.00000 | 4.00000 | +95,000 | 0 | +95,000 | +97,500 | +23,750 | +24,375 |
| 1 | 4.00000 | 4.00000 | 0 | 3,000 | 3,000 | 1,500 | 750 | 375 |
| 2 | 4.00000 | 4.00000 | 0 | 3,000 | 3,000 | 1,500 | 750 | 375 |
| 3 | 4.00000 | 4.00000 | 0 | 3,000 | 3,000 | 1,500 | 750 | 375 |
| 4 | 4.00000 | 4.00000 | 0 | 3,000 | 3,000 | 1,500 | 750 | 375 |
| 5 | 4.00000 | 4.00000 | 0 | 3,000 | 3,000 | 1,500 | 750 | 375 |
| 6 | 4.00000 | 4.00000 | 0 | 3,000 | 3,000 | 1,500 | 750 | 375 |
| 7 | 4.00000 | 4.00000 | 0 | 3,000 | 3,000 | 1,500 | 750 | 375 |
| 8 | 4.00000 | 4.00000 | 100,000 | 3,000 | 103,000 | 101,500 | 25,750 | 25,375 |

In this mark bond the initial costs are DM100,000 × 5% = DM5000. Thus the effective bond capital received is DM100,000 − 5000 = DM95,000.

Interest is charged per year on the total bond value, i.e. DM100,000 × 3% = DM3000 p.a. The only capital payment is the full face value of the mark bond. Thus DM100,000 is repaid at the end of year 8.

The after-tax interest payments are DM3000 × (1 − 0.5) = DM1500 p.a. These are translated back into pounds at the nominal rate in that period, where

$$\text{nominal exchange rate in period t} = \left(\begin{array}{c}\text{nominal (actual) exchange rate in period 0}\end{array}\right)\frac{1 + \text{change in foreign inflation rate in period } t}{1 + \text{change in domestic inflation rate in period } t}$$

Thus, using period 0 as the base period, the nominal exchange rate in period 1 is 4.00(1.06)/(1.06) = 4DM/£, and that in period 2 is 4.00(1.06)$^2$/(1.06)$^2$ = 4DM/£. Thus in this example, of equal inflation rates and purchasing power parity holding, there is no change in the nominal or real exchange rate over the duration of the debt.

The after-tax sterling cash flows are discounted at 8 per cent to arrive at a *debt value of £8713.*

*Varying balance loan*
The cash flows are as follows:

| Period (year) | Balance due (DM) | Capital repaid (DM) | Interest paid (DM) | Before-tax cash flows (DM) | After-tax cash flows (DM) | Total re- payments (£) | After-tax cash flows (£) |
|---|---|---|---|---|---|---|---|
| 0 | 100,000 | +95,000 | 0 | +95,000 | +97,500 | +23,750 | +24,375 |
| 1 | 87,500 | 12,500 | 3,000 | 15,500 | 14,000 | 3,875 | 3,500 |
| 2 | 75,000 | 12,500 | 2,625 | 15,125 | 13,813 | 3,781 | 3,453 |
| 3 | 62,500 | 12,500 | 2,250 | 14,750 | 13,625 | 3,688 | 3,406 |
| 4 | 50,000 | 12,500 | 1,875 | 14,375 | 13,438 | 3,594 | 3,359 |
| 5 | 37,500 | 12,500 | 1,500 | 14,000 | 13,250 | 3,500 | 3,313 |
| 6 | 25,000 | 12,500 | 1,125 | 13,625 | 13,063 | 3,406 | 3,266 |
| 7 | 12,500 | 12,500 | 750 | 13,250 | 12,875 | 3,313 | 3,219 |
| 8 | 0 | 12,500 | 375 | 12,875 | 12,688 | 3,219 | 3,172 |

In this mark term loan the initial costs are DM100,000 × 5% = DM5000. Thus the effective loan capital received is DM100,000 − 5000 = DM95,000.

The capital is repaid in equal instalments over the eight years, i.e. DM100,000/8 = DM12,500 p.a.

The initial debt balance in period 0 is DM100,000; the balance in period 1 is DM100,000 − 12,500 = DM87,500; that in period 2 is DM87,500 −12,500 = DM75,000; and so on.

The interest paid in period 1 is DM100,000 × 3% = DM3000; that in period 2 is DM87,500 × 3% = DM2625; that in period 3 is DM75,000 × 3% = DM2250; and so on.

The after-tax interest payments are adjusted by the tax factor of (1 − 0.5) per period to find the after-tax cash flows. These are translated back into pounds at the nominal rate in that period. In this example, of equal inflation rates and purchasing power parity holding, there is no change in the nominal or real rate of 4DM/£ over the duration of the debt.

The after-tax sterling cash flows are discounted at 8 per cent to arrrive at a *debt value of £5096.*

## Deutschmark debt, scenario 2: Germany 2%, UK 6% inflation

The bond and loan mark cash flow calculations are the same here as in scenario 1, except that the nominal exchange rate changes in each period:

$$\begin{array}{c}\text{nominal}\\\text{exchange}\\\text{rate in}\\\text{period } t\end{array} = \left(\begin{array}{c}\text{nominal (actual)}\\\text{exchange}\\\text{rate in period 0}\end{array}\right)\dfrac{1 + \text{change in foreign inflation rate in period } t}{1 + \text{change in domestic inflation rate in period } t}$$

Thus, the nominal exchange rate in period 1 is $4.00(1.02)/(1.06) =$ $3.849\text{DM}/\pounds$, and that in period 2 is $3.849(1.02)/(1.06) = 3.7038\text{DM}/\pounds$, or $4.00(1.02)^2/(1.06)^2 = 3.7038\text{DM}/\pounds$. This nominal mark apppreciation increases the pound interest and capital repayments per period for both the bond and the loan and thus reduces the value of each type of debt compared with scenario 1 when discounted at 8 per cent. The real exchange rate remains unchanged in scenario 2 as nominal exchange rates fully reflect inflation differences per annum.

*Bullet bond*
The cash flows are as follows:

| Period (year) | Nominal exchange rate (DM/£) | Real exchange rate (DM/£) | Capital repaid (DM) | Interest paid (DM) | Total repayments (DM) | After-tax cash flows (DM) | Total repayments (£) | After-tax cash flows (£) |
|---|---|---|---|---|---|---|---|---|
| 0 | 4.00000 | 4.00000 | +95,000 | 0 | +95,000 | +97,500 | +23,750 | +24,375 |
| 1 | 3.84906 | 4.00000 | 0 | 3,000 | 3,000 | 1,500 | 779 | 390 |
| 2 | 3.70381 | 4.00000 | 0 | 3,000 | 3,000 | 1,500 | 810 | 405 |
| 3 | 3.56404 | 4.00000 | 0 | 3,000 | 3,000 | 1,500 | 842 | 421 |
| 4 | 3.42955 | 4.00000 | 0 | 3,000 | 3,000 | 1,500 | 875 | 437 |
| 5 | 3.30013 | 4.00000 | 0 | 3,000 | 3,000 | 1,500 | 909 | 455 |
| 6 | 3.17560 | 4.00000 | 0 | 3,000 | 3,000 | 1,500 | 945 | 472 |
| 7 | 3.05577 | 4.00000 | 0 | 3,000 | 3,000 | 1,500 | 982 | 491 |
| 8 | 2.94045 | 4.00000 | 100,000 | 3,000 | 103,000 | 101,500 | 35,029 | 34,518 |

The after-tax sterling cash flows are discounted at 8 per cent to arrive at a *debt value of £3469.*

## Varying balance loan

The cash flows are as follows:

| Period (year) | Balance due (DM) | Capital repaid (DM) | Interest paid (DM) | Before-tax cash flows (DM) | After-tax cash flows (DM) | Total re-payments (£) | Ater-tax cash flows (£) |
|---|---|---|---|---|---|---|---|
| 0 | 100,000 | +95,000 | 0 | +95,000 | +97,500 | +23,750 | +24,375 |
| 1 | 87,500 | 12,500 | 3,000 | 15,500 | 14,000 | 4,027 | 3,637 |
| 2 | 75,000 | 12,500 | 2,625 | 15,125 | 13,813 | 4,084 | 3,729 |
| 3 | 62,500 | 12,500 | 2,250 | 14,750 | 13,625 | 4,139 | 3,823 |
| 4 | 50,000 | 12,500 | 1,875 | 14,375 | 13,438 | 4,192 | 3,918 |
| 5 | 37,500 | 12,500 | 1,500 | 14,000 | 13,250 | 4,242 | 4,015 |
| 6 | 25,000 | 12,500 | 1,125 | 13,625 | 13,063 | 4,291 | 4,113 |
| 7 | 12,500 | 12,500 | 750 | 13,250 | 12,875 | 4,336 | 4,213 |
| 8 | 0 | 12,500 | 375 | 12,875 | 12,688 | 4,379 | 4,315 |

The after-tax sterling cash flows are dicounted at 8 per cent to arrive at a *debt value of £1781.*

## Deutschmark debt, scenario 3: ERM and real exchange rate changes

The bond and loan mark cash flow calculations are the same here as in scenarios 1 and 2. The nominal exchange rate in periods 1, 2 and 3 changes in the same way as in scenario 2. However, the nominal rate is fixed after period 3 at 3.5DM/£. This alters the real exchange rate in periods 4 to 8. The real rate can be expressed as

$$\begin{array}{l}\text{real} \\ \text{exchange} \\ \text{rate in} \\ \text{period } t \end{array} = \left( \begin{array}{l}\text{nominal (actual)} \\ \text{exchange rate} \\ \text{in period } t \end{array} \right) \frac{1 + \text{change in domestic inflation rate in period } t}{1 + \text{change in foreign inflation rate in period } t}$$

Using year 0 as a base period, the real rate is as follows:

in period 1:  $3.8496(1.06)/(1.02)$ $= 4.00\text{DM}/£$
in period 2:  $3.70381(1.06)^2/(1.02)^2$ $= 4.00\text{DM}/£$
in period 3:  $3.56404(1.063)^3/(1.02)^3$ $= 4.00\text{DM}/£$
in period 4:  $3.50000(1.06)^4/(1.02)^4$ $= 4.082\text{DM}/£$
in period 5:  $3.50000 (1.06)^5/(1.02)^5$ $= 4.2422\text{DM}/£$

and so on. Or, using year 4 as a base period, the real rate is as follows:

in period 4:   $3.50(1.06)/(1.02)$          $= 3.637DM/\text{\pounds}$
in period 5:   $3.50(1.06)^2/(1.02)^2$     $= 3.7799DM/\text{\pounds}$

and so on. Here, year 0 has been used as the basis for the real rate calculations to show the real exchange rate change over the duration of the debt.

The real rate change fixes the sterling repayments for the mark debt after period 4 and thus makes this debt more valuable (less costly) than the mark debt under scenario 2.

### Bullet bond
The cash flows are as follows:

| Period (year) | Nominal exchange rate (DM/£) | Real exchange rate (DM/£) | Capital repaid (DM) | Interest paid (DM) | Total repayments (DM) | After-tax cash flows (DM) | Total repayments (£) | After-tax cash flows (£) |
|---|---|---|---|---|---|---|---|---|
| 0 | 4.00000 | 4.00000 | +95,000 | 0 | +95,000 | +97,500 | +23750 | +24375 |
| 1 | 3.84906 | 4.00000 | 0 | 3,000 | 3,000 | 1,500 | 779 | 390 |
| 2 | 3.70381 | 4.00000 | 0 | 3,000 | 3,000 | 1,500 | 810 | 405 |
| 3 | 3.56404 | 4.00000 | 0 | 3,000 | 3,000 | 1,500 | 842 | 421 |
| 4 | 3.50000 | 4.08217 | 0 | 3,000 | 3,000 | 1,500 | 857 | 429 |
| 5 | 3.50000 | 4.24225 | 0 | 3,000 | 3,000 | 1,500 | 857 | 429 |
| 6 | 3.50000 | 4.40862 | 0 | 3,000 | 3,000 | 1,500 | 857 | 429 |
| 7 | 3.50000 | 4.58150 | 0 | 3,000 | 3,000 | 1,500 | 857 | 429 |
| 8 | 3.50000 | 4.76117 | 100,000 | 3,000 | 103,000 | 101,500 | 29,429 | 29,000 |

The after-tax sterling cash flows are discounted at 8 per cent to arrive at a *debt value of £6538.*

## Varying balance loan

The cash flows are as follows:

| Period (year) | Balance due | Capital repaid | Interest paid | Before-tax cash flows | After-tax cash flows | Total repay- ments | After-tax cash flows |
|---|---|---|---|---|---|---|---|
| | (DM) | (DM) | (DM) | (DM) | (DM) | (£) | (£) |
| 0 | 100,000 | +95,000 | 0 | +95,000 | +97,500 | +23,750 | +24,375 |
| 1 | 87,500 | 12,500 | 3,000 | 15,500 | 14,000 | 4,027 | 3,637 |
| 2 | 75,000 | 12,500 | 2,625 | 15,125 | 13,813 | 4,084 | 3,729 |
| 3 | 62,500 | 12,500 | 2,250 | 14,750 | 13,625 | 4,139 | 3,823 |
| 4 | 50,000 | 12,500 | 1,875 | 14,375 | 13,438 | 4,107 | 3,839 |
| 5 | 37,500 | 12,500 | 1,500 | 14,000 | 13,250 | 4,000 | 3,786 |
| 6 | 25,000 | 12,500 | 1,125 | 13,625 | 13,063 | 3,893 | 3,732 |
| 7 | 12,500 | 12,500 | 750 | 13,250 | 12,875 | 3,786 | 3,679 |
| 8 | 0 | 12,500 | 375 | 12,875 | 12,688 | 3,679 | 3,625 |

The after-tax sterling cash flows are dicounted at 8 per cent to arrive at a debt value of £2920.

## Summary of calculations

The expected values (EVs) of the Deutschmark debt are calculated as follows:

EV of DM bond = (0.25 × £8713) + (0.35 × £3469) + (0.40 × £6538)
    = £6007.6
EV of DM loan = (0.25 × £5096) + (0.35 × £1781) + (0.40 × £2920)
    = £3065.35

The after-tax sterling debt cash flow discounting and NPV calculations are summarized in figure 12.2.

There are several points to note about these results. Firstly, the mark debt under scenario 1 is more valuable than the mark debt under scenarios 2 and 3; the mark debt under scenario 3 is more valuable than the mark debt under scenario 2. This is because, in scenario 1, purchasing power parity holds and no change occurs in the real or the nominal exchange rate over the eight years. Thus the mark and the pound effectively operate as one currency over the duration of the debt, and the 3 per cent mark rate is very low compared with the 7 per cent rate quoted in sterling terms. German controls over nominal interest rates suggest that real interest rates differ in this scenario for Germany and the UK. This would suggest that capital market segmentation occurs when purchasing power parity is holding. This seems most unlikely in the case of the mark and the pound.

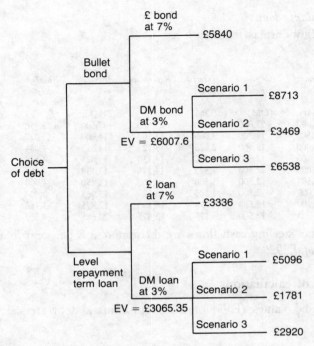

**Figure 12.2** Summary of example financing choices

However, it may occur in some domestic capital markets where the government controls interest rates and where capital (flow) controls are in force but the exchange rate is allowed to float freely.

In scenario 2, purchasing power parity holds and the nominal exchange rate declines from 4DM/£ to 2.94045DM/£ over the eight years. The real rate remains unchanged over the life of the debt at 4DM/£. German interest rates are not controlled and the interest rate differences between Germany and the UK reflect inflation differences. The real interest rate appears to be the same in both countries and nominal interest rates reflect local inflation.

In scenario 2, the appreciating mark (nominal) in years 1 to 8 combines with fixed mark capital and interest payments to increase the sterling cost of debt (capital and interest payments) over time. This reduces the value of the debt compared with sterling bond and loan equivalents. The mark repayments (interest and capital) are fixed at the start of the contract and so each year Exco has to find more pounds to pay off the fixed mark repayments. This occurs, in varying degrees, in both scenarios 2 and 3 and explains why the value of the debt falls under both circumstances relative to scenario 1. In scenario 3, the nominal mark appreciation is halted after period 4. This reduces the effects of the increasing sterling cost and thus the debt is of higher value than in scenario 2.

In scenario 3, purchasing power parity holds in periods 1 to 3 and thus the nominal rate adjusts and the real rate remains constant. However, in period 4 the pound and the mark are fixed in the ERM at the nominal rate of 3.5DM/£. The inflation differences still remain between the UK and Germany and so the real rate appreciates from 4DM/£ in period 4 to 4.762DM/£ in period 8. Exco (from period 4) can now exchange a fixed amount of pounds for its fixed mark payments and these pound payments do not increase in the same way as in scenario 2. The ERM arrangement has effectively increased Exco's ability to purchase appreciating marks (with increasing purchasing power) with the same number of pounds. The net result is that mark debt raised under scenario 3 is more valuable than debt raised under scenario 2.

The second point about the results is that sterling loan funding dominates mark loan funding, mark bond funding dominates sterling bond funding, and the mark bond provides maximum value. The mark bond should therefore be chosen as the funding source. These valuation effects are caused by the differences in the capital and interest repayments between the bond and the term loan. Mark term loans have capital repayments in periods 1 to 8. Thus the mark appreciations in scenarios 2 and 3 both increase the sterling cost of paying for the fixed mark repayments. This occurs early on in the life of the loan and this factor makes the loan less valuable (more costly in sterling terms) than the mark bond. The mark bond pays back the full capital in period 8 at the worst exchange rate in both scenarios 2 and 3. However, this is so far into the future that the impact on bond debt value is much reduced by discounting.

Thirdly, the analysis ignores the value implications of using the funding currency decision to avoid currency risk or to avoid political risks in Germany. Thus a reduction in NPV losses from these risk sources may be feasible by funding a mark asset with mark debt. The avoidance of these risks may make mark financing more attractive than the example suggests. This seems most unlikely given the stable German political system and the potential links between the pound and the mark in the ERM in the 1990s.

Fourthly, if varying interest mark and sterling debt are available, German and UK interest rates may fully reflect DM/£ expectations, thus making sterling debt and mark debt more comparable.

Fifthly, in practice it is unlikely that there will be many positive net present value financing opportunities between sterling and mark funding choices. These currencies and the various forms of risk capital denominated in marks and pounds are valued in competitive foreign exchange and international capital markets. International Fisher is likely to hold on a before-tax basis and, given harmonization of EC tax rates and systems, it may also hold an after-tax rate. Thus positive net present value financing opportunities are only likely to arise through transient and limited imperfections in mark and sterling capital markets, probably stemming from tax system changes. In general, most large internationally involved enterprises will be indifferent between sterling and mark funding, despite the possible range of exchange rate circumstances. If political conditions alter in the EC, factors such as currency and political risk may become more prominent in the funding decision. As a result, the problem does illustrate some of the major issues that can arise when funding in several currencies.

Finally, the example has assumed many common data for the bond and term loan and for tax rates. This has provided a clear basis to compare the choices open to Exco. However, Exco may be able to vary many of these financing parameters. Thus sensitivity analysis on differences in terms – e.g. coupon or nominal interest rate, duration, different ways of repaying capital, tax differences – will be important in such an analysis. This issue highlights the significance of a spreadsheet financial model to perform the above calculations and to create the capability to conduct such sensitivity analysis. This issue will be addressed in the following section.

## 12.4 Developing a Computer Based Financing Model

### Imperfections and model building

The problem of selecting a currency or currencies in order to maximize the net present value of financing decisions does not arise if world capital markets are integrated and efficient. For most investors (lenders) there will be no opportunity to achieve consistently superior rates of return in these capital markets. Unless imperfections are present (e.g. taxes) the firm faces a series of financing opportunities with zero NPVs. It should therefore be indifferent between various funding sources.

It is the existence of imperfections such as tax system asymmetries between countries, the availability of soft loans from governments, and deviations from ideal parity conditions that create positive financing NPVs. For example, a wide range of events associated with deviations from parity can occur over the life of a loan. These could include:

- changes in national tax rates and systems between parent home country and subsidiaries' countries creating after-tax deviations from parity
- IRP, UBFR, IFE holding for some periods but not for others
- the emergence or decline of forward markets in some currencies
- changing government policies with respect to controls over the flow of capital, soft loans, interest subsidies and expropriation.

The number of combinations here can be very large, and this in turn creates the complex computational and analytical problems identified above. These are solved by managers employing simple heuristics (Jilling and Folks 1977) to reduce the problem to manageable proportions. Such heuristics could include a decision to concentrate on imperfections that are expected to persist over the life of the loan. Thus some domestic tax systems may both be stable and provide beneficial tax treatments of financial cost, even when equilibrium relationships are working on a before-tax basis. Another decision might be to limit financing opportunities to those currencies that are suitable for hedging currency risks or for avoiding political risk.

## Approaches to model building

Various model building approaches have been suggested to solve these computational problems. For example, Vinso (1982) has proposed a goal programming approach to the financing problem. The particular virtue of this model is that it allows managers to assess the trade-offs between conflicting goals as well as to seek optimal financing combinations. However, such optimization models are generally difficult to implement and managers have shown a strong preference to develop simple simulation models as their first step in model building (Holland 1981). Shapiro (1984) has also demonstrated the power of analytic models in assessing the impact of tax on long term borrowing decisions. His models are particularly valuable in finding the interest rate, exchange rate and tax conditions which equate FC and HC borrowing. This analytic approach makes several simplifying but restrictive assumptions, such as constant appreciation or depreciation of the exchange rate over the life of the debt, and these may be inappropriate for corporate specific analyses. Despite the limitations, optimization and analytic models are of value in indicating the general features of a financing simulation model and the appropriate set of key financial variables.

The basic structure of a simple simulation financing model can be illustrated as in figure 12.3. The logic of this model has been derived from the equations in section 12.1 on the debt financing decision and is implied in the calculations in the Exco financing problem in section 12.3. These calculations form a simple design basis for a spreadsheet model, and building such a model is a useful exercise. In appendix 3 a working version of this type of model is listed in the BASIC programming language. This model was designed in a similar manner to the capital budgeting model demonstrated in the case in chapter 10. In particular its design has been restricted in many simplifying ways. The model is designed around the NPV rule and assumes nominal loan cash flow calculations, nominal discount rates, two types of loan repayment schedule, and simple corporate income and capital tax systems. The financing model is therefore designed mainly for teaching and learning purposes and needs considerable adaptation to become a practical decision aid for corporate treasurers. Corporate treasurers will have to adapt the model to their unique and probably more complex circumstances. For example, if major deviations from the parity relationships are expected then the input to the model will have to vary to correspond to this more complex situation. The use of the DATA statements from 8000 onwards is recommended for this purpose.

Further extensions to the model (and program) might include extra debt types, a more sophisticated analysis of the loan cash flows, and many other features unique to a particular decision. A financing simulation model could also be used in tandem with a capital budgeting model to explore the implications of joint investment and financing decisions. Thus we could calculate the net franc financing required by the StrathKelvin case in chapter 10 as fr18,500,000 capital outlay less fr1,500,000 released funds less fr5,000,000 cheap loan, i.e. fr12,000,000, and use a spreadsheet financing model to investigate various franc financing alternatives. A key issue here would be how the asset net after-tax cash flows could be used to pay off the capital and interest. The model could therefore be used to investigate such interactions between investment and financing decisions. Both use the

NPV model as a conceptual basis and so these interactions can be explored using a common theoretical model.

The financing model could also be extended to become a full liability portfolio model, and could be used to transfer data to, and receive data from, a company-wide capital budgeting model. A global tax model may be required to optimize corporate world tax payments. The overall corporate model would therefore provide the computational support for sensitivity analysis of corporate financial plans and the financing strategy to be outlined in chapter 13.

In appendix 4, this model has been used to calculate the value of the

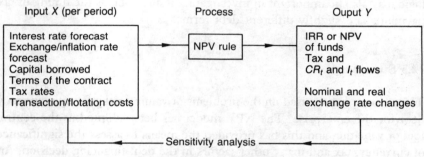

Figure 12.3 Simple simulation financing model

mark bond under exchange rate scenario 2 in section 12.3. The detailed problem in the text, and the example in the appendix, provide clear design guidelines for a spreadsheet model. This is recommended as a simple spreadsheet model building exercise for the reader.

## Sensitivity analysis

Once the model has been fully tested in terms of logic and accuracy, many variations are possible in the input data. For example, managers may vary some of the following input data (variable $X$ in figure 12.3):

- corporate income tax rates
- life or horizon of the loan
- inflation forecasts
- currency of funding to include US dollars or french francs
- amount of the loan or bond

- the way in which capital is repaid
- deviations from parity, especially international Fisher
- capital market segmentation as expressed in different real rates for identical risk securities as funding sources
- the impact of interest rate subsidies.

As indicated previously, tax is likely to be a key variable affecting most of the model output and so sensitivity analysis of tax data may be a major preoccupation of the financial manager. Alternatively, one can reverse the sensitivity analysis and seek the appropriate tax system which provides a required level of NPV. Finally, small changes in the spreadsheet model logic may also be important in investigating issues such as the timing of tax payments and slightly different debt forms.

## 12.5 Summary

This chapter has focused on the problems of valuing risky foreign currency debt for the enterprise. The NPV model has been adopted as the central tool of valuation and this has provided the means to assess the significance of currency, tax and many other factors in the debt financing decision. An extensive financing case problem was explored to illustrate the overseas financing problem in some depth. The complexity of this problem highlighted the significance of financial modelling in the funding decision. The design of such a model was discussed and its role in supporting the financing decision outlined.

# 13

# Global Financing Decisions

In this chapter we consider how an MNC can finance its world-wide operations. This requires an initial consideration in sections 13.1, 13.2, and 13.3 of the complexities of the global funding decision and an analysis of funding implications of efficient and inefficent financial markets. In section 13.4 financing tactics are analysed under varing economic circumstances.

In section 13.5, the capital structure decision for the MNC is investigated. The identification of the overall corporate capital structure and local subsidiary capital structure norms are key ingredients in the financing decision. They provide the boundaries within which the firm can pursue a value maximization goal for the financing decision. In section 13.6 the role of relationship banks in providing flexibility in the external supply of funds is considered.

In section 13.7 many of the above factors are brought together in an analysis of the global financing problem. The funding decision is closely related to many issues of risk management for the MNC. The terms of the funding decision create interest rate payments or exposure to interest rate risk. This cash outflow is exposed to volatile interest rates which may reduce or alter the expected level or volatility of corporate cash flows. In addition, currency exposure risks and the political risks of asset expropriation are often linked to funding decisions and interest rate risks. The primary focus of this chapter will be the funding decision: in section 13.7, interactions with these other decision areas will be considered as part of the development of a global financing plan.

In section 13.8 a detailed case study of ICI's global financing policy is outlined and discussed.

## 13.1 Complexities of Global Funding

The wide diversity of both domestic and international capital markets discussed in chapters 2 and 11 is both a major source of complexity and opportunity for the MNC treasurer dealing with the international financing decision. Key characteristics of the international economic environment which create these problems and opportunities include the following:

- major differences in tax systems across countries and their implications for after-tax cash flows, especially tax differences on types of funds (debt versus equity)
- governmental subsidies and penalties on sources of funds
- governmental influence and direct interference in domestic capital and banking markets
- joint governmental actions on exchange rates, and on the transfer of domestic funds to offshore markets
- the possibility of segmentation of domestic markets from offshore and perhaps other domestic markets.

## 13.2 Issues for the Overseas Financing Decision

These additional complexities raise the following issues for the overseas financing decision:

1  To what degree is the range of domestic capital markets and offshore capital markets efficient? It is important to the firm to know whether it should accept market prices or whether it should exploit any oopportunities within or across these markets to reduce the costs of financing the MNC.
2  To what extent can the MNC treasury function cover these markets and use its external (market) transacting capability to arbitrage between markets and its internal financial transfer and transacting capability to exploit funding opportunities?
3  Can any combination of debt or equity raised in these international capital markets add value to the firm?
4  How can an MNC deal with the value interactions implicit in the joint pursuit of funding, risk management and capital structure goals?
5  What is the influence, if any, of the financing decision on capital budgeting and currency risk management decisions?

If management can understand these issues of market efficiency, the capital structure decision, and the relationship between funding and other financial decisions, then the ground can be laid for coherent financing plans for the MNC.

The emphasis in this chapter will be on the external financing decision in capital markets. In particular the focus will be on the capital structure problem, the debt financing decision in international capital markets, and the development of a financing plan explicitly dealing with interactions between funding and risk management aims. The issue of internal funds transfer was considered in chapter 6. The issue of the interrelationships between the broader funding, capital budgeting and capital structure decisions will be discussed in chapter 14 as part of financial planning.

## 13.3 Efficient and Inefficient Capital Markets

Market efficiency is conventionally defined in three different forms. First of all, weak efficiency refers to a situation where past prices cannot be used to make excess returns. Semi-strong efficiency refers to a situation where excess returns or superior returns cannot be made on the basis of publicly available information (the public set of information). Finally, strong capital market efficiency exists when prices fully reflect all the information that can be obtained by the most careful sophisticated analysis (i.e. the total set of information).

Brealey and Myers (1981: 264–72) outline the six major lessons of capital market efficiency. These generally refer to semi-strong efficient capital markets, and state that:

1 Capital markets have no memory, and as a result past prices contain no information about future unknown changes. To this we can add that current prices contain information about anticipated events. Information about unanticipated events is, by definition, unknown and it arrives in markets in a random manner, affecting prices accordingly.

2 Market participants should trust market prices, in that they impound all available information and it is extremely difficult for most investors to earn superior returns.

3 There are no financial illusions in this marketplace. Thus investors are not confused by various accounting techniques and other forms of window dressing of publicly available information. They are only

368 Global Financing Decisions

concerned with their share of corporate cash flows.

4 In capital markets there is always the 'do-it-yourself' alternative. For example, investors will not pay for a firm to diversify by acquiring other firms when the investors can do this themselves perfectly well in capital markets.

5 Shares in stock markets are assumed to have almost perfect substitutes for each other, so the demand for any given company's stock is very elastic.

6 Prices in stock and bond markets reflect investors' expectations about the future. Thus futures or forward market prices, or implied market prices such as the term structure of interest rates, tell us how market participants expect prices to move in the future. These markets therefore provide us with free forecasts. As indicated previously, these are based on the public set of information on anticipated events.

These lessons are likely to apply to the major domestic capital markets of the world, in particular those of the United States, Japan, the United Kingdom, Germany, France and Hong Kong. They can also be applied to the offshore capital markets, such as the Eurocurrency and Eurobond markets, as well as the markets in the major currencies. The competition here is fierce and informational efficiency is likely to be fairly high. Arbitrage between offshore markets say in dollar Eurobond and domestic dollar bond equivalents (or offshore dollar bank deposit and domestic dollar deposit equivalents) ensures that segmentation is unlikely across these markets.

As one turns away from these particular markets, then questions begin to arise about the efficiency of other world markets. Solnik (1973a; 1973b) found that deviations from a random walk were more marked in the behaviour of stock prices of eight European capital markets than in those of the United States, i.e. the serial correlation for European stock market prices was found to be higher than those of the United States, and this would suggest a lesser weak form efficiency for most European stock markets at this time. However, this departure from a true random walk did not suggest that it was possible to make gains from historic share price data. In the 1990s, with increased integration occurring in Western European stock markets and cross-trading with the US market, the possibility of departure from weak efficiency or semi-strong efficiency within and between these markets seems increasingly unlikely.

Samuels (1981) pursues this point about different levels of market efficiency and argues that, as we move away from Western stock markets to stock markets emerging in the newly developing countries such as Nigeria, it is highly likely that informational inefficiencies exist. His argument revolves round the existence of major structural imperfections in these equity markets. This would include variables such as

- size of market
- wide and differing risk preferences amongst investors
- lack of adequate market regulation
- poor country-wide communication systems
- few analysts.

It is intuitively appealing that structural features of capital markets will affect the availability of information (public and total information sets) and informational efficiency. As a result, it may be possible to associate such features with informational inefficiencies in these capital markets. However, it is also possible that, even with structural problems, weak and semi-strong efficiencies will prevail. The set of publicly available information in developing countries may be much reduced by structural problems, but the local capital market may still efficiently impound this limited set of public information in its market prices. As a result the lessons of market efficiency are likely to have some value even in the capital markets of developing countries. However, it should be noted that the existence of lower quality public information sets, relative to the total information set, may mean that insider trading will be a much more significant activity in these capital markets. The existence of active insider trading may, in the long run, move such markets towards a broader reflection of the total information set and towards the semi-strong efficiency levels that exist elsewhere in the world stock markets.

Samuels (1981) does not provide evidence of the existence of inefficient capital markets but does point up the possibility that such markets may exist. Empirical research is therefore required to extend Solnik's work (1973a) to determine the relative levels of informational efficiency within all world stock and bond markets. This requires an operational measure of the relative quality of both public and total information sets across countries, as well as the more conventional measures of the degree to which prices reflect these information sets.

More traditional tests of LDC stock market efficiency include the following. Cooper (1982) carried out random walk tests on a series of 50 world stock markets including several from LDCs such as Kenya. He was unable to reject the random walk hypothesis, especially when transaction costs were taken into account. Barnes (1986) studied the 30 stocks of the Kuala Lumpur Stock exchange. He only found serial correlations in historic prices for two stocks. Muragu (1990) studied weak efficiency in the Kenyan Stock Exchange and found that the random walk model provided a good description of Kenyan stock prices. These results indicate that weak form efficiency is possible and likely in developing country stock markets.

However, if inefficient capital markets do exist within certain countries then we can reverse the lessons of market efficiency outlined by Brealey and Myers. For example:

1   There may be information to be gained from historic prices in these markets.
2   It may not be sensible to trust market prices in that they may not fully impound available information.
3   The markets may not be able to see through cosmetic accounting practices when corporations formally report information to the market.
4   Within these domestic markets, investors may not be able to diversify when corporations can.
5   The elasticity of stocks within a country may be lower than is generally to be found in OECD stock markets.
6   The forecasts available from market prices may be biased or misleading.

Under these circumstances both the domestic corporation and the multinational will be facing exploitable funding opportunities within such a domestic market for equity and bond securities. The MNC may be able to exploit these market based opportunities directly via market transactions or indirectly via the internal transfer of funds within the MNC. The latter possibility was discussed in chapter 6; market transactions are the focus of attention in this chapter.

In the following section, we explore possible market imperfections in more detail and assess their implications for funding and risk management decisions.

## 13.4 Economic Circumstances and Overall Strategies for Funding and Risk Management

In this section we explore how aspects of the firm's financing policy may vary with specific changes in the economic circumstances facing the firm. This section employs a somewhat static analysis in that it identifies robust decision rules for each specific set of economic circumstances. It does not explore the value interactions possible between funding, capital structure and risk management decisions. These will be considered in section 13.7. However, the framework employed in this section does provide considerable insight into which class of financing rules are appropriate for particular economic circumstances. It therefore provides one important basis from which to critically appraise components of an MNC's financing policy. Thus matching rules, interest rate risk rules and opportunistic funding can be assessed for each set of economic circumstances.

Table 13.1 summarizes the general economic conditions or circumstances under which various deviations from market efficiency and parity may occur. It also includes details of the appropriate funding and risk management policies and tactics to be employed under these conditions. The economic conditions begin with idealized market conditions and progress through a range of changing corporate circumstances, parity deviations and market imperfections. It should be noted that some of these circumstances appear unlikely given the efficiency of world capital and foreign exchange markets. It is unlikely that a firm will, over a long period, have superior forecasts of financial prices, will face segmented capital markets, or will be able to exploit major imperfections in international capital and banking markets. These contingencies are included for completeness. In addition, it should be noted that firms are more likely to face short lived combinations of these circumstances than a single set.

Two overall funding and risk management strategies can be identified in table 13.1 depending on the circumstances in the firm's economic environment:

1  a passive strategy
2  an active opportunistic strategy, which has two subsets: either with real decisions a priority and financial decisions in support; or with treasury as an arbitrageur and risk taker, and finance as a major source of value.

**Table 13.1** Strategies for global financing management

| | *Efficient* | *Efficient but unique corporate advantages or circumstances* | | *Major imperfections* |
|---|---|---|---|---|
| | 1 | 2 | 3 | 4 |
| Economic circumstances | Efficient integrated world markets. Parity relationships working | Efficient and integrated markets but: (a) firm has default risks (b) firm has superior forecasts | IRP, IFE, UBFR and Fisher effect functioning well but not at the level of specific firms. IFE does not work for firm. Firm in unique tax position | Financial parity deviations and market segmentation creating real interest differences and risk/return trade-offs between domestic markets and with offshore markets. Inefficiencies in some domestic/offshore markets |
| Funding tactics | Positive financing opportunities do not exist. Source and timing of funds irrelevant. Fund when firm has valuable projects | (a) Avoid fund sources which increase risk. (b) If have excess funds, can choose to fund when rates are historically low. Fund extra at this time and invest for high rate periods | Seek funds that exploit unique corporate tax advantages and after-tax IFE deviations | Exploit rate differences between markets or mispricing in markets to reduce funding costs. Location of funds very important. Exploit domestic sources unavailable to MNC competitors. Fund overseas subsidiaries with funds not available to domestic firms |
| Risk management tactics | Self-insurance allows gains and losses on interest rate changes to cancel out over time | (a) Match assets and liabilities in size, timing of cash flows. If still exposed then hedge to reduce default risk (b) Create exposed positions to exploit forecasting skills. Borrow fixed (floating) funds when expect rate increase (decline) | Hedge to reduce unique rate risks faced by firm | Diversify funding sources to reduce interest rate volatility. Use whole range of funding sources and risk management methods to exploit imperfections in financial markets and to deal with funding and risk problems |
| Attitudes to risk and financing policy | | A balanced policy in 2, 3 and 4 is concerned with dynamic value trade-off between cheap funding, managing risks, and altering some real decisions | | |
| | | A conservative policy would place risk reduction before cheap funding | | |
| | | A risky policy has sole focus on treasury profits, with treasury as speculator and arbitrageur in world financial markets | | |
| | | Circumstances 3, 3 and 4 are the major conditions for novel funding opportunities and interest rate risk problems/opportunities. Use full range of financing methods to deal with funding and interest rate risks | | |
| Strategy | Passive | Active opportunistic | | |

In the table we explore these two financing and risk management strategies within four general categories of economic circumstances. The latter are identified in the top row of the table, with the funding and risk management tactics described in the body of the table. As can be seen, this has strong similarities to the currency risk management decision and the economic circumstances surrounding this decision (section 4.1).

The passive strategy is suitable when a firm believes that it is operating in circumstances 1 in the table, in which there are integrated and efficient domestic and world capital markets, and all of the parity relationships hold. When markets are efficient and no biases exist in market rates, market based forecasts should be accepted as valid. No expected gain will result from changing the timing or currency of borrowing or investing funds. Under these conditions, the active pursuit of cheap funds or active interest rate risk management is of no value to shareholders. Managers can assume that after funding the firm's operations and new investment plans in efficient and fairly priced capital markets, a policy of doing nothing is acceptable to shareholders. In efficient capital markets, equity and debt securities are fairly priced, and as a result the purchase or sale of an equity or debt security is a zero net present value transaction. It is therefore difficult for the firm to secure funds and to generate cheap funds (positive net present financing values) at the same time. The funding decision cannot add additional value to the firm and the concept of identifying cheap funds is an illusion. A policy of self-insurance against unanticipated interest rate changes assumes that any gains and losses on unhedged positions will cancel each other out over a long period. Conventional decisions to insure against unexpected interest rate losses by using interest rate futures, interest rate swaps or other suitable market instruments as hedges are wasteful of managerial time and effort, and in addition the firm will incur unnecessary transaction costs.

The active opportunistic financing and risk management policy is appropriate under circumstances 2, 3 and 4 in table 13.1, occurring either singly or in combination. In circumstances 2 and 3, world capital markets are assumed to be integrated and efficient and the financial parity relationships are assumed to hold. However, the firm may find itself in a unique position relative to these well functioning financial markets.

For example, in circumstances 2(a) the specific nature of the firm's business may mean that its overseas cash flows are expected to be subject to many unanticipated exchange rate and interest rate changes. As such managers, creditors and shareholders may perceive a very high default risk. Corporate matching and hedging to reduce the high variability expected in liability or funding cash flows is justified here if it can reduce the potential shareholder wealth losses associated with financial distress. Financial managers should attempt to match borrowings and investments by matching the size, timing and currency of asset and liability cash flows as far as is possible (Dufey and Giddy 1978b: 76). This will, to some degree, ensure that any unanticipated changes in asset returns will be offset by similar unanticipated changes in interest rates or the effective costs of liabilities. This matched funding produces both interest rate risk and currency risk management benefits. If managers cannot fully match in this way then hedging using financial market instruments is justified to reduce the risks of financial distress.

Banks that are wholly transaction oriented and are not interested in a long term economic relationship with the firm may also be avoided as primary suppliers of funds. The lack of stability in supply here could be a contributory factor in financial distress under certain economic conditions. Thus managers may take the view that developing close relations with fund suppliers (normally large international banks) and matching and hedging interest rate risk are the least cost (liability management) means of reducing the risks associated with volatile corporate cash and income flows, even though the same level of cash flows is expected to occur. However, if managers can, through funding and interest risk management decisions, either increase expected corporate cash flows or reduce the systematic risk for the same expected cash flows, then this would clearly be of value to shareholders.

Under these efficient market circumstances, but with default risk, managers should concentrate on securing a flexible and stable supply of funds and on reducing financial and political risks to manageable levels. This should allow managers to concentrate their efforts on real decisions as the primary source of shareholder wealth.

In circumstances 2(b) in table 13.1, if management believes that it has unique information that enables it to out-forecast the market, then it should act on the forecasts when the risks of so doing are offset by the expected gains (Dufey and Giddy, 1978b: 79). If the firm has superior interest rate forecasting skills relative to the capital market, then it can create exposed interest rate positions and exploit its unique skills. Thus it can increase the proportion of floating rate funding if it is thought that interest rates are near the top of their limit for the current funding period. In contrast, if rates are considered to be at a historical low and are expected to show a continuing if fluctuating rise in the financing period ahead, then increasing the proportion of fixed low rate funding is desirable. It must be noted that the evidence suggests that it is very difficult for a firm to acquire such knowledge of interest rate cycles, and there is little reason to believe that the firm has a better forecast of the term structure of interest rates than that already implied in say bond prices traded in an efficient market. Furthermore, if the firm somehow does acquire this forecasting skill, its acts of arbitrage when exploiting this are likely to quickly erode this advantage.

In circumstances 3 in table 13.1, if international Fisher holds, then the before-tax costs of debt will be the same between countries. However, asymmetries in national tax systems and the unique ability of an MNC to exploit these differences may mean that the after-tax costs of debt will vary between some countries. Depending upon the tax difference, this will favour one mode of funding and interest rate risk management instrument over another. For example, if countries differ on their tax treatment of interest expense then funding in these markets may be preferable to internal transfers.

In circumstances 4 in table 13.1, major deviations in financial parity, market segmentation and in some cases market inefficiency are considered possible. Management will have profit opportunities when exchange rates or interest rates deviate in a systematic way from the markets' expectations. These imperfections may be due to governmental credit or exchange rate controls. If an MNC has the capacity to circumvent such controls (through its internal financial transfer system) then it may decide that the potential gains are worth any extra risk (Dufey and Giddy, 1978b: 78). If such financial parity deviations exist and real changes in interest rates have occurred or are likely to occur, then the firm has a whole host of funding and risk management tactics at its disposal.

The combination of possible segmented, efficient, inefficient, domestic and offshore markets means that the firm has the following wide range of external and internal financing sources to consider:

1 Efficient capital markets consisting of
  (a) the major Western domestic loan, bond and equity markets
  (b) the offshore or Euro loan, bond and equity markets
  (c) weak efficiency domestic capital markets and government controlled domestic loan and bank deposit markets.
2 Inefficient capital markets, which are presumed to exist in those developing countries where structural limitations prevent market efficiency arising.
3 Integrated world markets, which at best consist of all of the capital

markets in category 1 and at worst do not exist at all.
4    Non-market sources, which mainly consist of government subsidized funds. Subsidies can be in the form of reduced interest rates, loans with long maturities, grants for land and equipment and generous export credit facilities.
5    Funds externally generated by subsidiaries with unique access to local supplies of capital. In addition funds can be internally generated by these overseas subsidiaries. Both sources can be transferred via the internal financial system of the company and so can serve as a key source of financing. The internal financial transfer system and internal funding were discussed in chapter 6.

If for the present we concentrate on exploiting market sources, then the firm has to make judgements about funding cost opportunities in domestic markets and between various domestic and offshore capital markets. These markets may in turn be efficient or inefficient. It has therefore to decide whether opportunities exist for reducing funding costs by arbitraging within or between specific capital markets.

As discussed in chapter 3, these cheap funding opportunities do not seem to exist within the sophisticated capital markets of the United States, the UK etc. and the offshore markets. These markets appear to generally fall into a semi-strong efficiency category and opportunities for arbitrage within these markets is very limited.

This is also likely to be true when considering arbitrage between these markets except when governments erect stringent and effective capital control barriers. Generally, arbitrage between these major domestic markets for say bank deposits (or equity, bonds or loans) and their offshore equivalents in the same currency will ensure that differences in the cost of these funding sources only reflect transaction costs.

In a similar fashion, arbitrage between the foreign exchange markets and offshore markets for capital will maintain similar real prices for capital irrespective of the different nominal rates quoted in each currency. Thus differences in interest rates for say one year dollar bank deposits and one year sterling bank deposits will be reflected in the £/$ forward premium or discount. Arbitrage in the currency swaps markets is likely to ensure that interest rate parity will prevail over longer periods than in the forward market.

In addition, loan markets in the Western economies are likely to be integrated with risk pricing mechanisms in security markets through arbitrage in interest rate swaps between loan and bond markets. This arbitrage is most active in the offshore loan and bond markets but is likely to feed into equivalent domestic interest rates.

Empirical tests designed to identify integration or segmentation in world capital markets have already been discussed in chapter 3. It appears that models which explicitly include barriers to investment offer the best hope of understanding this issue (Stulz 1981a). As we have seen, this issue is currently unresolved when considering empirical evidence on asset pricing. However, the arbitrage possibilities identified above suggest that any differences in prices of capital (of the same risk) between these large domestic international markets is likely to be short lived.

As a result segmentation is unlikely to occur between market categories 1(a) and 1(b) listed above, except under major disturbances or governmental interference. Thus most forms of corporate funds within and across these markets are likely to be fairly priced, and cheap money will be an illusory concept under these competitive arbitrage conditions. This is an important attribute of these markets. Access from domestic financial systems to these external loan, bond, commercial paper and Euroequity markets has improved throughout the 1980s. This has meant that many more European, Japanese and US firms have access to these competitively priced markets for international capital.

However, as the level of imperfection grows, in particular because of short lived tax opportunities and because of barriers at the boundaries between countries (e.g. government regulation of capital flows or taxes on capital flows between countries), lower (than world market) cost financing opportunities may become more apparent between say the first two market categories 1(a) and 1(b) and the third category 1(c). Opportunities for arbitrage within markets may in turn become more abundant as one moves from capital markets in Western economies to those in developing countries or those shedding their old centrally planned systems. Government controls over domestic banking markets, especially deposit and loan rates, or controls over access to capital may also create opportunities for subsidiaries (and thus the parent) to acquire domestic funds at rates below world market rates. Alternatively, the parent may be able to exploit its access to world markets to fund its subsidiary at lower than domestic costs. In both situations the MNC is achieving a competitive funding advantage over its global competitors or domestic competitors.

If some capital markets are considered to be segmented, the MNC may be able to identify opportunities for funding supply and interest rate risk diversification which are not available to investors. Diversification of the company's financing base by financing in more than one currency and in more than one capital market is also more likely to be reversible and can also be used to hedge aspects of economic, transaction and translation currency exposures.

Finally, we can consider the possibility of combinations of circumstances 2, 3 and 4 in table 13.1. For example, it is more likely that the firm will be able to out-forecast markets under circumstances 4 than under circumstances 2. If it can, then these are the joint conditions under which it can profitably exploit timing and location opportunities both in funding and in interest rate risk management decisions.

The value impact, if any, of the above range of financing decisions will depend on the economic circumstances surrounding the firm. The degree of imperfections will affect the composition of the financing methods portfolio according to the individual ability of each financing method to reduce financing costs, reduce interest rate and currency risks, and protect or add to value under each set of circumstances. As a result, we can expect to see considerable variety amongst firms in terms of the choice of financing methods and in the emphasis placed on cheap funding versus interest rate risk management aims.

In all of the above funding and risk management decisions, attempts should be made to satisfy both the overall financial structure goals of the firm and local capital structure norms. The nature of this constraint will be discussed in section 13.5. This is followed in section 13.6 by a discussion of the importance of flexibility of external supply of funds, and in section 13.7 by an analysis of the value interactions between funding, capital structure and risk management decisions.

## The role of treasury in the active opportunistic funding strategy

A variant of the active opportunistic strategy is when the firm or its treasury takes the view that there are many exploitable opportunities in world capital and banking markets, i.e. circumstances 4 in table 13.1, and the firm has the capacity to take full advantage of these opportunities. As a result it may decide to borrow and invest funds when deviations from financial parity are expected or when it believes it has unique information. Centralized control over external borrowing and the internal collection of funds are essential ingredients in such a policy. If the firm does adopt this risky strategy, it will have become an active financial intermediary, borrowing funds to invest in profitable financial assets rather than to support real operations, or arbitraging perceived price differences in markets for interest rate options, swaps, forwards etc. However, the basic competitive advantages of the firm are likely to lie in imperfect international product and factor markets rather than in exploiting perceived mispricing or abundant capital supply in international banking and capital markets.

If treasury takes this view, then it has begun to think and act as a bank, by arbitraging perceived mispricing of funds or risk management instruments in financial markets or by betting against the future direction of interest rates and the availability of funds. Treasury may be very wrong in this view of markets and it may also lose sight of its primary role in securing funding and providing financial risk management services and advice to the rest of the enterprise. The danger here is that treasury will pursue profits in this role as a speculator and arbitrageur to the detriment of its other support roles in the firm. As a result, funding policy and responses to interest rate currency risk may be uncoordinated as the treasury sees financial decisions as about arbitrage and profit alone.

In addition, a long term practice of exploiting any capital market opportunity that arises may earn the MNC the reputation of being a poor corporate citizen in a host country. This, in turn, may lead to increased political interference in the decision making of the hostage subsidiary and ultimately to a reduction in the NPV of the asset.

This chapter presumes that the major funding and interest rate risk problems facing firms are best dealt with by using various combinations of funding and risk management tactics set within an active opportunistic financial management policy. This policy is dominated by strategic and shareholder wealth concerns. Treasurers should carefully weigh the evidence for and against imperfections and potential profitable opportunities. The likely efficiency of world capital and foreign exchange markets, allied with the likely short lived nature of financial parity deviations and exploitable tax differences across countries, suggests that scepticism and conservatism are appropriate attitudes towards perceived profit opportunities in these financial markets. Thus most firms should adopt a coherent funding and risk management policy primarily designed to support the achievement of strategic and operational goals. Treasury should play a major role in providing cash flow, funding and interest rate forecasts and financial advice to those managers making strategic and operational decisions. It should act as the specialist corporate function designed to buffer the firm against uncertainty in financial markets. As we move from economic circumstances 1 to 4 in table 13.1, the funding and risk management problems become increasingly complex. As a result the information provision, advisory, funding and active hedging roles of

380 Global Financing Decisions

treasury are likely to increase in complexity and significance for the firm. Only the very largest MNCs with sophisticated treasury functions are likely to be able to exploit such imperfections on a regular basis. However, even here, the use of scarce and costly treasury management skills to pursue financial market profits as a priority can be seen as potentially detrimental to a treasury role in which it contributes to the creation of wealth from the firm's world-wide production sites and its sourcing and selling activities in its global factor and product markets.

## 13.5 Capital Structure Decisions

The capital structure decision is concerned with the relative proportions of debt and equity employed in financing the firm. In the orthodox (primarily domestically oriented) financial management field there is a major debate amongst theoreticians about the relevance or otherwise of capital structure. The consensus is that there is an optimal capital structure. Ideally, in a world with no taxes and no market imperfections, the value of the firm would only depend upon the investment decision. Capital structure is irrelevant because asset and liability cash flows are independent and the latter have no effect upon the value of the firm. However, in the real world such value dependencies can occur. As the firm increases its debt relative to equity it increases the value of tax benefits but it also increases the cost of bankruptcy. At some point the marginal tax benefits are outweighed by the marginal costs of bankruptcy and the optimal capital structure is reached.

There are some flaws with this theory, especially since debt existed prior to these tax benefits. Furthermore the cost of bankruptcy appears small (Warner 1977). Miller (1977) also argues that the tax advantages of debt appear small, because as firms issue debt to exploit tax advantages they reach a point where they satisfy the demand on the part of zero tax paying investors. If they issue debt beyond this point they will have to pay a higher rate of interest to attract higher tax payers. Thus the rate of interest on debt will rise to a point where it cancels out the tax advantage. Masulis (1980) tested whether these tax advantages existed or not. He looked at firms which changed their capital structure but kept their asset structure unchanged. Business risk was therefore held constant and the change in capital structure was the only variable capable of changing firm value. He found a beneficial effect on firm value when debt was substituted for equity and suggested that this was due to the tax deduction for interest payments. Masulis did not find any evidence for the hypothesized bankruptcy effect.

Agency theory provides some additional help in understanding this problem of capital structure. From this theory we can deduce that as the firm's ownership structure changes from 100 per cent manager ownership to the introduction of external equity and debt, the size and risk of asset cash flows and therefore the value of the firm become dependent, in part, upon capital structure. Agency problems occur when a principal (or group of principals such as shareholders and debtholders) employ an agent (manager) to perform decision making services. Both managers and suppliers of capital are assumed to act in their own self-interest and are seeking to maximize their wealth.

Barnea et al. (1981: 8) classify the agency problems in the capital structure decision as arising from three sources. Firstly, there is a problem of informational asymmetry in that market imperfections may prevent managers from costlessly revealing the nature of the firm to debt and equity holders. Secondly, the existence of debt financing under conditions of limited liability generates shareholder incentives to take decisions which may transfer wealth from debtholders to equity holders or which may prevent the firm accepting profitable new investments. Thirdly, as the firm's ownership changes from 100 per cent manager ownership to increased ownership by external debt and equity holders, the owner manager has an increased incentive to consume corporate resources as perquisites.

Capital markets can to some degree resolve the conflicts of interest identified above. Barnea et al. (1981) outline the various market mechanisms open to shareholders and bondholders to exercise pressure on management to make decisions on their behalf. However, residual problems remain and the external suppliers of capital incur additional costs to ensure control over managerial decision making. These include the costs associated with writing restrictive provisions into debt contracts, and maintaining incentive schemes such as share options for managers. The costs of monitoring and controlling will increase both as managerial ownership declines and as debt is substituted for equity. At some capital structure level the combination of marginal bankruptcy and agency costs will exceed the marginal tax benefits and so the optimal capital structure is reached.

A similar case to that outlined for the domestic firm can be made for the MNC raising most of its equity and debt capital in one capital market, i.e. its home country market. Dufey (1983: 5) points out that such MNCs exhibit significant home country factors in their capital structure. If domestic conditions such as tax laws affect the tax advantage of debt and other local factors affect monitoring costs for suppliers of capital and the local cost and probability of bankruptcy, then this will accentuate the home country determination of the MNC's overall corporate structure. This does not mean that subsidiaries of other MNCs operating in these countries will have to conform to local norms. The subsidiaries will only have separate capital structures (from the parent) if the parent is prepared to allow the subsidiary to default with no call on corporate resources. If legal or explicit moral obligations exist to prevent default by a subsidiary, then it does not have an independent capital structure. Its true capital structure is equal to that of the whole enterprise. The world-wide capital structure recognized by the home market is therefore taken as dominating all subsidiaries' capital structures. The subsidiaries are seen as contributing to the world-wide capital structure and affecting the home currency market view of tax benefits, bankruptcy costs and agency costs.

Given that most of an MNC's equity is generally held by shareholders in its home country, the choice of capital structure norms by reference to this market can be seen as appropriate. This may be justified under the assumption of an integrated world capital market, if the further assumption is made that the reference domestic market is a satisfactory proxy for the world market. In the case of the US capital market this may be a valid assumption, but in the case of an MNC with several significant national sources of equity and debt capital the choice of the appropriate reference capital structure country becomes problematic. The emergence of many companies in the latter category and the possible establishment of world industry norms for capital structure may provide the necessary guidelines for financial managers of MNCs in the future. However, few MNCs have yet to fully broaden their equity base in this way. Those that have done so will find it necessary to discuss their capital structure range with international institutional investors and bankers operating in the major world capital markets.

In the case of an MNC with largely home country shareholders, the corporate goal under either segmentation or integration is to achieve or maintain the MNC capital structure within the requirements of the home country capital market. In the case of an MNC with many shareholders in overseas equity markets, the aim of the firm is to keep its capital structure within the perceived requirements of the international financial community. In all of these cases the MNC has considerable flexibility in varying the capital structures of its subsidiaries to achieve these parent capital structure goals. Specifically, it can vary local capital structures within national norms and constraints. These include (Dufey 1983: 6)

1 statutory law which prescribes a minimum equity level
2 tax laws which treat interest payments differently to dividend payments
3 exchange controls which may be less restrictive on interest payments than on dividend payments.

Both 2 and 3 provide an incentive for MNCs to finance overseas subsidiaries predominantly with debt securities. In particular, national tax laws can also significantly differ in their treatment of interest tax deductions and in their treatment of capital gains and losses due to exchange rate changes. Such asymmetries in national tax laws may create major imperfections which in turn create opportunities for the MNC in its debt financing decision. As a result MNCs have shown a strong preference to issue debt rather than equity overseas.

However, Jeffcoat and Southern (1983) have argued that incentives also exist to issue more equity overseas. These include a better corporate image in the host country and improved access to local capital markets. These factors and the growing internationalization of major domestic markets have meant that by the 1990s MNCs have begun to seek equity capital from outside their home country. The emergence of the Euroequity market and the enhanced possibility of raising equity capital in the main world financial centres have made these important new sources of risk capital for the MNC. This is a further stage in MNC development, in that all assets and liabilities can now be created on a world-wide basis rather than being biased towards one home country.

It is clear from the above that the identification of the overall corporate capital structure and local capital structure norms are key ingredients in the financing decision. They provide the boundaries within which the firm can pursue a value maximization or cost minimization goal for the global financing decision.

## 13.6 Flexibility of External Supply of Funds

MNCs operate in a volatile and rapidly changing business and financial environment. They must therefore establish a flexible and responsive external system for the supply of funds. Large international banks are the primary providers of loans, overdrafts and commitments as well as the primary arrangers and underwriters of bonds, commercial paper, equity and other securitized sources of funds. It is here that we can see the possibilities for close bank relationships in providing this flexibility in the funding decision.

Donaldson (1969) has described how bank relationships are a key component in dealing with financial uncertainty. Most finance officers in his sample placed considerable emphasis on the importance of cultivating a close relationship with the lending officer, a relationship usually regarded as a highly personal one, involving mutual trust and continuous communication. As a rule, normal funds resource planning worked on the basis that established lines of credit and borrowing limits on unsecured bank debt allowed a comfortable margin of safety.

Holland (1992a) extends this concept of financial mobility to many relationship banks and to the context of international financial markets. The large international firms in this study selected a portfolio of banking relationships. This involved the use of first tier or relationship banks as well as second and third tiers or circles of banks; ranking banks within each tier; establishing the role (if any) of dominant lead or house bank(s) within the first tier; and the use of transaction banks to keep the whole portfolio in touch with the market. Considerable variation existed within the bulk of these cases in terms of the overall number of banks dealt with, the number of banks per tier and the role of transaction banks in introducing market forces to the portfolio of banks. In the bulk of the cases the first tier banks or close relationship banks ranged from five to fifteen banks. This model of multiple bank relations for MNCs was fundamentally the same throughout the bulk of the cases. The complex aims and rationales for this portfolio approach to bank relations included the alleviation of a wide range of information asymmetries with international financial markets and the firm's portfolio of banks; the securing of stable long term supplies of a wide range of funds and financial services; and the creation of a flexible, responsive supply capacity relative to uncertainty in this market.

The prevalence of relationship banking as a central component of MNC's financing policy (see Ireland 1987 for a survey) can be seen as an extension of Donaldson's (1969) concept of a 'strategy of least resistance sourcing' across many international banks. This strategy is based on a primary concern for ease of negotiation. The treasurer first uses internal funds and reserves under his direct control, then proceeds to negotiate funds and other financial services from familiar and friendly sources especially relationship banks, and lastly negotiates with unfamiliar sources. Closely related to the corporate concern for ease of negotiation is the predictability or certainty of the source. When these two concerns are taken together they provide a powerful motivation in the sequence of use. This matches a bank's ability to use the close relationship to gain confidential information. This in turn allows the bank to carefully assess the expected performance of the loan and default risks with its relationship clients (Holland 1994). In Holland (1992a), multinational firms saw relationship banks as flexible, friendly, relatively predictable sources of funds and financial services. In contrast, transaction oriented or 'arm's length' banks were much less predictable and sympathetic suppliers. As a result, there was a clear preference to source internally, followed by relationship banks, followed by transaction banks.

A portfolio of bank relationships provides crucial extra degrees of freedom for the MNC treasurer in the global funding decision. The existence of a tier or 'inner circle' of close relationship bankers provides many more stable fund and financial service supply options than indicated by Donaldson (1969). The existence of a group of regular transaction banks further expands the financial service and funding supply options open to the MNC.

The long established and difficult to acquire relationships with commercial and investment bankers can be seen as providing a valuable insurance scheme against risks of inflexibility in funding supply. These risks include the difficulties a firm faces in creating a (bank provided) contingency reserve of standby funds to exploit short lived competitive opportunities or to deal with competitive threats, in the rapid mobilization of funds for takeover bids or defences, and in acquiring a steady and reliable source of funds to cope with the growth of the business. Close bank relations are not required to deal with a perceived risk of credit rationing or the non-availability of funds at any price. Credit rationing seems unlikely for the financially healthy firm, and funds are likely to be available for this firm's strategic and competitive purposes either directly from capital markets or from non-relationship or transaction oriented banks. However, in periods of credit shortage or low confidence and activity in security markets, the price may be very high both in terms of interest rates or returns required and in terms of controls such as covenants required by these sources. In contrast the relationship bank, knowing the detailed state of financial health of the enterprise, may be able to provide loan or security based funds much more quickly and at a lower cost to its relationship clients.

A high quality relationship bank may also provide the firm with special access to rapidly mobilized, large scale, relatively cheaper sources of funds. Thus an AAA rated bank operating in the high quality tiers of the Euro inter-bank market for bank deposits can rapidly supply its quality relationship clients with funds. If the MNC client is regularly employing the bank for a large proportion of its banking business, then it is more likely that the bank will share part of its competitive funding advantage with the firm.

Flexibility in funding supplies is of considerable significance to the treasurer of the MNC. This strategic advantage can be further enhanced by using the relationship bank as a funding source to inflate corporate borrowings over and above those required for current operations and known investment plans. The relationship bank could also be used as the source of additional committed bank (fund) facilities. In both of these cases, the additional funds or additional funding capacity are arranged to deal with currently unknown funding contingencies or urgent unanticipated calls on funds. This need may arise because the firm operates in an industry where the prediction of corporate cash flows is difficult in terms of both timing and volume, and this leads to similar difficulties in forecasting future external funding needs. Alternatively, this need may arise if the firm operates in an active market for corporate control and thus actively searches for new corporate acquisitions. The relationship bank is the most likely source for such 'buffer' funding or the pre-funding of requirements because it knows enough about the firm's prospects to justify lending on the basis of currently unknown projects or contingencies. However, there will be an interest cost or a commitment fee cost associated with contingency funding. This is only justified if the firm can demonstrate shareholder wealth benefits and the firm will not move outside its preferred capital structure range. The benefits may include

- reduced costs of rapid mobilization of funds when required
- reduced costs of lost competitive or acquisition opportunities
- reduced costs of dealing with competitive or takeover threats.

Clearly, the building up of excess unused funds on the firm's balance sheet may also have major costs. The costs of securing the funds and managing their reinvestment may be a waste of treasury skills and time. Relationship banks may also react if they think that the firm is using the excess funds to exploit arbitrage opportunities in markets. Such costs suggest that extensive contingency funding could undermine relationship banking benefits and reduce shareholder wealth.

The firm may have considerable difficulty in valuing the close bank relationship and its attendant flexible supply insurance scheme. However, it is essential that minimum requirements be established here in terms of the overall role of relationship bankers in the provision of funds, before the treasurer is allowed to minimize the cost of funds by seeking funds from transaction oriented least cost suppliers. The loss of this relationship funding advantage may create strategic problems for the MNC that have negative value implications for shareholders.

## 13.7 A Global Financing Strategy

Up to this point we have considered

- funding and risk management policies under economic circumstances ranging from market efficiency to many imperfections in financial markets
- the unique features of the capital structure decision for the MNC
- the need for a flexible and responsive external supply system
- the wide choice and variety of financing methods open to the MNC (chapter 11).

These complexities illustrate the need for a firm to develop a financing strategy to cope with the inevitable problems and to exploit any opportunities. In particular the MNC must consider

- how funding decisions can be made
- how they interact with risk management decisions and capital structure constraints
- how these decisions can together alter the riskiness of the firm's cash flows and the value of the firm.

The following stepwise strategy attempts to investigate how global financing decisions can be made, and how value interactions between funding, risk management and capital structure decisions can be dealt with by the MNC. The first stage consists of developing basic information on financing needs and identifying the constraints imposed by capital structure decisions. In the second stage, financing is arranged to maximize the net present value (or minimize the total costs) of the overall financing package subject to these needs and constraints.

## Overall financing needs: opportunities and constraints

The first stage of the strategy consists of the following parallel activities:

1   The assessment of world-wide financing requirements and surpluses stemming from existing operations and from new investment plans. Financing requirements will flow from an analysis of policies on acquisition, organic growth, portfolio investment in firms, and disinvestment. This analysis (see chapter 8) should help the firm in assessing by how much total expenditure will exceed internal cash generation, and therefore the scale of the external financing problem.

2   Internal flexibility and control over resources depend on the degree of sophistication of the MNC's internal financial transfer and information system. A highly developed system will allow the MNC to exploit internal (and some external ) financing opportunities arising in one part of the world and to use the funds elsewhere in its world-wide operations, and will be crucial to the generation of internal cash flows.

3   The identification of the range over which the parent capital structure is allowed to vary in the home country capital market. Alternatively, if the firm raises its equity and debt in a core group of major Western capital markets, then it must identify the capital structure range deemed appropriate by these suppliers of capital. This may be achieved by comparing the firm with other international firms operating in similar global industries. Direct discussions with capital market participants such as financial analysts and international bankers will also be of value. The capital structure range will provide the basic information to plan required levels of external equity and debt financing.

4   The exploitation of a flexible and responsive external funding system.

The above provide basic data and key decision parameters for the second stage of the strategy.

## Constructing the overall financing package: trade-offs between financing objectives

In the second stage of the strategy the firm has to satisfy a wide range of objectives concerning the global financing decision (figure 13.1). Firstly, the firm must achieve its funding objectives:

- To secure the volume of funds required for existing operations, new projects, and currently unknown business contingencies. This is the primary link between funding and real strategic decisions.
- To secure funds at lowest cost for each type of funds, i.e. bonds versus loans.
- To maintain a flexible and stable supply of funds from relationship banks and capital markets in which the firm has a good credit rating.
- To exploit other links with real decisions, by using the funding decision as a strategic tool and by adapting real decisions to alter funding needs.

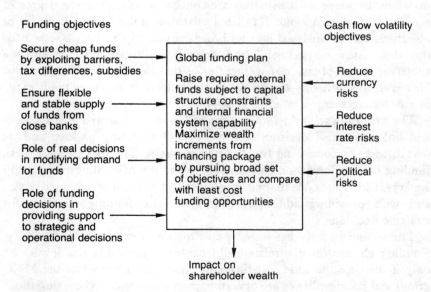

**Figure 13.1** The trade-off of objectives in a global financing decision

Secondly, the firm must reduce the impact of financial and political risks on the volatility of operating cash flows by achieving its risk management objectives:

- To reduce the interest rate risk facing the firm.
- To reduce the currency risk facing the firm.
- To use the funding decision to minimize political risks.

The common thread running through all of these objectives is their impact on the net present value of the overall financial package chosen by the firm. The pursuit of each objective will have its own differential impact on wealth, and thus an overall trade-off has to be established between these objectives.

For example, the pursuit of cheap funds as the sole objective may produce a large and obvious beneficial impact on the value of the overall financing package. It may be very tempting for the firm to fully exploit all opportunities here as the sole priority in global financing. However, such a funds cost minimization policy may also expose the firm to a wider range of financial and political risks and these may undermine overall corporate strategy. Thus the negative value consequences of cost minimization must be considered in a global financing policy.

In the following sections the assumption is that least cost funding decisions are made such that they are consistent with a desired degree of achievement of each major set of objectives identified above. Each set of objectives can be analysed and its broad wealth implications assessed for the whole financing package. The latter will be difficult in the case of the valuation effects of risk management or of the use of close bank relations. However, this difficulty should not lead to a decision to ignore the benefits of risk management or of close relations.

The firm can assess the implications of funding needs, risk management and links with real decisions for the overall financing package and its overall costs by comparing two funding packages. The first package seeks funding cost minimization consistent with the use of existing relationship bankers, with acceptable (to managers) levels of political and financial risks, and with providing additional (non-immediate funding) support for strategic decisions.

The second package has funding cost minimization as the sole priority. Funding choices involve relationship bankers, acceptable risk levels etc. only if they are the least cost financing solutions. Thus when the MNC group and its subsidiaries are operating in circumstances where deviations from parity prevail, the parent should satisfy the financing requirements of the group and subsidiaries by exploiting the unique opportunities open to it to reduce the costs of its financing decisions. It should therefore attempt to profit from market distortions created by governmental interference, to exploit tax differences between countries, to speculate using perceived inside information, and to exploit the company's unique ability to transfer funds internally.

Thus the extra funding costs of

- a flexible and secure funds supply via relationship banks
- reduced financial and political risks
- the provision of additional support for real decisions

can be compared with the benefits (wealth impact) of achieving these objectives. In this way, financing cost minimization can be recognized as a dominant and central aim of global financing, without it becoming the sole aim of such a planning activity.

*Funding decisions in the MNC*
Funding practices vary across MNCs and include conservative versus risk taking decisions on:

- relative proportions of external versus internal funding
- low versus high gearing
- relative proportions of short term versus long term debt
- relative proportions of fixed rate versus floating rate debt
- degree of currency mismatching between assets and liabilities
- extent of pre-funding and opportunistic funding.

In section 13.8 a detailed case considers how ICI, a large UK MNC, makes these decisions.

The raising of finance is primarily for funding existing or future operations, or for possible contingencies. However, there are many other interactions between the funding decision and strategic decisions. These include the use of the funding decision as a strategic tool, and adapting strategic decisions to modify demand for funds.

Funding as a strategic tool includes the use of the funding decision to provide additional support (non-funding) to strategic and operational decisions. A firm may therefore use cheap funds or surplus currency arising elsewhere in the business to 'sweeten' a major sales contract by providing the cheap funds or scarce currency to the customer. An aircraft manufacturer rich in dollar revenues may be able to provide an airline customer with dollar funds or spot dollars at better than market rates. Alternatively a firm may use the funding decision to raise the profile of the firm in overseas markets. For example, it could issue yen denominated equity or debt to raise the company's profile in Japan and aid penetration of the Japanese market for goods and services. This could also achieve name recognition amongst the Japanese financial community and thus improve access to a key financial market.

In the second case the firm may adapt the strategic and operational decisions to reduce funding problems. In one example, the firm could pre-sell many products to accelerate sales cash flows and thus reduce its need for external funds. In another example, the firm could reduce the scale of its investment decisions to reduce financing needs or it could change the investment location and hence access to domestic capital markets.

*Cash flow volatility and political and financial risks*
As indicated above, much of the firm's funding requirements may be satisfied via normal channels such as its relationship banks and its established routes for domestic and overseas security issues. These fund raising sources can also be used to manage the financial and political risks facing the firm subject to explicit objectives in these respects.

When the MNC group and its subsidiaries are operating in countries with efficient capital markets, the parent should fund itself and the subsidiaries locally and ensure that assets and liabilities are matched in terms of currencies and interest rate exposures. This rule means that many problems of currency risk, interest rate risk and political risk are minimized. The firm should therefore arrange its financing to reduce the riskiness of operating cash flows.

However, if the MNC faces many cheap funding opportunities stemming from various imperfections in financial markets, it must assess the risk implications created by exploiting these. These may include increased loan default risk stemming from significant new currency, interest rate or political risk exposures. Shareholders will expect managers to manage these financial and political risks on their behalf to reduce the impact on their returns. These risk levels can be reduced by altering the interest rate and currency of denomination terms of financing decisions. Interest rate risk exposures can be altered by adjusting the mix of floating rate versus fixed rate interest financing to match the asset cash flow characteristics. This may be achieved in the initial financing decision or may be subsequently changed by the use of interest rate swaps or other market instruments such as forward rate agreements or interest rate options. Political risk exposures may be altered by financing assets located in risky political zones with local funds. Currency risk exposures can be altered by funding asset revenue cash flows with financing cash flows of the same timing, currency and volume. The reduction of exposure to these risks should be assessed by their impact on the value of the global financing package as well as their impact on the riskiness of MNC cash flows. The imposition of managerial risk preferences here may lead to suboptimal decisions for shareholders and should therefore be avoided.

## Economic circumstances, financing methods and financing aims

Once the firm has established its minimum and expected requirements for ensuring flexible funds supply, for managing risk, and for exploiting the role of financing in strategy and operational decisions, it can then assess the possibility of full exploitation of cheap funds. Once priorities have been established among this broader set of funding related goals, treasury will have a clear idea of the extent to which the global funding plan can be altered to take advantage of cheap sources. This pursuit of cheap funds within a broader set of global financing goals and priorities is in stark contrast to the pursuit of a financing cost minimization policy alone.

Before the treasury embarks on this policy it should also clearly identify whether cheap funds do exist. As discussed in section 13.4, these opportunities are likely to depend on tax differences between countries, on deviations from parity in international and domestic capital markets and on the possibility that the firm may have unique information or access relative to a particular market. Scepticism and conservatism should guide the treasurer here, especially in the light of the empirical evidence presented in chapter 3 and the ever present need to keep the requirements of the real business at the forefront of treasury funding activities.

Finally, the firm must assess the influences, if any, of the financing decision on capital budgeting and economic exposure decisions. The relationship between capital budgeting and financing decisions has been explored at the level of one project in chapter 10. Many value interactions were identified here and were incorporated in the APV rule. Similar issues arise with the firm's long term strategic plan, its set of capital budgeting projects and their financing needs. This is a financial planning and strategic planning issue. This will be discussed in chapter 14 when financial planning and MNC strategy development are discussed. Given that dependencies do exist between the major IFM decision areas for the MNC, an explicit trade-off is also required here.

The global financing procedure discussed here, and the financial planning procedure outlined in the next chapter, are heuristics designed to capture the main elements of the decision problem concerned. They incorporate a set of steps such that all of the major issues are dealt with in a logical sequence with subsequent iteration to allow for learning through the sequence. In practice MNCs will differ in their financing policies and financial planning procedures. This may be due to a host of factors. However, long term organizational learning through time and many periods of crisis and success is probably the strongest determinant of each firm's policy. Some firms may feel that caution on funding is vital for the success of the firm and emphasize internal funds first. Conglomerate firms may emphasize financial goals and funding aims before real investment aims. However, they will all, at some point, have to deal with the central elements of the global financing policy discussed in this chapter, and the overall financial planning policy outlined in chapter 14. Thus firms will make decisions similar to the global financing strategy and financial planning outlined in these chapters but possibly in a different order. ICI will be used as a case example to illustrate one firm's experience in developing a global financing policy.

## 13.8 ICI Case and Global Financing Policy

ICI's experience over many years in global financing illustrates some of the practical difficulties faced by an MNC in this policy area. In this case we see how ICI has learnt over many years how to establish trade-offs between internal and external funding, between cheap funds and the need to support organic growth and acquisition led growth, between short and long term funds, between variable and fixed interest funding, and between the various risks faced by the firm. All of these rules constitute a learnt financial policy which is designed to support the strategic aims of ICI and which management argue are the appropriate decision guidelines to boost long term growth in shareholder wealth in a range of economic circumstances.

A firm such as ICI is subject to much public comment and analysis. In addition its senior executives have written many articles on this issue: thus Clements (1985; 1988) and Henderson and Rogerson (1987) are key sources. External commentators include Freeman (1990) and Singleton-Green (1991).

## Basic principles of ICI's financial policy

ICI has identified four basic principles to guide its global financing:

- to maintain as much control as possible over the group's cash position, particularly at the group centre
- to ensure that funds are as mobile as possible and can be moved quickly within the group
- to maintain long term group gearing levels at less than 30 per cent debt to total assets
- to build as much flexibility as possible into external financing so as to withstand sudden changes in the firm's position or in financial markets: this is achieved by keeping a top credit rating and by maintaining the confidence of relationship bankers.

These principles provide the context for a wide set of financing objectives and rules employed in capital markets:

*Funding*   Proactive funding in advance of needs; opportunistic funding relative to novel and cheap financing opportunities.
*Cash flow volatility*   Choosing maturity and repayment patterns to smooth the repayment profile of the existing portfolio of borrowings.
*Interest rate risk*   Percentage of fixed versus floating rate funding; percentage of long versus short term funding.
*Currency risk*   Matching of assets and liabilities in the same currency.

Together these broad financial policy principles and market financing rules form a set of decision heuristics that have been found to work for ICI management over the past two decades. Thus ICI has a global financing policy that has shareholder value seeking and value protecting aims at its heart. Cheap funding aims are traded off against a conservative attitude to supply risks, currency risks, interest rate risks and political risks, all subject to group capital structure constraints. The components of this policy are outlined below.

## Cash flow forecasts and generation

At the start of each year the ICI group reviews its expected cash flows and capital expenditures from existing operations. It also uses its long term strategic plans to assess the aggregate cash flow forecasts and funding implications of its investment, divestment and acquisition policies in the UK business and in overseas territories (Hodgson 1980).

Given the forecasts and budgets projected for ICI's existing assets, its operating businesses or territorial units around the world, the question is: how much controllable cash flow can the company expect to generate over the next three years after taxes, interest payments, and dividend payouts? The cash flow remaining after these deductions is considered to be the net cash flow that will be available to finance the major part of the company's strategy, i.e. capital expenditure plus additional working capital.

Long term operating experience has enabled ICI to build up a guideline which says in effect that its own internal cash generation must represent at least 75–80 per cent of the total expenditure anticipated. The combination of net internal cash flows and this rough guideline for the scale of internal funding of expansion plans effectively sets an upper limit on the scale of investment plans and the scale of external financing. For example, £200 million of internal cash flows and a 75 per cent internal financing rule means that £267 million is the investment limit and £67 million will be raised in external capital.

This internal funding rule is not followed in a slavish manner. Expenditure will be cut back if the internal funds are not there to fund 75–80 per cent, but this will be on a gradual smoothing basis over two to three years. In other periods, such as the mid 1980s, internal cash exceeded the investment volume. However, this moved backed to 75–80 per cent as ICI has identified new areas for investment.

The 75–80 per cent internal funding rule reduces ICI's activity in loan and bond markets relative to its size or that of comparable competitors. Despite this its annual funding needs are very large. In 1990 it had £1.7 billion of medium term and long term borrowings.

## Treasury centralization

Treasury centralization in ICI has produced control and information advantages for the financing decision:

*Centralization of external group financing*

Group financing is centralized to ensure that ICI can borrow in large amounts. This is presumed to reduce financing costs and ensures that the lowest cost markets can be sought out and exploited. ICI learnt the need for this centralized function during its large expansion programme in Europe in the 1960s. The combination of UK exchange controls, the possibility of uncoordinated funding by subsidiaries, and the emergence of the Eurobond market led to this development.

*Centralization of internal funding*

ICI has a sophisticated internal financial transfer and information system. This facilitates the sourcing of some funds internally as well as bulk external purchasing of funds and their redistribution internally. ICIs centralized and coordinated control over internal cash flows and capital resources can only be employed when ICI has 100 per cent ownership of its subsidiaries. This is one reason why ICI prefers full ownership of the bulk of its subsidiaries and why it avoids joint ventures. This high degree of centralization ensures maximum group control over internal resources, and with it an increased capacity to fund investment projects.

## Gearing levels

ICI has a clear policy to maintain long term group gearing levels at less than 30 per cent debt to total assets. The gearing and internal funding rule may combine to constrain ICI's development. For example, in the 1990s it appears that ICI will have to increase the size of its pharmaceutical operations to match those of its now very large international competitors. These firms have merged to achieve the economies of scale in R&D and in marketing now considered necessary in this industry. Joint ventures do not appeal to ICI because of the loss of control over its key knowledge advantage in the drugs field. The demerger of bioscience operations and the formation of Zeneca in June 1993 reflected, in part, these financing constraints.

To avoid this joint constraint on the development of new investment opportunities, ICI may also decide to go down the acquisition route. An exception to gearing over 30 per cent can be made when an important and large acquisition requires a large amount of external debt. The increase in gearing will be tolerated if it can be quickly reduced by disposals or by rapid repayment of debt from internal sources. Short to medium debt is preferred for funding of acquisitions with the remaining balance funded by longer term funds. For example, the $2 billion acquisition of Stauffer, the US chemicals company, was initially funded by short term funds and the proceeds of $1 billion of disposals, with the remaining balance coming from long term funds.

## Flexibility and certainty of external supply

These policies together provide the basis for boosting the confidence of external suppliers of capital in ICI. The 1981–2 crisis revealed to ICI how important these external 'reserves' could be when capital markets suffered a downturn at the same time as the firm's fortunes. Thus maintaining flexibility and responsiveness in external supply is a major financing aim for ICI.

### Credit rating

ICI adopts sound investment decisions, and these internal financing rules, gearing ratios, strong control over internal cash flows and centralized external funding, because it believes these combine to create the confidence for external agencies to rate ICI at A or AA and above. This high quality credit rating is supported by ensuring that interest payments are covered at least six times by profits. The high credit rating in turn is expected to maintain ICI's access to external funding markets at terms ICI can afford even when times are bad in the economy.

### Careful management of banking relations

ICI can do little in terms of external influence over its credit rating by the various agencies. It must focus on the quality of its assets and the other financial policy variables mentioned above. In contrast, ICI can externally manage and influence its bankers to ensure that confidence in ICI remains high here.

In the 1980s ICI had a vast number of bank relationships. Group treasury tried to avoid the costs of over-banking, but growth of the business through acquisitions and new banks arriving in London swelled the numbers. In 1987, ICI cut its large number of 60 to 70 commercial bankers down to a core group of 12. It now distributes 80 per cent of its custom to this select group world-wide (*Economist*, 17 November 1990, p. 134). This rationalization has had the dual effect of reducing bank relationship costs as well as providing a smaller, more responsive core of close relationship banks.

These house or relationship banks are global in scope. They must have a London or other world financial centre presence. They must also have a wide geographic spread to match that of ICI in various regions of the world. In the UK, ICI uses all four English commercial banks (clearers) as house banks. ICI also employs at least one commercial bank per major country of operation. Other banks are geographical or product specialized.

The basic policy with the house banks is one of close relationship rather than a transaction orientation. The group treasury co-ordinates and manages long term funding relationships for the group across the world. It also co-ordinates long term funding for overseas subsidiaries in consultation with local management. Local capital markets are also used for this funding activity. ICI finance, acting as profit centre or in-house bank and under the control of group treasury, handles all currency exposures and short/medium term funding. This treasury group manages the short/medium term funding aspects of banking relationships around the world for both the group's and the overseas subsidiaries' needs.

Given ICI's internal funding behaviour and high credit rating, it does not rely on bank finance and has considerable power relative to its bankers. It is also wary of the dangers it perceives as arising from excessive use of bank loans instead of other forms of funding. These dangers include influence on or limits to corporate decision making owing to bank loan covenants or, even worse, direct bank control in periods of financial distress. However, despite this policy, ICI is careful enough to provide the UK clearers and other house banks with forecasts of likely use of committed facilities provided by these banks for periods of a year and beyond. There are regular meetings with these house banks and they are informed in some detail of the group's current position and its major borrowing requirements for the future. This is a deliberate policy to ensure that ICI continues to have good access to this source of funds if required. ICI has recognized that this is a key element of its global financing policy. These banks have had a tendency to turn back to quality credits such as ICI when times get tough, and this source of 'reserves' has proved invaluable to ICI in the past. ICI will therefore continue to do its best to maintain the confidence of its house banks.

## External financing rules and policies

These general financing principles provide the context for funding behaviour in financial and banking markets. At this point, cost, currency and maturity issues dominate the funding decision, with location of market, method of funding and the choice of parent versus subsidiary to do the funding coming a close second.

Group investment, divestment and acquisition plans provide ICI treasury with some idea of the scale of external funds required in the years ahead.

## Proactive funding

ICI has a proactive funding policy, in that it tries to obtain funds in advance of its needs. This enhances the already high degree of flexibility in financing and ensures that ICI can withstand sudden changes in the firm's position or in financial markets.

## Funding mixture and interest rate risks

In its borrowing portfolio ICI tries to establish a stable mixture of fixed and floating rate funding such that floating funds do not exceed more than 30 per cent of total external debt. The group's medium and short funds are all variable rate funds. Long term funds are primarily fixed.

Floating rate funds are a small proportion (less than 30 per cent) of external debt and total debt is less than 25 per cent of funds. Thus floating rate funds are a very small proportion (less than 7.5 per cent) of total internal and external funding and have short and medium term maturities. This indicates that ICI faces very little interest rate risk from this source. The low proportion of variable rate funding is quite deliberate on ICI's part. Clements (1988) believes that ICI's asset cash flows are not inflation proof. Variable interest rates may increase to reflect increasing inflation or inflationary expectations but asset cash flows may only adjust slowly. In the 1970s and 1980s in a period of continuing inflation, the prices of many of ICI's products declined because of overcapacity in the chemicals industry. High variable rate funding in these circumstances could lead to questions about ICI's ability to service the debt and thus affect its all important credit rating. As a result ICI prefers to avoid this source of interest rate risk.

Fixed rate funds form less than 17.5 per cent of total funds generated internally and externally (i.e. 70 per cent of debt funds are fixed rate, and less than 25 per cent of all funds are debt). ICI believes that its business requires a relatively high percentage of fixed long term funding in its borrowing portfolio. This is presumably to gain some of the benefits of interest payments as a tax shelter, and to match interest payments with the 100 per cent certain component of asset cash flows. Given the low proportion of overall borrowing, the certain component of asset cash flows will exceed these interest payments many times over.

These fixed rate funds could be a significant source of interest rate risk if ICI secured these funds (primarily long term) when market rates were high and they subsequently turned out to be unexpectedly low. However, given the abundance of internal funds, ICI's treasury believes it can wait until it thinks long term fixed rates are at a historical low. Freeman (1990) provides some graphical evidence to suggest that ICI has been successful in avoiding raising long term funds in periods of very high interest rates. ICI has, in the 1970s and 1980s, been able to tap the UK and US long bond markets when nominal rates were low and avoid these markets when rates peaked.

As a result of these policies, ICI does not believe that it has a major interest rate risk problem and so it does not make much use of interest rate swaps, forward rate agreements and other interest rate insurance services available from the market.

### Opportunistic funding

The above example reveals that ICI does adopt an opportunistic policy with the prices and availability of funds raised externally. Given the relatively small amount of ICI's total funds involved, it is clear that ICI is quite risk averse even with this aspect of its funding policy. However, some funds are genuinely cheaper because of a host of imperfections such as tax. ICI continuously monitors the Eurobond and Eurocommercial paper markets and the large domestic markets to identify 'windows of opportunity' for cheap funding. If a cheap funding opportunity emerges (relative to market rates for the same level of risk), ICI has the capacity to rapidly produce the bond or loan prospectus and the close bank relations to rapidly arrange the funding. These opportunities for cheaper than market rate funding may arise from relationship banks identifying a short lived tax advantage in a market, or novel funding ideas may arise from non-relationship banks. The bank that identifies the cheap funding benefits will be allowed to lead the placement. In this way ICI creates a market for novel funding ideas. This policy, if taken too far, may undermine the core banking relationships to some extent.

### Maturity of long term funding and smoothing the repayments from the borrowing portfolio

ICI also tries to use its long term fixed rate funding decisions to produce a level repayment profile from its overall borrowing portfolio. The avoidance of large lumpy repayments in the short or medium term means that internal cash flows can continue to be used to fund expansion in a predictable manner. This can be difficult to achieve in periods when long term funding markets become thin. If the markets are active, then ICI will seek maturities and repayment profiles in new debt issues that fill in gaps in the existing schedule of repayments of borrowings. Thus the decision on maturity of long term debt is determined in part by market conditions and in part by the maturity structure of ICI's existing borrowing portfolio.

*Matching and currency risk*

At present, ICI seeks to match the currency exposures of its long term assets and liabilities as much as possible and to make as little use of the currency swaps markets as possible. It has tried to adopt this policy as best it can given market supply conditions. It has faced difficulties at times in securing sterling funds to match its extensive sterling assets. In the 1970s and up to the mid 1980s, the sterling bond market was quiescent. The growth of sterling Eurobonds solved this problem to some extent. In 1989, ICI faced difficulties with the restrictive covenant requirements of prospective UK institutional purchasers of ICI's Eurosterling bonds. This led ICI to issue two Australian dollar bonds to fund sterling assets. These were then both swapped into sterling at rates lower than the London inter-bank rate. This demonstrates the power of a stable, cash rich enterprise such as ICI relative to external suppliers. Currency swaps are generally used to alter the currency composition of the existing borrowing portfolio or of new loans so to achieve the aim of matching the currencies of assets and liabilities. Swaps are not used to make bets against exchange rate changes.

## Financial policy: a discussion

Long term organizational learning by ICI managers through periods of crisis and success has been a major determinant of this policy.

The recession of 1979–80 had a severe effect on ICI's profits and cash flows. The cutting of dividends in 1980 and low profits and cash flow levels in 1981 and 1982 meant that financial objectives such as return on shareholders' capital, margins on sales, and cash generation became a much higher priority in the 1980s and 1990s. The central control of cash provided early warning signs at group level and was one of the factors that allowed ICI to weather this storm in 1981–2. This recession caused a major restructuring of the group in the 1980s. ICI initially cut back on investment and built up its internal resources. Good financial results in 1984 heralded new expansion plans. From the beginning of a second recession in 1990–1, ICI implemented another extensive policy of cost cutting and restructuring. This accelerated in 1992 as the threat from Hanson Trust hovered over ICI (*Economist* 1992).

Organic growth within the existing subsidiaries appears to have been the basis for most investment decisions prior to the 1981–2 crisis. However, in

1984 ICI set up an acquisitions team. This team, managed (from 1986) by Alan Clements, the Finance Director of ICI, was given the task of identifying good acquisitions targets for ICI so that the firm could catch up on the ground lost in the early 1980s. This expansion need, expressed through the acquisition route, altered financing patterns in the 1980s in that ICI began to make extensive short term and medium term use of international capital markets. However, once an acquisition has been made, ICI has sought to return quickly to its conventional gearing levels and the heavy use of internal funds for expansion.

The indications are that ICI uses internal funds plus advance debt funding primarily to finance organic growth within the subsidiaries. Acquisitions are funded through quickly repaid short term debt, some long term debt and some internal funds. Thus funding is matched to the ability to pre-plan investments with certainty. In the first case, ICI can plan funding some years ahead and can thus fully deploy its internal financial advantages in financing organic growth. In the case of acquisitions or of opportunistic funding, ICI may have to raise funds at very short notice. Good credit ratings and excellent relationships with its core bankers mean that ICI can do this with confidence. The use of this combination of funding techniques appears to have been learnt in the 1980s and has created considerable flexibility in ICI's financing policy.

The firm has learnt over a much longer period that its business is inherently cyclical and that it is a capital intensive enterprise. This has led to periodic heavy demands for capital and with it the possibility that projects could be too large for ICI to finance. ICI, however, has a scientific knowledge basis that it does not wish to see dissipated through too many partnerships, collaborations or joint ventures. Many of the projects are of such a large scale that the project management skills of ICI managers and the financial controls of the ICI group are essential for project success. ICI group therefore seeks as full a control as is possible of its overseas subsidiaries and their new projects. This capability to fund a large proportion of these projects from internal funds has therefore become a central feature of ICI strategy.

This can be interpreted as ICI's means to stabilize the long term funding of its investment projects. This can be compared with its German and Japanese competitors with their heavier reliance on external bank debt and lead bank relations. ICI internalizes such lead bank relations by creating its own long term and stable internal capital market. In so doing, it creates a high degree of confidence with external suppliers of capital. This enhances its credit rating and thus the confidence of buyers of its securities such as Eurobonds and sterling and dollar commercial paper, as well as equity suppliers in the UK, the US, Europe and Japan. It also bolsters the confidence that the core group of relationship banks has in ICI. These capital supply advantages are important firm specific advantages (FSAs) for a firm operating in a global industry with strong German, Japanese and US competition.

ICI's approach bears some similarity to Donaldson's (1969) work on financial mobility in that it emphasizes the need to plan for the availability of funds for unanticipated demands. It differs in its much heavier emphasis on internal sources of funds, on the development of internal systems designed to identify, generate and move these funds, and on the imposition of a constraint on external funding and investment plans based on these internal funding levels.

As indicated previously, given the abundance of internal funds, ICI's treasury believes it can wait until it thinks long term fixed rates are at a historical low, and Freeman (1990) provides some support for this assertion. ICI treasury may be wrong in its timing expectation, in that long term rates may plummet after a major long term bond issue or fixed rate loan has been agreed. It may also mistake differences in nominal rates over time for the same real rate and should deflate nominal interest rates by historic inflation rates to see if the real rate has varied over these financing periods. It seems most unlikely that informationally efficient Euromarkets for bonds will provide ICI with cheap funds through timing alone. In addition, these funds may be supporting assets with different inflation characteristics and thus expose ICI to additional (net) inflation risk. This financing behaviour could also conceal a lack of good investment opportunities, or perhaps the possibility that ICI took a conservative view and delayed valuable projects in periods of high nominal interest rates and so did not need the external 'top up' funding. Alternatively, ICI could have made greater use of less publicly visible bank overdrafts and other short to medium term funds at these times, in order to avoid the high fixed interest rates for long term funds.

Finally, we should note that ICI's activity in debt markets involves very large deals. However, they are not the central funding decisions for ICI. The internal funding rule and the gearing rule dominate funding choices. ICI therefore has a conservative funding policy in that it minimizes its reliance on external suppliers and always tries to maintain itself in a dominant position relative to international financial markets and banks. It also uses its internal funding strength to acquire long term fixed rate debt in low interest periods, and both of these factors combine to reduce interest rate risk. Currency swaps are used to complete the currency matching of assets and liabilities. It is difficult to know if this is the optimum financing policy as far as shareholders are concerned. A heavier and riskier (from the managers' viewpoint) use of external funds in the 1970s might have allowed ICI to pursue its internationalization aims and increased profitability to the point where it could have avoided many of the problems encountered in the 1980–2 crisis. Alternatively, a riskier funding policy could have meant a loss of control for ICI management with some joint ventures or perhaps the whole firm. If shareholders' value depends crucially on the gradual development of managerial and scientific talent in the group and this is matched by the equivalent growth of internal funds, then the existing funding rules could be the best way for ICI to exploit its unique firm specific advantages.

Together these financial policy principles and funding rules form a set of decision heuristics that have been found to work for ICI management over the past two decades. They form a package of rules designed to provide the necessary funds to run the business and to avoid financial distress, illiquidity and insolvency. In general, they reflect the conservative, risk averse attitude of ICI to its funding problem and to interest rate risk and currency risk. They are considered by senior managers to be in the shareholders' interests, in that pursuit of these principles allows ICI to concentrate on maximizing value from its real business.

## 13.9 Summary

This chapter has focused on the external financing decision for the international firm. The concept of efficient (and inefficient) capital markets was discussed, and the possibility of capital market arbitrage by MNCs was identified. Financing and risk management decision rules were discussed in several different sets of economic circumstances.

This set the context for the discussion of the capital structure problem. This decision was seen to be dominated by home country capital markets, agency costs and transnational tax considerations. Given a corporate-wide capital structure decision, a very flexible range of subsidiary capital structures was possible. These sections provided the basis to analyse the global financing policy of the MNC. This policy considered how funding decisions can interact with risk management decisions and capital structure constraints and how together they can alter the riskiness of the firm's cash flows and the value of the firm. The ICI case provided further insight into these issues and revealed the amount of organizational learning over many decades involved in the formulation of a global financing policy.

# 14

# Financial Planning and Corporate Strategy

Chapters 1 to 13 have been concerned with analysing the major international corporate financial decisions. Each major decision area was viewed individually and implications were drawn for each area using conceptual frameworks drawn from finance theory, MNC theory and concepts of strategy.

These chapters will be briefly summarized in the following pages prior to considering joint investment, financing and exposure decision making. The latter analysis will be concerned with integrated financial planning issues and value interactions between investment, financing and currency risk decisions. In addition, the strategic context discussed in chapter 8 will provide the basis for considering the relationship between corporate strategy and financial planning in the MNC.

## 14.1 Summary of Previous Chapters

Chapter 1 began with a discussion of the nature of the MNC and the field of study of international financial management (IFM). The multinational was defined initially by its high degree of involvement in the world economy and its degree of control over its international operations. This simple classification scheme was supported by an attempt to describe the main features of multinationality. This was followed by an analysis of the international economic environment using three different but complementary sets of assumptions about markets and firms. This provided some insight into how changes in the economic circumstances faced by the firm or created by the firm can alter the significance of IFM decisions. The major issues and decision problems of IFM were then identified and the central concepts of finance and their primary areas of application in IFM decision making were briefly outlined. Finally, the nature of the treasury function in the MNC was discussed. Chapters 2 to 13 considered these issues in some detail, highlighting the role of central concepts of finance theory and unique aspects of IFM decision making.

In section 2.1 we began by investigating the nature of the international financial and monetary system. This section was primarily concerned with describing the system, by identifying its major institutional elements and the manner in which they relate to each other. In section 2.2 we described recent changes in this system.

In chapter 3, section 3.1 the neo-classical equilibrium theories linking interest rate changes, inflation and exchange rates were briefly outlined. These relationships were discussed in the context of the markets in which they were thought to prevail. Thus the Eurocurrency, Eurobond, equity and other international financial markets described in chapter 2 formed the institutional background for discussing interest rate (equity return) parity, the international Fisher effect, the unbiased forward rate effect and the international capital asset pricing model. To complete the framework, the purchasing parity theory was outlined.

In section 3.2 this neo–classical framework was then applied to three key decision areas in international financial management: foreign exchange risk management, financing decisions and capital budgeting decisions. If the equilibrium or parity relationships held then many of the issues of international financial management were shown to be illusions. Coping with the problems of IFM therefore became a question of using existing finance theory to see through these illusions to the fundamental financial problems common to all firms.

Few thinkers in the field of IFM urge the wholesale adoption of the neo-classical approach. It is generally seen in the literature as a valuable reference point, but in need of adaptation according to circumstances. The specific circumstances, and the appropriate management response, formed the focus of attention in chapters 3 to 13.

The rest of chapter 3 concentrated on imperfections in these international financial markets. It identified four major classes of parity deviation, and presented the evidence for and against the equilibrium framework. These discussions provided the basis for analysing the implications of such deviations for exposure management, financing and capital budgeting decisions in chapters 4 to 13.

From this analysis it was clear that under certain circumstances there were additional issues unique to international financial management. The central concern for management was to identify such circumstances, and to assess their significance for the firm, depending on its level of international involvement. The equilibrium framework was still considered valuable under the imperfections paradigm. Despite the problems outlined it was seen as a powerful pedagogic aid and managerial problem solving tool. It allowed managers to efficiently assimiliate very complex IFM phenomena and, if used in tandem with an explicit analysis of deviations, it encouraged managers to identify and respond to opportunities and threats in key IFM decision areas. It therefore enabled managers to look at IFM financial decisions from a common framework, and one that made extensive use of the central concepts of established finance theory such as efficient market notions, capital asset pricing and value additivity. Within this view there was no need for an alternative theory of IFM. What was required was the adaptation and application of existing finance theory to the additional complexities of the international environment and an explicit approach for dealing with deviations.

Chapters 4, 5, 6 and 7 demonstrated the range and complexity of foreign exchange risk management (FERM) methods available to the firm. Managers have to decide how to choose a combination of such methods to cope with the complexity of their unique FERM problem.

Chapter 8, section 8.1 considered the various theories of direct foreign investment (DFI) and sought to explain the corporate rationale behind these decisions, in particular the manner in which overseas projects are likely to generate additional wealth for the owners of the firm. Section 8.2 considered the nature of political risk and its impact on the overseas investment decision. Section 8.3 assessed how these theory sources could be used to guide the search for valuable overseas investment opportunities. Section 8.4 looked at how MNCs have developed their global strategy and the relationship between global strategy and the search for overseas investment opportunities.

Chapter 9 was concerned with analysis of the overseas capital budgeting decision. The global capital strategic analysis discussed in the previous chapter provided a key context for this chapter in that it aided the search for valuable overseas investment opportunities. The aim of chapter 9 was to try to combine the best insights of extant financial theory with the unique problems of the overseas corporate investment decision. This was done in such a way as to produce usable decision rules that fully employed available information.

Chapter 10 consisted of a case study in international capital budgeting. This case illustrated the difficulties managers face in generating basic information on project cash flows. The case included a detailed example of the capital budgeting problem faced by StrathKelvin. The example data were illustrated using the wide class of cash flow categories from the APV model. This provided the basis for the design of a simple spreadsheet financial model. The approach adopted in the case therefore provided managers with both the technology and a robust conceptual framework to tackle this complex decision area.

Chapters 11, 12 and 13 focused on the external financing decision for the international firm. Chapter 11 described the nature of international financial centres and other key sources of funds for the MNC. Chapter 12 dealt with the valuation of debt financing and the role of financing simulation models, and the potential for the development of a corporate financial planning model was identified. Chapter 13 began with the concept of efficient (and inefficient) capital markets. The possibility of capital market arbitrage by MNCs was identified. This set the context for the discussion of the capital structure and financing decisions. The former decision was seen to be dominated by home country capital markets, agency costs and transnational tax considerations. Given a corporate-wide capital structure decision and a very flexible range of subsidiary capital structures, a global financing strategy was outlined. ICI was employed as a detailed case to consider some of the practical difficulties in this decision area.

In chapters 3 to 13, an active opportunistic strategy was proposed for management facing deviations from equilibrium. The financial manager was seen as a reactive decision maker responding to externally created problems. In chapter 8, the financial manager was viewed as a member of an enterprise which was able to create and maintain such market imperfections. This view, in which the firm exercises considerable power, was in sharp contrast to the market perspective adopted in chapters 2 to 7 and 9 to 13. The MNC was seen as a firm that straddled many product, factor and capital markets. It had a unique knowledge of these markets and of transnational production decisions. This allowed it to influence allocations in these external markets, to supplant inefficient external markets with internal corporate markets, and to create internal markets when none existed externally. These strategic choices were seen to be constrained by the risks of political interference in the firms. The combination of strategic choice and political constraint had significant implications for the FERM, financing and capital budgeting decisions.

## 14.2 Developing a Corporate Financial Strategy

In chapters 4 to 13 the major international financial decisions have each been viewed as partially independent of the others. This has been a necessary step in understanding the unique international features of these decision areas. However, the senior financial managers of the internationally involved enterprise have to plan the joint effects of investment, financing and FERM decisions. Brealey and Myers (1981: 646) give three major reasons for developing financial plans:

1   The central financial decision areas interact and should be considered together.
2   Integrated financial planning can help managers to avoid foreseeable 'surprises' and to think ahead about how they can react to unavoidable surprises.
3   Financial planning helps establish concrete goals to motivate managers and provide standards for measuring performance.

Financial planning, then, is a process involving integrating the key financial decisions so as to avoid surprises and to make concrete financial choices. Such planning focuses on aggregate investment by division or line of business, and avoids getting bogged down in detail (p. 637). With these thoughts in mind we will turn to financial planning for the internationally involved company. This will focus on the aggregate investment, financing and exposure decisions. The aim is to develop a coherent corporate financial strategy to include insights from finance theory and the literature on the MNC and strategy. This involves integrating the major IFM decision areas such that progress can be made towards the shareholder wealth maximization goal.

### Neo-classicism and IFM planning

In the ideal world portrayed in section 3.1, a variety of market imperfections were ignored. These included taxes, capital market segmentation and various governmental actions.

In the neo-classical paradigm we are dealing with an ideal or 'first best' situation. The corporate finance objective of stockholder wealth maximization and the associated decision rules are logically linked to the underlying equilibrium theories of risky asset choice in efficient capital markets. These decision rules and shareholder wealth maximization are therefore internally consistent and emphasize the independence of the investment and financing decisions.

Under these ideal conditions, only the investment decision determines the value of the firm. Capital structure and currency risk management decisions are irrelevant. Managers should therefore expend their energies in seeking suitable investment opportunities in the pursuit of maximizing shareholder wealth. The sources of funds, interest rates and currency risks are considered irrelevant as they do not affect shareholder wealth. In this situation, financial planning is restricted to the identification and acquisition of investment opportunities. There are no problems of coping with interactions with other financial decision areas. The capital market performs this function and also provides the mechanism by which corporate performance is assessed. Firms that do not obey the very limited normative rules in section 3.1 for FERM, capital budgeting and financing decisions will be rapidly penalized by an omniscient capital market.

## Financial planning and imperfections

It is unlikely that managers, whilst acknowledging the power of market forces, would accept the above view of financial planning. In this they are supported by the evidence concerning deviations from parity and the inconclusive debates about the integration of world capital markets.

In a world in which there are imperfections in some domestic capital markets, in international goods markets and at the level of the firm, we are now dealing with 'second best' circumstances relative to the ideal of orthodox finance. These difficulties lead managers to employ simplifying solutions to the complexities of financial planning.

McInnes and Carleton (1982) investigated the use of financial theory and financial models in financial planning in large international companies. In their study they found a large gap between theory and practice in terms of the integration of investment and financing decisions. One of the fundamental propositions of normative theory is that strategic financial planning should treat investment and financing jointly, and integration should be achieved by means of constrained optimization based on shareholder utility. In practice, in their case firms there was often considerable separation between financing and investment decisions. The common logical pattern was to proceed from a plan for existing operations to a plan for new investments, and finally to a plan to finance these investments. Some information was recycled back through the planning process but the sequential process seemed to restrict a full consideration of the joint set of opportunities and constraints (p. 968). The authors argue that their work points to a substantial gap between theory and practice. Three major problems exist at this interface:

1   Actual financial planning systems do not generally provide the data for the analyses proposed by theory.
2   The theoretical treatment of uncertainty does not correspond in a satisfactory manner to the form in which it is experienced by financial managers.
3   There are major difficulties in formulating the financial planning problem in an optimizing framework.

It is clear from McInnes and Carleton's work that international financial managers are adopting crude 'rules of thumb' in their financial planning exercises as their solution to the limitations of financial theory and the very real informational, computational and risk management problems present in financial planning. These informational and computational problems and the problems of managing total risk mean that financial managers must develop some guidelines for overall financial policy and financial planning. These are the 'second best' circumstances in which managers and scholars agree there is a need for financial planning. There are now presumed to be value dependencies or interactions between investment, financing and FERM decisions. The major task for senior financial management is to identify these as part of a strategic analysis of the threats and opportunities facing the enterprise. The core problem of financial planning concerns the relationships between these decisions and the overall corporate financial goals. The international corporate finance literature generally advises the adoption of operational goals for each of the major financial decisions such that they are consistent with the goal of shareholder wealth maximization. This literature employs decision rules drawn from established concepts of finance. These are adapted to IFM circumstances such that shareholder wealth maximization is achieved by employing them. In the investment decision the goal is to accept positive NPV projects. For foreign exchange risk management decisions the operational goal is to minimize the impact of unexpected variations in real exchange rates on the home currency cash flows, and in financing it is to maximize additions to NPV. Thus all of these three decision areas are assumed to affect the level of net expected corporate cash flows and their riskiness and ultimately to affect the value of the firm. These sources of NPV can be identified for each decision area and for each major interaction.

Given these decision rules and operational goals, the financial planning task is to analyse the trade-offs between the central decision areas so that progress towards shareholder wealth maximization is achieved. Interactions and desirable trade-offs between these decision areas can be partially assessed within a financial plan by employing the fundamental decision rules of corporate finance. For example, the APV rule is a variant of the NPV rule designed to cope with the unique aspects of the overseas investment decision as well as to explicitly consider the value interactions between the investment and financing decisions in a project. The FERM decision has to be considered with both the investment and financing decisions. Thus a decision to match the currencies of assets and liabilities may affect project NPVs and financing costs. The explicit trade-off here is between loss of NPV and reduced currency risk. The reduced effect or influence of unanticipated real exchange rate changes on corporate value may therefore be offset by a decreased set of valuable financing opportunities.

It is apparent from the above that international corporate finance scholars are advocating second best solutions for second best (imperfections) financial policy decision situations. The selection of subgoals and second best decision rules involving trade-offs between investment, financing, capital structure and exposure decisions is, in part, a response to the severe analytical problems this poses for theory. These choices concerning appropriate financial planning decision rules are necessary because, in the current state of theory development, it is difficult to know how far away the second best situations (e.g. segmented capital markets) are from the first best situations (integrated markets). The evidence on the pricing relationships in international capital and foreign exchange markets, whilst inconclusive in many respects, does provide some support for the belief that under certain circumstances (e.g. in the major Western capital markets) the first best situation is close. However, when we consider capital markets outside the OECD countries it is very difficult to assess how suitable the subgoals (e.g. minimize variations in home currency returns due to unexpected real exchange rate changes) are for the second best situation. The difficulty of measuring the proximity of the latter situation to the ideal raises questions about the decision rules employed for financial planning decisions. For example, the APV rule may be maximizing a first best goal in circumstances far removed from first best conditions.

However, as Myers (1984) asserts, if finance theory is applied correctly it provides the best 'state of the art' decision rules for financial planners and strategic analysts. It still suffers from the problems outlined above, and clarifying a comprehensive financial planning framework under these conditions is a very complex task. Factors such as tax and intermittent government interference in markets mean that financial scholars have yet to make explicit a framework for analysing the trade-offs over time between the international capital budgeting, financing and foreign exchange risk management decisions.

In order to compensate for some of these problems, financial planners and strategic analysts can draw on developments elsewhere in economics and strategic analysis. From these perspectives firms are no longer seen solely as imperfections in markets. For example, the strategic perspective of chapter 8 can be seen as an alternative but complementary view of financial planning.

In addition, the financial planning problem can be broken down into manageable sections by adopting a simple planning sequence. Orthodox finance theory suggests that interactions between the major financial decision areas should be dealt with in a simultaneous manner. However, as McInnes and Carleton (1982) indicate, the informational, computational and risk management problems faced by MNC financial managers necessitate a separation between financing and investment decisions. Thus dealing with each decision area in relative isolation, followed by an analysis of interactions between all major decisions, can simplify some of these problems.

## 14.3 Financial Planning Sequence

Given the above arguments, the following financial planning sequence is proposed for an MNC:

1  Generate the set of new global investment projects and identify the levels of existing operations and areas of disinvestment expected over the plan period.
2  Satisfy global financing needs subject to opportunities and constraints.
3  Identify currency risk issues arising from this investment financing plan and outline the planned response.
4  Consider interactions between these decision areas.

5 Repeat steps 1 to 4 until managers feel that they have fully exploited all major information sources in the pursuit of shareholder wealth.

Investment decision making as the basic source of value is considered first, followed by the funding decision. Currency risk management, as an ancillary decision problem, is considered third. In each of steps 1, 2 and 3, one IFM decision area is dominant but the primary interactions with the other two areas are broadly considered. In step 4, all potential value interactions in the global investment, financing and currency risk plan are considered. This may lead to a major reconsideration of steps 1 and 2, and so on until a satisfactory plan is arrived at.

## Generating the set of global investment projects

A simple procedure to guide a global strategic analysis of overseas expansion opportunities was outlined in chapter 8.

The initial step is to identify world-wide opportunities for overseas expansion and to assess the strength and persistence of the imperfections underlying them. For example, if managers believe, on an *a priori* basis, that market growth and production cost economies are more likely in the Pacific Rim, Russia, Ukraine, Poland and Romania, and that these offer the best prospects for improving shareholder wealth, this can act as a guide to a much reduced global search for overseas investment opportunities. Alternatively, if the firm has the resources it can systematically scan world markets and production locations to identify investment opportunities.

Dunning's (1979) work on the eclectic theory of international production can be used to give further detailed guidance on the above search. It may be particularly valuable in identifying how combinations of ownership specific, location specific and internalization advantages create investment opportunities. This may be useful in combating the limitations of orthodox finance theory in identifying positive NPV opportunities. An understanding of the firm's unique ownership specific advantages is an essential element in the investment opportunity search process. These advantages may derive from unique corporate attributes such as heavy investment in research and development and in the general marketing function. According to Dunning, they may also be attributed to industry and country characteristics. Thus factors such as home market size and extent of product differentiation in an industry may contribute to the ownership specific advantages held by a firm.

In the second step of the global investment strategy, managers can employ the ownership, location and internalization factors to distinguish DFI opportunities from disinvestment, licensing and exporting opportunities. This requires an examination of the perceived opportunity to see if location and ownership specific advantages are likely to persist and an assessment of the relative costs of transacting in the firm and in the overseas market. In addition, the firm should assess its potential for achieving transaction cost economies relative to the market being considered. This may be achieved through the introduction of new organizational structures which reduce internal research, contracting and monitoring (hierarchical control) costs.

The third step in the global strategy involves evaluating each overseas expansion choice. Thus DFI, disinvestment, licensing and exporting options can be defined as different capital budgeting projects. The final step of this strategic analysis involves the choice of projects on the basis of their positive NPV contributions to the firm.

The simple strategic procedure outlined above can be extended to include corporate assessments of political risk in each step of the analysis. In general, the issues here can best be addressed by considering the impact of likely government actions on ownership specific, location specific and internalization advantages.

The formal strategy outlined above can serve as a central co-ordinating device for capital budgeting in the MNC. The outcome of this process is a set of new projects, an assessment of existing operations and a package of disinvestment decisions which together are likely to require extensive internal and external financing.

## Global financing needs: opportunities and constraints

The first part of the global financing strategy consists of two parallel activities. One is the assessment of world-wide financing requirements and surpluses stemming from existing operations and from new investment plans. Financing requirements will flow from an analysis of policies on acquisition, organic growth, portfolio investment in firms and disinvestment. This analysis should help the firm in assessing by how much total expenditure will exceed internal cash generation, and therefore the scale of the external financing problem. The role of the MNC's internal financial transfer and information system in exploiting internal (and some external) global financing opportunities arising will be crucial to this analysis.

The other activity is the identification of the range over which the parent capital structure is allowed to vary in the home country capital market. Alternatively, if the firm raises its equity and debt in a core group of major Western capital markets, then it must identify the capital structure range deemed appropriate by these suppliers of capital. This may be achieved by comparing the firm with other international firms operating in similar global industries. Direct discussions with capital market participants such as financial analysts and international bankers will also be of value. The capital structure range will provide the basic information to plan required levels of external equity and debt financing.

Assuming that financing decisions (especially debt) are made within the constraints imposed by corporate capital structure requirements, the funding sequence is as follows:

1   Finance initially with internal funds.
2   Fund the residual financing requirements via the close relationship banks. Thus loans provided directly by the relationship banks and bonds underwritten or possibly purchased and sold by these banks will be the next source of funds.
3   Fund the remaining debt finance requirements from the marketplace via transaction oriented banks. Thus loans may be raised from banks with whom no business has been done in the past. New bank partners may provide additional underwriting and placing services for publicly issued corporate bonds.

The mix between close bank suppliers and transaction bank suppliers of loans will depend on a variety of factors including bank capacity, corporate requirements for the influence of market prices, and treasury sophistication or the capability to search and negotiate many funding sources.

## Currency risk issues

Given the initial analysis of the global investment and financing plans, the firm can assess to what extent these plans expose it to unanticipated changes in real exchange rates. This risk assessment can be interpreted through the firm's FERM goals and policy and this leads to a set of planned corporate responses to currency risk.

The firm can make alterations to its existing global investment plans, its overall financial policy, and its expected set of operational policies. This is the first logical priority response to currency risk, and it leaves the firm free to plan to use internal and external financial techniques to deal with the remaining elements of its potential currency risk management problem.

The overall value impact of all major FERM methods is the final guiding criterion for choice. Each FERM method will have a different impact on corporate value, but it is the overall impact of all methods chosen that must be used to assess the effectiveness of the FERM methods mix.

Strategic and operational changes are a vital first means to deal with the currency risk consequences of potential real changes in exchange rates. Strategy is the dominant focus of corporate decision making, followed by real operational decisions. Strategic investment and real operating decisions are the basic source of wealth for the enterprise. They are central to the survival and growth of the firm and are made with the aim of maximizing shareholder wealth. Given that they are the basic source of value for the firm, they are the priority point at which to begin FERM decision making before the firm employs internal or external financial techniques. This is a logical priority rather than a time based priority. In practice the firm must simultaneously employ both real and financial responses to currency risk in the same period.

Thus managers should incorporate existing forecasts of changes in exchange rates, in exposure and in demands for financial services into the development of strategy. Alterations can be made to strategy to reflect these expected changes. The strategic decisions can also be made in such a way as to ensure that strategy is not a 'hostage to (foreign exchange rate) fortune'. Thus some thought should be given at the planning stage to increasing the responsiveness of strategic (operational and financial policy) decisions to unknown changes in exchange rate.

The aim here is to protect real decisions as the basic source of wealth or to adjust them to enhance this wealth. The financial policy aim is to protect or increase the expected cash flows resulting from real decisions or to stabilize or reduce the variability of these cash flows (or both). In a currency risk context this can be interpreted as aiming to reduce the impact of unanticipated (real) exchange rate changes on the firm's expected home currency cash flows. The more stable these HC cash flows and the higher their expected value then the more valuable they become.

## Overall interactions between investment, financing and FERM decisions

The shareholder wealth relationships between investment, financing and FERM decisions and the overall corporate financial goals are shown in figure 14.1.

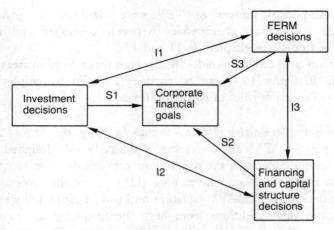

**Figure 14.1** Shareholder wealth relationships

The conventional goal of corporate finance, conceived within the field of domestic finance theory, is to maximize shareholder wealth. In the field of IFM and under the assumption of market imperfections, this is conventionally taken as an ideal to aim for. Shareholder wealth maximization is seen as a desirable target to move towards but one that is not fully achievable with existing theoretical prescriptions.

In the investment decision the goal was to accept positive NPV projects. For FERM decisions the goal was to minimize the impact of unexpected variations in exchange rate on the HC cash flows, and in financing it was to maximize additions to NPV. Thus all of these three decision areas are assumed to affect net expected corporate cash flows and their riskiness and ultimately to affect the value of the firm. These sources of NPV (S1, S2, S3 in figure 14.1) have been identified in previous chapters for each decision area and for each major interaction.

For example, in capital budgeting, positive NPVs stem both from firm specific advantages such as unique firm knowledge, technology and market power and from location specific advantages (see chapter 8 for details of the sources of positive NPV in the overseas capital budgeting projects). In the currency risk exposure decision, potential losses of NPV were identified in situations where PPP held generally between economies but where a firm's specific input/output prices deviated from parity. In circumstances where a firm has more control over its economic exposure than competitors (e.g. through more control over market prices), additions to NPV are possible through the FERM decisions (see chapters 4 and 5). In the financing decision, additional sources of NPV were identified in government subsidized funds, tax asymmetries between countries and internal transfers of funds (see chapters 6, 11 and 12).

Interactions and desirable trade-offs between these decision areas (i.e. I1, I2 and I3 in figure 14.1) can be partially assessed by employing the fundamental decision rules of corporate finance.

*Capital budgeting and value interactions with financing and FERM decisions*
For example, the APV rule is a variant of the NPV rule designed to cope with the unique aspects of the overseas investment decision as well as to explicitly consider the value interactions (I2) between the investment and financing decisions. The APV equation outlined in chapter 9 specifically identifies the value additions from both the financing and investment decisions as well as including other sources of value. Thus cheap funds, additions to debt capacity and other valuable financing implications of a project can be assessed.

Currency risk may have a serious effect on the expected level and riskiness of home country project cash flows. In the case of non-contractual project cash flows, if purchasing power parity holds, an analysis based upon cash flows stated in units of constant purchasing power and discounted at a real rate of interest (plus a systematic risk premium) seems appropriate. Alternatively, PPP may hold generally between economies, but there may be significant changes expected in project specific (relative) prices. These relative prices can have a large impact on the value of the project compared with deviations from PPP and they will therefore need to be considered in the (real) analysis above. In both cases, the additions or reductions to project value must be incorporated in the analysis.

An analysis of the interactions between capital budgeting and other major financial decisions is crucial for both the evaluation and management of the set of planned new projects. In the latter case, this information can help the board and project managers to assess project responsiveness to unanticipated events such as real exchange rate changes, interest rate changes or changes in the availability of funding. If, at this stage, managers feel that the proposed set of projects cannot respond flexibly to a wide range of uncertain and risky contingencies this may colour the way in which they evaluate the set of projects. Specifically, they may adjust these data to reflect the risk management problem associated with the project or choose decision models which allow them to control the choice of risky projects. Such a focus on the total risk of the firm and its new set of projects and the managerial capacity to deal with total risk is inconsistent with the orthodox precepts of financial theory, but it is consistent with avoiding shareholder wealth penalties caused by not managing total risk. Wilson (1988) provides some recent UK insight into such managerial behaviour. In his sample he showed how many UK MNCs separated out risk and return decisions and in some cases pursued risk minimization as the primary goal of international capital budgeting.

It is clear from McInnes and Carleton's (1982) and Wilson's (1988) empirical research that international financial managers are adopting crude 'rules of thumb' in their capital budgeting planning exercises. These are their managerial solutions to the limitations of financial theory in dealing with the interactions between international capital budgeting, financing and foreign exchange risk management decisions and with potential problems of managing many risky projects.

*Financing decisions and value interactions with FERM and capital budgeting decisions*

The global funding policy is conducted subject to the following needs:

- to secure funds at lowest cost for each type of funds, i.e. bonds versus loans
- to maintain a close link with and a stable supply of funds from banks and capital markets
- to exploit links between financing and real decisions
- to reduce currency, interest rate and political risks facing the firm.

The common thread running through all of these objectives is their impact on the present value of the overall financial package chosen by the firm. The pursuit of each objective will have its own differential impact on wealth, and thus an overall trade-off has to be established between these objectives. For example, the pursuit of cheap funds may undermine long established and difficult to acquire relationships with commercial and investment bankers. These relationships may be providing a valuable insurance scheme against funding supply risks.

The firm can assess the implications of funding needs, risk management and links with real decisions for the overall financing package and its overall costs by comparing two funding packages. One is based on funding cost minimization consistent with the use of existing relationship bankers, with acceptable (to managers) levels of political and financial risks, and with providing additional support for strategic decisions. The other is based on funding cost minimization as the sole priority. Funding choices involve relationship bankers, acceptable risk levels etc. only if they are the least financing cost solution.

Thus the extra funding costs of a flexible and secure funds supply via relationship banks, reduced financial and political risks, and the provision of additional support for real decisions can be compared with the benefits (wealth impact) of achieving these objectives. In this way, financing cost minimization can be recognized as a central aim of global financing, without it becoming the sole aim of such a planning activity.

Finally, major interactions can occur between financing and capital structure decisions. In chapter 13 the size and risk of expected asset cash flows and therefore firm value were shown to be dependent in part upon capital structure. This also is considered to be the case for an MNC raising most of its equity and debt capital in one capital market, i.e. its home currency market. The world-wide capital structure recognized by this market is therefore taken as dominating all subsidiaries' capital structures. These are seen as contributing to the world-wide capital structure and affecting the home currency market view of financial distress, tax benefits and agency cost. The corporate goal under these circumstances is to achieve or maintain the MNC capital structure within the requirements of the home currency capital market. The MNC has considerable flexibility in varying the capital structures of its subsidiaries to achieve this goal. It can therefore vary local capital structures within national norms and constraints. These provide the boundaries within which the firm can pursue a value maximization goal for the financing decision.

### ✗ FERM decisions and interactions with financing, investment and other real decisions

The FERM decision has to be considered with both the investment and financing decision (I1 and I3 in figure 14.1). Thus the decision to match assets and liabilities may affect project NPVs and financing costs. The explicit trade-off here was between loss of NPV and reduced currency risk. The reduced effect or influence of unanticipated exchange rate events on corporate value may therefore be offset by a decreased set of valuable financing opportunities.

The following illustrates the shareholder wealth questions to be asked concerning interactions between strategic and operational real decisions and currency risk:

1   Is basic value protected or enhanced by relocation, R&D, or new product and market niche decisions to reduce the impact of currency risk?

2   Are pricing, sourcing, and production changes for currency risk etc. a short term source of profit?

3   Are they at the expense of long term sources of value from strategic decisions?

4   Compare the NPV of new projects before and after managing currency risk through real changes: has the penalty value loss of not managing risk been reduced?

5   Does investment outlay on treasury and internal financial systems produce returns or added value that are otherwise unavailable to the firm?

6   Can treasury exploit major imperfections to make profit and add unique value from finance?

7   Does the use of treasury systems reduce currency risk, the variability of HC cash flows and default risk at the expense of basic value?

The portfolio of FERM methods can create a time overlap between available methods and offer unique solutions to unique problems. In some cases market based methods may create time or flexibility for strategic and operational responses. In contrast, strategic methods such as currency risk sharing amongst project partners may be the means to counteract lack of availability or flexibility of risk instruments. Strategic decisions may also create the conditions for operational flexibility. Finally, the sophistication of internal financial transfer systems can have a strong impact on the need for external financial risk instruments. We can therefore see that the beneficial interactions possible within the whole portfolio of methods may be of considerable value to an enterprise and shareholders and can greatly enhance corporate flexibility relative to currency risk. These benefits are only available if the firm can employ the full set of methods open to it.

## 14.4 Basic Framework of the Book

This book has been primarily concerned with the unique international aspects of corporate financial decision making. As such it has drawn heavily on the existing theory of corporate finance. In addition alternative theory constructs have been introduced both to explain IFM phenomena and to provide operational decision rules for the international financial manager.

Figure 14.2 summarizes the basic framework employed in this book. The use of particular elements of this framework is common throughout the IFM literature. However, the parity theories and the domestic financial

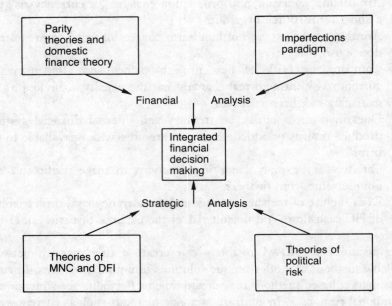

**Figure 14.2** IFM framework used in this book

management (DOFM) theory are usually the only explicit theory constructs employed. Imperfections are generally dealt with on an *ad hoc* basis and so the classification scheme outlined in chapter 3 is valuable in that it offers a more structured approach to the manager. Political risk analyses and theories of MNC economic behaviour are conventionally employed with respect to the investment decision alone, and their broader role in comprehending the problems associated with all major IFM decisions is ignored.

The framework shown is therefore explicit in two novel ways. Firstly, some elements such as the imperfections paradigm are employed across all major financial decisions. Secondly, their interrelationships have been explored at the level of the individual IFM decision and at the level of integrated financial planning.

This framework has proved invaluable in exploring the significance of the field of study of IFM and the relevance of existing domestic corporate finance theory for IFM problem solving. It has also been central to this chapter in which financial planning has been considered from a neo-classical perspective, an imperfections paradigm perspective and finally from a strategic perspective. The emphasis in the third view has been: given certain economic theories about the MNC and a framework for political risk analysis, how should a firm identify strategic aspects of the overseas capital budgeting, financing and exposure decisions? This is one point of departure for placing financial planning within the context of global strategic planning by the MNC. A second approach considers what is generally known about such global planning and considers how financial planning might be related to corporate strategy. This descriptive view of global strategic planning was considered in chapter 8.

International financial planning as outlined in previous sections must also be analysed within the context of a global plan to ensure that the financial aspects of strategic planning are consistent with the basic aims and philosophy of the business, its competitive posture in international markets, the major opportunities and risks currently known, the action programmes of the business and the contingency strategies currently adopted. Overseas capital budgeting projects must therefore be analysed within the general global strategy of the firm, with the NPV rule being used to question the basic assumptions of the strategy and its general direction. In a similar fashion, financing and exposure plans must be consistent with the global strategy by ensuring that the full financial benefits of these decisions are achieved subject to the operational action programmes and contingency plans. Sections 14.2 and 14.3 and indeed much of the content of this book can therefore be seen as providing the essential financial discipline in the global planning exercise of the multinational firm. In particular, the ability of finance to impose more explicit goals on the global planning process, and in many cases, clear modes of analysis may help managers of the multinational enterprise to obtain a clearer view of the woods rather than the trees.

This book therefore identifies the detailed financial aspects of global financial planning in chapters 2 to 13. In chapter 8 the search for valuable overseas investment projects and the nature of global strategic planning were investigated. In this chapter the essential links between financial planning and strategic plans have been identified. These, when placed within the context of a global planning exercise, can stimulate an iterative interchange of information and ideas within the financial and strategic planning framework. This approach can release corporate finance from its relative isolation from other developments in corporate decision theory and allow the unique insights of finance to be exploited on a wider stage. Finally, placing IFM decision making within the context of the theories and strategic analyses of chapter 8 may help counteract some of the limitations identified in financial theory in the key area of integrated financial planning.

# Appendix 1: Linear Programming Run for Netting Problem

See section 6.4. Units: X and PAY/REC in £million, transfer costs in weight $\times 10^4$, objective in £ $\times 10^{-2}$.

TABLEAU BEFORE ANY ITERATIONS

| X1 | X2 | X3 | X4 | X5 | X6 | X7 | X8 | X9 | | | | | | | PAY/REC |
|----|----|----|----|----|----|----|----|----|----|----|----|----|----|----|---------|
| 1 | 1 | 1 | 0 | 0 | 0 | 0 | 0 | 0 | 1 | 0 | 0 | 0 | 0 | 0 | 19 |
| 0 | 0 | 0 | 1 | 1 | 1 | 0 | 0 | 0 | 0 | 1 | 0 | 0 | 0 | 0 | 52 |
| 0 | 0 | 0 | 0 | 0 | 0 | 1 | 1 | 1 | 0 | 0 | 1 | 0 | 0 | 0 | 10 |
| 1 | 0 | 0 | 1 | 0 | 0 | 1 | 0 | 0 | 0 | 0 | 0 | 1 | 0 | 0 | 54 |
| 0 | 1 | 0 | 0 | 1 | 0 | 0 | 1 | 0 | 0 | 0 | 0 | 0 | 1 | 0 | 17 |
| 0 | 0 | 1 | 0 | 0 | 1 | 0 | 0 | 1 | 0 | 0 | 0 | 0 | 0 | 1 | 10 |
| -10 | -10 | -11 | -8 | -7.5 | -8.8 | -11 | -11 | -12 | 0 | 0 | 0 | 0 | 0 | 0 | 0 |

CHOSEN COL. IS 1 CHOSEN ROW IS 1 AND RATIO IS 19
PIVOT VALUE = 1

TAB. AFTER ONE ITERATION

| 1 | 1 | 1 | 0 | 0 | 0 | 0 | 0 | 0 | 1 | 0 | 0 | 0 | 0 | 0 | 19 |
|----|----|----|----|----|----|----|----|----|----|----|----|----|----|----|-----|
| 0 | 0 | 0 | 1 | 1 | 1 | 0 | 0 | 0 | 0 | 1 | 0 | 0 | 0 | 0 | 52 |
| 0 | 0 | 0 | 0 | 0 | 0 | 1 | 1 | 1 | 0 | 0 | 1 | 0 | 0 | 0 | 10 |
| 0 | -1 | -1 | 1 | 0 | 0 | 1 | 0 | 0 | -1 | 0 | 0 | 1 | 0 | 0 | 35 |
| 0 | 1 | 0 | 0 | 1 | 0 | 0 | 1 | 0 | 0 | 0 | 0 | 0 | 1 | 0 | 17 |
| 0 | 0 | 1 | 0 | 0 | 1 | 0 | 0 | 1 | 0 | 0 | 0 | 0 | 0 | 1 | 10 |
| 0 | 0 | -1 | -8 | -7.5 | -8.8 | -11 | -11 | -12 | 10 | 0 | 0 | 0 | 0 | 0 | 190 |

CHOSEN COL. IS 4 CHOSEN ROW IS 4 AND RATIO IS 35
PIVOT VALUE = 1

TAB. AFTER 2 ITERATIONS

| | | | | | | | | | | | | | | | |
|---|---|---|---|---|---|---|---|---|---|---|---|---|---|---|---|
| 1 | 1 | 1 | 0 | 0 | 0 | 0 | 0 | 0 | 1 | 0 | 0 | 0 | 0 | 0 | 19 |
| 0 | 1 | 1 | 0 | 1 | 1 | -1 | 0 | 0 | 1 | 1 | 0 | -1 | 0 | 0 | 17 |
| 0 | 0 | 0 | 0 | 0 | 0 | 1 | 1 | 1 | 0 | 0 | 1 | 0 | 0 | 0 | 10 |
| 0 | -1 | -1 | 1 | 0 | 0 | 1 | 0 | 0 | -1 | 0 | 0 | 1 | 0 | 0 | 35 |
| 0 | 1 | 0 | 0 | 1 | 0 | 0 | 1 | 0 | 0 | 0 | 0 | 0 | 1 | 0 | 17 |
| 0 | 0 | 1 | 0 | 0 | 1 | 0 | 0 | 1 | 0 | 0 | 0 | 0 | 0 | 1 | 10 |

| 0 | -8 | -9 | 0 | -7.5 | -8.8 | -3 | -11 | -12 | 2 | 0 | 0 | 8 | 0 | 0 | 470 |

CHOSEN COL. IS 2 CHOSEN ROW IS 2 AND RATIO IS 17

PIVOT VALUE = 1

TAB. AFTER 3 ITERATIONS

| | | | | | | | | | | | | | | | |
|---|---|---|---|---|---|---|---|---|---|---|---|---|---|---|---|
| 1 | 0 | 0 | 0 | -1 | -1 | 1 | 0 | 0 | 0 | -1 | 0 | 1 | 0 | 0 | 2 |
| 0 | 1 | 1 | 0 | 1 | 1 | -1 | 0 | 0 | 1 | 1 | 0 | -1 | 0 | 0 | 17 |
| 0 | 0 | 0 | 0 | 0 | 0 | 1 | 1 | 1 | 0 | 0 | 1 | 0 | 0 | 0 | 10 |
| 0 | 0 | 0 | 1 | 1 | 1 | 0 | 0 | 0 | 0 | 1 | 0 | 0 | 0 | 0 | 52 |
| 0 | 0 | -1 | 0 | 0 | -1 | 1 | 1 | 0 | -1 | -1 | 0 | 1 | 1 | 0 | 0 |
| 0 | 0 | 1 | 0 | 0 | 1 | 0 | 0 | 1 | 0 | 0 | 0 | 0 | 0 | 1 | 10 |

| 0 | 0 | -1 | 0 | .5 | -.8 | -11 | -11 | -12 | 10 | 8 | 0 | 0 | 0 | 0 | 606 |

CHOSEN COL. IS 7 CHOSEN ROW IS 5 AND RATIO IS 0

PIVOT VALUE = 1

TAB. AFTER 4 ITERATIONS

| | | | | | | | | | | | | | | | |
|---|---|---|---|---|---|---|---|---|---|---|---|---|---|---|---|
| 1 | 0 | 1 | 0 | -1 | 0 | 0 | -1 | 0 | 1 | 0 | 0 | 0 | -1 | 0 | 2 |
| 0 | 1 | 0 | 0 | 1 | 0 | 0 | 1 | 0 | 0 | 0 | 0 | 0 | 1 | 0 | 17 |
| 0 | 0 | 1 | 0 | 0 | 1 | 0 | 0 | 1 | 1 | 1 | 1 | -1 | -1 | 0 | 10 |
| 0 | 0 | 0 | 1 | 1 | 1 | 0 | 0 | 0 | 0 | 1 | 0 | 0 | 0 | 0 | 52 |
| 0 | 0 | -1 | 0 | 0 | -1 | 1 | 1 | 0 | -1 | -1 | 0 | 1 | 1 | 0 | 0 |
| 0 | 0 | 1 | 0 | 0 | 1 | 0 | 0 | 1 | 0 | 0 | 0 | 0 | 0 | 1 | 10 |
| 0 | 0 | -12 | 0 | .5 | -11.8 | 0 | 0 | -12 | -1 | -3 | 0 | 11 | 11 | 0 | 606 |

CHOSEN COL. IS 3 CHOSEN ROW IS 1 AND RATIO IS 2

PIVOT VALUE = 1

TAB. AFTER 5 ITERATIONS

| | | | | | | | | | | | | | | | |
|---|---|---|---|---|---|---|---|---|---|---|---|---|---|---|---|
| 1 | 0 | 1 | 0 | -1 | 0 | 0 | -1 | 0 | 1 | 0 | 0 | 0 | -1 | 0 | 2 |
| 0 | 1 | 0 | 0 | 1 | 0 | 0 | 1 | 0 | 0 | 0 | 0 | 0 | 1 | 0 | 17 |
| -1 | 0 | 0 | 0 | 1 | 1 | 0 | 1 | 1 | 0 | 1 | 1 | -1 | 0 | 0 | 8 |
| 0 | 0 | 0 | 1 | 1 | 1 | 0 | 0 | 0 | 0 | 1 | 0 | 0 | 0 | 0 | 52 |
| 1 | 0 | 0 | 0 | -1 | -1 | 1 | 0 | 0 | 0 | -1 | 0 | 1 | 0 | 0 | 2 |
| -1 | 0 | 0 | 0 | 1 | 1 | 0 | 1 | 1 | -1 | 0 | 0 | 0 | 1 | 1 | 8 |
| 12 | 0 | 0 | 0 | -11.5 | -11.8 | 0 | -12 | -12 | 11 | -3 | 0 | 11 | -1 | 0 | 630 |

CHOSEN COL. IS 5 CHOSEN ROW IS 3 AND RATIO IS 8

PIVOT VALUE = 1

TAB. AFTER 6 ITERATIONS

| | | | | | | | | | | | | | | | |
|---|---|---|---|---|---|---|---|---|---|---|---|---|---|---|---|
| 0 | 0 | 1 | 0 | 0 | 1 | 0 | 0 | 1 | 1 | 1 | 1 | -1 | -1 | 0 | 10 |
| 1 | 1 | 0 | 0 | 0 | -1 | 0 | 0 | -1 | 0 | -1 | -1 | 1 | 1 | 0 | 9 |
| -1 | 0 | 0 | 0 | 1 | 1 | 0 | 1 | 1 | 0 | 1 | 1 | -1 | 0 | 0 | 8 |
| 1 | 0 | 0 | 1 | 0 | 0 | 0 | -1 | -1 | 0 | 0 | -1 | 1 | 0 | 0 | 44 |
| 0 | 0 | 0 | 0 | 0 | 0 | 1 | 1 | 1 | 0 | 0 | 1 | 0 | 0 | 0 | 10 |
| 0 | 0 | 0 | 0 | 0 | 0 | 0 | 0 | 0 | -1 | -1 | -1 | 1 | 1 | 1 | 0 |
| .5 | 0 | 0 | 0 | 0 | -.3 | 0 | -.5 | -.5 | 11 | 8.5 | 11.5 | -.5 | -1 | 0 | 722 |

NOW FEASIBLE: LOOK FOR IMPROVEMENTS

CHOSEN COL. IS 1 CHOSEN ROW IS 2 AND RATIO IS 9

PIVOT VALUE = 1

TAB. AFTER 7 ITERATIONS

| | | | | | | | | | | | | | | | |
|---|---|---|---|---|---|---|---|---|---|---|---|---|---|---|---|
| 0 | 0 | 1 | 0 | 0 | 1 | 0 | 0 | 1 | 1 | 1 | 1 | -1 | -1 | 0 | 10 |
| 1 | 1 | 0 | 0 | 0 | -1 | 0 | 0 | -1 | 0 | -1 | -1 | 1 | 1 | 0 | 9 |
| 0 | 1 | 0 | 0 | 1 | 0 | 0 | 1 | 0 | 0 | 0 | 0 | 0 | 1 | 0 | 17 |
| 0 | -1 | 0 | 1 | 0 | 1 | 0 | -1 | 0 | 0 | 1 | 0 | 0 | -1 | 0 | 35 |
| 0 | 0 | 0 | 0 | 0 | 0 | 1 | 1 | 1 | 0 | 0 | 1 | 0 | 0 | 0 | 10 |
| 0 | 0 | 0 | 0 | 0 | 0 | 0 | 0 | 0 | -1 | -1 | -1 | 1 | 1 | 1 | 0 |

| | | | | | | | | | | | | | | | |
|---|---|---|---|---|---|---|---|---|---|---|---|---|---|---|---|
| 0 | -.5 | 0 | 0 | 0 | .2 | 0 | -.5 | 0 | 11 | 9 | 12 | -1 | -1.5 | 0 | 717.5 |

CHOSEN COL. IS 6 CHOSEN ROW IS 1 AND RATIO IS 10

PIVOT VALUE = 1

TAB. AFTER 8 ITERATIONS

| | | | | | | | | | | | | | | | |
|---|---|---|---|---|---|---|---|---|---|---|---|---|---|---|---|
| 0 | 0 | 1 | 0 | 0 | 1 | 0 | 0 | 1 | 1 | 1 | 1 | -1 | -1 | 0 | 10 |
| 1 | 1 | 1 | 0 | 0 | 0 | 0 | 0 | 0 | 1 | 0 | 0 | 0 | 0 | 0 | 19 |
| 0 | 1 | 0 | 0 | 1 | 0 | 0 | 1 | 0 | 0 | 0 | 0 | 0 | 1 | 0 | 17 |
| 0 | -1 | -1 | 1 | 0 | 0 | 0 | -1 | -1 | -1 | 0 | -1 | 1 | 0 | 0 | 25 |
| 0 | 0 | 0 | 0 | 0 | 0 | 1 | 1 | 1 | 0 | 0 | 1 | 0 | 0 | 0 | 10 |
| 0 | 0 | 0 | 0 | 0 | 0 | 0 | 0 | 0 | -1 | -1 | -1 | 1 | 1 | 1 | 0 |

| | | | | | | | | | | | | | | | |
|---|---|---|---|---|---|---|---|---|---|---|---|---|---|---|---|
| 0 | -.5 | -.2 | 0 | 0 | 0 | 0 | -.5 | -.2 | 10.8 | 8.8 | 11.8 | -.8 | -1.3 | 0 | 715.5 |

NO FURTHER IMPROVEMENT POSSIBLE

ANSWERS TO NETTING

PRIMAL VARS:

| VARIABLE | VALUE | OBJECT | NAME |
|---|---|---|---|
| 1 | 19 | 10 | X1 |
| 4 | 25 | 8 | X4 |
| 5 | 17 | 7.5 | X5 |
| 6 | 10 | 8.8 | X6 |
| 7 | 10 | 11 | X7 |

DUAL VARS:

VARIABLE VALUE

REAL VARIABLES:

| 2 | -.5 | X2 |
|---|---|---|
| 3 | -.2 | X3 |
| 8 | -.5 | X8 |
| 9 | -.2 | X9 |

VALUE OF OBJECTIVE: 715.5

**Sensitivity Analysis**

RANGE IS:
(UKP) 54 to 64
(FRP) 17 to 27
(WGP) 0 to 10
(AUSR) 9 to 19
(HKR) 42 to 52
(USR) 10 to infinity

*SENS. ON OBJ. COEFFS*

(VARIABLE: X1)
THE DECREASE IS NOT BOUNDED.
BOUND ON INCREASE IS .1999998 .
IE RANGE IS 10 PLUS OR MINUS ABOVE

(VARIABLE: X2)
BOUND ON DECREASE IS .5 .
THE INCREASE IS NOT BOUNDED.
IE RANGE IS 10 PLUS OR MINUS ABOVE

(VARIABLE: X3)
BOUND ON DECREASE IS .1999998 .
THE INCREASE IS NOT BOUNDED.
IE RANGE IS 11 PLUS OR MINUS ABOVE

(VARIABLE: X4)
BOUND ON DECREASE IS .1999998 .
THE INCREASE IS NOT BOUNDED.
IE RANGE IS 8 PLUS OR MINUS ABOVE

(VARIABLE: X5)
THE DECREASE IS NOT BOUNDED.
BOUND ON INCREASE IS 0.499999
VAR. 5 WILL LEAVE BASIS.
IE RANGE IS 7.5 PLUS OR MINUS ABOVE

(VARIABLE: X6)
BOUND ON INCREASE IS .19999998
THE DECREASE IS NOT BOUNDED.
IE RANGE IS 8.8 PLUS OR MINUS ABOVE

(VARIABLE: X8)
BOUND ON DECREASE IS .5 .
THE INCREASE IS NOT BOUNDED.
IE RANGE IS 11 PLUS OR MINUS ABOVE

(VARIABLE: X9)
BOUND ON DECREASE IS .1999998 .
THE INCREASE IS NOT BOUNDED.
IE RANGE IS 12 PLUS OR MINUS ABOVE

# Appendix 2: BASIC Listing of Capital Budgeting Model

The BASIC program has a very simple structure, as outlined in chapter 10:

1  Statements 10 to 2000 are dedicated solely to the input of data. This is achieved by direct input at the computer keyboard in response to questions on the screen.
2  Statements 2000 to 4000 are dedicated to the calculation sequence. Each element of the APV equation occupies a unique and relatively independent segment of the program. For example, lines 2300 to 2550 calculate the operating cash flows. Each segment is separated by a REM (remark) statement describing its calculation purpose. Additional segments can be added for further PV elements in an APV equation.
3  Statements 5000 to 5710 are dedicated to output of the results of the calculation sequence. This is again designed on a segmented basis, with each output segment corresponding to a calculation segment or APV element. The user accesses the desired output via a menu located at the start of the output module.

The program has been written in standard Microsoft BASIC and does not use files. It should therefore run on most computers with little or no adaptation.

```
10 DIM B5(25)
11 DIM S2(25)
12 DIM S3(25),S4(25)
200 REM input of data
210 PRINT "LIFE OF PROJECT"
```

```
215 INPUT T1
220 PRINT "CAPITAL OUTLAY FC"
230 INPUT C0
240 PRINT"ADDITIONAL & RESTRICTED FUNDS RELEASED
BY PROJECT FC"
250 INPUT C1
260 PRINT "SPOT RATE FC per units of HC"
265 INPUT S0
270 S0 = 1/S0
300 PRINT "INFLATION FORECASTS"
310 PRINT "HOME COUNTRY"
320 INPUT I1(0)
340 PRINT "FOREIGN COUNTRY"
350 INPUT I2(0)
400 PRINT "PRODUCT SALES PER ANNUM "
410 INPUT X(0)
500 PRINT "PRICE PER UNIT YEAR 1 FC"
510 INPUT P(0)
550 PRINT "ANNUAL GROWTH RATE OF SALES"
560 INPUT G1(0)
600 PRINT "COST PER UNIT YEAR 1"
610 INPUT C(0)
700 PRINT "DISCOUNT RATE FOR OPERATING CASH FLOWS"
710 INPUT D1
800 PRINT "PRODUCT SALES REPLACED DUE TO PROJECT"
810 INPUT R(0)
820 PRINT "DECLINE IN REPLACED SALES (PER ANNUM)"
830 INPUT B(0)
850 PRINT "HC PROFITS PER UNIT ON REPLACED SALES"
860 INPUT Q(0)
870 PRINT "RESIDUAL VALUE OF PLANT,BUILDINGS & LAND"
872 PRINT "IN HC & TODAYS' VALUES"
873 PRINT "AS % OF CAPITAL OUTLAY"
874 INPUT R9
878 R9 = R9*C0
880 PRINT "DISCOUNT RATE FOR RESIDUAL VALUES"
885 INPUT R7
900 PRINT "HOME COUNTRY CORPORATE TAX RATE"
910 INPUT U0
920 PRINT "HOME COUNTRY CAPITAL GAINS TAX RATE"
```

```
930 INPUT T1(0)
940 PRINT "FOREIGN COUNTRY CORPORATE TAX RATE"
950 INPUT U1
960 IF U0 > U1 THEN T(0)=U0
970 IF U1> U0 THEN T(0)=U1
1100 PRINT "DISCOUNT RATE FOR DEPRECIATION TAX
ALLOWANCES"
1110 INPUT D3
1300 PRINT "INCREASE IN CORPORATE BORROWING CAPA-
CITY (HC)"
1310 INPUT B5
1320 PRINT "HC BORROWING RATE FOR THESE FUNDS"
1330 INPUT B6
1340 PRINT "HC RISKLESS RATE"
1350 INPUT B7
1600 PRINT "FC GOVERNMENT SUBSIDIZED LOAN"
1610 INPUT L0
1620 PRINT "FC BORROWING RATE"
1630 INPUT D4
1640 PRINT "GOVERNMENT LOAN RATE"
1650 INPUT L1
1800 PRINT "EXTRA TAX SAVINGS p.a from deferrals & transfer
pricing HC"
1810 INPUT S4
1820 PRINT "DISCOUNT RATE FOR EXTRA TAX SAVINGS"
1830 INPUT D5
1900 PRINT "ADDITIONAL REMITTANCES pa HC"
1910 INPUT S5
1920 PRINT "DISCOUNT RATE "
1930 INPUT S6
2000 REM CALCULATION SEGMENTS
2100 REM EXPECTED EXCHANGE RATE PER PERIOD
2110 FOR T = 1 TO T1
2120 I1(T)= I1(0)
2130 I2(T)= I2(0)
2140 I8=(1+I1(T))^T
2145 I9=(1+I2(T))^T
2150 I8=I8/I9
2160 S(T) = 10000000#*S0*I8
2162 S(T)= INT(S(T))
```

```
2164 S(T) = S(T)/10000000#
2180 NEXT T
2300 REM OPERATING CASH FLOWS
2310 FOR T =1 TO T1
2320 X(T)=X(0)
2325 C9= (1+I2(T))^T
2330 G1(T)=G1(0)
2335 G8 = (1+G1(T))^T
2340 P(T) = P(0)*C9
2350 C(T) = C(0)*C9
2355 X(T) = X(T)*G8
2360 W(T)= X(T)*(P(T)-C(T))
2365 W(T)=S(T)*W(T)
2400 B(T)=B(0)
2410 C8=(1-B(T))^T
2420 R(T)=R(0)*C8
2430 C7=(1+I1(T))^T
2440 Q(T)=Q(0)*C7
2450 Y(T)=R(T)*Q(T)
2460 W(T) = W(T)-Y(T)
2480 T(T)=T(0)
2500 W(T) = W(T)*(1-T(T))
2505 S5(T) = W(T)
2510 F1=(1+D1)^T
2520 W(T)=W(T)/F1
2530 S9 = S9+W(T)
2550 NEXT T
2570 REM RESIDUAL VALUE OF PLANT, EQUIPMENT, BUILD-
INGS & LAND
2580 C7 = (1+I1(T1))^T1
2590 F7 = (1 + R7)^T1
2595 T1(T1) = T1(0)
2600 R8 = R9*C7
2605 R8 = R8*(1-T1(T1))
2610 R5 = R8/F7
2700 REM TAX ALLOWANCES FOR DEPRECIATION
2705 C3 = S0*C0
2710 FOR T = 1 TO T1
2715 D(T) = C3/T1
2720 T9(T)= D(T)*T(T)
```

```
2725 F3 = (1+D3)^T
2730 D9(T) = T9(T)/F3
2735 Z3 = Z3 +D9(T)
2750 NEXT T
2765 PRINT
2800 REM INCREASE IN CORPORATE BORROWING CAPACITY
2820 FOR T= 1 TO T1
2830 T7(T) = B5*B6*T(T)
2840 F2 =(1+B7)^T
2850 T8(T)= T7(T)/F2
2860 Z2 = Z2 + T8(T)
2900 NEXT T
2910 PRINT
3000 REM CONCESSIONARY LOAN
3010 B5(1) = L0
3020 FOR T = 1 TO T1
3030 C5(T) = L0/T1
3040 I(T) = B5(T)*L1
3050 B5(T+1) = B5(T) - C5(T)
3060 T5(T) = C5(T) + I(T)
3070 F4 = (1 + D4)^T
3080 D5(T) = T5(T)/F4
3082 Z4 = Z4 + D5(T)
3085 W4 = Z4
3100 NEXT T
3105 PRINT
3120 PRINT
3144 Z4 =L0-Z4
3152 PRINT
3155 Z4 = Z4*S0
3300 REM EXTRA TAX SAVINGS FROM DEFERRALS &
TRANSFER PRICING
3305 S2(1)=S4
3310 FOR T = 1 TO T1
3315 I6 =(1+I1(T))^T
3320 S2(T+1)=S4*I6
3330 F5 = (1+D5)^T
3340 S1(T)=S2(T)/F5
3350 Z5 =Z5 + S1(T)
3370 NEXT T
```

```
3500 REM ADDITIONAL REMITTANCES
3505 S3(1)= S5
3510 FOR T = 1 TO T1
3520 I6 = (1+I1(T))^T
3530 S3(T+1) = S5*I6
3540 F7=(1+S6)^T
3550 S4(T)=S3(T)/F7
3560 Z7 =Z7 + S4(T)
3570 NEXT T
5000 REM OUTPUT OF RESULTS
5010 PRINT
5020 PRINT
5030 PRINT "OUTPUT OF RESULTS":PRINT:PRINT
5040 PRINT "CHOOSE ONE OF THE FOLLOWING RESULTS BY"
5050 PRINT "INPUTTING THE APPROPRIATE RHS NUMBER"
5060 PRINT:PRINT
5070 PRINT "OPERATING CASH FLOWS 1"
5080 PRINT "TAX ALLOWANCES FOR DEPRECIATION 2"
5090 PRINT "INCREASES IN BORROWING CAPACITY 3"
5100 PRINT "LOAN FROM GOVERNMENT 4"
5110 PRINT "EXTRA TAX SAVINGS 5"
5115 PRINT "EXTRA REMITTANCES 6"
5120 PRINT "TOTAL OF NPVs 7"
5130 PRINT "NO MORE RESULTS 8"
5140 INPUT X
5150 ON X GOTO 5160,5250,5330,5410,5560,5630,5640,5710
5160 REM OPERATING CASH FLOWS
5165 PRINT "PER","EX RATE","OP CF","DISC CF"
5170 FOR T =1 TO T1
5175 E0 = 1/S(T)
5180 PRINT T,E0,S5(T),W(T)
5190 NEXT T
5200 PRINT
5210 PRINT "NPV OF OPERATING CASH FLOWS IS" S9
5220 PRINT
5225 PRINT "PV OF RESIDUAL PLANT, BUILDINGS & LAND,
AFTER CG TAX"R5
5230 INPUT O0
5240 GOTO 5030
5250 REM TAX ALLOWANCES FOR DEPRECIATION
```

```
5255 PRINT "PER","DEP HC","TAX ALL HC","DISC ALL"
5260 FOR T = 1 TO T1
5270 PRINT T,D(T),T9(T),D9(T)
5280 NEXT T
5290 PRINT "HC PV OF DEPRECIATION TAX ALLOWANCES "Z3
5300 PRINT
5310 INPUT O0
5320 GOTO 5030
5330 REM INCREASE IN CORPORATE BORROWING CAPACITY
5335 PRINT "PER","TAX BENEFITS","DISC BEN"
5340 FOR T= 1 TO T1
5350 PRINT T,T7(T),T8(T)
5360 NEXT T
5370 PRINT
5380 PRINT "HC PV OF INCREASE IN BORROWING CAPACITY
"Z2
5390 INPUT O0
5400 GOTO 5030
5410 REM CONCESSIONARY LOAN
5415 PRINT " HC VALUES OF"
5420 PRINT "BAL","CR","INT","TR","DISC"
5430 FOR T = 1 TO T1
5440 PRINT B5(T),C5(T),I(T),T5(T),D5(T)
5450 NEXT T
5460 Z4 =W4
5470 PRINT"FC PV of loan int+cap rep ="Z4
5480 PRINT
5490 Z4 =L0-Z4
5500 PRINT "FC NPV of loan =",Z4
5510 PRINT
5520 Z4 = Z4*S0
5530 PRINT "HC NPV of loan "Z4
5540 INPUT O0
5550 GOTO 5030
5560 REM EXTRA TAX SAVINGS FROM DEFERRALS &
TRANSFER PRICING
5565 PRINT "PER","TAX SAVINGS","DISC"
5570 FOR T = 1 TO T1
5580 PRINT T,S2(T),S1(T)
5590 NEXT T
```

```
5600 PRINT
5610 PRINT "HC PV OF EXTRA TAX SAVINGS DUE TO
DEFERRALS/TRANSFER PRICING "Z5
5620 INPUT O0
5625 GOTO 5030
5630 REM EXTRA REMITTANCES
5632 PRINT "PER","EXTRA REM","DISC"
5633 FOR T = 1 TO T1
5634 PRINT T,S3(T),S4(T)
5635 NEXT T
5636 PRINT
5637 PRINT "PV OF ADDITIONAL REMITTANCES "Z7
5638 INPUT O0
5639 GOTO 5030
5640 REM TOTAL NPV or APV FOR PROJECT
5645 PRINT " PV SUMMARY "
5647 PRINT
5650 Z0 = 0
5660 Z0 = -S0*C0
5670 Z0 = Z0 + (S0*C1)
5675 C0 = C0*S0: C1 = C1*S0
5680 Z0 = S9+Z3+Z2+Z4+Z5+Z0
5681 Z0 = Z0 + R5 + Z7
5682 PRINT "PV OF CAPITAL OUTLAY "C0
5684 PRINT "PV OF RELEASED FUNDS "C1
5686 PRINT "NPV OF OPERATING CASH FLOWS IS "S9
5687 PRINT "PV OF RESIDUAL PLANT, BUILDINGS & LAND,
AFTER CG TAX "R5
5688 PRINT "HC PV OF DEPRECIATION TAX ALLOWANCES "Z3
5689 PRINT "HC PV OF INCREASE IN BORROWING CAPACITY
"Z2
5690 PRINT "HC NPV of loan "Z4
5691 PRINT "HC PV OF EXTRA TAX SAVINGS (DEFERRALS &
TRANSFER PRICING) "Z5
5692 PRINT "PV OF ADDITIONAL REMITTANCES "Z7
5693 PRINT
5695 PRINT "TOTAL OF NPVs "Z0
5697 INPUT O0
5700 GOTO 5030
5710 END
```

# Appendix 3: BASIC Listing of Financing Model

The BASIC program has a very simple structure based upon the design discussed in chapter 12, and bears a strong resemblance to the structure of the capital budgeting model outlined in chapter 10. Thus:

1  Statements 10 to 2000 are dedicated solely to the input of data. Input is achieved by user replies via the computer keyboard in response to questions displayed on the screen.
2  Statements 2000 to 3900 are dedicated to the process calculation sequence. Each segment within this block of statements is separated by a REM (remark) statement describing its calculation purpose. Additional segments can be added for further debt types. The segments are as follows:
   (a) Statements 2000–2190 are for foreign exchange rate calculations and are based on purchasing parity.
   (b) Statements 3000–3200 are for the term loan calculations including balance outstanding, interest charges, total repayments and transaction costs. Currency of denomination and currency of translation values are calculated.
   (c) Statements 3500–3700 are for similar bond calculations.
   (d) Statements 3700–3900 are for the calculation of capital gains or losses on either of the debt forms and also for the calculation of tax implications.
3  Statements 5000 to 5710 are dedicated to output of the results of the calculation sequence. This is again designed on a segmented basis, with each output segment corresponding to a calculation segment.

The user accesses the desired output via a menu located at the start of the output module.

4   Statements 6000–7630 are subroutines dedicated to NPV and IRR calculations.

5   Statements from 8000 onwards are for DATA statements containing foreign exchange rate forecasts. This is an alternative to the purchasing parity direct input method and is designed for analysis of deviations from PPP.

As with the capital budgeting model, this program has been written in standard Microsoft BASIC and does not use files. It should therefore run on most computers with little or no adaptation.

```
10 DIM B5(25)
11 DIM S2(25)
12 DIM S3(25),S4(25)
15 DIM T(25),T2(25),T3(25),T5(25),S7(25)
200 PRINT "horizon"
203 INPUT T1
205 PRINT "CURRENCY OF DENOMINATION": INPUT D$
207 PRINT "CURRENCY OF TRANSLATION": INPUT T$
210 PRINT "EXCHANGE RATE FORECAST"
212 PRINT "DIRECT OR VIA PP"
215 PRINT " INPUT 1 or 2 "
220 INPUT P8
221 IF P8 = 2 THEN 260
223 FOR T = 0 TO T1
225 READ E0 : S(T) = 1/E0
227 PRINT E0,S(T)
230 NEXT T
245 GOTO 600
260 PRINT " SPOT RATE ";D$;" per units of ";T$
265 INPUT S0
270 S0 = 1/S0
300 PRINT "INFLATION FORECASTS"
310 PRINT T$;" COUNTRY"
320 INPUT I1(0)
340 PRINT D$;"COUNTRY"
350 INPUT I2(0)
600 PRINT " CORPORATE TAX RATE"
```

```
610 INPUT T(0)
700 PRINT "CAPITAL GAINS & LOSSES TAX RATE"
705 PRINT " INPUT ZERO (O) IF NOT APPLICABLE"
707 PRINT "ZERO IF GAIN NOT TAXED"
708 PRINT "ZERO IF LOSS NOT ALLOWED"
710 PRINT "ON GAINS"
720 INPUT G0
730 PRINT "ON LOSSES"
740 INPUT G1
1000 PRINT "TERM LOAN or BOND ISSUE? input 1 or 2 "
1005 INPUT B7
1007 IF B7 = 2 THEN 1700
1600 PRINT D$;" LOAN AMOUNT"
1610 INPUT L0
1640 PRINT " LOAN RATE"
1650 INPUT L1
1655 PRINT "INITIAL FEE AS % OF LOAN"
1657 INPUT F7
1660 GOTO 2000
1700 PRINT D$;" BOND AMOUNT"
1710 INPUT L2
1740 PRINT " COUPON RATE"
1750 INPUT L4
1760 PRINT "FLOTATION CHARGE as % of BOND ISSUE"
1770 INPUT F7
2000 REM CALCULATION SEGMENTS
2001 IF P8 = 1 THEN 2190
2100 REM EXPECTED EXCHANGE RATE PER PERIOD
2105 S(0) = S0
2110 FOR T = 1 TO T1
2120 I1(T)= I1(0)
2130 I2(T)= I2(0)
2140 I8=(1+I1(T))^T
2145 I9=(1+I2(T))^T
2150 I8=I8/I9
2160 S(T) = 10000000#*S0*I8
2162 S(T)= INT(S(T))
2164 S(T) = S(T)/10000000#
2180 NEXT T
2190 IF B7 = 2 THEN 3500
```

```
3000 REM TERM LOAN
3005 F(0) = L0*F7
3007 C5(0) = F(0)
3008 T5(0) = C5(0)
3009 T2(0) = F(0)*T(0)
3010 T3(0) = T5(0)-T2(0)
3011 S7(0) = T5(0)*S(0)
3012 B5(0) = L0
3020 FOR T = 1 TO T1
3030 C5(T) = L0/T1
3040 I(T) = B5(T-1)*L1
3050 B5(T) = B5(T-1) - C5(T)
3060 T5(T) = C5(T) + I(T)
3065 S7(T) = T5(T)*S(T)
3090 T2(T) = ( I(T) + F(T) ) * T(0)
3095 T3(T) = T5(T) - T2(T)
3100 NEXT T
3105 PRINT
3120 PRINT
3144 Z4 =L0-Z4
3152 PRINT
3155 Z4 = Z4*S0
3200 GOTO 3700
3500 REM BOND ISSUE
3510 F(0) = L2*F7
3512 C5(0) = L2*F7
3520 FOR T = 0 TO T1-1
3530 B5(T) = L2
3540 I(T) = L2*L4
3550 I(0) = 0
3560 T5(T) = C5(T) + I(T)
3565 S7(T) = T5(T)*S(T)
3570 F4 = (1 + D8)^T
3580 D5(T) = T5(T)/F4
3582 Z4 = Z4 + D5(T)
3585 W4 = Z4
3590 T2(T) = (I(T) + F(T))*T(0)
3593 REM AFTER TAX CASH FLOWS T3(T)
3595 T3(T) = T5(T) - T2(T)
3600 NEXT T
```

```
3605 PRINT
3607 I(T) = L2*L4
3610 C5(T) = L2
3611 T5(T) = C5(T) + I(T)
3618 B5(T) = B5(T-1)-L2
3620 S7(T) = T5(T)*S(T)
3625 T2(T) = I(T)*T(0)
3630 T3(T) = T5(T)-T2(T)
3635 D6(T) = T3(T)/F4
3652 PRINT
3700 REM CALCULATION OF CAPITAL GAIN/LOSS & TAX
IMPLICATIONS
3705 FOR T= 0 TO T1
3720 G9(T) = C5(T)*((S(0)/S(T))-1)
3750 IF G9(T) > 0 THEN 3770
3751 REM G9(T) IS A CAPITAL LOSS
3754 T1(0) = G1
3756 T3(T1) = T3(T1) + (G9(T)*T1(0))
3765 GOTO 3784
3770 REM G9(T) IS A CAPITAL GAIN
3774 T1(0) = G0
3778 T3(T1) = T3(T1) + (G9(T)*T1(0))
3784 NEXT T
5000 REM OUTPUT OF RESULTS
5010 PRINT
5020 PRINT
5030 PRINT "OUTPUT OF RESULTS":PRINT:PRINT
5040 PRINT "CHOOSE ONE OF THE FOLLOWING RESULTS BY"
5050 PRINT "INPUTTING THE APPROPRIATE RHS NUMBER"
5060 PRINT:PRINT
5070 PRINT"Exchange rate forecast 1"
5100 PRINT"LOAN OR BOND CASH FLOWS 2"
5120 PRINT"Tax details 3"
5125 PRINT"IRR and NPV values 4"
5130 PRINT"NO MORE RESULTS 5"
5140 INPUT X
5150 ON X GOTO 5160,5410,5640,6000,6999
5160 REM EXCHANGE RATE FORECAST
5165 PRINT "PER","EX.RATE ";D$;" per ";T$
5170 FOR T = 0 TO T1
```

```
5175 E0 = 1/S(T)
5180 PRINT T,E0
5190 NEXT T
5195 INPUT O0
5200 GOTO 5030
5410 REM output of bond or term loan details
5415 PRINT " ";D$; " VALUES OF"
5420 PRINT "BAL.OUT","CAP.REP","INTEREST","TOT.REP","AT
CFS"
5430 FOR T = 0 TO T1
5440 PRINT B5(T),C5(T),I(T),T5(T),T3(T)
5450 NEXT T
5532 INPUT O0
5538 PRINT "PER","TR","TR","AT TR"
5539 PRINT "",D$,T$,T$
5540 FOR T = 0 TO T1
5542 T8(T) = T3(T)*S(T)
5545 PRINT T,T5(T),S7(T),T8(T)
5547 NEXT T
5548 INPUT O0
5550 GOTO 5030
5640 PRINT " ";D$ ; " VALUES OF"
5641 PRINT "PERIOD","CAPITAL","TAX","INTEREST","TOTAL"
5642 PRINT "","GAIN/LOSS","CHANGE","TAX ","TAX"
5643 PRINT ""," + / -","","BENEFIT","CHANGE"
5644 PRINT"_____"
5645 PRINT
5646 FOR T= 0 TO T1
5649 PRINT T,G9(T),-G9(T)*T1(0),T2(T),T2(T)-G9(T)*T1(0)
5655 NEXT T
5657 PRINT
5697 INPUT O0
5700 GOTO 5030
6000 REM CALCULATION OF IRR & NPV - BEFORE & AFTER
TAX
6001 PRINT "BEFORE TAX VALUES"
6505 J1 = T1
6506 IF B7 = 2 THEN P1 = L2
6507 IF B7 = 1 THEN P1 = L0
6508 PRINT "CAPITAL BORROWED =" ;D$ ;P1
```

```
6509 PRINT "DEBT REPAYMENTS " ; D$
6510 FOR T = 0 TO T1
6520 G(T) = C5(T) + I(T)
6525 PRINT G(T),
6527 NEXT T : PRINT
6530 PRINT "DISCOUNT RATE",
6532 INPUT R0
6534 GOSUB 7500
6536 PRINT "NPV OF BOND OR LOAN =";Y2
6540 GOSUB 7000
6545 PRINT "IRR OF BOND OR LOAN";100*R;"%"
6550 N1 = Y2
6552 R1 = 100*R
6553 PRINT
6555 REM IRR & NPV BEFORE TAX
6560 P1 = P1*S(0)
6562 PRINT "CAPITAL BORROWED =" ;T$ ;P1
6563 PRINT "DEBT REPAYMENTS " ; T$
6565 FOR T = 0 TO T1
6568 G(T) = S7(T)
6569 PRINT G(T),
6570 NEXT T : PRINT
6571 PRINT "DISCOUNT RATE",:INPUT R0:GOSUB 7500
6572 PRINT "NPV OF BOND OR LOAN = ";Y2
6573 GOSUB 7000
6574 PRINT "BEFORE TAX IRR HC =" 100*R,"%"
6576 R2 =100*R
6578 N2 = Y2 :PRINT:PRINT
6580 PRINT "AFTER TAX VALUES"
6585 P1 = P1/S(0)
6590 PRINT "CAPITAL BORROWED = " ;D$ ;P1
6595 PRINT "NET DEBT REPAYMENTS " ; D$
6600 FOR T = 0 TO T1
6620 G(T) = T3(T)
6625 PRINT G(T),
6630 NEXT T: PRINT
6633 PRINT "DISCOUNT RATE",
6635 INPUT R0
6637 GOSUB 7500
6640 PRINT " AFTER TAX NPV OF BOND OR LOAN = ";Y2
```

```
6660 GOSUB 7000
6700 PRINT "After tax IRR of Bond or Loan"; 100*R,"%"
6715 R3 = 100*R
6718 N3 = Y2
6800 REM AFTER TAX IRR OF HC CASH FLOWS
6810 P1 = P1*S(0)
6812 PRINT
6815 PRINT "CAPITAL BORROWED = " ;T$ ;P1
6817 PRINT "NET DEBT REPAYMENTS " ; T$
6820 FOR T = 0 TO T1
6830 G(T) = T8(T)
6835 PRINT G(T);
6850 NEXT T : PRINT
6852 PRINT "DISCOUNT RATE",:INPUT R0
6854 GOSUB 7500
6856 PRINT "AFTER TAX NPV OF BOND OR LOAN =";Y2
6860 GOSUB 7000
6880 PRINT " AFTER TAX IRR = ",100*R,"%"
6882 N4 = Y2
6885 R4 = R*100
6887 PRINT
6900 PRINT " IRR VALUES"
6910 PRINT
6920 PRINT "",D$,T$
6930 PRINT "BEFORE TAX",R1,R2
6940 PRINT "AFTER TAX",R3,R4
6980 INPUT O0
6990 PRINT " NPV VALUES"
6991 PRINT
6992 PRINT "",D$,T$
6993 PRINT "BEFORE TAX",N1,N2
6994 PRINT "AFTER TAX",N3,N4
6995 INPUT O0
6998 GOTO 5010
6999 END
7000 Y9 = 0
7040 R = 0
7050 FOR J = 1 TO 5
7060 Z1 = (.1)^J
7070 R = R + Z1
```

```
7075 IF R = .00001 THEN 7190
7080 Y1 = 0
7090 FOR T = 0 TO T1
7095 Y1 = Y1 + G(T)/(1+R)^T
7110 NEXT T
7117 X = Y1 -P1
7120 IF Y1-P1 > 0 THEN 7070
7130 R = R-Z1
7140 NEXT J
7150 IF R > 0 THEN 7190
7160 IF R < 0 THEN 7190
7180 GOTO 7050
7190 RETURN
7500 REM NPV CALCULATION SUB
7510 Y2 = 0
7550 FOR T = 0 TO T1
7580 Y2 = Y2 + G(T)/(1+R0)^T
7590 NEXT T
7610 Y2 = P1 -Y2
7630 RETURN
7999 REM FOREIGN EXCHANGE RATES
8000 DATA 1.75,1.665,1.580,1.495
8010 DATA 1.410,1.325,1.240,1.155
8020 DATA 1.1,1.05,1.01
```

# Appendix 4: Simulation Run Using the Financing Model

The results of a financing simulation are presented here. The computer output has been edited to delete irrelevant output. The example chosen is the Deutschmark bond under exchange rate scenario 2 in section 12.3. This run is shown here to demonstrate the power of the financing model.
GERMAN BOND - ISSUED BY GERMAN SUBSIDIARY

horizon
? 8
CURRENCY OF DENOMINATION
?D-Marks
CURRENCY OF TRANSLATION
?£ Sterling
EXCHANGE RATE FORECAST
DIRECT OR VIA PP
　　INPUT 1 or 2
? 2
SPOT RATE D-Marks per units of £ Sterling
? 4
INFLATION FORECASTS
£ Sterling COUNTRY
? .06
D-Marks COUNTRY
? .02
CORPORATE TAX RATE
? .5
CAPITAL GAINS & LOSSES TAX RATE

   INPUT ZERO (O) IF NOT APPLICABLE
ZERO IF GAIN NOT TAXED
ZERO IF LOSS NOT ALLOWED
ON GAINS
? 0
ON LOSSES
? 0
TERM LOAN or BOND ISSUE? input 1 or 2
? 2
D-Marks BOND AMOUNT
? 100000
   COUPON RATE
? .03
FLOTATION CHARGE as % of BOND ISSUE
? .05


OUTPUT OF RESULTS

CHOOSE ONE OF THE FOLLOWING RESULTS BY
   INPUTTING THE APPROPRIATE RHS NUMBER

| | |
|---|---|
| Exchange rate forecast | 1 |
| LOAN OR BOND CASH FLOWS | 2 |
| Tax details | 3 |
| IRR and NPV values | 4 |
| NO MORE RESULTS | 5 |

? 1

| PER | EX.RATE |
|---|---|
| | D-Marks per £ Sterling |
| 0 | 4 |
| 1 | 3.849057 |
| 2 | 3.70381 |
| 3 | 3.564044 |
| 4 | 3.429551 |
| 5 | 3.300134 |
| 6 | 3.175601 |
| 7 | 3.055767 |
| 8 | 2.940454 |

? 2

D-Marks VALUES OF

| BAL.OUT | CAP.REP | INTEREST | TOT.REP | AT CFS |
|---|---|---|---|---|
| 100000 | 5000 | 0 | 5000 | 2500 |
| 100000 | 0 | 3000 | 3000 | 1500 |
| 100000 | 0 | 3000 | 3000 | 1500 |
| 100000 | 0 | 3000 | 3000 | 1500 |
| 100000 | 0 | 3000 | 3000 | 1500 |
| 100000 | 0 | 3000 | 3000 | 1500 |
| 100000 | 0 | 3000 | 3000 | 1500 |
| 100000 | 0 | 3000 | 3000 | 1500 |
| 0 | 100000 | 3000 | 103000 | 101500 |

| PER | TR D-Marks | TR £ Sterling | AT TR £ Sterling |
|---|---|---|---|
| 0 | 5000 | 1250 | 625 |
| 1 | 3000 | 779.4117 | 389.7059 |
| 2 | 3000 | 809.9769 | 404.9884 |
| 3 | 3000 | 841.7406 | 420.8703 |
| 4 | 3000 | 874.7502 | 437.3751 |
| 5 | 3000 | 909.054 | 454.527 |
| 6 | 3000 | 944.703 | 472.3515 |
| 7 | 3000 | 981.7502 | 490.8751 |
| 8 | 103000 | 35028.6 | 34518.48 |

What is the discount rate for debt cash flows ? .08

IRR VALUES

| | D-Marks | £ Sterling |
|---|---|---|
| BEFORE TAX | 3.733999 | 7.802001 |
| AFTER TAX | 1.838001 | 5.831999 |

NPV VALUES

|  | D–Marks | £Sterling |
|---|---|---|
| BEFORE TAX | 23,233 | 311 |
| AFTER TAX | 34,853 | 3469 |

# References

Adler, M. and Dumas, B. 1983: International portfolio choice and corporation finance: a synthesis. *Journal of Finance*, 38, June, 925–84.

Adler, M. and Dumas, B. 1984: Exposure to currency risk: definition and measurement. *Financial Management*, summer, 41–50.

Agarwal, S. and Ramaswami, S. 1992: Choice of foreign market entry mode: impact of ownership, location and internalization factors. *Journal of International Business Studies*, 23(1), 1–28.

Aggarwal, R. and Soenen, L. 1989: Managing persistent real changes in currency values: the role of multinational operating strategies. *Columbia Journal of World Business*, 24(3), 60–7.

Bailey, R.W., Baillie, R.T. and McMahon, P.C. 1984: Interpreting econometric evidence on efficiency in the foreign exchange market. *Oxford Economic Papers*, 36.

Baillie, R.T. 1989: Econometric tests of rationality and market efficiency. *Econometric Reviews*, 8, 151–86.

Baillie, R.T. and Bollersley, T. 1990: A multivariate generalized ARCH approach to modeling risk premia in forward foreign exchange rate markets. *Journal of International Money and Finance* , 9(3) 309–24.

Baillie, R.T., Lippens, R.E. and McMahon, P.C. 1983: Testing rational expectations and efficiency in the foreign exchange market. *Econometrica*, 51.

Bain, A.D. 1970: *The Control of the Money Supply*. Penguin.

Barnea, A., Haugen, R. and Senbet, L. 1981: Market imperfections, agency problems and capital structure: a review. *Financial Management*, summer, 7–22.

Barnes, P. 1986: Thin trading and stock market efficiency: the case of the Kuala Lumpur Stock Exchange. *Journal of Business Finance and Accounting*. 13(4), 609–17.

Bartlett, C.A. 1983: MNCs: get off the reorganization merry-go-round. *Harvard Business Review*, March/April, 138–46.

Bar-Yosef, S. 1977: Interactions of corporate financing and investment decisions – implications for capital budgeting – comment. *Journal of Finance*,

32, March, 211–17.

Beerel, A. 1987: Setting up treasury as your in-house bank. *Accountancy*, June.

Belk, P and Glaum, M. 1990: The management of foreign exchange risk in UK multinationals – an empirical investigation. *Accounting and Business Research*, 21(81), 3–13.

Betts, Paul 1992: UK-German group in aero engine talks with MTU. *Financial Times*, 21 February.

Bickerstaffe, G. 1984: Banks start cashing in on faster money management. *International Management Europe (UK)*, 39(7), 33–5.

Bhoocha-oom, A. and Stansell, S. 1990: A study of international financial market integration: an examination of US, Hong Kong and Singapore markets. *Journal of Business Finance and Accounting*, 17(2), 193–212.

Bilson, J.F.O. 1981: The 'speculative efficiency' hypothesis. *Journal of Business*, 54, July.

Black, F. 1974: International capital market equilibrium with investment barriers. *Journal of Financial Economics*, 1, December, 337–52.

Black, F. and Scholes, M. 1972: The valuation of option contracts and a test of market efficiency. *Journal of Finance*, 27, May, 399–418.

Boddewyn, J.J. 1983: Foreign direct divestment theory: is it the reverse of FDI theory? *Weltwirtschaftliches Archiv.*, June.

Boisseau, Ch. de. 1990: The dynamics of the EMS in the light of European financial integration: some reflections from a French perspective. *Journal of Banking and Finance*, 14(5), 889–908.

Booth, L. 1982: Capital budgeting frameworks for the multinational corporation. *Journal of International Business Studies*, fall, 113–23.

Booth, L. and Rotenberg, W. 1990: Assessing foreign exchange exposure: theory and application using Canadian firms. *Journal of International Financial Management and Accounting*, 2(1), 1–22.

Brealey, R. and Myers, S. 1981: *Principles of Corporate Finance*. McGraw-Hill.

Breeden, D.T. 1979: An intertemporal asset pricing model with stochastic consumption and investment opportunities. *Journal of Financial Economics*, 27, September, 265–96.

Brown, M. 1984: Multinationals get a budget tax bonanza. *Sunday Times*, 25 March, 57.

Buckley, P.J. and Casson, M.C. 1976: *The Future of the Multinational Enterprise*. London: Macmillan.

Bui, N. and Pippinger, J. 1990: Commodity prices, exchange rates and their relative volatility. *Journal of International Money and Finance*, 9(1), 3–20.

Burmeister, H. 1981: The cost of financing to the firm in foreign exchange. In F. Derkinderen and R. Crum (eds), *Risk, Capital Costs and Financing Decisions*, Martinus Nijhoff, chapter 2.

Burnie, D. 1986: Capital asset prices and the Friedman hypotheses of inflation. *Journal of Business Finance and Accounting*, 13(4), 519–34.

456    *References*

Calvet, R.L. 1981: A synthesis of foreign direct investment theories and theories of the multinational firm. *Journal of International Business Studies*, spring/summer, 43–59.

Canaday, J. and Feenstra, F. 1991: Managing FX relationships. *The Treasurer*, April, 6–12.

Casson, M. 1982: Transaction costs and the theory of the multinational enterprise. In A.M. Rugman (ed.), *New Theories of the Multinational Enterprise*, London: Croom Helm, 24–43.

Castellanos, C. 1990: The changing dynamics of FX markets. *The Treasurer*, May, 11–15.

Caves, R.E. 1971: International corporations: the industrial economics of foreign investment. *Economica*, February, 1–27.

Channon, D.F. 1978: *Multinational Strategic Planning*. New York: Amacom.

Channon, D.F. and Jalland, M. 1979: *Multinational Strategic Planning*. Macmillan.

Clements, A. 1985: Problems and opportunities in the financing of multinational companies. Third Armitage and Norton Lecture, Huddersfield Polytechnic, 16 October (author Finance Director of ICI).

Clements, A. 1988: Interview. *Investor's Chronicle*, 22 July, 17 (subject Finance Director of ICI).

Coase, R.H. 1937: The nature of the firm. *Economica*, 4, November, 386–405.

Coggan, Philip 1991: A trend towards bi-lateral lending? *The Treasurer,* March, 10.

Collier, P. and Davis, E. 1985: The management of currency transaction risk by UK multi-national companies. *Accounting and Business Research*, autumn, 327–34.

Collier, P., Davis, E. Coates, J.B. and Longden, S.G. 1990: The management of currency risk: case studies of US and UK multinationals. *Accounting and Business Research*, 20(79), 206–10.

Contractor, F. 1984: Choosing between direct investment and licensing: theoretical considerations and empirical tests. *Journal of International Business Studies*, winter.

Cooper, J.C.B. 1982: World stock markets: some random walk tests. *Applied Economics*, 14, 515–31.

Cornell, B. 1977: Spot rates, forward rates and exchange market efficiency. *Journal of Financial Economics*, 5, August, 55–66.

Cornell, B. and Shapiro, A. 1985: Interest rates and exchange rates: some new empirical results. *Journal of International Money and Finance*, December, 431–42.

Cumby, R. E. 1990: Consumption risk and international equity returns: some empirical evidence. *Journal of International Money and Finance*, 9(2), 182–91.

Dahlman, C.J. 1979: The problem of externality. *Journal of Law and Economics*, 22, April, 141-62.

Daniels, J. and Radebaugh, L. 1992: *International business: environments and operations*, 6th edn. Addison-Wesley.

Davidson, W.H. 1982: *Global Strategic Planning*. Wiley, New York.

Davutyan, N., and Pippinger, J. 1985: Purchasing power parity did not collapse. *American Economic Review*, 75, December, 1151–8.

Donaldson, G. 1969: Strategy for financial emergencies. *Harvard Business Review*, November/December, 67–79.

Dornbusch, R. 1976: Expectations and exchange rate dynamics. *Journal of Political Economy*, 84, 1161–76.

Dufey, G. 1983: International financial management: the overall investment and financing plan. In *International Manager's Handbook*, Wiley, section 8.12, 4–17.

Dufey, G. and Giddy, I. 1978a: *The International Money Market*. Prentice-Hall.

Dufey, G. and Giddy I. 1978b: International financial planning. *California Management Review*, fall, 69–81.

Dufey, G. and Srinivasulu, S. 1983: The case for corporate management of foreign exchange risk. *Financial Management*, winter, 54–61.

Dunning, J.H. 1977: Trade, location of economic activity: a search for an eclectic approach. In B. Ohlin et al. (eds), *The International Allocation of Economic Activity*, Holmes and Meier.

Dunning, J.H. 1979: Explaining changing patterns of international production: in defence of the eclectic theory. *Oxford Bulletin of Economics and Statistics*, November, 269–95.

Dunning, J.H. 1981: Explaining the international direct investment position of countries: towards a dynamic or developmental approach. *Weltwirtschaftliches Archiv.*, 117(1), 30–44.

Dymsza, W.A. 1984: Global strategic planning: a model and recent developments. *Journal of International Business Studies*, fall, 169-83.

Eaker, M. 1977: Teaching international finance – an economist's perspective. *Journal of Financial and Quantitative Analysis*, November, 607–8.

*Economist* 1992: ICI – more discipline needed. *The Economist*, 23 May, 101–2.

Edison, H. J. 1987: Purchasing power parity in the long run: a test of the dollar/pound exchange rate (1890–1978), *Journal of Money, Credit and Banking*, 19(3), 376–87.

Edwards, J. 1988: Jaguar PLC's foreign exchange exposure and its presentation to the investor community. *The Treasurer*, February, 29–30.

Eiteman, D. and Stonehill, A. 1989: *Multinational Business Finance*, 5th edn. Addison-Wesley.

Fama, E.F. 1975: Short term interest rates as predictors of inflation. *American Economic Review*, 65, June, 269–82.

Fama, E.F. and Schwert, G.W. 1977: Asset returns and inflation. *Journal of Financial Economics*, 5, November, 115–46.

Feiger, G. and Jacquillat, B. 1982: *International Finance*. Allyn and Bacon.

Flexl, Judith 1985: Economic exposure. *The Treasurer*, September, 17–21.

Folks, W. and Advani, R. 1980: Raising funds with foreign currency. *Financial*

*Executive*, February, 44–9.

Freeman, Andrew 1990: ICI sticks with well oiled funding formula. *Financial Times*, 14 June.

Frenkel, J.A. 1981: The collapse of purchasing power parity in the 1970s. *European Economic Review*, 16, May, 145–65.

Friedman, M. 1977: Nobel lecture: inflation and unemployment, *Journal of Political Economy*, 85(3), 451–72.

Gaillot, H.J. 1970: Purchasing power parity as an explanation of long term changes in exchange rates. *Journal of Money, Credit and Banking*, 2, August, 348–57.

Garman, M.B. and Kohlhagen, S.W. 1983: Foreign currency option values. *Journal of International Money and Finance*, 2, 231–7.

Geske, R. and Roll, R. 1983: The fiscal and monetary linkage between stock returns and inflation. *Journal of Finance*, March, 1–30.

Gibson, W.E. 1970: Price expectations effects on interest rates. *Journal of Finance*, 25, March, 19–34.

Gibson, W.E. 1972: Interest rates and inflationary expectations. *American Economic Review*, 62, December, 854–6.

Giddy, I. 1977: A note on the macroeconomic assumptions of international financial management. *Journal of Financial and Quantitative Analysis*, November, 601–5.

Gultekin, N.B. 1983: Stock market returns and inflation: evidence from other countries. *Journal of Finance*, March, 49–65.

Hansen, L.P. and Hodrick, R.J. 1980: Forward exchange rates as optimal predictors of future spot rates: an econometric analysis. *Journal of Political Economy*, 88, October, 828–53.

Hansen, L.P. and Hodrick, R.J. 1983: Risk averse speculation in the foreign exchange market: an econometric analysis of linear models. In J.A. Frenkel (ed.), *Exchange Rates and International Macroeconomics*, Chicago: University of Chicago Press.

Hawkins, R.G. 1981: Discussion. *Journal of Finance*, 34(2), 442–4.

Henderson, D. and Rogerson, P. 1987: The chairman and the treasurer. *The Treasurer*, September, 6–11 (authors Chairman and Treasurer of ICI respectively).

Hodgson, M. Sir 1980: The corporate treasurer and the international development of a group. *The Treasurer*, November/December, 5–12.

Hodrick, R. J. 1987: *The Empirical Evidence on the Efficiency of Forward and Futures Foreign Exchange Markets*. Chur, Switzerland: Harwood.

Hodson, D. 1984: *Corporate Finance and Treasury Management*. Gee.

Holland, J.B. 1981: Problems in the development and use of managerial financial models. *Managerial and Decision Economics*, 2(1), 40–8.

Holland, J.B. 1990: Capital budgeting for international business – a framework for analysis. *Managerial Finance*, 16(2), 1–6.

Holland, J.B. 1992a: Relationship banking: choice and control by the multinational firm. *International Journal of Bank Marketing*, 10(2), 29–40.

Holland, J.B. 1992b: Foreign exchange risk management – a balanced portfolio. *Managerial Finance*, 18, (3/4), 2–20.

Holland, J.B. 1994: Bank lending relationships and the complex nature of bank–corporate relations. *Journal of Business Finance and Accounting*, forthcoming.

Hood, N. and Young, S. 1979: *The Economics of the Multinational Enterprise*. London: Longman.

Howe, J.S. and Madura, J. 1990: The impact of international listings on risk: implications for capital market integration. *Journal of Banking and Finance*, 14, (6), 1133–42.

Hsieh, D.A. 1982: *Tests of Rational Expectations and No Risk Premium in Forward Exchange Markets*. National Bureau of Economic Research, working paper, no. 843, January.

Hymer, Stephen 1960: *The International Operations of National Firms: a study of direct foreign investment*. Cambridge, MA: MIT Press (revised edition 1976).

Ibbotson, R.G., Carr, R.C. and Robinson, A.W. 1982: International equity and bond returns. *Financial Analysts Journal*, July/August, 61–83.

Ireland, L. 1987: Banking relationships. *Euromoney Corporate Finance*, July, 43–50.

Jacque, L.L. 1978: *Management of Foreign Exchange Risk: theory and praxis*. Lexington, MA: D.C. Heath.

Jacque, L.L. 1981: Management of foreign exchange risk: a review article. *Journal of International Business Studies*, spring/summer, 81–101.

Jeffcoat, A.E. and Southern, A.D. 1983: Why and how to court foreign shareholders, *Harvard Business Review*, July–August, 30–8.

Jilling, M. and Folks, W. 1977: Evaluation of foreign currency borrowing: a review of theory and practice. Paper at Academy of International Business, Annual Meeting, Florida, August.

Johnson, C. and Batchelor, G. 1988: Corporate treasury management. *Corporate Finance*, May.

Kaplanis, E. C. 1988: Stability and forecasting of the comovement measures of international stock market returns. *Journal of International Money and Finance*, 7, (1), 63–75.

Kim, W.C. and Hwang, P. 1992: Global strategy and multinationals' entry mode choice. *Journal of International Business Studies*, 23(1), 29–54.

Kindleberger, C.P. 1969: *American Business Abroad*. New Haven, CT: Yale University Press.

Knickerbocker, F.T. 1974: *Oligopolistic Reaction and Multinational Enterprise*. Cambridge, MA: Harvard Business School, Division of Research.

Knight, D. and Barnett, S. 1990: Making the connection. *Corporate Finance*, May, 45–7.

Kobrin, S. 1979: Political risk: a review and reconsideration. *Journal of International Business Studies*, spring/summer, 67–80.

Kobrin, S., Basek, J., Blank, S. and La Palombara, J. 1980: The assessment and evaluation of noneconomic environments by American firms: a preliminary report. *Journal of International Business Studies*, spring/summer, 32–47.

Kohlhagen, S. 1975: The performance of the foreign exchange markets 1971–1974. *Journal of International Business Studies*, fall, 33–9.

Kravis, I.B. and Lipsey, R.E. 1978: Price behaviour in the light of balance of payments theory. *Journal of International Economics*, 8, May, 193–246.

Krueger, A.O. 1983: *Exchange Rate Determination*. Cambridge University Press.

Lane, M. 1988: Damage control. *Risk*, 1(5), 34–8.

Lane, M. 1989: Driven to options. *Risk*, 2(5), 20–4.

Lessard, D. 1979: Transfer prices, taxes, and financial markets: implications of internal financial transfers within the multinational corporation. In *Research in International Business and Finance*, vol. 1, JAI Press, 101–35.

Lessard, D. 1980: International diversification. In S. Levine (ed.), *The Investment Manager's Handbook*, Dow-Jones-Irwin, chapter 11.

Lessard, D. 1981: Evaluating international projects: an adjusted present value approach. In R.L. Crum and F. Derkinderen (eds), *Capital Budgeting under Conditions of Uncertainty*, Martinus Nijhoff, chapter 6.

Lessard. D. 1989: Corporate finance in the 1990s – implications of a changing competitive and financial context. *Journal of International Financial Management and Accounting*, 1(3), 209–31.

Levich, R.M. 1983: Exchange rate forecasting techniques. In A. George and I. Giddy (eds), *International Finance Handbook*, Wiley, section 8.1, 1–30.

Levich, R.M. 1979: Are forward exchange rates unbiased predictors of future spot rates? *Columbia Journal of World Business*, winter, 49–61.

Levich, R.M. 1978: Tests of forecasting models and market efficiency in the international money market. In J.A. Frenkel and H.G. Johnson (eds), *The Economics of Exchange Rates*, Reading, MA: Addison-Wesley.

Lewent, J. and Kearney, A. 1990: Merck and Co – a case in foreign exchange risk management. *Journal of Applied Corporate Finance*, 2(4), 19–28.

Lewis, M.K. and Davis, K.T. 1987: *Domestic and International Banking* Philip Allan.

Magee, S.P., 1976: Technology and the appropriability theory of the multinational corporation. In J. Bhajwati (ed.), *The New International Economic Order*, Cambridge, MA: MIT Press.

Maldonado, R. and Saunders, A. 1981: International portfolio diversification and the inter-temporal stability of international stock market relationships. *Financial Management*, autumn, 54–63.

Masulis, R.W. 1980: The effect of capital structure changes on security prices. *Journal of Financial Economics*, March.

McDermott, M. 1984: Private Communication, Glasgow University, October.

McInness, J. Morris and Carleton, Willard J. 1982: Theory, models and implementation in financial management. *Management Science*, 28(9), 957–78.

McRae, T.W. and Walker D.P. 1980: *Foreign Exchange Management*. Prentice-Hall.

Meher, M. 1990: An international comparison of prices and exchange rates: a new test of purchasing power parity. *Journal of International Money and Finance*, 9(1), 75–91.

Meric, I. and Meric, G. 1989: Potential gains from international portfolio diversification and intertemporal stability and seasonality in international stock market relationships. *Journal of Banking and Finance*, 13(4/5), 627–40.

Millar, W. 1990: New directions in financial risk management. In W. Millar and B. Asher (eds), Strategic risk management, *Business International*, January.

Miller, M. 1977: Debt and taxes, *Journal of Finance*, 32, 261–75.

Moazzami, B. 1990: Interest rates and inflationary expectations. *Journal of Banking and Finance*, 14(6), 1163–70.

Modigliani, F. and Miller, M. 1963: Corporate income taxes and the cost of capital: a correction. *American Economic Review*, 53, June, 433–43.

Muragu, K. 1990: *Stock Market Efficiency in Developing Countries: a case study of the Nairobi Stock Exchange*. PhD thesis, University of Glasgow.

Myers, S.C. 1974: Interactions of corporate financing and investment decisions – implications for capital budgeting. *Journal of Finance*, 29, March, 1–25.

Myers, S.C. 1977: Reply. *Journal of Finance*, 32, March, 218–20.

Myers, S.C. 1984: Finance theory and financial strategy. In Arnoldo Hax (ed.), *Readings in Strategic Management*, Cambridge, MA: Ballinger, 177–88.

Officer, L.H. 1976: The purchasing parity theory of exchange rates: a review article. *IMF Staff Papers*, March, 1–60.

Oxelheim, L. and Wihlborg, C. 1989: Competitive exposure: taking the global view. *Euromoney Corporate Finance*, February.

Peel, D.A. and Pope, P.F. 1988: Stock returns and expected inflation in the UK: some new evidence. *Journal of Business Finance and Accounting*, 15(4), 459–67.

Prindl, A.R. 1976: *Foreign Exchange Risk*. London: Wiley.

Porter, M.E. 1980: *Competitive Strategy: techniques for analyzing industries and competitors*. New York: Free Press.

Raymond, A. and Weil, G. 1989: Diversification effects and exchange rate changes. *Journal of Business Finance and Accounting*, 16(4), 454–66.

Robbins, S. and Stobaugh, R., 1973: *Money in the Multinational Enterprise*. New York: Basic Books.

Robinson, J. 1983: *Multinationals and Political Control*. Gower.

Robock, S.H. and Simmonds, K. 1983: *International Business and Multinational Enterprises*, 3rd edn. Illinois: Irwin.

Rodriguez, R. 1981: Corporate exchange risk management – theme and aberrations. *Journal of Finance*, 34(2), 427–39.

Roll, R. 1977: A critique of the asset pricing theory's test. Part I: On past and potential testability of the theory. *Journal of Financial Economics*, 4, March, 129–76.

Roll, R. 1979: Violations of the law of one price and their implications for differentially denominated assets. In *International Finance and Trade*, vol. 1, Cambridge, MA: Ballinger.

Roll, R. and Solnik, B. 1975: *A Pure Foreign Exchange Asset Pricing Model*. European Institute for Advanced Studies in Management, working paper no. 75.

Root, F.R. 1977: *Entry Strategies for Foreign Markets: from domestic to international business*. New York: Amacom.

✓Rugman, A., Lecraw, D. and Booth, L. 1986: *International Business: firm and environment*. McGraw-Hill.

Rush, M. and Husted, S. 1985: Purchasing power parity in the long run. *Canadian Journal of Economics*, 1, February, 137–45.

Rutenberg, D.P. 1970: Maneuvering liquid assets in a multinational company: formulation and deterministic solution procedures. *Management Science*, 16(10), 671–84.

Rutenberg, D.P. 1982: *Multinational Management*. Boston: Little Brown.

Samuels, J. 1981: Inefficient capital markets and their implications. In F. Derkinderen and R. Crum (eds), *Risk, Capital Costs and Financing Decisions*, Martinus Nijhoff, chapter 8.

Savage, R. 1990: Quoted in editorial. *The Treasurer*, May, 8–9.

Scott, I. 1987: Managing economic exposure – Jaguar cars. *The Treasurer*, February, 19–21.

Shapiro, A. 1978a: Payments netting in international cash management. *Journal of International Business Studies*, fall, 51–8.

Shapiro, A. 1978b: Capital budgeting for the multinational corporation. *Financial Management*, spring, 7–16.

Shapiro, A. 1984: The impact of taxation on the currency of denomination decision for long term foreign borrowing and lending. *Journal of International Business Studies*, spring/summer, 15–25.

Singleton-Green, Brian 1991: World class financial control. *Accountancy*, July, 106–8.

Soenen, L.A. and Aggarwal, R. 1989: Cash and foreign exchange management: theory and corporate practice in three countries. *Journal of Business Finance and Accounting*, 15(5), 599–619.

Solnik, B. 1973a: A note on the validity of the random walk for European stock prices. *Journal of Finance*, 28, 1151–9.

Solnik, B. 1973b: *European Stock Markets*. Lexington, MA: Lexington Books.

Solnik, B. 1974: The international pricing of risk – an empirical investigation of the world capital market structure. *Journal of Finance*, 29, May, 365–79.

Solnik, B. 1977: Testing international asset pricing: some pessimistic views. *Journal of Finance*, 32, May, 503–11.

Solnik, B. 1983: The relation between stock prices and inflationary expectations: the international evidence. *Journal of Finance*, 38(1), 35–48.

Stanley, M. 1981: Capital structure and cost of capital for the multinational firm. *Journal of International Business Studies*, spring/summer.

Stehle, R.H. 1977: An empirical test of the alternative hypothesis of national and international pricing of risky assets. *Journal of Finance*, 32(2), 493–502.

Stulz, R.M. 1981a: On the effects of barriers to international investment. *Journal of Finance*, 34(4), 923–34.

Stulz, R.M. 1981b: A model of international asset pricing. *Journal of Financial Economics*, 9, December, 383–406.

Sweeney, A. and Rachlin, R. 1984: *Handbook of International Financial Management*. McGraw-Hill.

Van Horne, J. 1980 *Financial Management and Policy*. Prentice-Hall.

Vernon, R. 1966: International investment and international trade in the product cycle. *Quarterly Journal of Economics*, May, 190–207.

Vernon, R. 1983: Organizational and institutional responses to international risk. In R. Herring (ed.), *Managing International Risk*, Cambridge University Press, chapter 5.

Vernon, R. and Wells, L.T. 1981: *Manager in the International Economy*. Englewood Cliffs, NJ: Prentice-Hall.

Vinso, J. 1982: Financial planning for the multinational corporation with multiple goals. *Journal of International Business Studies*, 443–58.

Viren, M. 1989: The long run relationship between interest rates and inflation: some cross country evidence. *Journal of Banking and Finance*, 13(4/5), 571–88.

Warner, J. 1977: Bankruptcy costs: some evidence. *Journal of Finance*, May.

Wickens, M.R. 1984: *Rational Expectations and Exchange Rate Dynamics*. Centre for Economic Policy Research, discussion paper no. 20, June.

Wihlborg, C. 1980: Currency exposure: taxonomy and theory. In R.M. Levich and C. Wihlborg (eds) *Exchange Risk and Exposure: current developments in international financial management*, Lexington, MA: D.C. Heath and Lexington Books, 23–44.

Williamson, O.E. 1975: *Markets and Hierarchies*. New York: Free Press.

Williamson, O.E. 1977: Firms and markets. In S. Weintraub (ed.), *Modern Economic Theory*, Oxford: Blackwell.

Wilson, M. 1988: An empirical investigation of the use of a conceptual framework of risk and return in international capital budgeting by United Kingdom based multinationals. Paper presented at September meeting of the British Accounting Association Northern Accounting Group Conference.

Wymeersch, E. 1983: Securities market regulation in Europe. In A. George and I. Giddy (eds), *International Finance Handbook*, Wiley, section 6.2, 1–51.

# Index

accounting exposure *see* translation/
    accounting exposure
adjusted present value rule (APV)  268–9
Adler, M.  88, 99, 119, 122, 130
Advani, R.  340
Agarwal, S.  239
agency theory  381
Aggarwal, R.  221
Allied Lyons, speculative trading by
    treasury in $/£ currency
    options  219–20
American depository receipts (ADRs)  108
appropriability theory  237
arbitrage  49, 62
Australia, exchange control  142–3

Baillie, R. T.  102, 104
Bain, A. D.  63
Baker, James  71
bankers  17–18
banking
    deregulation  69
    EC Second Banking Directive  70
    international  63, 67–8, 75
    regulation  68–70
    relationship  383–7
    Single European Act 1986  69–70
banks  62–3
    changing roles of investment and
      commercial  67–9
    financial innovations  66–7
    source of currency risk management
      instruments  222–3
Bar-Yosef, S.  267
Barnea, A.  381
Barnes, P.  370

Barnett, S.  21
barriers to trade, financial services
    markets  179–80
Bartlett, C. A.  258
Basle Committee  69
Batchelor, G.  18
Beerel, A.  22
Belk, P.  210, 214, 215, 217, 224
beta values  270
Betts, Paul  134, 150
Bhoocha-oom, A.  106
Bickerstaffe, G.  192
Bilson, J. F. O.  102
Black, F.  111
Black-Scholes option model  56
Boddewyn, J. J.  240
Bollersley, T.  104
Booth, L.  267
Brady, Nicholas  71
Brealey, R.  86, 88, 102, 109, 255, 268–9,
    367, 370, 410
Breeden, D. T.  112
Bretton Woods system  32–3
brokers, foreign exchange  42
Buckley, P. J.  232, 235, 236–7
Bui, N.  101
Burmeister, H.  90
Burnie, D.  110
business environmental risk index
    (BERI)  244

call option  45
Calvet, R. L.  94–5, 232–3, 235
Canaday, J.  214, 221, 222
capital adequacy  69

capital asset pricing model (CAPM)
13–14, 270
*see also* international capital asset pricing
model
capital budgeting 90–2, 265–87, 420–1
case study: The StrathKelvin
Company 288–317
decision model 267–75
discount rates 270–5
capital markets
domestic and international 60–2
efficient and inefficient 367–78
regulation 62
capital structure 380–3
Carleton, Willard J. 411–12, 414, 421
case studies
Allied Lyons 219–20
financing decision problem 348–60
ICI 5–6, 168–9, 394–405
Jaguar 172–3
Merck & Co. 226–8
Rolls-Royce 133–6, 150–6, 211–12
The StrathKelvin Company 288–317
cash flows 13, 275–86
Casson, M. 180, 232, 235, 236–7
Castellanos, C. 31
Caterpillar Tractor 250–1
Caves, R. E. 232, 234
Channon, D. F. 18, 263
Chicago International Money Market
(IMM) 44
chief accountant 17
chief financial executive 15
clearing banks *see* commercial banks
Clements, A. 394, 400, 403
Coase, R. H. 180
Coggan, Philip 325
Collier, P. 210, 214, 217
commercial banks 62–3, 67–9
Contractor, F. 240
Convention on Biological Diversity 248
Cooke Committee 69
Cooper, J. C. B. 369
Cornell, B. 102, 110
Cumby, R. E. 112
currency options markets 45–6, 206–10
valuation 54–7
currency risk 10–12, 87–9, 417–18
defining 131–3
hedging 88, 120, 204–10

internal and external financial techniques
in dealing with 182–7
internal financial techniques 188–99
managerial attitudes 215–19
MNC's strategy to reduce 147–50
currency swaps 107, 335–7

Dahlman, C. J. 180
Daniels, J. 263
Davidson, W. H. 263
Davis, E. 210
Davis, K. T. 58
Davutyan, N. 101
dealing rooms, currency 41
debt financing 339–64
case study 348–60
choices 346–8
model building 360–4
debt for equity swaps 337–8
definitions, multinational corporation 2
deregulation 69
direct foreign investment (DFI) 5, 11
distinguishing between DFI, licensing
and exporting choices 257–8
market imperfections 94, 232–41
product life cycle theory 234
discount rates, capital budgeting 270–5
dividends
multinational corporations 12
dollar standard 33
domestic financial management
(DOFM) 24, 92, 424
domestic internal financial system
(DIFS) 182
Donaldson, G. 187, 384, 385, 404
Dufey, G. 63, 85, 90, 102, 106, 118, 120,
121–2, 157, 374
Dumas, B. 88, 99, 119, 122, 130
Dunning, J. H. 232, 235, 236, 238, 240,
256, 415
Dymsza, W. A. 263

Eaker, M. 93
economic exposure 88, 129
adapting and modifying operational
policies 156–63
case study of Rolls-Royce 133–6, 150–6
Edison, H. J. 100
Edwards, J. 212
Eiteman, D. 243
employees, EC Social Chapter 250

environment, multinational
    corporations  246–8
equity return parity (ERP) theorem  98,
    108
Eurobanks  63
Eurobonds  57, 59–60, 66, 321, 325
    agent banking  331
    as a source of corporate funds  327–32
    difference from foreign bonds  56, 327
    negotiating terms  328–30
    secondary market  59, 331
    selling the bonds  330–1
    withholding tax exemption  60
Eurocommercial paper  64–5, 326, 331–2
Eurocurrency market  57–60, 321–32
    interest rates  59
    regulation  58
Eurodollars  321
Euroequities  67, 107
Euroloans  321–6
Euromarkets, securitization  326–7
Euronotes  64, 331–2
European central bank  39
European Commission
    anti–trust measures  95–7
    Second Banking Directive  70
European Community (EC)  246, 251
    internal market  233
    Social Chapter  250, 260
European Currency Unit (ECU)  37–8, 95
European monetary system (EMS)  31, 32,
    36, 37
    crisis of September 1992  75, 143
    devaluation or revaluation of
        currencies  37–9
    managed  144
exchange control  39
    Australia  142–3
exchange rate mechanism (ERM)  36
    sterling  37–9
exchange rate risk *see* currency risk;
    foreign exchange risk management
    (FERM)
exchange rates
    control  36–40
    current practices  33–4
    floating  35
    forecasting  140–5
    government intervention  36–40, 118,
        141–2, 144
    history of systems  32

parity relationships  79–84
    volatile  56
    *see also* foreign exchange
exporting, distinguishing between DFI,
    licensing and exporting choices
    257–8
exposure management  128–40
    ICI  148–9, 223
    operational policies  156–63
    *see also* economic exposure; transaction
        exposure; translation/accounting
        exposure

Fama, E. F.  110
Feenstra, F.  214, 221, 222
Feiger, G.  58, 61, 92, 99, 112
finance
    basic concepts  13–14
    international sources  318–38
finance director  15, 17–18
financial centres  318–21
financial planning for the MNC  410–23
    imperfections  411–14
    neo–classicism  410–11
financial services markets, barriers to
    trade  179–80
financing debt *see* debt financing
financing decisions, multinational
    corporations  365–405
firm, the, decision to invest overseas
    10–13, 238–41
Fisher hypothesis *see* international Fisher
    effect; one country Fisher effect
Flexl, Judith  134, 150
Folks, W.  340, 361
forecasting
    foreign exchange rates  140–5
    inflation rates  140
foreign bonds, difference from
    Eurobonds  56, 327
foreign exchange, bid and offer rates  48–9
    direct quote  46
    financing debt  342–4
    forward quotes  49–54
    indirect quote  46–7
    market  40–64
    market forces  78–83
    market imperfections  93–7, 180–1
    quotation convention  46–57
    unbiased forward rate (UBFR)
        theorem  79, 84–5, 102–5

*see also* currency risk; exchange rates;
   foreign exchange risk management
foreign exchange dealing   216
foreign exchange risk management
   (FERM)   118–46, 417–23
   active opportunistic policy   182–8
   case study of Rolls-Royce   133–6, 150–6
   choice of methods   163–73
   combined internal and external financial
      techniques   182–7
   constraints on choice of methods   169–73
   corporate management   118–21
   exposure management   128–40
   external risk management
      instruments   202–30
   fragmented   188
   goal of the corporate treasurer   121–2
   ICI   168–9
   internal financial techniques   188–99
   strategies   123–8, 147–56
   use of external financial
      techniques   224–6
forward markets
   currency   44, 49–54
   hedging   204–5, 208–10
forward quotes, premiums and
   discounts   49–54
Freeman, Andrew   395, 400, 404
Frenkel, J. A.   100
Friedman, M.   110
futures markets, currency   44

G7 (group of seven largest industrialized
   countries), currency co-operation
   36–7
G10 (group of ten industrialized countries),
   bank supervision   69–70
Gaillot, H. J.   100
Garman-Kohlhagen model   56
General Agreement on Tariffs and Trade
   (GATT)   37
Geske, R.   110
Gibson, W.E.   109
Giddy, I.   63, 78–9, 85, 90, 102, 106, 374
Glaum, M.   210, 214, 215, 217, 224
global warming   246–7
gold standard   32
government intervention
   exchange rates   36–40, 118, 141–2, 144
   market distortion   233
Great Depression   32

Gultekin, N. B.   110

Hansen, L. P.   102, 112
Hawkins, R. G.   186, 190
hedging   88, 119–20
   banks as source of currency risk
      management instruments   222–3
   constraints   220–1
   continuous   213–14
   forward market   204–5, 208–10
   Jaguar's policy   212–13
   managerial attitudes to transaction
      exposure   215–19
   Merck & Co.   226–8
   money market   205–6, 208–10
   Rolls-Royce's policy   211–12
   translation/accounting exposure   210
Henderson, D.   6, 223, 394
Hodrick, R. J.   102, 104, 112
Hodson, E.   17
Holland, J. B.   186, 222, 275, 315, 323,
   361, 384, 385
Hood, N.   232
Howe, J. S.   113
Hsieh, D. A.   102
Husted, S.   101
Hwang, P.   240, 254
Hymer, Stephen   232

Ibbotson, R. G.   60
ICI
   case study   5–6
   case study of financing policy   394–405
   centralised treasury   20, 223, 396–7
   choice of FERM methods   168–9
   internal FERM techniques   199
   strategy to reduce exposure to currency
      risk   148–9, 223
in-house bank (IHB)   22–3, 223
industrial organization theory   235–6
inflation rates
   forecasting   140
   parity relationships   79–84
interest rate parity (IRP)   79, 85–6, 105–7
interest rate swaps   107, 333–5
interest rates
   Eurocurrency   59
   forecasting currency valuations   56
   parity relationships   79–84
   risk   21

internal financial system *see* domestic
      internal financial system (DIFS);
      multinational internal financial system
      (MIFS)
internal organization theory   236-7
internal rate of return (IRR)   340
international capital asset pricing model
      (ICAPM)   90-2, 98, 111-14
international capital markets   60-2
      1992   72-4
   equilibrium relationships   86-7
   financing decisions   89-90
   market imperfections   93-7, 180-1
international financial management (IFM)
   market forces assumptions   7-9, 78-87
   market imperfections   7-9, 92-114,
      179-82, 411-14
   neo-classical assumptions   7-9, 87-92,
      410-11
   theory   13-14
international Fisher effect (IFE)   79, 85-6,
      89-90, 109-10
International Monetary Fund (IMF)   31
   exchange rate monitoring   34
   role in co-ordinating currency co-
      operation   36
   special drawing right (SDR) basket of
      currencies   33
internationalization of business   21
investment banks   67-9
Ireland, L.   384


Jacque, L. L.   142-3
Jacquillat, B.   58, 61, 92, 99, 112
Jaguar
   constraints on choice of FERM
      decisions   172-3
   hedging policy   212-13
Jalland, M.   18
Japan, equity market   61
Jeffcoat, A.E.   383
Jilling, M.   361
Johnson, C.   18


Kaplanis, E. C.   114
Kearney, A.   171, 226
Kim, W. C.   240, 254
Kindleberger, C. P.   232
Knickerbocker, F. T.   234
Knight, D.   21
Kobrin, S.   242-3, 245, 251, 252

Kohlhagen, S.   105
Kravis, I. B.   99
Krueger, A. O.   32-3, 99-101


lagging *see* leading and lagging
Lane, M.   212
leading and lagging   189-90
less developed countries (LDCs)
   debt   72
   exchange rate systems   34
Lessard, D.   90, 114, 175-6, 179, 181-2,
      269, 283-4
Levich, R. M.   85, 103, 105, 141, 144
Lewent, J.   171, 226
Lewis, M. K.   58
licensing, distinguishing between DFI,
      licensing and exporting choices
      257-8
Lipsey, R. E.   99
location theory   235-6
London as a financial centre   319-21
London inter-bank offering rate
      (LIBOR)   57
London International Financial Futures
      Exchange (LIFFE)   44
London Traded Options Market
      (LTOM)   44
Louvre Accord, 1987   35


McDermot, M.   251
McInness, J. Morris   411-12, 414, 421
McRae, T. W.   25, 130, 145, 174
Madura, J.   113
Magee, S. P.   237
Maldonado, R.   108
market efficiency *see* capital markets
Masulis, R. W.   345, 380
matching   190-1
Meher, M.   101
Merck & Co., financial hedging in
      FERM   226-8
Meric, G.   114
Meric, I.   114
Millar, W.   221
Miller, M.   267, 345, 380
mismatching   191
MNC *see* multinational corporation
Moazzami, B.   109
Modigliani, F.   267
money market hedge   205-6, 208-10
multinational corporation (MNC)

case study of ICI 5–6, 168–9, 394–405
classification system 2–3
co-ordination 3
definition 2
dividends 12
environmental issues 246–8
ethical guidelines by world
    institutions 246, 251
finance and treasury function 14–23
financial planning 410–23
financing decisions 365–405
foreign exchange trading 42–3
identifying overseas investment
    opportunities 255–7
impact of the Maastricht proposals 250
internal financial system *see* multinational
    internal financial system
operational responses to currency
    risk 161–3
political risk 241–52, 259–61
product differentiation 149
strategic planning practices 261–3
strategies to reduce exposure to currency
    risk 148–50
strategy for co-ordinating investment
    decision making 252–61
multinational internal financial system
    (MIFS) 174–82
exploiting market imperfections 181–2
problems in using internal financial
    system 187–8
Muragu, K. 370
Myers, S. 86, 88, 102, 109, 255, 267,
    268–9, 367, 370, 410

net present value (NPV) 13–14
netting 188–9, 191–9
new products 234
New York as a financial centre 319
New York Plaza Agreement, 1985 35
note issuance facilities (NIFs) 64–5, 326,
    331–2

Officer, L. H. 100
oligopoly 234
one country Fisher effect 79, 86, 108–9
options
    currency 45–6, 54–7, 206–10
    over the counter (OTC) 46
organization, treasury and finance
    function 17–18

Organization for Economic Co-operation
    and Development (OECD)
    Caterpillar Tractor 250–1
    code of conduct for MNCs 246, 251,
        260
    *Financial Trends* 72
over the counter (OTC) options 46
Oxelheim, L. 130, 153

Peel, D. A. 110, 140
petrodollars 65
pharmaceutical industry 171
Philadelphia Stock Exchange 45–6
Pippinger, J. 101
political risk 11, 97, 241–52, 259–61
political system stability index (PSSI) 244
Pope, P. F. 110, 140
Porter, M. E. 152, 263
price controls 171, 226
Prindl, A. R. 25, 174
product differentiation 149, 234
    Rolls-Royce 153–4
production costs 234
project risk 270–5
purchasing power parity (PPP)
    theorem 79–84, 99–102
put option 45

Rachlin, R. 20
Radebaugh, L. 263
Ramaswami, S. 239
Raymond, A. 114
regulation
    banking 68–70
    capital markets 62
    Eurocurrency markets 58
    Single European Act 1986 69–70
research and development
    Rolls-Royce 153–4
    strategy to reduce exposure to currency
        risk 149
revolving underwritten facilities
    (RUFs) 64–5
Rio de Janeiro Earth Summit 246
risk
    interest rate 21
    political 11, 97, 241–52, 259–61
    *see also* currency risk; foreign exchange
        risk management
risk asset model (RAM) 69
risk management, strategies 371–8

Robbins, S.  175
Robinson, J.  97, 251
Robock, S. H.  263
Rodriguez, R.  182–6
Rogerson, P.  6, 223, 394
Roll, R.  100, 105, 110, 113
Rolls–Royce
  economic exposure  133–6, 150–6
  hedging policy  211–12
  transaction exposure  135–6, 211–12
Root, F. R.  262
Rugman, A.  242, 263
Rush, M.  101
Rutenberg, D. P.  175, 199

Samuels, J.  369
Saunders, A.  108
Savage, Richard  168
Schwert, G. W.  110
Scott, I.  172
securitization  21, 64–74
  Euromarkets  326–7
Shapiro, A.  110, 267, 273, 361
Simmonds, K.  263
single currency  39
Single European Act 1986, banking
  regulation  69–70
Singleton–Green, Brian  395
Smithsonian Agreement  33
Soenen, L.  221
Solnik, B.  105, 110, 111, 113, 368, 369
Southern, A. D.  383
spot market  43
Srinivasulu, S.  118, 120, 121–2
Stanley, M.  90
Stansell, S.  106
Stehle, R. H.  111
sterling, exchange rate mechanism  37–9
Stobaugh, R.  175
Stonehill, A.  243
StrathKelvin Company, The, capital
  budgeting case study  288-317
Stulz, R.  111–12, 113, 377
swaps market  66, 107, 332–8
Sweeney, A.  20

taxation
  debt financing decision  341, 345–6, 375
  multinationals  249–50
Tokyo Stock Exchange, market

  capitalization  61
transaction costs, barriers to trade  180–1
transaction exposure  88, 129
  ICI  168–9
  managerial attitudes  215–19
  Rolls–Royce  135–6, 211–12
translation/accounting exposure  88, 129
  hedging  210
treasurer  17–18
treasury function
  centralized  11, 18–20, 22–3, 223–4
  decentralized  20
  development  20–2
  funding strategy  378–80
  hedging policy  218
  ICI  20, 223, 396–7
  in-house bank (IHB)  22–3, 223
  multinational corporations  14–23
treasury staff  15
  financial role  16
  information provision  16

unbiased forward rate (UBFR)
  theorem  79, 84–5, 102–5
United Nations  246, 251
  Conference on Environment and
    Development  246
United States, equity market  60–1

Van Horne, J.  267
Vernon, R.  232, 234, 242, 262
Vinso, J.  361
Viren, M.  109

Walker, D. P.  25, 130, 144, 174
Warner, J.  380
weighted average cost of capital
  (WACC)  267–8
Weil, G.  114
Wells, L. T.  262
Wickens, M. R.  101
Wihlborg, C.  129, 130, 153
Williamson, O. E.  9, 235
Wilson, M.  421
workers, EC Social Chapter  250
World Bank  31
world debt crisis  64–5, 70–2
Wymeersch, E,  97

Young, S.  232